Public Policy

Why ethics matters

Public Policy

Why ethics matters

Edited by Jonathan Boston, Andrew Bradstock,
and David Eng

E PRESS

the Australia and New Zealand
School of Government

Published by ANU E Press
The Australian National University
Canberra ACT 0200, Australia
Email: anuepress@anu.edu.au
This title is also available online at: http://epress.anu.edu.au/ethics_matters_citation.
html

National Library of Australia Cataloguing-in-Publication entry

Title: Public policy : why ethics matters / edited by Jonathan Boston,
                 Andrew Bradstock, and David Eng.

ISBN: 9781921666735 (pbk.) 9781921666759 (eBook)

Series: ANZSOG series.

Notes: Includes bibliographical references.

Subjects: Ethics.
                 Decision making--Moral and ethical aspects.
                 Political ethics.
                 Social values.

Other Authors/Contributors:
                 Boston, Jonathan, 1957-
                 Bradstock, Andrew.
                 Eng, David L., 1967-

Dewey Number: 170

Cover design by ANU E Press

Printed by Griffin Press

Funding for this monograph series has been provided by the Australia and New
Zealand School of Government Research Program.

John Wanna, *Series Editor*

Professor John Wanna is the Sir John Bunting Chair of Public Administration at the Research School of Social Sciences at The Australian National University and is the director of research for the Australian and New Zealand School of Government (ANZSOG). He is also a joint appointment with the Department of Politics and Public Policy at Griffith University and a principal researcher with two research centres: the Governance and Public Policy Research Centre and the nationally funded Key Centre in Ethics, Law, Justice and Governance at Griffith University.

Contents

Part I: Ethical foundations of public policy

Part II: Ethics of climate change

Part III: Perspectives on ethics and the economy

Preface

This edited volume brings together a selection of 12 papers that were originally delivered at a major conference – Ethical Foundations of Public Policy – in December 2009 in Wellington, New Zealand. The conference was co-hosted by the Institute of Policy Studies and the Philosophy Programme at Victoria University of Wellington, and the Centre for Theology and Public Issues at the University of Otago, and was sponsored by the School of Government Trust. The conference was very well attended with some 350 participants, of whom about 50 delivered papers.

The purpose of the conference was to encourage and facilitate debate about the ethical basis for policy making. This includes, of course, the ethical principles that should inform our behaviour, whether as citizens, voters, policy analysts, or decision makers, as well as the normative considerations that should guide our choices over the substantive content of particular policies – whether fiscal policy, health policy, or foreign policy.

To facilitate such a dialogue, the conference brought together a variety of policy makers, including politicians, government officials, and political advisers, together with academics from various disciplines, including economics, law, philosophy, politics, religious studies, and theology. The mix of disciplines was deliberate. Discussions concerning the ethical foundations of public policy must not, in our view, be the prerogative exclusively of moral philosophers or theologians. On the contrary, the subject is of universal relevance and deserves the attention of all those who wish to contribute to public life.

The conference had five main sub-themes: speaking truth to power (or the ethics of advice giving), the ethics of decision making, protecting the global commons, issues of equality and justice, and measuring progress. But there were also contributions on other subject areas, including ethics and economics, and ethics and health care, with papers on such issues as vulnerability, autonomy and justice, making fair funding decisions for high-cost health care, and the role of consumers in making health policy.

As highlighted by the contributions to the conference, ethical analysis remains a vigorously contested field. There are many competing moral philosophies and theologies. In our view, public debate on the merits of the different approaches is critical. After all, the ethical framework we adopt has major consequences for policy making: it shapes the questions we ask, the methodologies we use, the values we embrace, the weighting we give to different ethical principles, and hence the policy choices we make.

The chapters in this book cover all but one of the five main sub-themes addressed during the conference. The exception concerns the measurement of progress, and this subject will be covered, together with several other topics, in a separate edited volume to be published by Victoria University Press.

We would like to thank all those who contributed to the production of this book: the authors of the 12 chapters for their diligent and rapid re-crafting of their conference papers, Belinda Hill for her assistance with copy-editing, and John Butcher for advice and encouragement. We would also like to thank the School of Government Trust, the Philosophy Programme at Victoria University of Wellington, and the Centre for Theology and Public Issues at the University of Otago for their generous financial support.

Jonathan Boston
Andrew Bradstock
David Eng
July 2010

Biographies of contributors

Jonathan Boston is Professor of Public Policy and Director of the Institute of Policy Studies at the School of Government, Victoria University of Wellington. He has published widely in the fields of public management, tertiary education, social policy, comparative government, New Zealand politics, and climate change policy, including 24 books and over 170 journal articles and book chapters.

Andrew Bradstock is Howard Paterson Professor of Theology and Public Issues and Director of the Centre for Theology and Public Issues at the University of Otago. Previously he co-directed the Centre for Faith and Society at the Von Hügel Institute, St Edmund's College, Cambridge, and was Secretary for Church and Society with the United Reformed Church in the United Kingdom.

David Bromell is a principal adviser with the New Zealand Ministry of Social Development, a senior associate of the Institute of Policy Studies at the School of Government, Victoria University of Wellington, and the author of *Ethnicity, Identity and Public Policy: Critical perspectives on multiculturalism* (2008) and 'Recognition, redistribution and democratic inclusion' (in R. Openshaw and E. Rata (eds), *The Politics of Conformity in New Zealand*, 2009).

John Broome is White's Professor of Moral Philosophy at the University of Oxford. He was previously Professor of Philosophy at the University of St Andrews and Professor of Economics at the University of Bristol. His books include *The Microeconomics of Capitalism* (1984), *Weighing Goods* (1991), *Counting the Cost of Global Warming* (1992), *Ethics out of Economics* (1999), *Weighing Lives* (2004).

Tom Campbell is Director of the Centre for Applied Philosophy and Public Ethics, an Australian Research Council Special Research Centre, at Charles Sturt University. He was formerly Dean of Law at the Australian National University and Professor of Jurisprudence at the University of Glasgow. His books include *The Left and Rights* (1983), *Justice* (2001), and *Rights* (2006).

Ramon Das is a senior lecturer in philosophy at Victoria University of Wellington. He is especially interested in questions about ethics and international relations, as well as questions about what responsibilities ordinary citizens have to alleviate global suffering. His other research areas include philosophy of law, philosophy of economics, and moral psychology. He is writing a book on the ethics of globalisation.

David Eng is a consultant for the Tertiary Education Commission in New Zealand and was previously a lecturer in philosophy at Victoria University of Wellington. Before that, he was an assistant professor at California State University Bakersfield for three years. When he moved to New Zealand in 2003, he worked for the Tertiary Education Commission until 2007. His areas of research include epistemology, social epistemology, philosophy of mind, aesthetics, and philosophy of evaluation.

Howard Larsen is a principal analyst with the New Zealand Ministry for the Environment, where he has a particular interest in the effective use of science in policy development. He has earlier worked extensively in atmospheric physics research, both in New Zealand and overseas. His particular area of research was clouds, storms, and rain.

Xavier Márquez is a lecturer in political theory at Victoria University of Wellington. His research interests range from ancient political thought (especially Plato and Cicero) to more general questions about power, democracy, and expertise. He is currently writing a book about Plato's political thought.

Julia Maskivker is Assistant Professor of Political Science at Rollins College, Florida. She holds a PhD from Columbia University. Her areas of specialisation include analytical ethical and political theory, theories of justice, theories of social citizenship, and modern political thought.

Michael Mintrom is an associate professor of political studies and coordinator of the master of public policy degree at the University of Auckland. He is a specialist in the politics of policy innovation, policy entrepreneurship, and change leadership. He is the author of *Contemporary Policy Analysis*, forthcoming from Oxford University Press.

David Rea is a principal adviser with the New Zealand Ministry of Social Development and a research associate of the Institute of Policy Studies at the School of Government, Victoria University of Wellington. Previously he was general manager of the New Zealand Ministry of Youth Development and general manager of older people's policy in the Ministry of Social Development.

Andy Reisinger is a senior fellow with the New Zealand Climate Change Research Institute at the School of Government, Victoria University of Wellington. He works on a variety of issues, including climate policy as well as vulnerability and adaptation to climate change. Previously he worked for the Intergovernmental Panel on Climate Change and as a senior adviser for the New Zealand Ministry for the Environment. He is the author of *Climate Change 101: An educational resource* (2009).

Simon Smelt is working with the Centre for Law and Economics at the Australian National University on governance and regulation of financial institutions. Previously he has worked for the New Zealand Treasury (1986–94) on the reform of ports, Tomorrow's Schools, labour market legislation, and capital markets. As a consultant, he worked internationally on financial management and regulatory reform.

John Uhr is Professor of Public Policy at the Crawford School of Economics and Government, Australian National University. He teaches ethics and public policy and runs the Parliamentary Studies Centre. His books include *Terms of Trust: Arguments over ethics in Australian government* (2005). He has published extensively on ethics and government.

Dan Weijers is a PhD student in the Philosophy Programme at Victoria University of Wellington. His masters and doctoral theses are in the field of ethics. He is particularly interested in happiness and well-being, subjects he has published and lectured on.

1. Ethics and public policy

Jonathan Boston, Andrew Bradstock, and David Eng

Introduction

This book is about ethics and public policy. Such a topic immediately raises at least three questions. First, what is ethics? Second, what is public policy? And third, how, and in what ways, are ethics and public policy connected? All three questions have, unsurprisingly, generated large literatures.

Put simply, ethics is about what we ought to do or ought not to do. That is, it is concerned with what is good and bad, right and wrong, just and unjust, or noble and ignoble, and how we can tell the difference. There are many different and often competing ethical frameworks, theories, and principles, and there is certainly no complete agreement about the ethical standards and behaviour that should apply in specific contexts. However, it is generally accepted that the domain of ethics embraces not merely the discrete actions of individuals but also the actions of groups of individuals – whether these groups are small, such as families, or large, such as nations and the international community. Hence, ethical inquiry – or what is often called moral philosophy – is not confined to the private sphere of life;[1] it is equally relevant to the public realm, including the decisions of those who act on behalf of the public, whether at the national or sub-national level.

Public policy has been defined in many ways, but a relatively uncontroversial approach is to suggest that it is about what governments choose to do and or not to do.[2] Hence, public policy is concerned primarily with *governmental* action and inaction. This of course includes both *empirical* and *normative* questions. At the empirical level, there are the issues of what governments do in practice and how this varies over time and between jurisdictions. At the normative level, key issues include what governments ought to do and ought not to do, and what principles should guide decision making. From this perspective, then, ethics lies at the heart of public policy and is relevant, as Michael Mintrom argues persuasively in this volume, to all aspects of the policy-making cycle

1 Note that there has been much debate about whether a distinction can be made between ethics and morality, as is highlighted by John Uhr's contribution to this volume.
2 For instance, Mark Considine (1994, p. 3) defines a public policy as 'an action which employs government authority to commit resources in support of a preferred value'.

– including the tasks of defining the problem, identifying and assessing the available options, decision making, implementation, evaluation and – where justified – termination.

This of course does not mean that public policy is solely about ethics. Many aspects of policy analysis lack an ethical dimension. For instance, whether a particular country has a policy on nuclear weapons, climate change, refugees, or agricultural subsidies is an empirical matter, for which there is usually a straightforward factual answer. But whether it *should* have a policy on such matters and, if so, what this policy ought to be, are fundamentally ethical questions. They thus require careful ethical analysis if they are to be answered in a rigorous and justifiable manner.

Just as not all aspects of public policy have an ethical dimension, not all values are *ethical* values. Mathematical values, for instance, are different in nature and purpose to ethical values. At the same time, we need to be alert: particular statistics or metrics, such as gross domestic product or the consumer price index, often embody or reflect certain ethical assumptions and values, or may be used to justify a certain policy stance, which in turn reflects a particular ethical purpose. Equally, as is widely recognised, the market price of a good or service may not equate to its 'true' worth to society – perhaps because the price fails to take into account the positive and negative externalities associated with the production of the good or service in question. But of course the question of how we should determine the 'true' worth of something raises many profound ethical issues.

This introductory chapter surveys some of the key issues at the interface of ethics and public policy and summarises the main concerns and arguments of the contributors to this volume.

We discuss the relevance of ethics to public policy and explore the various ways in which ethical inquiry is relevant to policy analysis and governmental decision making. We also briefly examine some of the ethical challenges that face public policy practitioners – whether policy analysts, senior advisers, or decision makers – including the problem of conflicting moral imperatives. In so doing, we draw upon and highlight the perspectives of the contributors to Part I of this volume – Tom Campbell, Michael Mintrom, David Bromell, and John Uhr.

We then focus on one of the great moral challenges of the 21st century, namely how the global community should address the problem of human-induced climate change. The policy issues here are many and varied, and the ethical dilemmas facing humanity are complex and profoundly difficult. For instance, what responsibilities do those living today have to future generations and other species? What constitutes a 'dangerous', or alternatively 'safe', amount of climate change? What kind and magnitude of risks are ethically acceptable? How should the burdens of mitigation and adaptation be shared across the international community? And what discount rate should be applied to analyses of the costs and benefits of actions to address climate change? Such questions are discussed by the contributors to Part II of this volume – John Broome; Andy Reisinger and Howard Larsen; Dan Weijers, David Eng, and Ramon Das; and Xavier Márquez.

In the final part of this chapter, we turn to the subject of ethics and the economy. Here, as with climate change, ethics impinges on the nature, regulation, and outcomes of economic activity in multiple ways. What, for instance, is the purpose of economic activity? How does ethical conduct, or the lack thereof, impact on the financial performance of a firm or the economic performance of a nation? For what ends, to what extent, and by what means should we seek to regulate economic activity? To what extent, if at all, has the recent global financial crisis been the product of unethical behaviour, especially by key actors in the financial markets? What policy instruments are available to encourage, or perhaps enforce, particular ethical standards, and what are the costs and benefits of the various regulatory options? Further, it is clear that markets generate unequal outcomes: some people, through their skills, effort, or good fortune, secure substantial wealth; other people, through bad luck, limited capability, or low motivation, remain very poor. But are such unequal outcomes morally acceptable? What are the requirements of distributive justice? And to what extent and by what means should governments redistribute income, whether between people or over the course of a person's lifetime? Further, where the state provides assistance of various kinds to citizens, should such support be conditional or unconditional? Such questions form the heart of the final part of this book and are addressed by Andrew Bradstock, David Rea, Simon Smelt, and Julia Maskivker.

Ethical foundations of public policy

Let us return, then, to the relationship between ethics and public policy: in what ways is ethics relevant to policy makers and those who advise them? There are at least two issues that are central to policy analysis and that are fundamentally ethical in nature. First, what is policy for? Or, to put it differently, what ends should governments strive to achieve? Second, what are the appropriate means or policy instruments for achieving these ends? Bear in mind that ends and means are closely interrelated: some ends, for instance, are simultaneously the means for achieving other purposes.

With respect to the purpose of public policy, any answer necessarily entails ethical values. The problem, however, is to determine which particular values should be pursued and what the end should be. On this matter moral and political philosophers have offered many different answers over the centuries. One common approach has been to say that public policy should be directed towards the goal of building *the good society*, or at least a better one than we currently experience. Others, such as John Rawls (1971), have given pride of place to the quest for *justice*. Others have argued that the overarching aim should be to realise *the common good* or *the public interest*. Still others have invoked theological categories and argued that the role of the state is to uphold the divine will or build the *Kingdom of God*. And yet others, notably utilitarians such as John Stuart Mill (see Robson 1966), have emphasised the need to maximise utility, happiness, or welfare or achieve the greatest good for the greatest number.

A key issue for many of these approaches is that they beg the question of what is 'good', 'valuable', or 'just'. What, for instance, constitutes a 'good' or 'just' society? What kinds of 'values' – pleasure, happiness, well-being – should be maximised? But setting aside the issue of providing a theory of the good, justice, or value, a related issue is what constitutes a *good policy*. From the perspective of moral philosophy, there are two broad approaches to answering this question. The first, which is a consequentialist approach, is to assess the goodness or otherwise of a policy solely on the basis of its consequences. But the consequences of a policy are often difficult to discern or may not be fully evident for many years or even decades. Moreover, the consequences may include both positive and negative impacts, and the weighing up of these is often highly controversial. Hence, judging the worth of a policy solely on the basis of its consequences is fraught with problems.

The second approach is to adopt a non-consequentialist or deontological approach, and thus assess a policy not on the basis of its consequences but on whether it is consistent with certain agreed ethical principles. But this raises the issue of what particular principles should count, and, if there are conflicts between the relevant principles, how these should be resolved. Not merely do deontologists favour different ethical principles but they also support different decision-rules for resolving ethical conflicts: some favour giving absolute priority to one particular principle; others favour the use of maximin or maximax rules;[3] while yet others favour some kind of weighting.

---

3 Under the maximax approach, the decision rule involves choosing the course of action (or policy option) under which the most fully realised ethical value (across a range of options) is as fully realised as possible. By contrast, under the maximin approach the aim is to choose the course of action (or policy option) where the least fully realised value (across a range of options) is most fully realised.

Hence, both consequentialist and non-consequentialist approaches encounter problems. How, then, is progress to be made? In the face of ethical doubt and uncertainty, some might argue that the best way forward is for the state to do very little and rely as much as possible on individuals transacting voluntarily through lightly regulated markets. To justify such an approach one or more of the following assumptions might be advanced: that individuals are the source of value (or the sole criterion of value); that all human wants, desires, and preferences are equally meritorious, so have an equal right to be satisfied; and that individuals are the best judges of their own interests. But whether or not such assumptions are justified, the suggestion that by doing very little the state can somehow avoid exercising an ethical judgement concerning what are good or bad policies, or what are good or bad outcomes, is simply flawed. Ethical neutrality by the state is not an option. Choosing to undertake very few tasks involves no less of an ethical judgement than choosing to do a great deal. And both may be wrong.

The only alternative, therefore, is to embrace a particular ethical stance – whether one wants or not. This applies to all levels of government – including national and sub-national government, and to both the political and bureaucratic levels (that is, departments and agencies). A good example of a government *department* adopting a specific ethical stance is the 'well-being framework' endorsed by the Australian Commonwealth Treasury. To quote Dr Ken Henry, the secretary to the Treasury, in a major speech in late 2009 (pp. 6–7):

> Treasury's advice on fiscal policy – as in all other policy areas – is informed by the wellbeing framework that sits at the core of our mission statement. ...
>
> The Treasury's wellbeing framework has five dimensions:
>
> - centrally, the level of freedom and opportunity that people enjoy;
> - second, the aggregate level of consumption possibilities;
> - third, the distribution of consumption possibilities;
> - fourth, the level of risk that people are required to bear; and
> - fifth, the level of complexity that people are required to deal with.

Henry goes on to say (p. 7):

> Treasury's perspective on freedom and opportunity has been heavily influenced by the work of Amartya Sen on the contribution that 'substantive freedoms' make to development.

> According to Amartya Sen, the true measure of human development is the capabilities that an individual has to choose a life they have reason to value. … Capabilities allow an individual to fully function in society. They are not income and, while they include basic civil rights and political freedoms, they are not limited to 'rights'.

Later Henry notes (p. 12):

> It would be an exceptional case in which a policy intervention would be considered unambiguously positive across all five dimensions. Indeed, the wellbeing framework reflects our conviction that trade-offs matter deeply, emphasising the importance of assessing policy interventions in broad terms.

This is not the proper place to evaluate the Treasury's well-being framework, but several points deserve mention. First, advisory bodies such as treasuries, line departments, and policy taskforces inevitably rely on analytical frameworks in formulating their policy advice to governments. Such frameworks are either explicit and transparent, as in the case of the Australian Commonwealth Treasury, or implicit and opaque. More transparency is arguably better than less. If nothing else, it facilitates easier public scrutiny and more informed democratic debate. Second, analytical frameworks are not ethically neutral. On the contrary, they entail important ethical commitments – that is, commitments about what is valuable and what is not, or what is good and what is bad. The Treasury's framework places a high value on human freedom, opportunities, and capabilities. This represents an ethical choice. Many other choices are possible.

In considering the ethical rationale for any particular policy proposal or objective, it is important to recognise that in many situations it is possible to advance several different justifications. In some cases these may be distinctive and competing, in others overlapping and/or mutually reinforcing. Tom Campbell's contribution to this volume highlights such matters with respect to the challenge of alleviating global poverty. As he observes, it has been common over recent decades for poverty eradication to be justified ethically on the basis of considerations of global justice; indeed, for some, this is the sole justification. But while the pursuit of justice is a critically important ethical imperative, Campbell argues that it is not the only, and perhaps not even the most significant, value of relevance to the issues of global poverty. Instead, he suggests that a more important ethical motivation for reducing poverty is what he calls 'humanity' – that is, the moral duty to alleviate severe suffering for its own stake. In other words, the imperative to relieve hunger and starvation arises out of a basic concern for the well-being of other human beings. This goal of 'humanity', Campbell maintains, is distinct from considerations of justice, and ought to serve as a fundamental ethical driver of public policy.

Additionally, Campbell advances the proposition that in order to justify and develop a satisfactory policy approach for eradicating global poverty we need to embrace what might be termed 'virtuous prudence' — which he sees as a moral virtue that is distinct from both justice and humanity. Virtuous prudence, in Campbell's view, entails something more than simply enlightened self-interest and includes the notion of mutually beneficial conduct and a concern to provide assistance to the poor and disadvantaged in ways that will minimise dependency and generate increased self-sufficiency. Hence, policy measures to alleviate global poverty need to be designed and implemented with care. While the central goal must be kept sharply in focus, it is also important to recognise that the various policy instruments that are available may have very different implications, including different impacts on the longer-term capabilities and wherewithal of those receiving assistance.

At least two important lessons concerning the relationship between ethics and public policy can be drawn from Campbell's analysis. First, being able to justify policies on multiple ethical grounds has significant potential benefits: not merely does it strengthen the moral case for governmental action and increase the likely level of public support, but it also helps to ensure policies are appropriately crafted to take into account the full range of relevant ethical values. Second, the means and the ends of public policy are closely coupled. They both have ethical dimensions, and these need to be considered simultaneously rather than sequentially.

Ethical policy analysis and advice giving

For policy makers and their advisers serious ethical reflection on both the purpose of policies and how they should be designed is crucial. But a range of other ethical issues also arise in policy-making contexts. For instance, what norms and values should guide the behaviour of those involved in the policy process? What procedures should be adopted in the event of conflicts of interest? How should the need for secrecy — which is essential for frank and confidential discussions — be balanced against the desirability of openness and public participation? Further, for departmental officials working for a democratically elected government, there are a variety of quite specific ethical issues. For example, to what extent is it legitimate for officials to challenge the priorities and policies of the government? What are the boundaries of free and frank advice or loyal and obedient service? Is it appropriate for officials to advocate for particular social, cultural, economic, or environmental outcomes within the performance of their public duties?

Such issues are explored by two contributors to this volume — Michael Mintrom and David Bromell — both of whom have worked as government officials and within an academic context. In his chapter 'Doing ethical policy analysis', Mintrom highlights five ethical principles that should guide policy analysts: integrity, competence, responsibility, respect, and concern. In so doing he emphasises the importance of policy analysts being well connected to the communities that their policies affect and alert to the impacts of their work on the lives of others. Meanwhile, David Bromell proposes a chalcedonian 'distinction without division or separation' between the roles of analysis, advice giving, and advocacy – that is, the interplay between information, interests, and ideology. He identifies principles to guide public servants in maintaining such distinctions and exercising moral judgement within inevitably imperfect democratic processes and institutions, and within a real-world context in which conflicts over facts and values, means and ends, are inescapable. Such an applied ethics requires the active cultivation of what Kenneth Winston (2009) terms 'moral competence in public life'.

The first part of this volume concludes with timely reflections by John Uhr on the limits to ethics in the policy realm. Uhr is not of course suggesting that policy makers should ignore ethical considerations or that we should abandon the task of constructing policies on secure ethical foundations. But he levels three warnings regarding their application. First, he argues that an over-emphasis on moral theory runs the risk of dragging the ethics of public policy in the wrong direction towards a world of uncompromising absolutes. The solution is to make a distinction between belief-based morality and practice-based ethics so that we can focus on the practical 'role ethics' of policy makers. Second, central government agencies can promote unrealistic versions of official ethics with a 'one size fits all' approach. The solution, he suggests, is to ensure the 'ethics of office' are appropriately dispersed or context-specific rather than inappropriately uniform or standardised. Third, he cautions policy makers against bypassing the democratic process and using what he calls 'stealth ethics' to guide policy choices. The solution is to put democracy back into ethics by insisting on an ethics of fair procedure as a core foundation of public policy.

Ethics of climate change

The second part of this volume focuses on the ethics of climate change. As the chapters in this part illustrate, the complex issues related to the problem of climate change and the pressing need to agree on how to avoid its damaging consequences make this problem perhaps the most challenging facing humanity today.

Climate change is both an important *ethical* issue and a *public policy* issue. It is an *ethical* issue simply because it raises the normative question about what we *should* do given that our actions (or our failure to act) have the potential to cause significant harm to ourselves and future generations, as well as other species and the environment. Unlike previous generations, our generation is in the unique position of both knowing the potentially catastrophic consequences of our actions and having the ability to do something about it. If our generation fails to prevent the potentially catastrophic consequences of climate change, this will likely be one of humanity's greatest moral failings.

Climate change is also a critical *public policy* issue. It is a classic example of a commons dilemma at the global level, a kind of problem where a common property resource or collective good is damaged as a result of individuals in the collective acting in their own self-interest. As such, the problem is one that affects all of us and that all of us can affect. The global scope of the problem means any effective solution can be achieved only through an international agreement that requires individuals and nations to look beyond their immediate self-interest and take into account the interests of others, the broader collective, and future generations. But the causes of this problem go far beyond the actions of particular individuals. They are deeply rooted in institutional practices and structures. The extensive reliance on polluting resources in developed countries goes to the heart of how individuals in these countries live (Jamieson 1992). The fundamental changes that are necessary, therefore, can be achieved only through effective policies and agreements at the national and international levels.

Several factors make the problem of climate change enormously complex from both ethical and public policy perspectives. As already noted, from a purely ethical perspective, climate change raises a wide range of questions. At the most fundamental and theoretical level, there is the question of what is the right or appropriate moral theory to adopt in analysing the problem – a deontological approach that focuses on duties, a consequentialist approach that focuses on consequences, or a virtue theory that focuses on character traits.

The standard approach in environmental economics and public policy has been to use a broadly consequentialist approach, and in particular, a utilitarian cost–benefit analysis, as most prominently illustrated by the review conducted for the British government by Nicholas Stern (2006). The success of this kind of approach, not simply as an economic analysis but one that appropriately reflects ethical values and considerations depends on two broad issues. First, the approach needs to address traditional problems that have been raised for consequentialist/utilitarian approaches, such as whether it is possible to take into account rights, special obligations, and prioritising certain individuals. Second, the approach also requires a plausible theory of value that addresses issues such as (a) how to assess the moral value of current and future people's deaths and our extinction or population collapse and (b) whether the environment has any intrinsic moral value.

John Broome addresses some of these issues, such as how to assess the moral value of our extinction or population collapse. Although we tend naturally to think that such a consequence is intrinsically bad, Broome argues that preventing a life, or a set of lives, from existing would be bad only if the level of well-being of these potential lives is greater than a neutral level of well-being. Moreover, he argues that even if we assume that future lives have a greater than neutral level of well-being, considerations about our extinction and population collapse can wrongly dominate our analysis of how to respond appropriately to climate change. We can mistakenly think that the most important thing to do is to avoid the unlikely consequence of our extinction or population collapse. Using an expected utility analysis, Broome shows that the small chance of utterly catastrophic climate change (for example, warming of 8°C or more) should not dominate our ethical analysis. Instead, we should be equally, if not more, concerned about the harm that moderate to severe climate change will inflict.

Xavier Márquez, in his chapter, explores the merits, tensions, and limitations of using a virtue theory approach in conjunction with the three broad kinds of solutions to collective action problems: technical, external/incentive, and internal/educational (Hardin 1968). In particular, Márquez notes that the research suggests that conditional virtues – virtues that are fragile and sensitive to context – are much more prevalent than robust virtues that are unconditional and less sensitive to context. If Márquez is correct, reliance on a virtue approach and conditional virtues highlights tensions with technical, incentive, and educational-based solutions to commons and collective action problems. For example, technical solutions, such as geoengineering, have the adverse effect of decreasing the inculcation of virtues; individuals have fewer opportunities and less motivation to develop virtuous habits if there is an effective technology for 'solving' the commons problem. And although incentive schemes tend to be more compatible with virtuous behaviour if the appropriate motivations and information are provided, an over-emphasis on external motivating factors can negatively affect the internalisation of virtues.

As a collective action problem, climate change raises ethical challenges that are much broader than simply determining what is ethically right for individuals to do in light of the consequences of their actions, or their duties, or what are virtuous character traits. For instance, it is also morally relevant that some individuals and countries have had a greater role in causing the problem, that some have a greater capability to solve the problem, and that still others are more vulnerable or likely to benefit from any mitigation actions that are taken. In short, one of the fundamental ethical issues raised by climate change is about distributive justice or fairness: what is, and how do we determine, the most just or fair way of distributing the responsibilities of dealing with climate change in light of considerations such as those above?

As a problem of distributive justice, climate change is perhaps the most complex ethical problem that humanity has ever faced. In addition to raising theoretical issues about what principles and theories of justice – whether egalitarian, utilitarian, or desert-based – should be used, the problem raises a wide range of ethical considerations given the global and intergenerational dimensions of the problem. How do we account for historical, non-culpable polluting caused by previous generations? Should we prioritise the needs of countries that are worst off and are most vulnerable to the effects of climate change? Do citizens of states have a default entitlement to their current level of well-being? How does a country balance its obligations to its citizens compared with the citizens of other countries? Should future individuals, goods, and services be given the same moral weight as current individuals, goods, and services? As discussed by Andy Reisinger and Howard Larsen, and Dan Weijers, David Eng, and Ramon Das, the success of any of the theoretical approaches to justice depends on whether countries can address these questions, and thus identify the relevant ethical principles (for example, historical and/or culpable responsibility, capability, basic rights and needs, vulnerability, status quo entitlements, equity) and how these should be prioritised.

At the heart of the negotiations on climate change has been the principle of common but differentiated responsibilities and respective capabilities, which has been central to the approach under the United Nations Framework Convention on Climate Change, negotiated in 1992. Although the principle has been almost universally endorsed by the international community, there is no agreement on how it should be interpreted and, in particular, on how the responsibilities should be differentiated. In their chapter, Weijers, Eng, and Das argue for an interpretation of the principle that emphasises basic needs, ability, and culpable responsibility. The two main claims of their view are as follows. First, countries whose citizens do not meet a minimum average level of well-being are licensed to knowingly pollute. Second, all other countries, in proportion to their respective capabilities, bear a three-fold responsibility, namely to account for a) the culpable polluting that they currently cause, b) all non-culpable historical polluting, and c) the permissible polluting caused by the countries whose citizens do not meet a minimum average level of well-being.

For public policy makers, many of the significant challenges are not simply theoretical or ethical. Any real solution to the problem of climate change, in addition to being just, needs to be effective, practical, and politically achievable. For example, the problem of justifying why we should prioritise climate change over other pressing aims, such as the recent global financial crisis, presents a significant political challenge for public policy makers and officials. Large parts of the population continue to raise the issue of empirical uncertainty, so continue to be sceptical about the science of climate change and whether we can be certain about its causes and effects. Although these doubts are not surprising – especially given the impact that policies such as emissions trading schemes and emissions taxes are likely to have on large parts of the population – they are irrational. On any reasonable cost–benefit analysis of the problem, the magnitude of the harmful consequences of climate change and the risks of the impacts far outweigh any concerns about empirical uncertainty.

The far more daunting challenge facing public policy makers arises from the interdisciplinary nature of the problem. Beyond the purely ethical complexities described earlier, any effective solution obviously needs to rely on a scientific analysis to identify the causes and effects of climate change as well as effective strategies for mitigation and adaptation. At the same time, public policy makers need an economic analysis of the costs and benefits of potential strategies and policies. The issues that arise from analysing the problem from each of these perspectives are, of course, enormously complex.

The interdisciplinary nature of the problem of climate change does not arise merely from the fact it requires analyses from many different perspectives – scientific, economic, ethical, and political. As Reisinger and Larsen discuss, many of the key concepts at the heart of the debate on climate change are inherently interdisciplinary. 'Key vulnerabilities', 'dangerous climate change', and 'acceptable risks', for example, can be defined only on the basis of both scientific and ethical analyses. Likewise, determining the appropriate discount rate – a key concept in any cost–benefit analysis that reflects the value of goods and service in the future compared with today – can be informed only by both economic and ethical analyses. Of course, drawing on different disciplinary perspectives is not without its challenges, but, as highlighted in this volume, it can enrich our understanding and deepen our appreciation of the complexity and gravity of the issues at stake. Arguably, the problem of climate change illustrates this better than any other contemporary ethical or policy dilemma.

Perspectives on ethics and the economy

The final part of this book looks at issues related to 'economics', in particular the relationship between ethical behaviour and the functioning of markets, the question of how far markets should be regulated, the moral dilemma of 'freeloading' in systems that allocate welfare benefits unconditionally, and the challenges posed by rising economic inequality. Forming a backdrop to this section is the global financial crisis that first shook the world in 2008, and three of the chapters engage directly with that crisis. Many commentators viewed this crisis as a consequence of highly *unethical* behaviour on the part of people in the financial and banking industry, prompting calls for a radical re-examination of the way markets operate and a fresh look at issues such as accountability, regulation, and control. These calls directly and indirectly inform the contributions to this part.

It is tempting to conclude that the global economic downturn offered a stark illustration of what can happen when ethics gets uncoupled from economics, when markets are allowed to operate in a totally 'unfettered' way. In the ever more brutal 'dog eat dog' world of contemporary capitalism what matters most is securing global brand recognition, improving shareholder returns, and discovering ever more imaginative ways of 'making money from money'. The voices seeking to highlight the human consequences of economic activity, or calling for moral restraint in the interests of 'the common good', seem like ever fainter cries in a more and more inhospitable wilderness. Yet it was not ever thus, for as R. H. Tawney reminded his readers nearly a hundred years ago, the gradual separation of ethics from economics was really only set in train with the development of capitalism. Until then, Tawney noted, economic thought had been understood as part of a hierarchy of values embracing all human interests and activities (cited in Gorringe 1994, pp. 31–2). Now we could say that the situation is reversed to the extent that, for many economists and politicians, the global economy is the system within which *everything else* is subsumed. As such, the global economy is able, as Jonathon Porritt writes, to 'define its own operational boundaries' (Porritt 2007, p. 56), to effectively close down space for ethical questions rooted in a discourse situated outside those boundaries. As Washington-based commentator Jim Wallis has argued, we have now succeeded in substituting 'market value' for 'moral values', with the market replacing 'much of the moral space of society, even questioning the value of having "moral space" where the market does not reach' (Wallis 2010, p. 28).

When a former UK prime minister, Gordon Brown, suggested that 'the unsupervised globalisation of our financial markets did not only cross national boundaries [but] moral boundaries too' (Brown and Rudd 2009), he reflected the view of many influential figures in politics, the academy, the media, and the church that 'the market' and 'ethics' needed to become reacquainted. Calls for greater regulation of markets, for measures to ensure more responsible lending, for action to restrain what was seen as the 'greed' of banks and finance houses, were voiced in parliaments, in pulpits, in news-rooms, and on the streets. Developments such as the introduction of a currency transaction levy in the United Kingdom, essentially a tax on the banking sector to raise new money for international development, suggest these calls have not entirely fallen on deaf ears. Yet as the contributors to this volume argue, the issues behind the global crisis were multifaceted and diverse, and the ethical questions they raised complex and involved.

Simon Smelt considers the oft-recited claim that the root of the crisis lay in the 'greed' of people operating in the market, as if this were somehow a new phenomenon (as in Alan Greenspan's assertion in 2008 that people 'got greedy' (cited in Goodman 2008)). Greed, Smelt notes, is hardly new, and in fact we have developed over the years a better idea of how to harness it: legislation has been in place for years to curb excessive pay and benefits for bankers, for example. We just did not ensure it was enforced. The question of governance and regulation in the banking sector is also more complex than sometimes imagined, Smelt argues, since it was the better governed and regulated banks that got themselves into the most trouble, not those we might see as 'laggard'. The technology was there but, again, it failed when needed. Indeed, Smelt notes, after considering a range of factors in the crisis, the root of the crisis lay not in any lack of regulation or risk analysis in the financial sector but in 'the practice of ethical policy and governance through established principles of day-to-day fairness applied so as to build and earn trust'. The 'moral dimension' underlying the economic crisis, in other words, stemmed from a weakness in the commutative justice that underpins the marketplace. This was not a crisis brought about by a shortage of 'trust' – another myth Smelt seeks to challenge – but by trust in modern sophisticated risk analysis and regulatory techniques being misplaced.

David Rea offers a different but complementary take on the question of how ethical behaviour can be understood within an economic context, arguing that a direct relationship exists between such behaviour and economic efficiency. Starting, as Smelt did, with the global financial crisis and the debate around its origins and causes, Rea argues that the crisis provides us with a compelling example of how poor ethical standards within business can result in adverse economic consequences. For Rea, ethical behaviour in the context of economic activity involves individuals balancing their personal self-interests and the interests of others – forgoing, perhaps, a course of action that would benefit them in favour of one that benefits others – and he argues that, while selfish behaviour can lead to markets functioning badly or failing altogether, ethical behaviour can be seen to increase their efficiency. Taking as a case study the practice of contracting, Rea shows how, for example, the construction of safeguards against the risk of opportunism on the part of the other party can be costly, and how the costs involved not infrequently mean that parts of the process, or indeed of the contract itself, are left incomplete. Thus, the extent to which individuals act selfishly is material to the overall cost of contracting, and where ethical behaviour is more prevalent, the process is both cheaper and more efficient. Rea adduces evidence to show that countries where ethical behaviour is more widespread tend to be richer than those with lower measured ethics. He argues that New Zealand, despite already having a relatively high ranking on the 'index of ethical behaviour', might be able to reach the income levels of Australia if it had a level of ethical behaviour akin to that of Switzerland.

Given the focus of his chapter, Rea notes, but chooses not to develop, the argument that ethical behaviour in an economic context might lead to a 'fairer' distribution of resources. Smelt, too, touches on the issue of 'distributive justice', although he suggests the pursuit of such a goal through the market can be shown to weaken its 'workings', even that attempts to pursue it may have exacerbated the global crisis. In his chapter, Andrew Bradstock does indeed see tackling economic inequality as an ethical imperative, and argues that both on theological and sociological grounds the case can be made for governments to pursue policies aimed, not just at reducing poverty, but at narrowing the gap between 'rich' and 'poor'. Bradstock's case rests on two lines of reasoning. First, the Judaeo-Christian principle that all people are created with equal value places a responsibility on communities to ensure that none of their members is unable to meet their basic needs. Second, current research in the area of public health demonstrates that one of the key factors behind dysfunctional societies is their level of economic inequality. Just as the biblical narratives suggest that measures to prevent economic inequality becoming entrenched will enhance the health and well-being of a community and its individual members, contemporary research indicates that even small reductions in inequality can result, not just in fewer poor people, but in safer, more trusting, and more cohesive societies to the benefit of all their members. Therefore, countries with relatively high levels of inequality, such as New Zealand, Australia, and the United Kingdom, could usefully consider measures aimed at reducing inequality, and while these will inevitably involve a degree of central coordination, they do not imply a return to the 'big state'. Indeed, Bradstock argues, a wide variety of mechanisms might be adopted to narrow inequality, and only an approach that moves beyond old ideological divisions would be likely to succeed.

One area that Bradstock suggests will need to be addressed if inequality is to be tackled effectively is the provision of social assistance (or social welfare). Julia Maskivker examines this subject in detail in her chapter, focusing on the debate over whether the provision of 'unconditional' welfare is compatible with well-accepted principles of justice. Is it fair, for instance, for people to enjoy the benefits of the system without contributing to it? And is it reasonable for hardworking taxpayers to fund the benefits of those who opt not to work when in practice they could? Maskivker notes the force of this 'free-rider' argument against unconditional welfare benefits, and highlights the fact that defenders of unconditionality have yet to come up with a satisfactory rebuttal.

The strongest counter-argument thus far is that the option to exit cooperation is not unjust because it is equally available to everybody. But Maskivker criticises this contention on the grounds that assessing the 'justness' of a given situation cannot be undertaken simply by evoking 'a distributive criterion as the primordial index of fairness'. Free-riding, in other words, could be said to be by nature unjust, regardless of how many people are in a position to take advantage of it.

Taking up the challenge to find a better refutation, and drawing on the work of John Rawls (1972) and H. L. A. Hart (1955), Maskivker develops her own response to the 'free-rider' objection to unconditional welfare benefits. Her argument, in short, is that freedom from cooperation in the generation of social benefits is justified on the basis of injustice in the design of the cooperative scheme and the non-voluntary nature of that scheme.

Like Bradstock, Maskivker also places a high priority on the fulfilment of 'basic human needs', and one conclusion to draw from this section is that the ultimate ethical criterion for measuring economic arrangements must be the extent to which they enhance and promote the good life for all. This brings us back to Campbell's assertion at the beginning of this book, and which runs like a leitmotif throughout each of its parts, that a primary ethical driver of public policy must be a basic concern for the well-being of others.

References

Brown, G., and K. Rudd. 2009. 'Speech and Q&A at St Paul's Cathedral.' London, 31 March. http://webarchive.nationalarchives.gov.uk/+/number10.gov.uk/news/speeches-and-transcripts/2009/03/pms-speech-at-st-pauls-cathedral-18858.

Considine, M. 1994. *Public Policy: A critical approach*. South Melbourne: Macmillan.

Goodman, P. 2008. 'Taking hard new look at a Greenspan legacy.' *New York Times*, 8 October. www.nytimes.com/2008/10/09/business/economy/09greenspan.html.

Gorringe, T. J. 1994. *Capital and the Kingdom: Theological ethics and economic order*. Maryknoll, NY: Orbis.

Hardin, G. 1968. 'The tragedy of the commons.' *Science* 162(3859): 1243–8.

Hart, H. L. A. 1955. 'Are there any natural rights?' *Philosophical Review* 64(2): 175–91.

Henry, K. 2009. 'Fiscal policy: More than just a national budget.' Address to the 2009 Whitlam Institute Symposium, 30 November. www.treasury.gov.au/documents/1678/HTML/docshell.asp?URL=Whitlam_Institute_Speech.htm.

Jamieson, D. 1992. 'Ethics, public policy, and global warming.' *Science Technology and Human Values* 17(2): 139–53.

Porritt, J. 2007. *Capitalism as if the World Matters*. London: Earthscan.

Rawls, J. 1972. *A Theory of Justice*. London: Oxford University Press.

Robson, J (ed.). 1966. *John Stuart Mill: A selection of his works*. New York: Odyssey Press.

Sen, A. 2009. *The Idea of Justice*. London: Allen Lane.

Stern, N. 2006. *The Economics of Climate Change: The Stern Review*. Cambridge, UK: Cambridge University Press.

Wallis, J. 2010. *Rediscovering Values: On Wall Street, Main Street, and Your Street*. New York: Howard Books.

Winston, K. 2009. *Moral Competence in Public Life*. Occasional paper 4. Melbourne: Australia and New Zealand School of Government and State Services Authority. www.ssa.vic.gov.au/CA2571410025903D/WebObj/OccPaper_04_Winston/$File/OccPaper_04_Winston.pdf.

Ethical foundations of public policy

2. Justice, humanity, and prudence

Tom Campbell

Introduction

This chapter examines the concepts of justice, humanity, and prudence in the context of justifying policies, especially policies aimed at reducing global poverty, by which I mean extreme poverty approached as a global issue and requiring the urgent attention of national governments and international organisations. My thesis is that there are good reasons not to classify this matter morally as primarily a matter of global justice; nor, however, should it be considered as based primarily on what is called 'humanitarianism', a term that is closely associated with emergency aid in kind. Rather, I suggest, we need to develop and include a contemporary moral notion of what I call 'humanity', that is the duty (and the motivation) to relieve extreme suffering for its own sake. Something like a moral principle of humanity, combined with elements of justice and what may be called 'virtuous prudence', is required if we are to articulate a satisfactory approach to selecting the objectives, justifications, motivations, and techniques for developing policies aiming at eradicating global poverty.

There are many divergent good reasons for pursuing a policy and justifying its political objectives and methods. In some cases, such as the elimination of extreme poverty, it is likely to be 'the more the merrier' as far as rationales for reducing poverty are concerned. It is in this spirit that I approach the task of gathering together considerations of humanity, justice, and prudence in the cause of reducing global deprivation. The hope is that, by bringing together these distinctive moral rationales, we may strengthen the case and perhaps also the motivations for achieving an evidently good end. If one approach does not convince the critics or stir the apathetic, perhaps another will. And if one approach is accepted as a relevant moral reason, perhaps the other approaches will join in to add greater moral force to back it up. This line of thought suggests that it is unwise to rely on any one moral basis when advocating such a good and urgent cause.

In general, I take this view, and my principal objective in this chapter is to warn against relying on justice as the sole ethical justification for poverty eradication, commending the significance of what I call humanity, and adding some thoughts about the moral relevance of prudence. However, we need to consider also whether the substance of one moral foundation can erode the force of others. Thus, overplaying humanity may distract us from the task of laying blame and enforcing fair competition, while the covert appeal to self-interest associated with the concept of prudence may undermine the unselfish and guilt-based motivations that go with humanity and justice, respectively.

Articulating the moral grounds for taking action to reduce global poverty raises questions both of moral rightness and of moral motivation. Indeed the question of how best to frame the moral basis for poverty reduction is bound to raise questions as to which moral basis is likely to stimulate the most effective responses. That is as much a matter of psychological and economic analysis as it is as about normative ethics. The pursuit of policy goals has to take into account the motivations that are required to garner support for the adoption and implementation of policies. Nevertheless, my primary philosophical interest here is in identifying the morally best goals and the morally preferred means to reach the desired objective and to do this by means of moral reflection rather than the associated matter of how to maximise moral suasion.

Within normative ethics itself, important implications arise when we introduce a variety of moral foundations to support a policy objective. A plurality of values may affect the specific content of the policies that we should adopt by altering our priorities and affecting the mechanisms that are appropriate for the achievement of our ultimate objectives. In the context of global poverty, for instance, different but overlapping moral approaches may affect who should have priority in poverty relief, how this relief should be managed, and who should bear the burdens that are associated with the process.

Moreover, specific objectives may change in the light of the alternative moral foundations introduced into the moral and practical debate with which we are concerned. Thus, considerations of humanity, that is the relief of suffering for its own sake, can lead to a different vision of what it is that constitutes poverty, while considerations of prudence may point us away from drawn out investigations into culpability, compensation, and responsibility for the suffering of others and towards the promotion of mutual benefit. Further, the choice of moral principles for use in developing policies relating to global poverty has considerable relevance for the choice of appropriate mechanisms for attaining our chosen objectives.

Justice

The eradication of world-wide extreme poverty is standardly regarded as being a matter of 'global justice' (Caney 2005; Brock 2009). This may lead us to assume that justice is the sole moral basis for the obligations to remedy poverty, rather than one amongst several moral considerations, all of which have relevance to poverty eradication. Here, I take Thomas Pogge as the exemplar since he is an influential theorist who places great emphasis on global poverty as a violation of justice. Pogge does not confine his attention to ideas of justice in relation to global poverty, but he does make it the centre piece of his moral approach. In brief, the Pogge picture is that Rawls's theory of justice (Rawls 1971) is basically sound but needs to be extended beyond its national applications within independent states to an international or cosmopolitan context in a world that, from the moral point of view, has no borders (Pogge 2008).

Pogge's core position is that extreme poverty is primarily a consequence of a biased trading system and abuses of power, economic and military, that skew the global economic system to the advantage of the better-off and to the grave disadvantage of the very poor. The institutions of international and domestic trade are controlled by the rich for their own benefit. Or, more generally and less starkly, some countries benefit from the institutions of the global economy in a way that is disproportional and therefore unfair.

Further, Pogge holds to a sharp moral distinction between harming and not preventing harm, between killing and letting die (Pogge 2005). For him, the violations that give rise to our obligations with respect to poverty must be positive acts of harming others in such a way as to have caused their poverty in a culpable manner. He holds that, once we have come to grips with the horrendous phenomenon of global poverty, the crucial factor to be determined is the degree to which government, citizens, and corporations, are complicit in systems that cause such poverty. The evil is not so much the poverty itself as the fact it is the result of human institutions and collective choices: 'We should not, then, think of our individual donations and of possible institutional poverty eradication initiatives … as helping the poor, but as protecting them from the effects of global rules whose injustice benefits us and is our responsibility' (Pogge 2008, p. 23). He, therefore, argues that 'the relevant analogue for torture is, then, not poverty, but rather a certain kind of impoverishment that other agents are causally and morally responsible for' (Pogge 2007, p. 15).

It follows that these institutions should be reformed and those who have benefited and are benefiting from their unreformed operations are at fault and have thereby unjustly enriched themselves, so ought to rectify the harm they have caused. It is, thus, a matter of justice that there should be a redistribution of resources to something like the situation that would have been the outcome of fair trade, fair politics, and fair educational opportunities. Those responsible for actively bringing about this situation should be held accountable with respect to taking the positive actions necessary to rectify the appalling situation they have brought about or from which they have unfairly benefited.

The attractions of this approach to global poverty are evident. Rectification can be demanded as of right. There is a (rough) basis for calculating the extent of the goods to be redistributed. There is a way to identify those who have the responsibility of putting right the wrongs they have done. Further, there is hope for the future in the prospect of correcting the distortions of the past. For recipients of aid there is dignity in being compensated for the deprivation of what is rightly theirs.

Moreover, there is a powerful rhetorical force to the language of injustice as something that is morally intolerable. It also accords with the common view that, by and large, unless we have special responsibilities, we are culpable for the harm we do rather than the harm we fail to prevent. This makes for a more secure basis for moral claims and makes it more likely that people will respond well to the imposition of obligations to help those whom we are believed to have harmed.

Yet there are also disadvantages to having such a close association between poverty relief and remedial justice. Not all extreme poverty can be laid at the door of exploitation or unfairness. Many natural disasters are difficult to lay to the account of human beings, although, of course, the capacity to deal with natural disasters may be affected by the past immoralities of other people. Not all disasters arising from environmental change are 'natural' in the sense of produced by non-human facts, as we are becoming all too well aware in relation to global warming. Then, there is the unequal distribution of natural resources, which would appear to be as much a matter of luck as of bad behaviour, although of course we can see much of human history as a struggle between peoples for access to what were seen at the time as valuable natural resources. Further, there are the variable capacities of different cultures to generate materially beneficial activities, for which individuals and groups cannot reasonably be held to account. While all ways of life may (but of course need not) be regarded as equally valuable in terms of worthwhile forms of life, they are certainly not equal with respect to their capacity to create material prosperity. Moreover, it is very difficult if not impossible to calculate the harms caused on the basis of counterfactuals relating to what would have happened under different trading regimes and political systems. Most individuals who have benefited from maladjustments in global economies have little actual culpability for situations they were powerless to affect.

Such fault as there is, and there is a great deal of wrongdoing at work in the generation of global poverty, often lies with people who do not have the resources to provide effective poverty eradication. Offenders are not always winners. Then there is very significant disagreement as to the best means of reducing extreme poverty and, in this context, the best means may not be to demand the return of allegedly ill-gotten gains on unfair distribution. If it is achieving outcomes with which we are concerned, rather than rectifying past wrongs, then the pursuit of compensation may not be the most effective way to proceed.

In relation to the objection that few individuals have any clear responsibility for unfair trading and abuse of economic and political power, we may fall back on the weaker version of the justice approach to global poverty. This version is that there is a degree of moral culpability in being complicit in injustice, by going along with or acquiescing in the systems in place. It is argued, for instance, that in such situations there is 'unjust enrichment' in the sense that people have received rewards that they do not deserve at the expense of those who have been deprived of their moral entitlements, even though this was not the result of their actions or part of their conscious intentions.

Finally, there is a straightforward moral objection to prioritising rectificatory justice over the distinct and independent moral aim of relieving suffering for its own sake, whatever its causes and whoever, if anyone, is responsible for its occurrence. It is to the articulation and commendation of the latter principle that I now turn.

Humanity

An alternative view of global poverty sees it as an intolerable situation experienced by those who are poor rather than as an injustice arising out of the actions of the better-off. Poverty, it is argued, is morally unacceptable directly because of the suffering that it involves. It is the experiences of those in extreme poverty that founds the moral obligations to improve their situation. The misery of hunger, malnutrition, ill health, and premature death that goes with the lives of those who lack the basic means of subsistence is the prime issue at stake.

Straightforward utilitarian reasoning is sufficient to give rise to this morally uncomplicated analysis of human duties with respect to global poverty. Such reasoning is founded on a simple endorsement of a basic human concern for others that prompts us to relieve pain and suffering for its own sake, irrespective of its cause. Thus, Adam Smith contends that, as a matter of fact, which he endorses as also a fundamental moral norm, 'We cannot form the idea of an innocent and sensible being, whose happiness we should not desire, or to whose misery, when distinctly brought home to the imagination, we should not have some degree of aversion' (Smith 1790, VI.ii.3.1).

While moral theorists dispute the adequacy of utilitarian calculations as a total account of the content of morality, few would reject the contentions that human pleasures and pains have great moral significance and that the relief of suffering should be given priority over the promotion of pleasure. In relation to extreme poverty, it is relatively uncontroversial to affirm 'negative utilitarianism', which focuses on diminishing suffering rather than promoting pleasure, along the lines developed by moral 'prioritarians' (Parfit 2000). A contemporary version of this position is to be found in the work of Peter Singer, with respect to what he calls 'principles of assistance', according to which the moral duty to assist arises from the combination of severe need on the one hand and the ability to assist on the other (Singer 2009).

While the relief of suffering for its own sake is a very ancient moral imperative, it is not easy to fasten on a contemporary term to label the basic moral truth that we have compelling reason to relieve grave suffering as an end or objective in itself. 'Benevolence' seems too weak, and it highlights feelings, feelings of goodwill, pity, and empathy, rather than moral affirmation of right over wrong. Feelings are crucially important in motivating people to do the right thing in relation to poverty, but they do not feature directly in determining what it is that is morally right, or morally required, with respect to the duty of relieving the suffering of others. Identifying what it is right to do does not require having any particular motive for doing it. Therefore, we may not want to replace 'justice' with 'benevolence'. The term 'beneficence' is scarcely any better in this regard since it smacks of the gracious transfer of what is excess to requirements, or superfluity. 'Charity' carries its own baggage as being concerned with actions that are morally good but not morally required. It is not, at this time, part of the discourse of duty, and it is with duties rather than acts of supererogation that we are concerned here. 'Humanitarian' is closer to what the conceptual terminology is better suited to cover providing effective assistance to those in dire need, but it is too closely associated with a particular form of relief in kind in situations of extreme and abnormal (often natural) catastrophes, such as earthquakes and floods. For such reasons, I use the term 'humanity' as the label for actions done to relieve extreme suffering (Campbell 1974). This is not ideal, because 'humanity' is rather amorphous by itself and, like benevolence, is historically associated with the importance of having feelings of concern for others rather than being a moral principle requiring action. But it is a term with some potential to be filled with the imperatives of a progressive and developing contemporary global morality.

This apparent quibbling with words is important because the conceptual difficulties in articulating a contemporary global ethics are not localised and contingent. Rather, they flow from our working moral framework in which only the terminology of justice, with all its associations with desert, guilt, and fault, is taken to generate powerful and unconditional moral imperatives. We need, but do not yet have, a discourse that adequately expresses the moral imperatives deriving from remediable global poverty. Progressive moral development requires a distinctive language that readily fits the idea that relieving distress has at least equal, perhaps greater, moral weight to rectifying any injustices involved. In the interim, I suggest we speak of the principle of humanity when identifying the morally overriding principle of relieving suffering for its own sake.

There are, however, also instrumental reasons for the relief of distress. Living in extreme poverty makes it difficult to engage in a whole range of morally valuable activities. Survival and basic subsistence are necessary conditions of all other human goods (Shue 1996). In moral terms one such human good is the capacity and opportunity to act as a moral agent, making choices and carrying out projects on the basis of moral considerations rather than the immediate imperatives of survival. On this view, agents need to be alive and in a position to think rationally and choose effectively if they are to fulfil their nature as agents.

This neo-Kantian approach is exemplified in the work of Alan Gewirth who contends that (Gewirth 1982, pp. 201–3):

> by virtue of being actual or prospective agents who have certain needs of agency, persons have moral rights to freedom and well-being. Since all humans are such agents, the generic rights to freedom and well-being are human rights … It is obvious that starvation is a basic harm, a deprivation of basic well-being.

So much would seem to be implied by article 22 of the United Nations Declaration of Human Rights, according to which:

> Everyone, as a member of society, has the right to social security and is entitled to realization, through national effort and international cooperation and in accordance with the organization and resources of each State, of the economic, social and cultural rights indispensable for his dignity and the free development of his personality.

There is considerable moral insight in this analysis but it supplements rather than replaces the principle of humanity in the understanding of the moral evil of extreme poverty. Moral choice and human moral development are distinctive and vitally important moral considerations, but they do not displace the moral centrality of relieving suffering for its own sake. In making suffering morally secondary to the development of distinctively human capacities Gewirth's analysis distracts attention from a prior and more compelling vision of what is at stake with respect to extreme poverty. Focusing on the implications of moral agency for human moral development has the effect of diminishing the more immediate and demanding moral objective of removing the causes of human misery. Moral agency is of considerable significance, especially for philosophers looking for what is distinctive about human worth, but it is a serious practical mistake to make the relief of extreme poverty dependent solely on its connections with the realisation of this higher but morally less demanding value.

We are dealing here with a bundle of moral rationales that can be brought into relationship with each other through a process of moral reflection and conceptual adjustment. Clearly, moral duties arise from the culpable causation of poverty and there is good reason to bring these duties within a concept of justice in which desert plays an important role (Campbell 2010, pp. 20–36). Equally, there are other, poverty-related duties that are unrelated to the deserts of those involved that are better conceptualised as having to do with humanity. Further, there is no reason why balancing should always prioritise justice over humanity. It may be objected that justice is, by definition, the overriding moral criterion in the public sphere. This conceptual prioritisation of moral concepts in the political arena did not originate with Rawls, but in recent times it can be traced to the dominant influence of his work. Rawls stipulates that 'justice is the first virtue of social institutions, as truth is of systems of thought' (Rawls 1971, p. 3). This could be taken simply as a preliminary identification of his focus on the institutionally based distribution of the benefits and burdens of social co-operation, with 'justice' being the term he uses to label whatever is taken to be the most important moral considerations for this purpose. However, this conceptual prioritisation plays a more substantive part in his analysis when he comes to consider such matters as the place of natural (as opposed to institutionally created) desert as a relevant factor in such social distributions and argues for the exclusion of desert from the principles of justice. This has the double disadvantage of running up against the close relationship between justice and desert in moral discourse and diminishing the direct appeal to humanity as a core ingredient in determining social policy relating to distributive issues. In this situation, especially when we transfer Rawls's domestic concerns to the global sphere, it is best to question the automatic priority he gives to justice and, at the same time, to reconnect justice with concepts of responsibility and desert, thereby opening the way to giving greater prominence to humanity as a moral consideration that is at least on a par with justice as far as public policy is concerned.

The implication of this morally motivated conceptual shift is to give more impetus to redirecting policy priorities towards major redistributive goals. There are clearly many different ways in which such objectives might be implemented at the global level. Most of these are likely to be directed to promoting economic development rather than providing immediate 'humanitarian' aid in the form of food supplies and shelter. However, the funding of such programmes will always require significant levels of domestic taxation in more economically developed countries, the effectiveness of which will be largely dependent on obtaining working international agreements to co-operate in the raising and expenditure of such revenues.

This might be achieved, for instance, through the co-ordinated initiation of a global humanitarian levy based on the operationalisation of the principle of humanity. This could be a morally better based and politically more palatable enterprise to deal with global policy than one that seeks to extract such revenues from those who are deemed most responsible for the current state of affairs, the emphasis being more on the capacity to assist than the relative fault of the parties involved. The sort of scheme I have in mind is an earmarked tax on all personal incomes over a particular level of income (a 'supertax' in an erstwhile idiom), a levy on personal wealth above a prescribed level (a wealth tax), and equivalent corporate levies relating to both profits and wealth. These revenues would initially be imposed by states but could be implemented through an international organisation (Campbell in Pogge 2007, pp. 55–75, at pp. 67–9).

The political co-ordination problems of gaining the adoption of such schemes are dauntingly massive and I make no claim here as to the relative feasibility of alternatives. Drawing attention to the sort of policy arrangements to which the principle of humanity gives rise does, however, emphasise its distinctiveness as against the connotations of justice and 'humanitarianism'. With humanitarianism, the focus is on immediate aid in kind, while the principle of humanity serves as a basis for poverty relief through a wide range of mechanisms for promoting development and redistributing resources. The motivations may be similar but the practical conceptions are not. The foundational point that needs to be made is that the policy implications of the principle of humanity are no less complex and no less stringent than the principles of justice.

It is also worth adding that there is no necessary association between the principle of humanity and paternalism, either in the sense of the wiser and the more important seeing to the needs of the less able and less important or in the sense of the providers following their ideas of what is good for the beneficiaries, rather than taking account of the beneficiaries' own judgement as to the manner and methods of the development programmes involved. Outside the perspective of justice there is less basis for the assumption that those who have the resources are entitled to them because they have obtained them due to their merits.

Paternalistic attitudes are more likely to be nurtured within the perspective of justice than in the name of humanity, for it carries no presuppositions of relative merit, either good or ill.

A further source of scepticism about humanity as a moral principle is that it is too demanding, in that it seems to imply that the well-off should divest themselves of their relative wealth, even to the point of becoming poor themselves. In practice, this objection can be met by starting with redistributive schemes that involve the relatively well-off contributing only what they would be expected to contribute if everyone contributed their share. However, this seems a rather ad hoc and rationalised response to a profound moral challenge. Perhaps, in part for this reason, we need to broaden our moral range and turn to considering whether an element of prudence in addition to both humanity and justice should be incorporated within the moral foundations of policy formation in dealing with issues such as global poverty.

Prudence

We have seen that justice and humanity both overlap and diverge with respect to their implications for policy development. In this section I explore the suggestion that an element of prudence should be added to the moral sources on which we draw in relation to global poverty eradication.

Again, the choice of terms is difficult. 'Prudence' points in the direction of rationality concerning means and ends and carries with it regard for what we now talk of as sustainability, at least in respect to long-term rationality. Nowadays, this is usually understood as an amoral capacity that can serve good or ill, and indeed, because of a modern association with self-interest, is commonly contrasted with morality. On the other hand, the term has an ancient, medieval, and, for some of our contemporaries, an important, often central, place within morality as one of the fundamental virtues. According to this school, prudence is the exercise of wisdom in relation to human affairs, so is essential to the achievement of the human good. This analysis, which is derived from Aristotle and Aquinas (Westberg 1994; Hibbs 2001), takes prudence to be a virtue alongside justice and beneficence. However, I do not here adopt an analysis of prudence as a translation for 'phronesis', a form of Aristotelian practical wisdom that incorporates all the elements that are necessary for being a good moral judge. Rather, I adopt this rather old-fashioned term because of its connotations of virtuous self-interest. Virtuous prudence goes beyond the enlightened self-interest of individuals, and beyond even the rationality that serves the interests of social groups and, in principle, of the world at large, but still carries with it the connotation of intelligent objectivity and far-sightedness (Sidgwick 1907; Nagel 1970; Parfit 1981).

Those who want only to persuade rather than reach the right moral decisions, may manipulatively seek to convince those whom they believe ought to be contributing the solution to extreme poverty, by having recourse to the idea of enlightened self-interest. According to self-interest it is rational for individuals and groups to secure their own well-being through having some regard to the interests of other individuals and groups. Self-interest is often (but not universally) a more effective device for securing the co-operation of those who can contribute to the cause than appeals to either humanity or justice. That may be enough to justify the morality of the appeal to enlightened self-interest in the light of its beneficial consequences, in avoiding wars, social disruption, and economic decline.

Whether the indirect morality of appeals to self-interest would justify putting our false claims about the deleterious consequences of extreme poverty on the well-off, I do not speculate here. It can be cogently argued that, on a longer-term view, most people, or at least their families, will benefit one way or another in a material way from eliminating or reducing extreme poverty, although it is far from clear that it is in everyone's immediate interest to contribute to this effort. On the other hand, there is something less than promising in appealing to the prudent individual to acknowledge their obligation to contribute to the abolition of poverty. Prudent people, the stereotype has it, care more for their own future than for the present suffering of others. Prudent people are risk averse. That means they save, rather than donate, or vote for higher taxes.

However, I am more interested here in the direct moral case for prudence in the form of a moral virtue, not because I think this is a good motivation tactic, although it may be, but because prudence, may have something morally distinctive to add to considerations of justice and humanity. In particular, the analysis of prudence may help to bring the morality of justice and humanity into the domain of the everyday world in which we are all primarily concerned with our own projects, our own activities, and our own well-being. Normally we see the everyday world as legitimately concerned with our own (not necessarily either selfish or self-interested) projects, with morality coming in as a circle of limitations as to how we carry through our ordinary lives. However, we can also think in terms of practical morality embedded in our everyday rationality, as something *within* our agent—relative preoccupations: hence, the idea of 'virtuous prudence'. Again, this is partly a tactical matter, as moral appeals are not going to have much impact if they are perceived as discontinuous with the demands of the everyday world, but it is also a moral enquiry into how we can and should integrate our personal preoccupations and our wider duties.

The first barrier to be overcome in taking this approach is that the idea of virtuous prudence seems to be a contradiction in terms. Prudence is generally regarded as no more than being careful when your interests are at stake and having practical regard to your own future well-being. A skill it may be, requiring means–end rationality, self-control, and reflection on one's priority goals. Such skills may be 'virtuous' in a non-moral sense, but there would seem to be no element of moral good and bad or moral praise and blame involved. This position accords with an analysis of prudence as purely instrumental, a cluster of capacities that are useful in relation to a variety of ends of very different moral quality. There are prudent villains who avoid being caught as well as prudent business persons who make profits and prudent saints who look to the future well-being of those they love and care for.

Yet prudence has been regarded as a moral virtue by many thoughtful people. Why might this be so? One reason is that moral agents have a duty to cultivate prudence as a necessary capacity for the attainment of morally desirable goals. This is applicable to individuals pursuing their own morally legitimate interests, a complex matter requiring considerable experience, insight, and sagacity. However, it is equally a requirement of successfully attaining objectives that include the future well-being of the individual's immediate social group and indeed the wider communities in which a person lives. Therefore, one reason for seeing prudence as a policy virtue might be that prudence is an essential precondition for being morally useful where consequences, good and bad, are involved. That does take us as far as having a moral duty to develop our rationality as a skill that is necessary to achieve many morally desirable goals. This is particularly so when we are involved in working out the most effective ways to implement the demands either of global justice or global humanity. Prudence does not have to be intrinsically valuable to be morally commendable.

Another reason for regarding prudence as a virtue draws more on its self-interested focus. This line of argument is that by being self-interestedly prudent a person becomes less dependent on others, so does not make claims on scarce resources or depend on the goodwill and hard work of others. Morally, where possible, people ought to look after themselves and so avoid becoming dependent on others. This can certainly be used as an argument against impoverishing ourselves or our communities in an excess of humanity-inspired giving. It can also be seen as prompting us to devise ways of providing economic aid that do not have the deleterious consequence of creating dependency rather than generating self-sufficiency. Both the instrumental analysis of prudence in terms of successfully achieving morally good outcomes and what is in effect a particular instantiation of the same sort of analysis with respect to avoiding dependency may be seen as no more than sophisticated techniques for achieving moral success rather than independent moral grounds for engaging in poverty relief. Yet they may be developed into something like a counter-morality in which the pursuit of legitimate forms of self-interest by individuals and groups is seen, not as a way of life that is limited by external moral constraints, such as justice and humanity, but as an expression and manifestation of a different aspect of morality.

Here we are dealing with a sense of prudence in which it involves considered and committed effortful participation in the economic and social way of life of which individuals are a part and hence a social commitment of benefit to others, which can be undertaken at least in part for that reason. Arguably such involvement is prudent, in the narrow sense of enlightened self-interest, perhaps for the individual but certainly for the group. Mutually beneficial conduct is in that sense, prudent for any economic and social community. And, perhaps, on the larger scale, it is part of a global prudence that such commitments are valued and encouraged. Individuals flourish by participating in workforces and in family and other social groupings and networks. It is, therefore, imprudent for individuals not to be as actively involved as they can and imprudent for human groups not to encourage such participation. There is, therefore, a moral basis for encouraging involvement in and support for sustainable social groupings and organisations. Further, in so far as this is part of any model for successful human flourishing, it ought not to be discouraged or disparaged even in responding to other moral imperatives, such as the principle of humanity. A coherent model, which does not deal in an awkward clash of incommensurable moral values, might require us to bring an element of global prudence into co-operation with considerations of humanity and justice. This analysis has special application in market economies where generally self-interested economic conduct is a necessary ingredient of a successful market, that is, a market that maximises the availability of desired goods and services at the lowest prices compatible with sustaining a healthy and able workforce. This simplistic model is subject to many moral qualifications, but to the degree that it is accepted, the morality of market-based prudence can be seen as a constituent virtue within a successful economy.

Part of my earlier analysis, in distancing my position from Pogge's emphasis on justice, involved doubting that we can really blame participants in unequal markets who benefit as a result of that participation on the grounds that such participation cannot be regarded as informed and voluntary. Now the argument is rather that people do have an obligation to participate in unequal markets despite their moral deficiencies. Blame may attach where those involved have the capacity to improve the system in question but fail to do so, but that is a separate consideration. Making an overall assessment in an all-things-considered framework that takes into account all the origins and consequences of the system, citizens have obligations to participate in such critiques and in the politics that arises from them. Meanwhile, however, citizens ought to act prudently within markets, both as individuals and as collectives. Indeed, if developing markets is a necessary part of the solution to poverty, then acknowledgement should be given to this fact both with respect to virtuous prudence in economically developed societies and in relation to the methods and mechanisms adopted in seeking to promote development. Thus, markets can be seen as a partial expression of a humanity-based programme. In this case, a counter-morality is at work that, while it may be ultimately based on considerations of both humanity and justice, has at the level of policy analysis, an independent force that ought to be taken into account. According to this counter-morality, the moral status of markets and other less individualistic social institutions must be high (Sen 1985, p. 1; Machan 2009).

Such thoughts may be seen as undermining the moral bases of both the justice and the humanity approaches to global poverty. They certainly do diminish the force of some but not all of the justice analysis by undermining the extent of complicity. They also count against seeking to base global poverty policies on a simplistic idea of humanitarianism that bypasses the necessity to promote sustainable market economies. Whether or not we regard prudence as part of or as a supplement to the moral foundations of policy analysis, by bringing together the ideal of individual and collective rationality in a holistic framework that is ultimately justified by a model of the human good that prioritises humanity, the idea of virtuous prudence could be a useful addition to both justice and humanity. It may be worthwhile to take into account that every one has a duty to be a prudent participant in the economic and social life of their societies, not dependent on others, and, where possible, to generate the wealth that can be used to assist others either as part of the economic system or by way of other mechanisms. This could affect our thinking about how to incorporate the principle of humanity into our everyday concerns and have a salutary impact on devising the mechanisms of sustainable poverty relief by focusing our attention more on developing capacity than on donating goods. It is at least salutary to think through how these more grandiose moral norms could be melded in with the more pedestrian, but perhaps equally important, moral considerations that are associated with the everyday ideal of prudent participation in productive economies and stable societies.

References

Brock, G. 2009. *Global Justice: A cosmopolitan account.* Oxford: Oxford University Press.

Campbell, T. 1974. 'Humanity before justice.' *British Journal of Political Science* 4: 1–16.

Campbell, T. 2010. *Justice.* 3rd edn. London: Macmillan.

Caney, S. 2005. *Justice beyond Borders: A global political theory.* Oxford: Oxford University Press.

Gewirth, A. 1982. *Human Rights: Essays on justification and adjudication.* Chicago: University of Chicago Press.

Hibbs, T. 2001. *Virtue's Splendour: Wisdom, prudence and the human good.* New York: Fordham University Press.

Machan, T. R. 2009. 'The virtue of prudence as the moral basis of commerce.' *Reason Papers* 3: 49–61.

Nagel, T. 1970. *The Possibility of Altruism.* Oxford: Clarendon.

Parfit, D. 1981. *Reasons and Persons.* Oxford: Clarendon Press.

Parfit, D. 2000. 'Equality of priority.' In M. Clayton and A. Williams (eds). *The Ideal of Equality.* London: Macmillan, pp. 81–125.

Pogge, T. 2005. 'Severe poverty as a violation of negative duties.' *Ethics and International Affairs* 19(1): 55–83.

Pogge, T. (ed.) 2007. *Freedom from Poverty as a Human Right.* Oxford: Oxford University Press.

Pogge, T. 2008. *World Poverty and Human Rights: Cosmopolitan responsibilities and reforms.* 2nd edn. Cambridge: Polity Press.

Rawls, J. 1971. *A Theory of Justice.* Cambridge, MA: Harvard University Press.

Sen, A. K. 1985. 'The moral standing of the market.' *Social Philosophy and Policy* 2: 1–19.

Shue, H. 1996. *Basic Rights: Subsistence, affluence and US foreign policy.* 2nd edn. Princeton: Princeton University Press.

Sidgwick, H. 1907. *The Methods of Ethics.* 3rd edn. London: MacMillan.

Singer, P. 2009. *The Life You Can Save*. Melbourne: Text.

Smith, A. 1790. *The Theory of Moral Sentiments*. 6th edn. London: A. Millar.

Westberg, D. 1994. *Right Practical Reason: Aristotle, action and prudence in Aquinas*. Oxford: Oxford University Press.

3. Doing ethical policy analysis

Michael Mintrom

Introduction

In contemporary society, economic and social processes are shaped by vast numbers of complex and subtle interactions between private, decentralised activities and the activities of governments. Like the demand for many professional services, the demand for policy analysis arises from knowledge gaps. Government decision makers, such as cabinet ministers or councillors, continuously confront public problems for which solutions must be found. Typically, those decision makers adopt new public policies or adjust current policy settings to address the problems at hand. Outside of government, decision makers in many non-governmental organisations also seek policy analysis. Such decision makers rely on policy analysis to help them interpret how changes in government policies could affect their operating contexts, revenue streams, and the cost of doing business.

The knowledge gaps that drive demand for policy analysis also create problems of trust. Over the centuries, government decision makers have developed various ways of structuring bureaucracies and using systems of checks and balances to reduce concerns about the trustworthiness of advisers (Kelman 1988; Le Grand 2003). Yet even when such systems are in place to promote honest and high-quality work, verifying the merits of advice given by policy analysts can be costly. The good motives and actions of individual advisers, therefore, remain a key to good governmental decision-making processes. Decision makers must be assured that the policy analysts who advise them are acting with integrity. We can never be entirely sure that individual policy analysts will prove trustworthy. But steps can be taken to reduce the chances that they will behave badly. Those steps include carefully screening applicants for advice-giving roles, creating organisational cultures that promote truthfulness, and instructing policy analysts on good practice. This chapter contributes to good practice by offering suggestions for how to do ethical policy analysis.

For the purpose of the current discussion, the focus is placed on the work of policy analysts serving as advisers to elected and appointed decision makers in government. This simplification allows us to discuss the practice of policy analysis in the context where most of it is performed, without the need to continually discuss exceptions. Even so, much of what is said here will be relevant to policy analysts serving any clients, be they public or private decision makers. It is also useful to remember that ethical questions are almost always context-specific. Therefore, the broad treatment of ethical issues offered here is intended as an invitation to consideration of dilemmas in many instances.

The next section offers background to our explorations of policy analysis and ethical practice. It is followed by a general discussion of policy analysis and ethical practice. Consideration is then given to how aspects of ethical practice can inform each of the essential elements of policy analysis. The overall argument is that policy analysts should avoid shaping their work in ways that simply reinforce prevailing views in local policy conversations. Although such an approach is pragmatic in some ways, it can reduce the usefulness of policy analysis. At their best, policy analysts maintain critical distance from political debates – not to the extent that they become disengaged, but so they can view problems in fresh ways and offer evidence and insights capable of creating bold changes in policy thinking. Performing like this, policy analysts can exhibit trustworthiness while also infusing policy conversations with ideas and analyses that can promote significant, positive change in policy-making communities.

Policy analysis and ethical practice

The public expect government decision makers to address problems caused by private, decentralised aspects of social and economic interactions, others caused by governmental processes, and yet others caused by unintended, negative interactions between public and private activities. Those decision makers face knowledge gaps concerning the nature of the problems and how they might be resolved. Decision makers also must be careful that any responses to given problems represent workable solutions. As Charles Wolf cautioned, 'the cure may be as bad as the illness' (Wolf 1979, p. 133). Policy analysts are employed to close knowledge gaps that inhibit effective policy making. As the discipline of policy analysis has evolved, a consensus has emerged on how policy analysts conduct their work. Here, I follow Eugene Bardach's (2008) portrayal of that view, encapsulated in eight general steps. My wording differs slightly from Bardach's, but the nature and order of the eight steps does not. Policy analysts add value to decision-making processes when they:

• define the problem at hand

• assemble some evidence about the problem, its causes, and its effects

• construct a set of alternative ways to address the problem

• select the criteria for judging the relative merits of each alternative

- project the likely outcomes of each alternative, given the chosen criteria

- note the trade-offs associated with pursuing each alternative

- decide what alternative seems most appropriate, given the selected criteria, projected outcomes, and expected trade-offs

- present the findings of the analysis and the conclusions drawn from it.

My portrayal of policy analysts emphasises their role in closing knowledge gaps for government decision makers, but this work is rarely straightforward. Policy analysts have significant discretion when considering how to define a problem and the nature of the analytical work that flows from there. They also face many choices when they develop their policy reports and present their advice to their clients. Further, policy analysts face choices over the extent to which they consult with stakeholders during the policy development process. Even when requirements are made for consultation, everyone knows that stakeholder engagements can be perfunctory. Sometimes, consultation can be used primarily for pushing specific solutions rather than for genuinely listening to stakeholders and understanding their concerns.

Among other things, policy analysts acting ethically must strive to promote outcomes that are good for society. They must also be transparent about the choices embodied in their work. Contemporary notions of ethical practice are informed by a variety of philosophical and religious ideas that have been discussed and developed through the ages. Here, I draw from that tradition to develop five ethical principles that can guide the practices of individual policy analysts. However, before turning to those principles, it is useful to review three highly influential ethical perspectives: universalism, utilitarianism, and altruism.

Universalism tells us there are certain appropriate behaviours and that those behaviours should be followed without any reference to the mediating effects of context. The Ten Commandments fit the universalism model.[1] The Golden Rule offers another example of universalism and has been proposed by many religions and cultures. It is summed up in the words of Jesus: Do unto others as you would have them do unto you.[2] Immanuel Kant presented a variation of the Golden Rule, 'Act only on that maxim through which you can at the same time will that it should become a universal law'.[3] Universalism promotes persistence and consistency, but it is difficult to apply because exceptional circumstances abound. The focus is on strict adherence to a code of practice; the

---

1   See the Old Testament books of the Bible: Exodus 20: 1–17 and Deuteronomy 5: 5–21.
2   See the New Testament books of the Bible: Matthew 7: 12 and Luke 6: 31.
3   See Kant (1797) reproduced in Pasternack (2002).

assumption being that this will generate desirable outcomes. In public policy, having uniform standards that all applicants to university must meet to gain entry would represent a case of universalism.

Utilitarianism focuses on outcomes; the maximisation of pleasure and the minimisation of pain. Here, consequences of actions are considered to be more important than whether those actions fit a universal code of practice. The perspective is most closely associated with the thinking of Jeremy Bentham and John Stuart Mill.[4] Within the utilitarian perspective, individuals are expected to promote the attainment of the greatest good for the greatest number of people. There are many instances where deviations from a universal law would be justified within this perspective. For example, there may be times when failing to attend to the neediest people in a group allows effort to be devoted to securing the best outcome for the group as a whole. Utilitarianism is easily understood and is frequently used. However, outcomes are often difficult to predict, and people might have different views about the likely consequences of an action. In public policy, tying enrolment numbers for specific university degrees to labour market demand for graduates with those degrees would represent a case of utilitarianism.

Altruism requires that love of others serves as our ethical standard. People are not treated as the means to an end. People are what matter most. Altruism guides us to always take account of the position of the least-advantaged person and make that position as dignified and comfortable as possible. This perspective has been espoused by many people who have dedicated their lives to working among the poor, or who have used their political careers to promote the social circumstances of the least fortunate. Although informed by imperatives that characterise universalism, altruism takes account of context. Difficulties surround the application of this perspective, because people can disagree on what is best for others. In public policy, allowing exceptions to admissions standards to university so that individuals who do not meet those standards may enrol if they demonstrate maturity and profess a thirst for knowledge would represent a case of altruism.

The three ethical perspectives mentioned here offer distinctive views on what individuals should care most about. Should we follow a strict code of practice, focusing on good process? Should we care most about maximising the outcomes of society? Or should we attend most to the fair treatment of the least-advantaged person? A crucial part of the ethic of being a good policy analyst involves helping others to better understand the choices they face and the likely consequence of any given course of action. At the level of the individual professional, we also

---

4   See John Stuart Mill's *Utilitarianism* (1863) and *On Liberty* (1859), including Mill's Essay on Bentham and selections from the writings of Jeremy Bentham and John Austin, in Mill (1859).

need to be aware of the choices we face in our daily practices. When would it be appropriate for us to follow universal principles? When would it be more appropriate for us to focus on outcomes? When should we pay special attention to the situation of those who could be most harmed by the advice we give? Identifying the ethical dilemmas we face in our work and discussing them with others around us can serve to improve the overall quality of the analysis we do and the advice we give. We can be better people as a consequence of this kind of reflexivity and offer better support to government decision makers. Inevitably, though, there will be times when our efforts will fall short of what is expected of us. At such times, my suggestion is that we follow the advice of the great Stoic philosopher Epictetus, 'Human betterment is a gradual, two-steps-forward, one-step-back effort. Forgive others for their misdeeds over and over again ... Forgive yourself over and over and over again. Then try to do better next time'. [5]

Other policy scholars have considered how policy analysts might use ethical perspectives to guide their work. The literature falls into two camps. In one, consideration is given to the practices of policy analysts themselves. In the second camp, consideration is given to how policy analysts can integrate ethical frameworks and analysis into the development of policy advice. A common concern is that policy analysts do not make sufficient use of ethical analysis to guide their comparisons of policy options. The concerns of each camp were neatly represented in articles published back to back in an issue of the *Journal of Policy Analysis and Management* that appeared several decades ago.

Representing the camp concerned with doing ethical policy analysis, Guy Benveniste (1984) argued that a code of ethics should be developed for policy experts and advisers. Benveniste recognised the power and status that can accrue to policy analysts because of the knowledge they hold. He worried that individual policy analysts could become enamoured with playing the game of political influence. In doing so, they could undermine their legitimacy as sources of independent expert knowledge. Benveniste argued that an effective code of ethics would cover the scope of responsibilities, what should be done about identifying and managing conflicts of interest, how issues of secrecy and the exposure of information should be managed, how policy analysts should manage consultation with stakeholder groups, and how decision-making processes should be conducted during crises (Beneviste 1984, p. 569). Benveniste recognised that establishing a code of ethics would be difficult and that many clients and policy analysts would see little point in its adoption. He noted, for example, that recipients of policy advice are usually powerful political actors, which distinguishes them from the clients of other professionals, such as lawyers and doctors. In the latter cases, the asymmetries of power and

---

5   Epictetus (c. AD 55–135, p. 99).

knowledge between clients and professionals are more pronounced than in the case of policy advising and tend to run in the favour of the person rendering the services.

Representing the camp calling for more application of ethical principles as guides to the analysis of public policies was Douglas J. Amy (1984). Amy suggested the strong emphasis on policy analysis as a technical exercise, combined with issues of administrative structure, reduced the opportunities for consideration of ethical issues. In the decades since Amy wrote this, the contributions made by ethicists to policy debates across a variety of policy domains have grown significantly. For example, in their introduction to public policy, Michael E. Kraft and Scott R. Furlong (2007) note the ways ethical considerations inform aspects of health care policy, environmental policy, and foreign policy, along with public policies relating to other fields of human activity. Note also that many of the chapters in this volume offer examples of how ethical principles can be applied to the analysis of public policies.

The present chapter falls in the camp concerned with doing ethical policy analysis, the camp Benveniste (1984) defined. The goal here is to consider how policy analysts exhibit ethical behaviour in the conduct of their work. Models for this kind of exercise can be found in cognate areas of professional practice. For example, a literature exists exploring how social scientists can be ethical in their practices. As well as covering topics such as informed consent, confidentiality, and the researching of sensitive topics, this literature covers motivations for conducting social science research, the need for competency among researchers, and the appropriate reporting of research findings (Reynolds 1979; Frankfort-Nachmias and Nachmias 1996). Within the field of programme evaluation, efforts have been made to develop standards (Sanders et al. 1994). Among other things, these include standards for designing evaluations, collecting information, engaging in analysis, and reporting results.

Policy scholars David L. Weimer and Aidan R. Vining (2005) have offered a useful guide for how policy analysts might exhibit professional ethics through their work. To do so, Weimer and Vining proposed that policy analysts be viewed as performing one of three roles: the objective technician, the client's advocate, or an issue advocate. Each policy analyst can be seen as holding fundamental values. Those values can be a commitment to analytical integrity, responsiveness to the client, or adherence to one's conception of what is socially good. At any given time, policy analysts might view themselves as performing more than one of these roles and show joint commitment to analytical integrity, their client, and their own values, but ethical dilemmas often arise. Weimer and Vining explore how policy analysts might respond to values conflicts, noting available options. These range from discussion of those conflicts with the client to resigning from a given role and even showing disloyalty to the client.

This chapter explores how ethical challenges arise at each step in the process of doing policy analysis. As such, it offers the prospect of reducing the tendency for policy analysts to profess an ethical orientation and good intentions, while routinely engaging in practices that undercut the contributions they could make to improving policy discussions and promoting high-quality public decision making.

Ethical principles for policy analysts

Most general ethical principles hold relevance for people in both their private lives and vocational settings. Contributions to the contemporary literature on leadership and management emphasise the importance of ethical behaviour for supporting effective team processes, organisational transformation, and the emergence of cultures of excellence.[6] Here, five ethical principles are introduced: integrity, competence, responsibility, respect, and concern. In selecting this set, I have followed Thomas G. Plante (2004). Although other principles are relevant, these five offer a sound basis from which to explore how a focus on ethics can promote good practice among policy analysts. Having set out these principles for policy analysts, I use them to assess how policy analysts might act ethically at each step in the process of doing analytical work.

Integrity

When people act with integrity, they are directed by an internal moral compass. They strive to do the right thing in any given situation and to achieve consistency in their intentions and actions across contexts. Plante (2004, p. 61) has suggested that 'integrity is the foundation for living an ethical life'. In his view, people display integrity when they follow high standards of honesty and when they show commitment to the values of justice and fairness. People of integrity do not seek selfish, short-term gains through opportunistic actions that harm others. Rather, they take the view that their commitment to honesty and fairness will produce the best outcomes all around. Evidence from cognitive psychology suggests that people have fine-tuned skills for detecting when others are not being honest with them (Kramer 1999; Meyerson et al. 1996). As a result, acting with integrity can lay the foundations for building long-term relationships of trust and mutual support (Covey 2006).

Policy analysts are called to advise decision makers about the nature of the public problems they must confront and the relative merits of alternative

---

6   See, for example, Bennis (2003), Covey (1991, 2006), Fox (2002), Jones (1995), Kotter (1996), Maxwell (1999), Quinn (2000), and Sample (2002).

responses. In all cases, clients must have faith that the policy analysts have performed their work with integrity. Advice based on limited engagement with appropriate evidence, lack of consideration for how various policy approaches will affect different groups of people, and limited attention to good design and implementation could result in poor outcomes both for those affected by the policies and the decision makers who adopted them. That is why policy analysts must act with integrity. Adherence to the values of honesty, justice, and fairness is important. Being around others who exhibit integrity can also help to reduce the risk of behavioural lapses.

Competence

A strong relationship exists between competence and ethical behaviour. When you talk or act as if you can do something, then the qualities of honesty and integrity dictate that you can actually do it. It is dishonest for anyone to say they can do something when they cannot. Most professionals have specialised knowledge and skills, making them highly competent in a narrow set of areas. To undertake work outside your specialisation carries the risk that you could fail at it. In some professions, such as medicine and engineering, incompetence could result in serious injuries and the loss of lives.

In the field of policy analysis, the level of knowledge and skill required to perform competently will depend on the substantive area of focus. However, all policy analysts should aspire to delivering high-quality work, to do so without unnecessary cost, and to continuously improve their analytical skills. Seeking feedback from clients, working with mentors, and identifying high-quality work to emulate are some useful strategies that policy analysts can use to strengthen their competencies. Often, the nature of the analytical task will require that teams of policy analysts work together, so that all team members can contribute in their areas of expertise, without straying into territory where their skills would be inadequate. Policy analysts also have reason to form teams with specialists from other fields who possess substantive knowledge and skills relevant to the analytical task. The teamwork required by many policy tasks illustrates the importance of policy analysts building people skills that complement their technical expertise. The skills of working effectively in teams, communicating with a variety of stakeholders, and managing conflict are highly relevant to the work of policy analysts (Mintrom 2003).

Responsibility

Taking responsibility means acknowledging the part you play in contributing to expected or observed outcomes. It is commonplace for people to willingly accept the credit when good outcomes occur but to deflect blame for poor outcomes.

People who take responsibility do more than accept that they are accountable to others. They tend to be proactive, striving from the start to achieve good outcomes. They also quickly acknowledge instances where their actions or lack of action created problems. They then do what they can to make good on past mistakes. Making good can range from sincerely apologising for what happened to doing all that is necessary to address and fix the problem. Acknowledging problems you have caused and undertaking service recoveries takes courage. It can also mean spending valuable resources to make things right. However, when such actions are taken with good grace, they not only serve to mend endangered relationships but they can even strengthen them (Covey 2006; Quinn and Quinn 2009).

Policy analysts face many situations where responsible action is called for. They face choices about how thoroughly to investigate policy problems and explore creative ways to address them. When policy analysts recognise and respect the trust that decision makers place in them, they can scope their work and conduct it in ways that break with conventional wisdom and offer new insights for policy design and implementation. Of course, there will be times when policy problems are neither significant enough nor novel enough to justify extensive new work being performed. Part of being responsible involves taking the time to listen to clients and evaluate their willingness to pursue significant policy innovation. Responsible policy analysts work to develop good relations with their clients. They look for appropriate ways to close knowledge gaps. They also work quickly to defuse problems or misunderstandings that arise because of their actions.

Respect

When we show respect for others, we acknowledge their humanity, their dignity, and their right to be the people they are. Respect means being considerate and appreciative of others. It means treating others as you would like to be treated (Plante 2004). It is relatively easy for us to respect others when we like them, when we have known them for a long time, and when we share with them common views and interests. The tough part of respect is looking for the humanity, the good, and the reasonableness in people who our gut instincts lead us to despise. Hard as it is, part of being an ethical person involves seeking to understand others, to appreciate how they see things. The quality of forgiveness can be especially valuable as an aid in such efforts, so, too, can patience; particularly when it means slowing down the pace of our actions and listening hard.

Respecting others is an important attribute in policy analysts. First, policy analysts need to respect others who they engage with when they are conducting their analysis and developing ideas for ways to address policy problems. Often, policy debates grow heated because of the different interests at stake (Schön and

Rein 1994). Although it can be challenging, policy analysts can gain valuable insights into effective policy design by listening closely to others, even when they profoundly disagree with what they are hearing. Respecting others and turning conflicts into opportunities for learning can promote creative problem solving (Quinn and Quinn 2009). Second, policy analysts need to respect the lives, the needs, and the aspirations of the people who will be directly affected by policy change. Often, policy analysts work to develop policies that will significantly affect the lives of people with whom they share little in common. At such times, showing deep respect for the views, feelings, and hopes of others can be vital for resolving differences. Making conscious use of gender analysis or analytical strategies that take account of differences across racial groups and people of different ethnicities can serve as a useful starting point for recognising social differences and their policy implications. Marianne Williamson (2004, p. 175), who proposes love as a key to addressing the world's problems, has observed, 'It's amazing how positively people respond when they feel respected for their thoughts and feelings. Learning to feel such respect – and to actually show it – is key to a miracle worker's power'. We might add that, in the cut and thrust of policy disputes, showing respect for others can be both courageous and transformative.

Concern

Living an ethical life requires that we show concern for others, and not just those who are close family members or friends. Concern means caring about, showing an interest in, and being involved in the lives of others. When people devote their lives to working with and advancing the interests of the poor, they demonstrate exceptional levels of concern for others. Without making that level of sacrifice, many people – through their work, their philanthropy, and their acts of altruism – do an enormous amount to help others to live better lives.

Policy analysts often choose their vocation because they are concerned for the lives of others and they want to make a positive difference in the world. As such, many policy analysts share a people-focused orientation that has roots in the same goodwill towards others that can be found among people in the caring professions, such as doctors, nurses, teachers, counsellors, and social workers. However, the day-to-day work of policy analysis can easily become rarefied and removed from the lives of those who will be affected by policy change. This suggests that value lies in policy analysts gaining exposure to the communities that their policies affect. By keeping the lives of others salient to themselves, policy analysts can remain alert to the impacts of their work.

Doing ethical policy analysis

Policy analysts are called to close knowledge gaps faced by decision makers. Given inherent information asymmetries in these relationships, decision makers must place trust in policy analysts to act ethically. Having discussed five ethical principles for policy analysts, we now explore the implications those principles hold for the actions of policy analysts at each step in their work.

Ethical problem definition

Defining policy problems is inherently political work. Rarely do the objective facts of a problem receive uniform interpretations from all relevant stakeholders (Majone 1989; Rochefort and Cobb 1994). At this most preliminary stage of policy inquiry, policy analysts face choices about the conduct of their work. Those choices are significant, because how problems are defined strongly influences which policy responses are likely to gain serious attention and which will be brushed aside. How should ethical policy analysts act at the problem-definition step? First, they should identify relevant stakeholder groups and learn how members of those groups see the problem and how they would like it to be addressed. Second, they should assess their findings and identify the key lines of disagreement. Based on this information, they should collect more basic information about the nature of the problem, the problem's causes, and the feasible solutions that might be available to address the problem. All of this information should be assessed and synthesised into a problem statement. It should be shared and discussed with the client, with the goals of conveying potential risks associated with the development of policy solutions, achieving clarity around how the client views the problem, and getting support for moving ahead to other steps in the analytical process. High levels of integrity and competence are required of policy analysts at this stage to avoid conflicts based on stakeholder perceptions of exclusion or beliefs that a favoured solution has already been selected and that everything else will be spin.[7]

Ethical construction of alternatives

Introducing a range of alternative policy responses to a problem can be done in ways that significantly advance policy discussion and good decision making. The subject of how we identify relevant solutions to problems has been considered at length, both by scholars of decision making and political

---

7   James Verdier (1984, pp. 426–27) noted that 'analysis that comes early in the process can usually have much more impact than that which comes later … Economic analysis at this stage can help frame the terms of the debate and structure the options that are presented. At later stages, politics tends to dominate analysis. Economic analysis is then used the way a drunk uses a lamp post, for support rather than illumination'.

scientists (see, for example, Cyert and March 1963; Jones 2001; Kingdon 1995). Typically, solutions and problems come intertwined. That is, when feasible solutions become apparent, perceptions of problems change, and arguments are made that government action is necessary. For example, as treatments have been discovered for life-threatening diseases, arguments for government funding of those treatments have grown compelling. Likewise, evidence of the life-preserving effects of airbags in cars produced compelling grounds for airbags to become required features of all new cars. We see in these examples that the suitability of the fit between solutions and problems tends to change over time, predicated on the flow of evidence and of technical innovations. A challenge for policy makers involves avoiding the adoption of policy responses that lock in present technologies and potentially inhibit the discovery of improved solutions. Another challenge is the way that interest groups tend to promote their favourite solutions to problems, even when evidence would suggest that those solutions might not produce the best outcome for the greatest number of people.

What is an ethical approach to constructing the set of alternative policy solutions? First, we should acknowledge that there are limits to how many alternatives can be considered in any decision-making process (Schwartz 2004). Three or four would seem a reasonable number. To promote useful discussion, alternative approaches included within the set should each be quite distinctive, so decision makers can get a good sense of the range of possibilities open to them.

Second, we should include alternatives that appear most relevant, given the problem and discussions surrounding it. If an alternative is well known to be favoured by key stakeholders then it is appropriate to include it – or a close approximation to it – in the set. Decision makers will need to know how it stacks up against other alternatives.

Third, the set of alternatives should be constructed taking account of the broader financial context. For example, when government spending is highly constrained, there is little point in proposing costly policies without accompanying the proposal with suggestions for cost-savings in other areas.

Fourth, the construction of alternatives offers an opportunity for policy analysts to broaden policy discussions. Learning about approaches tried in other jurisdictions or in other related areas of policy can help analysts to devise innovative policy solutions (Mintrom 1997; Mintrom and Norman 2009). This shows evidence of both competence and concern.

Finally, we should treat our analysis as a vehicle for facilitating discussion of additional alternatives. If, on reviewing our advice, decision makers request more alternatives to be considered that build on those already presented, that should be treated as good feedback.

Ethical selection of criteria

Policy analysts are required to weigh up the relative merits of alternative policy responses to any given problem. To do this in a systematic fashion, they must establish a set of criteria for judging each alternative, and then make sure they assess the expected performance of each alternative on each criterion of interest. It is common for policy analysts to analyse policy alternatives using three criteria: efficiency, equity, and administrative simplicity. Taken together, these criteria lead us to consider the relative costs of each alternative, the fairness by which different groups of people are affected by each alternative, and the relative degree of burden that each alternative would place on those required to implement it and those required to comply with it. There is good reason to believe the use of these three criteria is both sound and ethical. However, focusing on only these criteria can limit policy analysis in unhelpful ways.

It is often important to assess policy alternatives in terms of their implications for personal freedom, human dignity, social harmony, and environmental sustainability. When should other criteria be introduced? The development of policy analysis as a discipline has seen increasing calls by various groups in society to have their interests and their concerns reflected in the criteria used to judge policy alternatives. While there is no conceptual limit to what criteria might be applied, in practice we need to keep our analysis manageable. Reflecting on the concerns expressed by stakeholder groups who have weighed in at the problem-definition stage is helpful here. It can lead to the development of a set of evaluative criteria that is appropriately suited to the context. Discussing with others what they care about and how their concerns could be captured in the evaluative criteria is a good way to show both respect and concern during the process of policy development.

Ethical prediction of outcomes

Decision makers need high-quality information on the likely effects of adopting specific policy solutions. The challenge for policy analysts is to generate that information, paying careful attention to the criteria judged most appropriate. Policy analysts can use various methods to gather information, generate information, and analyse the information to predict likely policy effects. Several ethical concerns arise.

First, all analytical work requires that we make simplifying assumptions, that we make estimates when good data are not present, and that we work with models that, at their best, only approximate real-world processes. None of this is a problem, so long as we carefully document our work and have others peer review it. Other people should be able to follow our analytical procedures and come to much the same conclusions. They should also be able to clearly understand the limits of our analysis. Strong technical work should be accorded value by decision makers. However, analysts should never try to hide behind technical matters, or try to win support for a favoured solution using opaque, but smart-sounding, analysis.

Second, because we know there is room for manipulating evidence, we should promote high standards of technical ability and clarity of explanation in our work. This raises the bar for those who would be happier to win policy disputes by playing fast and loose with the evidence.

Through the work of predicting outcomes, policy analysts will usually become clear about the relative merits of each alternative and the trade-offs associated with pursuing one over the others. It is important that these trade-offs be made explicit. Policy analysts should also be prepared to state their views on what policy alternative would be most appropriate in the given context. Doing so can be clarifying to decision makers. Just as importantly, it forces the analyst to work hard at making their arguments for the choice they favour. The most effective way to do this is to make the strongest possible argument for each alternative, rather than paying more attention to a favoured position and doing limited or sloppy analysis of the other alternatives. Exposing their work to peer review is a further check on the validity of the analysts' evidence and arguments.

Ethical reporting practices

Knowledge gaps can be closed only when relevant information is presented in ways that work for the clients. If a busy decision maker requests that all material be initially presented in an oral briefing and a one-page memo, then the onus is on the policy analyst to meet that requirement. Meeting such a requirement can take a lot of careful thought and effort. Policy analysts need to become adept at writing and presenting their work for multiple audiences (Mintrom 2003). It is both ethical and smart to tell the same story in multiple ways, so long as the story remains consistent across the audiences being reached. Having said this, it is clear that any organisational conventions around reporting must be met. Increasingly, policy analysts working in government settings find they must follow report templates that come with their share of positives and negatives. The key is to not let the conventions inhibit the development of effective communication with clients and stakeholders. Working at different ways to present your work to different audiences is an important means of showing respect to others. But throughout, policy analysts must be sure that they also have a version of their report that they feel most comfortable with, that pulls together in one place all the documentation associated with the analytical process. Increasingly, we can make use of technology to produce reports where different audience members can choose the features of the analysis that they wish to focus on. To do this well is likely to mean working with experts in website design, communications, and marketing. That is what is required when we take responsibility for improving policy discussions and when we desire to help others understand the problems they face and how policy changes can address them.

Conclusion

Knowledge gaps provide the primary rationale for the work of policy analysts. At its best, their work can enlighten decision makers about policy problems and effective ways to address them. Given the nature of these knowledge gaps, decision makers must trust that the information provided to them is based on sound, honest work. The asymmetries in expertise create the potential for problems to arise. For example, policy analysts might deliberately narrow the definition of a problem, limit the selection of alternatives to address the problem, or place undue weight on cost issues when other criteria should be made salient.

This chapter has discussed how policy analysts might develop and deliver their work in accordance with sound ethical principles. By adhering to the proposed approaches, policy analysts can find ways to advance and even transform policy conversations. It is important that policy analysts understand the political contexts within which they operate. But it is disappointing when apparent contextual constraints are used to justify analytical work that does little more than support the political consensus of the day. I have suggested that, when exploring alternative policy responses, policy analysts should aspire to being creative and look for innovative solutions from elsewhere that could usefully inform local policy discussions. This way of doing policy analysis does not depart greatly from standard approaches, but it sets us in a direction that can promote significant, positive change. More than most people in society, policy analysts can catalyse new thinking on policy issues. To do so is ethical. In a world filled with challenges, where routine responses yield limited gains, such work is urgently needed.

References

Amy, D. J. 1984. 'Why policy analysis and ethics are incompatible.' *Journal of Policy Analysis and Management* 3(4): 573–91.

Bardach, E. 2008. *A Practical Guide for Policy Analysis: The eightfold path to more effective problem solving.* 3rd edn. Washington, DC: CQ Press.

Bennis, W. 2003. *On Becoming a Leader.* 3rd edn. New York: Basic Books.

Benveniste, G. 1984. 'On a code of ethics for policy experts.' *Journal of Policy Analysis and Management* 3(4): 561–72.

Covey, S. M. R. 2006. *The Speed of Trust: The one thing that changes everything.* New York: Simon and Schuster.

Covey, S. R. 1991. *Principle-Centered Leadership.* New York: Free Press.

Cyert, R. M., and J. G March. 1963. *A Behavioral Theory of the Firm.* Englewood Cliffs, NJ: Prentice-Hall.

Epictetus. c. AD 55–135. *The Art of Living.* New interpretation by S. Lebell, 1994. New York: HarperCollins.

Fox, J. J. 2002. *How to Become a Great Boss.* New York: Hyperion.

Frankfort-Nachmias, C., and D. Nachmias. 1996. *Research Methods in the Social Sciences.* 5th edn. New York: St. Martin's Press.

Jones, B. D. 2001. *Politics and the Architecture of Choice: Bounded rationality and governance.* Chicago: University of Chicago Press.

Jones, L. B. 1995. *Jesus, CEO: Using ancient wisdom for visionary leadership.* New York: Hyperion.

Kant, I. 1797. 'Groundwork of the metaphysics of morals.' Translated by H. J. Paton. Reproduced in L. Pasternack (ed.). 2002. *Immanuel Kant: Groundwork of the metaphysics of morals, in focus.* London: Routledge, ch. 11.

Kelman, S. 1988. *Making Public Policy: A hopeful view of American government.* New York: Basic Books.

Kingdon, J. 1995. *Agendas, Alternatives, and Public Policies.* 2nd edn. Boston, MA: Little, Brown.

Kotter, J. P. 1996. *Leading Change.* Boston, MA: Harvard Business School Press.

Kraft, M. E., and S. R. Furlong. c. 2007. *Public policy: Politics, analysis, and alternatives.* 2nd edn. Washington, DC: CQ Press.

Kramer, R. M. 1999. 'Trust and distrust in organizations: Emerging perspectives, enduring questions.' *Annual Review of Psychology* 50: 569–98.

Le Grand, J. 2003. *Motivation, Agency, and Public Policy: Of knights and knaves, pawns and queens.* Oxford: Oxford University Press.

Majone, G. 1989. *Evidence, Argument, and Persuasion in the Policy Process.* New Haven: Yale University Press.

Maxwell, J. C. 1999. *The 21 Indispensable Qualities of a Leader.* Nashville, TN: Thomas Nelson Publishers.

Meyerson, D., K. E. Weick, and R. M. Kramer. 1996. 'Swift trust and temporary groups.' In R. M. Kramer and T. R. Tyler (eds). *Trust in Organizations: Frontiers of theory and research.* Thousand Oaks, CA: Sage Publications, ch.9.

Mill, J. S. 1859. *Utilitarianism and On Liberty.* 2nd edn. Edited and with an introduction by M. Warnock. 2003. Malden, MA: Blackwell Publishers.

Mintrom, M. 1997. 'Policy entrepreneurs and the diffusion of innovation.' *American Journal of Political Science* 41: 738–70.

Mintrom, M. 2003. *People Skills for Policy Analysts.* Washington, DC: Georgetown University Press.

Mintrom, M., and P. Norman 2009. 'Policy entrepreneurship and policy change.' *Policy Studies Journal* 37(4): 649–67.

Pasternack, L. (ed.) 2002. *Immanuel Kant: Groundwork of the metaphysics of morals, in focus.* London: Routledge.

Plante, T. G. 2004. *Doing the Right Thing: Living ethically in an unethical world.* Oakland, CA: New Harbinger Publications.

Quinn, R. E. 2000. *Change the World: How ordinary people can accomplish extraordinary results.* San Francisco: Jossey-Bass.

Quinn, R. W., and R. E. Quinn. 2009. *Lift: Becoming a positive force in any situation.* San Francisco: Berrett-Koehler Publishers.

Reynolds, P. D. 1979. *Ethical Dilemmas and Social Science Research.* San Francisco: Jossey-Bass.

Rochefort, D. A., and R. W. Cobb (eds). 1994. *The Politics of Problem Definition: Shaping the policy agenda.* Lawrence, KS: University Press of Kansas.

Sample, S. B. 2002. *The Contrarian's Guide to Leadership*. San Francisco: Jossey-Bass.

Sanders, J. R., et al. 1994. *The Program Evaluation Standards*. 2nd edn. Thousand Oaks, CA: Sage Publications.

Schön, D. A., and M. Rein. 1994. *Frame Reflection: Toward the resolution of intractable policy controversies*. New York: Basic Books.

Schwartz, B. 2004. *The Paradox of Choice: Why more is less*. New York: HarperCollins.

Verdier, J. M. 1984. 'Advising congressional decision-makers: Guidelines for economists.' *Journal of Policy Analysis and Management* 3(3): 421–38.

Weimer, D. L., and A. R. Vining. 2005. *Policy Analysis: Concepts and practice*. 4th edn. Upper Saddle River, NJ: Pearson Prentice Hall.

Williamson, M. 2004. *The Gift of Change: Spiritual guidance for living your best life*. New York: HarperCollins.

Wolf Jr, C. 1979. 'A theory of non-market failures.' *Public Interest* 55: 114–33.

4. The public servant as analyst, adviser, and advocate

David Bromell

Much of the work of public officials – elected or appointed – involves choices amongst values; indeed, it is this characteristic of their role in a liberal democracy that often makes their decisions contestable, debateable and requiring public justification. Therefore, nothing is more dangerous to the well-being of the body politic than a public official who is technically competent or strategically astute but ethically illiterate or unfit. (Preston 1994, p. 1).

Introduction

Public servants involved in policy making fulfil at least three distinct functions within Westminster-style parliamentary democracies: those of analyst, adviser, and advocate (cf. Gallagher 1981, pp. 72–3). These functions are not necessarily distinguished by role or position and correspond to the interplay between information, interests, and ideology in public policy making (Weiss 1983).

This paper explores tensions within and between analysis, advice giving, and advocacy, and proposes that the three functions be distinguished without separation or division. Maintaining appropriate distinctions is, in fact, encouraged in law and by convention, ethical codes of practice, and statements of public sector values. It requires above all, however, the intentional cultivation of what Kenneth Winston (2002, 2009) has termed 'moral competence in public life' and its institutionalisation through public sector management and leadership.

The analyst

As analyst, the public servant collects and analyses data and other information and provides this to ministers, parliament, and the public. Examples include preparing departmental annual reports for the portfolio minister to table in the House of Representatives, assisting Vote ministers with Estimates debates, providing information to and appearing as witnesses or advisers before select committees, assisting with responses to parliamentary questions and ministerial correspondence, providing briefings to ministers and their staff, and responding to requests made under the Official Information Act 1982. In this role, the public servant is expected to be technically competent and politically neutral.

Policy analysis also commonly requires public servants to articulate two or more options, using an appropriate 'evidence base' and analytical framework or frameworks, in order to enable the government to determine its preferred means to achieve its agreed ends. Those ends are defined by the manifesto commitments and electoral mandate of the party that leads the government, by coalition and confidence-and-supply agreements with minor parties, and by direction provided from time to time by ministers and cabinet. In this sense, the public servant is an implementer and 'rational functionary' (Parsons 1995, p. 7), who 'faithfully serves the government of the day' by aligning public administration with government priorities.

A positivist account of policy analysis, and of the role of social science in public policy, requires the separation of facts and values, means and ends. Callahan and Jennings (1983, p. xvii; cf. Moroney 1981, p. 81) describe this 1960s–1970s approach, whereby policy analysis was taken to be primarily an administrative, technical activity concerned with the efficient fitting of means to given ends:

> Having been assigned a particular goal by the policymaker (who, in turn, was acting on authority delegated by democratically elected representatives), the social scientist was to analyze particular policy options which, on the basis of empirically confirmed generalizations about human behaviour, could be evaluated in terms of their potential consequences, the relationship between costs and benefits, and their likely effectiveness.

State Services Commission guidance reflects this sort of approach (SSC 2007b, p. 13):

> The work we do must not be influenced by personal beliefs or commitments. These personal interests can be wide-ranging, including party political, religious, philosophical, and vocational, and can be shaped by all sorts of experiences and upbringing. What we do in our organisation must reflect State Services standards of integrity and conduct and not be undermined by any personal conviction or particular ethical viewpoint we may embrace.

The Frankfurt School, however, and Habermas in particular, has challenged scientistic conceptions of objectivity, which identify objectivity with neutrality and freedom from normative commitments (Nielsen 1983). It is increasingly accepted, as Callahan and Jennings (1983, p. xix) argue, that 'even the most quantitative and formalistic policy-analytic techniques contain concealed value choices and inextricable normative implications'.

This requires the public servant as analyst to manage tensions between the objective and the subjective nature of reality (and hence the empirical and the normative) and between short-term alignment to government priorities and longer-term responsibility to the public good. Quite apart from the incomplete and imperfect information we have to work with, no analyst is a purely 'rational functionary'. We all have complex interests, values, beliefs, ideologies, and goals of our own that cannot be entirely separated from 'evidence-based' public policy analysis (Parsons 1995, pp. 7, 87–8; Bardach 2000, p. xiii). These shape our perceptions of reality and influence, in particular, the critical 'problem definition' stage in policy analysis (Parsons 1995, p. 88, emphasis in original):

> policy analysts could be said to be in the business of problem-structuring and ordering so as to facilitate problem-solving by decision-makers. Politics arises because we do not share perceptions of what the problems are, or if we do, what follows from the definition in terms of what can be or should be done. *A definition of a problem is part of the problem.*

Geva-May (1997, p. 4) similarly reflects that:

> Casting and recasting the problem is one of the most important functions a policy analyst performs. Problems do not exist as objectively defined entities out there 'waiting to be solved'. Rather, a single set of conditions can yield any number of problems depending, among other things, on the reference frame of interested parties.

Analysts are, thus, not a species of social scientist in the (positivist) sense of 'technicians of the social life' (Nielsen 1983, p. 117); neither can the mere fact of electoral competition alone be expected to carry normative weight, given the imperfection of democratic institutions and processes (McPherson 1983, pp. 69, 75–6). The analysis of data and information is, therefore, somewhat indirect – 'one small piece in a larger mosaic of politics, bargaining, and compromise' (Callahan and Jennings 1983, p. xiii). Nevertheless, there is a continuing expectation that public sector analysis will be evidence-informed, professional, and politically neutral.

A further challenge for the public servant as analyst is to balance short-term priorities against long-haul thinking about hard questions and 'wicked problems' (Rittel and Webber, 1973; Australian Public Service Commission 2007). Public servants are required to be responsive to government priorities and to support their ministers in aligning policies, programmes, and services to those priorities. Ministers naturally tend to be focused on the short term and the three-year electoral cycle. The Westminster system of a permanent, professional public service also requires, however, investment in medium- to long-term analysis that may not be immediately important to the current government but may prove critical, nevertheless, to the public sector's ability to respond to future crises and priorities of the next government or the one after that. The system is based on the idea that governments, present and future, will be served well when the public service retains 'expertise, institutional memories and wisdom about good policy which is developed over years' (Scott 2008, p. 12).

The tension between short-term alignment and medium- to long-term policy development is highlighted when ministers themselves demand, on the one hand, alignment to current priorities, 'exploitation' rather than 'exploration' modes of research and evaluation (Lindquist 2009, p. 15) that enable rapid evidence assessment (*Rapid Evidence Assessment Toolkit* n. d.) and 'real-time learning' and, on the other hand, innovative and forward-thinking 'transformative' approaches to emerging challenges and 'wicked problems' (Baehler and Bryson 2009, pp. 15, 17).

The adviser

As adviser, the public servant is responsible for 'speaking truth to power' (Wildavsky 1987), providing advice to the government of the day that is 'free and frank' (SSC 2007a, 2007b, p. 14). In the Westminster system of government, this advice is to be professional, politically neutral, and of such integrity as to maintain the confidence of present and future ministers, parliament, and the public (SSC 2007b, pp. 13, 14, 16, 2008c, p. 4).

At the same time, public servants are required to 'faithfully serve the government of the day' by implementing its policy decisions, once made, without criticism or re-litigation (SSC 2008c, pp. 5–6). In doing so, public servants are further expected to uphold duties to the public to protect the interests of society generally through the manner in which policies are implemented and programmes and services delivered (Woodward 1994, p. 228).

This raises the question of what 'success' looks like in the policy advice role (Radin 2000, p. 28; cf. Bardach 2000, pp. 23–4). Is the adviser successful when the agreed policy 'outputs' have been delivered within the agreed timeframes? When decision makers have been convinced to adopt the adviser's recommendations? When decision makers are helped to understand the complexities and dimensions of a policy choice (which may result in a different policy being adopted)? When a policy adopted by decision makers has broad public support? When, with or without public support, a policy is endorsed by key stakeholders or academic experts? When the policy is consistent with the nature, aims, and purposes of public services and the values inherent in these? When policy once implemented can be demonstrated to have improved outcomes for citizens? The answer, of course, is some combination of all of the above.

This in turn implies that the public servant as adviser juggles conflicting demands from multiple clients. As Martin (1994, p. 106) explains:

> Currently the accepted expression in New Zealand of the duty of a public servant (within the law) is that 'the minister is my client'. This immediately throws into relief the claims of competing duties: to the government-as-a-whole? to the public? to the chief executive (who is the employer)? to values such as justice, democracy, efficiency or rationality?

Advice, moreover, has become highly contestable, with a growing demand from ministers for advice sourced from beyond the public service and an increasing number of 'political' (or 'ministerial') advisers being employed to support their ministers in advancing the government's political and policy agenda (Eichbaum and Shaw 2005, 2007, 2010; cf. SSC 2008c, pp. 7–8). Political advisers can play a useful role within New Zealand's mixed-member proportional electoral system, assisting with negotiations around the formation of a government, managing relationships between the government and its coalition and parliamentary support parties, and assisting ministers to prepare political (as distinct from factual) responses to parliamentary questions and ministerial correspondence. There are risks, however, that political advisers may filter and contaminate the free flow of information and communication between ministers and departmental officials, dilute the robustness of officials' advice, and provide ill-informed and uncritical second-opinion advice on policy proposals (Pollitt 2003, p. 87). Consequently, the employment of 'political advisers' in New Zealand, Australia, and the United Kingdom has not occurred without criticism (Uhr 2005, p. 25; Hood and Lodge 2006, p. 159; Lodge 2009, p. 53; Scott 2008, p. 5).

The challenge for the public servant as adviser is to balance *rigour* and *relevance* in the real-world hurly-burly of politics. As Gregory (2005, p. 26) puts it:

> Analysis can be rigorous (but of course it sometimes/often is not) but it may also be rigorously irrelevant (to actual policy-making) if it does not speak constructively to the agendas that are driving decision makers.

Neutrality is, in this sense, a naïve and even dangerous aspiration. Gregory (2005, p. 27) cites Brian Chapman (1959, p. 275):

Neutrality in public office tends in the end to moral corruption. If all governments are to be served with equal impartiality and loyalty there are no grounds at all for criticizing the German official who served Hitler to the best of his ability.

Consequently, Gregory (2005 p. 27) argues that:

> Government officials as individuals must retain, even nurture, a capacity for personal reflective judgement, even as they work in contexts and roles which by their nature insidiously limit that capacity.

Government officials ought, moreover, act to preserve and protect the integrity of the process and the broader democratic values they serve as public servants. McPherson (1983, p. 76) sums up the issue like this:

> We can catch some of the complexities here by saying that the adviser really has a three-sided obligation: (1) to serve his or her superiors honestly, (2) to promote better policies, and (3) to respect and improve the democratic process by which decisions are made.

The advocate

Public servants are to be 'imbued with the spirit of service to the community' (State Sector Act 1988, para (a) of the Long Title). A frequently voiced motivation, in fact, is the desire 'to make a difference', according to personal and (actual or assumed) collective understandings of such desired outcomes as 'social justice', 'the public interest', or 'the common good'.

Given the convention of offering 'free and frank' advice, can and should advice giving by permanent public servants extend to ends as well as means? Can public servants legitimately advocate for particular social and economic outcomes within the performance of their public duties? And how are public servants to balance their desire (and obligation) 'to do the best for New Zealand' with narrower policy agendas and demand for short-term fixes within typical government policy processes (Baehler and Bryson 2009, p. 17)?

Policy making involves, indeed requires, political *argument*. As Wildavsky (1987, p. 13) puts it, 'Analysis, which is in part rhetoric, should be persuasive'. If carried beyond the modelling and alternative design stages of the policy-development process, the analyst's search for rationality and neutrality can be nothing more than an ill-conceived attempt to side-step the demands of democratic contestation (Radin 2000, pp. 92, 104). To be effective, advisers must have regard for the authorising environment and the ideological and political preferences and perspectives of decision makers (Scott 2008, p. 2), and it is naïve to pretend otherwise. Geva-May (1997, p. 145) explains:

> Neutrality serves policy analysis well during evaluation conduct – at the modelling and alternative design stages – but it becomes impedimentary once findings and recommendations are presented, discussed and acted on by organizational actors. Then it becomes subjected to the power and politics of major organizational players. Lacking advocacy and organizational basis, proposals have little capacity of survival.

Moving into an advocacy role as a public servant, however, is a risky business. In an increasingly pluralistic society, whose 'common good' is the public servant advocating for? Whose interests, values, ideology, and vision of what is 'best for New Zealand' are to be voiced? And how are unelected officials accountable to the public for the advocacy they engage in?

Hawke (1993, p. 37) urges policy advisers to focus on the issue, not a routine application of individual beliefs, because, 'Working together may be damaged by officials following their own agendas rather than showing commitment to the policy process. Officials have varying beliefs and values, personality differences and distinctive professional backgrounds'. State Services Commission guidance further reminds us that (SSC 2008b, p. 3):

> A partisan statement made or position adopted by a State servant may not be forgotten easily and it could colour the way that Ministers (or future Ministers) relate to that State servant or to the agency employing that person. The consequences could be to reduce the credibility of the State servant and the agency (and the State Services generally).

What, then, are the options? Radin (2000, p. 101) identifies three.

- Move away from high-profile roles and assignments to less visible activity, and accept that one's impact will be only at the margin of decisions (the details of policy design and implementation) rather than the contours of the policy itself.

- Exit the public sector and become identified with particular political or value commitments; that is, move into an explicit advocacy posture.

- Attach oneself directly to political actors (for example, as a 'political adviser') or stand for elected office and move into a decision-making role.

There is, of course, a fourth option (most commonly pursued by public servants): live with and manage role proliferation and confusion (Baehler and Bryson 2000, p. 17) by exercising judgement on a case-by-case basis and seeking advice as required from one's manager, chief executive, or the State Services Commission (SSC 2008a, pp. 3, 8).

A Chalcedonian challenge

The fifth-century Christian churches were divided over whether, how, and to what extent the second person of the Trinity could be both fully human and fully divine. As in all disputes over big ideas, the arguments were as much political as doctrinal. In 451, the emperor Marcian issued a decree, on behalf also of the Western Emperor Valentinian III, calling an ecumenical council to address this and other issues.

The council met in October 451 in Chalcedon, a city in Bithynia in Asia Minor (now part of the greater city of Istanbul, on the Asian side of the Bosphorus). In the fifth session, held on 22 October, the bishops published the Chalcedonian Definition of the Faith, which asserts that 'the one and the same Christ, Lord, and only-begotten Son, is to be acknowledged in two natures without confusion, change, division, or separation (*in duabus naturis inconfuse, immutabiliter, indivise, inseparabiliter)*'.

Notwithstanding the resulting major schism between Eastern Orthodox and Western churches, I propose that public service functions of analysis, advice giving, and advocacy be similarly *distinguished without separation or division*. This is because the three functions correspond to an inescapable interplay between information, interests, and ideology (or fact, value, and theory) in public policy making (Weiss 1983; Gregory 2005; Rein 1983, p. 83).

The challenge for the public servant is to live creatively with the tensions within and between the three functions of analysis, advice giving, and advocacy, maintaining appropriate distinctions and exercising sound judgement – and to do so within inevitably imperfect democratic institutions and processes. Public sector policy making occurs within a real-world context of conflict over facts and values, information and power, means and ends, and where multiple, complex, and complicated 'public service bargains' (Hood and Lodge 2006) are operative.

What then, are the principles, values, and institutional arrangements that might guide and support public servants to make and maintain appropriate distinctions between analysis, advice giving, and advocacy, without separating or dividing them?

Public sector ethics

Public sector ethics are promoted, explicitly or implicitly, by:

- legislation and convention
- codes of conduct
- statements of public sector and organisational values.

Legislation and convention

The roles and requirements of the New Zealand public service are legislated in the State Sector Act 1988, Public Finance Act 1989, and Official Information Act 1982, as well as in statutes that govern particular agencies and their functions (for example, the Education Act 1989 and Children's Commissioner Act 2003). Legislation and convention support four broad propositions, as identified by the Right Honourable Sir Kenneth Keith in his introduction to the *Cabinet Manual* (Keith 1990, p. 4). Members of the public service are:

- to act in accordance with the law
- to be imbued with the spirit of service to the community
- (as appropriate) to give free and frank advice to ministers and others in authority and, when decisions have been taken, to give effect to those decisions in accordance with their responsibility to the ministers or others
- when legislation so provides, to act independently in accordance with the terms of that legislation.

Sir Kenneth adds (p. 5), 'Public servants meet those obligations in accordance with important principles such as neutrality and independence, and as members of a career service'. In other words, public service occurs within a democratic compact whereby society delegates coercive powers to the state but does so on the understanding that public powers are to be exercised for the public good, in accordance with the law, and with forbearance, good reason, and transparency.

Codes of ethics and conduct

In a pluralist society, individually generated moral beliefs, values, or principles are unlikely to constitute a coherent and consistent body of ethical guidance for public service. While public servants certainly have private lives, the ethics we are concerned with here relate primarily to the performance of public duties (Uhr 2005, p. 10). What is required is a set of norms that is socially constructed in such a way as to align individual behaviour with institutional purposes (Hardin 2006). These sets of norms are commonly articulated in the form of codes of ethics or conduct.

In an independent survey of New Zealand state services integrity and conduct (Ethics Resource Center 2007), 75 per cent of those who had observed misconduct believed it breached the organisation's standards of integrity and conduct, rather than the law or both combined. State servants commonly recognise, therefore, a distinction between what is legal and what is ethical.

In New Zealand, the first written public service code of conduct was issued by the State Services Commission in 1989 (Hicks 2007, p. 12). This was followed by a comprehensive guidance series (SSC 1995) on public sector ethics and standards. In 2001, a revised state services code of conduct was issued (SSC 2001), and accompanying guidance material later developed (SSC 2007a, 2007b).

In addition, many public sector agencies have their own codes of conduct. The Ministry of Social Development's code applies to all employees, contractors, and consultants who are working for the ministry on a full-time, part-time, temporary, or casual basis (MSD n. d., a). The code is both *aspirational*, setting out 'principles that guide the way we work', and *disciplinary*, establishing specific responsibilities and outlining investigation processes and the likely consequence of disciplinary action should the code be breached.

As Rhode (2006, p. 34) notes:

> Codes of conduct can clarify rules and expectations, establish consistent standards, and project a responsible public image. If widely accepted and enforced, codified rules can also reinforce ethical commitments, deter ethical misconduct, promote trust, reduce the organization's risks of liability, and prevent free riders (those who benefit from others' adherence to moral norms without observing them personally).

On the other hand, codes tend to restrict only the behaviour of those who are already ethical (Sampford 1994, p. 20). Codes also do not clarify the standards public servants should aspire to, and against which they will, or ought to be, assessed. As Uhr (2005, p. 38) comments:

> It is one thing to know that corruption means conduct falling below the standard; it is another to know how far above that standard official conduct should go, or aspire to go, in the direction of, for example, honesty and impartiality.

Moreover, as Uhr (2005 p. 140) adds, 'No code is any better than the competence of those empowered to investigate its breaches'. Rhode (2006, pp. 34–5) acknowledges that codes of conduct, in particular, are less effective in promoting ethical behaviour than are 'approaches that stress values by encouraging self-governance and commitment to ethical aspirations'.

Statements of organisational values

As well as codes of conduct, many agencies, including the Ministry of Social Development (MSD n. d., b) have statements that define organisational vision, purpose, and values. In addition, the ministry's leadership team developed a set of operating principles in 2008 that is reproduced on internal stationery and the ministry's intranet:

Ministry of Social Development (MSD) Principles

MSD PEOPLE:

- put people first
- team up to make a bigger difference
- act with courage and respect
- empower others to act
- create new solutions
- are 'can do', and deliver
- honour achievement.

Above all, we do the right thing for New Zealanders.

The OECD (2000, p. 2) advises that, 'Identifying core values is the first step to creating a common understanding within society of the expected behaviour of public office holders'. The eight most frequently stated core public service values in OECD countries in rank order are impartiality, legality, integrity, transparency, efficiency, equality, responsibility, and justice. A survey of public organisations in Canada (Kernaghan 1995) identified 19 core values in the following rank order: integrity and ethics, accountability and responsibility, respect, service, fairness and equity, innovation, teamwork, excellence, honesty, commitment and dedication, quality, openness, communications, recognition, responsiveness, trust, effectiveness, professionalism, and leadership.

As can be seen from these lists, values statements commonly contain a broad mix of *goal values* (where we want to go) and *conduct values* (how we will get there) (Starling 2008, p. 183). Pollitt (2003, p. 135) has further classified these as:

- *democratic values* (serving the common good rather than sectional interests, promoting public accountability, supporting elected representatives, always observing the law)

- *professional values* (promotion by merit, continuous improvement, impartiality, effectiveness, creativity, loyalty to professional colleagues, putting the client's interests first)

- *general ethical values* (integrity, honesty, equity, probity)

- *people values* (reasonableness, civility, respect for difference, kindness).

Statements of organisational values need to reflect and be integrated with the purpose of the agency, so that policy, programme, and process are coherent (Gawthrop 1984, p. 120; Rein 1983, pp. 86–7). Ideally, as Sampford (1994, p. 19) argues, they are created and reviewed regularly with and by the staff who are to work in accordance with them:

> If you want people to behave ethically and internalise the relevant values, you have to get the staff who will live by them to take an active part in their creation. Do not just give them the rules but ask them to look at the ways in which their practice is ethically vulnerable, to discuss such vulnerabilities and to reflect on the kinds of rules they should adopt for themselves.

Values statements are empty rhetoric unless they are embodied in and expressive of institutional design, work processes, recruitment, and performance management and are consistently modelled by chief executives and their senior staff.

Moral competence in public life

Distinguishing public service functions of analysis, advice giving, and advocacy without separating or dividing these functions is encouraged and supported by legislation and constitutional convention, codes of conduct, and the promotion of public sector and organisational values. In my experience as a public servant, however, even in combination these are necessary but not sufficient. They are more effective at drawing the line at unethical behaviour than at enabling staff consistently to exercise sound judgement in the normal course of their duties, let alone when we are put on the spot and must decide quickly how to respond or act. This is particularly the case because the hard choices in public policy making are 'not just between right and wrong, or good or bad, or just and unjust, but between right and most right, or ethical and most ethical' (Hicks 2007, p. 11).

'Walking the line' requires what Winston (2002, 2009) has termed 'moral competence in public life'. The generic attributes that Winston (2009, p. 1) regards as constituent components of moral competence are 'not character traits or personal virtues in the ordinary sense, but qualities of those acting in their official capacities'. In other words, public servants, like all citizens, cannot escape exercising 'personal reflective judgment' (Gregory 2005, p. 27), but the judgement required in the exercise of public service is about what the purpose and principles of the political order require in a particular case, rather than what the public servant might personally like or approve (McPherson 1983, pp. 77–8).Winston (2002, 2008, 2009) defines six components of moral competency.

1. *Civility* – the duty to act only on the basis of principles that citizens could reasonably accept (cf. Rawls 1999).

2. *Fidelity to the public good* – and the dual responsibility this implies to the 'appointing officer' and to broader considerations of the public good (that is, able to reconcile partial and general perspectives).

3. *Respect for citizens as responsible agents* – balancing concern for citizens' well-being with respect for citizens' individual and collective abilities to set goals, develop commitments, pursue values, and succeed in realising them.

4. *Proficiency in democratic architecture* – skilled in exercising deliberative judgement about the interplay between ends and means and in facilitating citizen participation in decision making.

5. *Prudence* – the practical wisdom to make sound moral judgements in concrete situations, including tolerance of moral ambiguity and the ability to learn from recurrent perplexities and tensions.

6. *Double reflection* – the ability to discern what a course of action might mean to another person when at variance with one's own understanding, and to contemplate with equanimity the contestability of one's own worldview.

To simplify matters, I propose that components 1 and 6 be merged, as also components 3 and 4. Thus, the moral competencies required for public service are fourfold: civility, fidelity to the public good, respect for citizens as responsible agents, and prudence.

Civility

Civility is the capacity to engage in reasoned, reflective judgement that makes itself accountable to a diverse public. That is, it requires the recognition of diversity and some level of commitment to a politics of difference and to democratic inclusion (Bromell 2008, 2009a, 2009b). It follows Dewey (1927, 1939) in understanding democratic decision making as a mode of communication and experimentation in which ideas are exchanged in a public manner and problems solved through experimentation, testing, and learning. It does not aspire to 'pure' rationality, but rather 'communicative rationality' (Habermas 1984), whereby people who live together in difference (and the conflicts this creates) engage in inter-subjective communication about facts, values, and preferences in order to arrive at a workable and more or less common understanding within a given social context at a particular point in time. This may require different modes of reasoning and argument, facility in dealing with incomplete and 'pluralist' rather than 'monist' information (Sen 1985), and different modes of communication; so while it will not be uniform, it is nevertheless internally consistent, transparent, and subject to contestation as public deliberation.

What must not be lost in the 'policy circus' (deLeon 1994, p. 202) with its less than rational stunts and tricks is precisely the imperative of *publicity*, or the liberal restraint principle. As Baehler (2005, p. 6) expresses this:

> Citizens (including officials) who propose policies that involve coercion of their fellow citizens ought to restrain from using non-public reasons to support those proposals, out of respect for each other and the democratic system. Public reasons are understood as the kinds of reasons that other reasonable people might accept as reasonable without necessarily having to agree with them.

Baehler (2005, p. 7) goes on to propose the following features of a public argument model for public policy, which usefully summarise some practical implications of civility.

- Establish clear principles and rules of thumb to distinguish public and non-public policy rationales.

- Scan the ideological and evidence terrain and build multi-dimensional cognitive maps of a policy field, including both descriptive data and competing policy approaches in ideological space.

- Develop better methods to build and test public arguments.

- Use evidence as one ingredient (linked with logic, linked with an appeal to people's values) to build and support the argument framework.

- Engage ministers in the shared goal of building public good arguments.

Fidelity to the public good

Fidelity to the public good requires skill and responsibility in dealing with vast complexity and dynamic change along the horizontal continuum of time, as distinct from being merely responsive to the demands of the present moment and to vertical accountabilities. Public sector organisations ought not to be merely reactive and incremental. Fidelity to the public good requires rather 'a sense of purpose that transcends the present and serves as a sense of direction in shaping public policies to improve the long-term well-being of society' (Gawthrop 1984, pp. 120–1). Fidelity to the public good requires a sense of purpose, a sense of consequence, a sense of history. It requires responsibility as well as responsiveness.

Fidelity to the public good means public servants go about their work in such a way as to maintain the confidence of future as well as present ministers, parliament, and the public. It means 'faithfully serving the government of the day' without being captured by it or losing longer-term perspectives inherent in being *public* (as distinct from government) servants. It means engaging in the sorts of research and evaluation that enable an estimation of trends in citizens' well-being over time. It requires attention to issues of intergenerational equity and to a horizontal sense of purposefulness over medium- to long-term timeframes that is convergent and consensus building. It requires building and maintaining a professional public service.

Respect for citizens as responsible agents

Respect for citizens as responsible agents is a necessary moral competence, if as a society we want to do better than implement paternalistic (or 'nanny state') welfarism through a cadre of technocratic bureaucrats and 'we know best' political masters and mistresses.

As Amartya Sen (1985, 1999; cf. 2009, ch. 13) has argued, both the 'well-being aspect' and the 'agency aspect' of persons are relevant to the assessment of states of affairs and actions. He distinguishes (1985, pp. 203–4) agency freedom as 'open conditionality':

> Whereas well-being freedom is freedom to achieve something in particular, viz., well-being, the idea of agency freedom is more general, since it is not tied to any one type of aim. Agency freedom is freedom to achieve whatever the person, as a responsible agent, decides he or she should achieve.

This open conditionality does not imply that a person's view of their own freedom is beyond challenge or constraint. Aims, objectives, and consequences for the public good all need to be assessed, and agency freedom exercised as *responsible* freedom. 'But', Sen (1985, p. 204) adds, 'despite this need for discipline, the use of one's agency is, in an important sense, a matter for oneself to judge'; that is, the substantive freedoms (the capabilities) to choose a life one has reason to value (Sen 1999, p. 74).

Respect for citizens as responsible agents requires skill in situating public policy between power and rationality (Arts and Van Tatenhove 2004), in managing increasing demands for subsidiarity, 'multi-actor' or 'network' governance, and citizen 'co-production' (Alford 2009a, 2009b), and in otherwise facilitating citizen participation in self-government. Wildavsky (1987, p. 255) argues that, 'Whatever else policy analysts may be ... they should be advocates of citizen participation. ... Designing policies that facilitate intelligent and effective participation is an essential task of policy analysis'.

Prudence

Prudence is the exercise of practical and not only technical reason to make moral judgements in concrete situations (that is, within the limits and opportunities of specific social and historical contexts) that can be challenged and defended through an exchange of public reasons.

Technical reason is the rational selection (using techniques such as cost–benefit analysis) of instrumental means to achieve given ends. Practical reason concerns the acceptance or rejection of norms, especially norms for action, the claims to validity of which can be supported or opposed with public reasons (Habermas 1974, p. 3).

Robert Bellah (1983, p. 55) argues that practical social science should take priority over technocratic social science and that the purpose of prudential practice 'is not to produce or control anything but to discover through mutual discussion and reflection between free citizens the most appropriate ways, under present conditions, of living the ethically good life'. Accordingly, its vocabulary is the common moral vocabulary of a free society, with *justice*, *equality*, and *freedom* among its basic terms (p. 62).

Practical social science can only ever hope to achieve 'disciplined knowing', not the degree of certainty that might be expected in the physical sciences. Prudence is required precisely because scientific demonstration is not possible (Bellah 1983, p. 64). Public policy making is, for this reason, more art and craft than science, 'a projection of frames of reference on reality, around which action is taken' (Geva-May 1997, p. xxii). It focuses, as per Socrates, on 'What ought one to do?' rather than on 'What is right, what is wrong?' or 'What is good, what is evil?' (Longstaff 1994, p. 142). It draws on cumulative experience to make strategic, contingent judgements in the full awareness of moral ambiguity, the fallibility of human planning, and the inevitability of unintended consequences (Winston 2009, p. 5; cf. Uhr 2005, ch. 3).

Prudence, however, does not replace the need for technical reason. We might rather follow Dewey in seeing the practical and the technical as two indispensable aspects or dimensions of policy making, rather than as two distinct and self-contained kinds of enterprise (McPherson 1983, p. 71). Policy making may be more art and craft than science (Wildavsky 1987, ch. 16), but the sound application of technical reason can help prevent the craft from being exercised in ways that are merely 'crafty'.

Moral leadership

How, then, might the cultivation of moral competence in public life be encouraged and supported, and institutionalised through public management and leadership?

In a career public service where everyone starts as a cadet and has opportunity for eventual promotion to leadership roles only by working their way up through the ranks, sound judgement can be cultivated through the accumulation of experience and relationships forged with one's seniors and peers, who have likewise had long-term exposure to the purpose, values, and principles that govern the agency and wider public service. Promotion and reward are tied, moreover, to behaviours aligned with the agency's ethos (cf. Hood and Lodge 2006, pp. 168–9).

In New Zealand, this model now applies only in the defence force and police. It has previously applied in the Ministry of Foreign Affairs and Trade, which has offered a 'lifetime career path', but even senior positions in the ministry are now being opened up to people with wider public or private sector experience. I myself came into the public service mid-career.

If we assume that, for various reasons, the days of a lifetime career public service are numbered, then the cultivation of moral competence in public life depends on staff recruitment, training, and development, and, above all, on the exercise and modelling of moral leadership by chief executives and their senior staff.

Recruiting and retaining a workforce with diverse professional backgrounds and academic training (arts and humanities as well as 'soft' and 'hard' sciences) is one protection against a 'group think' application of technocratic reason to public policy making. Ethics can also be taught – in the sense that public servants can learn to think more reflectively and systematically about professional practice and to engage with others in critical reflection on 'hard cases' (cf. Dworkin 1977, ch. 4). There certainly ought to be a place in the induction of new employees for an introduction to public sector ethics, the state sector code of conduct, and the agency's own code, purpose, values, and principles. This should be more than a cursory formality whereby the employee signs that they have received a copy and read it, but rather the initiation of a continuing process of critical reflection on the ethics of public service and the ethos of the employing agency. In the 2007 survey of New Zealand state services integrity and conduct, although 55 per cent of state servants believed their organisations provide training on standards of integrity and conduct, just more than one in five reported that they 'do not know' whether their organisation does (Ethics Resource Center 2007, p. 5). The Ethics Resource Center recommended (2007, p. 9), 'In order to promote a strong ethical culture and foster positive outcomes, establish programmes that are consistent, genuine, and relevant to the needs of State servants'.

As Preston (1994, p. 6) notes, however, 'The teaching of ethics to those determined to be corrupt or unethical is unlikely to make a difference'. Ethics is caught rather than taught, and if we concentrate only on the individual's behaviour, or narrowly focus on 'risk and assurance' in the prevention and detection of unethical behaviour, the impact on public sector ethics will be limited (Rhode 2006, pp. 34–5). What is required is rather the socialisation and institutionalisation of ethics within the structure, relationships, and distribution of power within public sector organisations (Preston 1994, p. 8; Sampford 1994).

I have myself benefited from opportunities to work alongside older and more experienced public policy practitioners. Trusting relationships with senior colleagues have provided me with 'sounding boards' and 'safe space' for critical reflection on 'doing the right thing' as a public servant. This implies deliberate attention to organising workplace teams in ways that maximise formal and informal contact and mentoring between 'wise hands' and less-experienced staff, and not so overloading principal analysts and advisers with project work that they are unable to contribute as mentors and coaches to more junior staff in any significant way or to provide robust second-opinion advice.

Ultimately, however, what makes or breaks public sector ethics is the tone created by chief executives and their senior staff. And what most counts is not what we say and do on the good days but how we conduct ourselves when confronted with ambiguity in the performance of our public duties – 'the disquieting internal tension that comes from competing duties, colliding considerations, and dissonant emotions' (Rhode 2006, p. 85). Rhode further reminds us that, 'No corporate mission statement or ceremonial platitudes can counter the impact of seeing leaders withhold crucial information, play favorites with promotion, stifle dissent, implement corrosive reward structures, or pursue their own self-interest at the organization's expense' (p. 39). She particularly urges senior managers to solicit diverse perspectives and dissenting views, on the grounds that a defining feature of moral leadership is a willingness to ask and to hear uncomfortable questions (p. 40).

Moral leadership demands going beyond responsiveness to responsibility; beyond doing no wrong, to doing the right thing (Hanson 2006, pp. 291–2; cf. Uhr 2005, ch. 8). And whether or not chief executives do in fact provide moral leadership will depend, in large part, on the incentives and accountabilities that apply to them and the transparency of those incentives and accountabilities.

Conclusion

This chapter has analysed tensions within and between public policy functions of analysis, advice giving, and advocacy. It has proposed that, because of the inescapable interplay between information, interests, and ideology in public policy making, the three functions need to be distinguished, without separation or division.

While maintaining appropriate distinctions can be encouraged in law and by convention, ethical codes of practice, and statements of public sector and organisational values, ethical policy making requires above all the intentional cultivation of 'moral competence in public life'. Four key competencies are civility, fidelity to the public good, respect for citizens as responsible agents, and prudence. The long-term integrity of a professional public service depends on the socialisation and institutionalisation of these competencies through public sector management and leadership that is moral and not narrowly or merely 'ethical'.

References

Alford, J. 2009a. *Engaging Public Sector Clients: From service delivery to co-production*. Basingstoke, Hampshire: Palgrave Macmillan.

Alford, J. 2009b. *Public Value from Co-production by Clients*. Working paper. Australia and New Zealand School of Government. http://ips.ac.nz/events/downloads/2009/Building%20the%20Public%20-%20Spring%20Series (accessed May 2010). (Forthcoming in J. Benington and M. Moore (eds). *In Search of Public Value*. London: Palgrave Macmillan.)

Arts, B., and J. Van Tatenhove. 2004. 'Policy and power: A conceptual framework between the 'old' and 'new' policy idioms.' *Policy Sciences* 37: 339–56.

Australian Public Service Commission. 2007. *Tackling Wicked Problems: A public policy perspective*. Barton, ACT: Commonwealth of Australia. www.apsc.gov.au/publications07/wickedproblems.htm (accessed May 2010).

Baehler, K. 2005. 'What are the limits to public service advising? The "public argument" test.' *Policy Quarterly* 1(3): 3–8.

Baehler, K., and J. Bryson. 2009. 'Behind the Beehive buzz: Sources of occupational stress for New Zealand policy officials.' *Kōtuitui: Journal of Social Sciences Online* 4: 5–23. www.royalsociety.org.nz/site/publish/journals/kotuitui/default.aspx (accessed May 2010).

Bardach, E. 2000. *A Practical Guide for Policy Analysis: The eightfold path to more effective problem solving.* New York and London: Chatham House Publishers.

Bellah, R. 1983. 'Social science as practical reason.' In D. Callahan and B. Jennings (eds). *Ethics, the Social Sciences, and Policy Analysis.* New York and London: Plenum Press, pp. 37–64.

Bromell, D. 2008. *Ethnicity, Identity and Public Policy: Critical perspectives on multiculturalism.* Wellington: Institute of Policy Studies, Victoria University of Wellington.

Bromell, D. 2009a. 'Diversity and democracy.' *Policy Quarterly* 5(4): 29–35.

Bromell, D. 2009b. 'Recognition, redistribution and democratic inclusion.' In R. Openshaw and E. Rata (eds). *The Politics of Conformity in New Zealand.* North Shore City: Pearson, pp. 231–55.

Callahan, D., and B. Jennings (eds). 1983. *Ethics, the Social Sciences, and Policy Analysis.* New York and London: Plenum Press.

Chapman, B. 1959. *The Profession of Government.* London: George Allen & Unwin.

deLeon, P. 1994. 'Democracy and the policy sciences: Aspirations and operations.' *Policy Studies Journal* 22(2): 200–12.

Dewey, J. 1927. *The Public and its Problems.* New York: Holt.

Dewey, J. 1939. *Freedom and Culture.* New York: Putnam.

Dworkin, R. 1977. *Taking Rights Seriously.* Cambridge, MA: Harvard University Press.

Eichbaum, C., and R. Shaw. 2005. 'Why we should all be nicer to ministerial advisers.' *Policy Quarterly* 1(4): 18–25.

Eichbaum, C., and R. Shaw. 2007. 'Minding the minister? Ministerial advisers in New Zealand government.' *Kōtuitui: Journal of Social Sciences Online* 2: 95–113. www.royalsociety.org.nz/site/publish/journals/kotuitui/default.aspx (accessed May 2010).

Eichbaum, C., and R. Shaw (eds). 2010. *Partisan Appointees and Public Servants: An international analysis of the role of the political advisor.* Cheltenham, UK: Edward Elgar Publishing.

Ethics Resource Center. 2007. *New Zealand State Services Integrity and Conduct Survey: August 2007.* Ethics Resource Centre: Washington, DC. www.ssc. govt.nz/display/document.asp?DocID=6276 (accessed May 2010). Results of a follow-up survey conducted in March 2010 are on the State Services Commission's website (www.ssc.govt.nz/display/home.asp).

Gallagher, J. 1981. 'Models for policy analysis: Child and family policy.' In R. Haskins and J. Gallagher (eds). *Models for Analysis of Social Policy: An introduction.* Norwood, NJ: Ablex Publishing Corporation, pp. 37–77.

Gawthrop, L. 1984. *Public Sector Management, Systems, and Ethics.* Bloomington: Indiana University Press.

Geva-May, I. 1997. *An Operational Approach to Policy Analysis: The craft – Prescriptions for better analysis.* Boston: Kluwer Academic Publishers.

Gregory, R. 2005. 'Politics, power and public policy-making: A response to Karen Baehler.' *Policy Quarterly* 1(4): 26–32.

Habermas, J. 1974. *Theory and Practice.* London: Heinemann.

Habermas, J. 1984. *The Theory of Communicative Action, Vol. 1: Reason and the rationalization of society.* London: Heinemann Education.

Hanson, K. 2006. 'Perspectives on global moral leadership.' In D. Rhode (ed.). *Moral Leadership: The theory and practice of power, judgment, and policy.* Hoboken: Jossey-Bass, pp. 291–300.

Hardin, R. 2006. 'Morals for public officials.' In D. Rhode (ed.). *Moral Leadership: The theory and practice of power, judgment, and policy.* Hoboken: Jossey-Bass, pp. 111–25.

Hawke, G. 1993. *Improving Policy Advice.* Wellington: Institute of Policy Studies, School of Government, Victoria University of Wellington.

Hicks, C. 2007. 'A case for public sector ethics.' *Policy Quarterly* 3(3): 11–15.

Hood, C., and M. Lodge. 2006. *The Politics of Public Service Bargains: Reward, competency, loyalty – and blame.* Oxford and New York: Oxford University Press.

Keith, K. 1990. 'On the constitution of New Zealand: An introduction to the foundations of the current form of government.' *Cabinet Manual 2008*. Wellington: Cabinet Office, pp. 1–6. www.cabinetmanual.cabinetoffice.govt.nz/introduction (updated 2008; accessed May 2010).

Kernaghan, K. 1995. 'The emerging public service culture: Values, ethics, and reforms.' *Canadian Public Administration* 37(4): 614–30.

Lindquist, E. 2009. *There's More to Policy than Alignment*. CPRN Research Report, Canadian Policy Research Networks. www.cprn.org/doc.cfm?doc=2040&l=en (accessed May 2010).

Lodge. M. 2009. 'Strained or broken? The future(s) of the public service bargain.' *Policy Quarterly* 5(1): 53–7.

Longstaff, S. 1994. 'What is ethics education and training?' In N. Preston (ed.). *Ethics for the Public Sector: Education and training*. Leichhardt, NSW: Federation Press, pp. 138–60.

Martin, J. 1994. 'Ethics in public service: The New Zealand experience.' In N. Preston (ed.). *Ethics for the Public Sector: Education and training*. Leichhardt, NSW: Federation Press, pp. 91–114.

McPherson, M. 1983. 'Imperfect democracy and the moral responsibilities of policy advisers.' In D. Callahan and B. Jennings (eds). *Ethics, the Social Sciences, and Policy Analysis*. New York and London: Plenum Press, pp. 69–81.

Moroney, R. 1981. 'Policy analysis within a value theoretical framework.' In R. Haskins and J. Gallagher (eds). *Models for Analysis of Social Policy: An introduction*. Norwood, NJ: Ablex Publishing Corporation, pp. 78–102.

MSD. n. d., a. *Code of Conduct*. Wellington: Ministry of Social Development.

MSD. n. d., b. *Our Vision, Values and Purpose*. Wellington: Ministry of Social Development. www.msd.govt.nz/about-msd-and-our-work/about-msd/our-vision-values-and-purpose.html (accessed May 2010).

Nielson, K. 1983. 'Emancipatory social science and social critique.' In D. Callahan and B. Jennings (eds). *Ethics, the Social Sciences, and Policy Analysis*. New York and London: Plenum Press, pp. 113–57.

OECD. 2000. *Building Public Trust: Ethics measures in OECD countries*. PUMA Policy Brief No. 7. Organisation for Economic Co-operation and Development.

Parsons, W. 1995. *Public Policy: An introduction to the theory and practice of policy analysis*. Aldershot, UK and Brookfield, US: Edward Elgar.

Pollitt, C. 2003. *The Essential Public Manager.* Philadelphia, PA: Open University.

Preston, N. (ed.). 1994. *Ethics for the Public Sector: Education and training.* Leichhardt, NSW: Federation Press.

Radin, B. 2000. *Beyond Machiavelli: Policy analysis comes of age.* Washington, DC: Georgetown University Press.

Rapid Evidence Assessment Toolkit. n. d. UK Government Social Research Service. www.civilservice.gov.uk/my-civil-service/networks/professional/gsr/resources/gsr-rapid-evidence-assessment-toolkit.aspx (accessed May 2010).

Rawls, J. 1999. *The Law of Peoples; with, The Idea of Public Reasons Revisited.* Cambridge, MA: Harvard University Press.

Rein, M. 1983. 'Value critical policy analysis.' In D. Callahan and B. Jennings (eds). *Ethics, the Social Sciences, and Policy Analysis.* New York and London: Plenum Press, pp. 83–111.

Rhode, D. (ed.). 2006. *Moral Leadership: The theory and practice of power, judgment, and policy.* Hoboken: Jossey-Bass.

Rittel, H., and M. Webber. 1973. 'Dilemmas in the general theory of planning.' *Policy Sciences* 4(2): 155–69.

Sampford, C. 1994. 'Institutionalising public sector ethics.' In N. Preston (ed.). *Ethics for the Public Sector: Education and training.* Leichhardt, NSW: Federation Press, pp. 14–38.

Scott, C. 2008. 'Enhancing quality and capability in the public sector advisory system.' Lecture to the Institute of Policy Studies Futuremaker Series, Victoria University of Wellington, 23 September 2008. http://ips.ac.nz/events/downloads/2008/ScottFuturemakers%2023-9-08.pdf%20 (accessed May 2010).

Sen, A. 1985. 'Well-being, agency and freedom: The Dewey Lectures 1984.' *Journal of Philosophy* 82(4): 169–221.

Sen, A. 1999. *Development as Freedom.* New York: Anchor Books.

Sen, A. 2009. *The Idea of Justice.* Cambridge, MA: Belknap Press.

SSC. 1995. *Principles, Conventions and Practice Guidance Series.* Wellington: State Services Commission. www.ssc.govt.nz/display/document.asp?docid=5798 (accessed May 2010).

SSC. 2001. *New Zealand Public Service Code of Conduct.* Reprinted 2005. Wellington: State Services Commission.

SSC. 2007a. *Standards of Integrity and Conduct: A code of conduct issued by the State Services Commissioner under the State Sector Act 1988, section 57.* Wellington: State Services Commission. www.ssc.govt.nz/display/document. asp?DocID=7063 (accessed May 2010).

SSC. 2007b. *Understanding the Code of Conduct: Guidance for state servants.* Wellington: State Services Commission.

SSC. 2008a. *Political Neutrality Fact Sheet No. 1: What is 'political neutrality' and what does it mean in practice?* Wellington: State Services Commission.

SSC. 2008b. *Political Neutrality Fact Sheet No. 2: Political views and participation in political activities.* Wellington: State Services Commission.

SSC. 2008c. *Political Neutrality Fact Sheet No. 3: The relationship between the public service and ministers.* Wellington: State Services Commission.

Starling, G. 2008. *Managing the Public Sector.* 8th edn. Boston, MA: Thomson Higher Education.

Uhr, J. 2005. *Terms of Trust: Arguments over ethics in Australian government.* Sydney, NSW: University of New South Wales Press.

Weiss, C. 1983. 'Ideology, interests, and information: The basis of policy positions.' In D. Callahan and B. Jennings (eds). *Ethics, the Social Sciences, and Policy Analysis.* New York and London: Plenum Press, pp. 213–45.

Wildavsky, A. 1987. *Speaking Truth to Power: The art and craft of policy analysis.* New Brunswick, NJ: Transaction Books.

Winston, K. 2002. *Moral Competence in the Practice of Democratic Governance.* KSG Faculty Research working paper series RWP02–048. http://web.hks. harvard.edu/publications/workingpapers/citation.aspx?PubId=1145 (accessed May 2010).

Winston, K. 2008. *What Makes Ethics Practical.* KSG Faculty Research working paper series RWP08–013. http://web.hks.harvard.edu/publications/ workingpapers/citation.aspx?PubId=5613 (accessed May 2010).

Winston, K. 2009. *Moral Competence in Public Life.* Occasional paper 4. Melbourne: Australia and New Zealand School of Government and State Services Authority. www.ssa.vic.gov.au/CA2571410025903D/WebObj/ OccPaper_04_Winston/$File/OccPaper_04_Winston.pdf (accessed May 2010).

Woodward, A. 1994. 'Making ethics part of real work.' In N. Preston (ed.). *Ethics for the Public Sector: Education and training.* Leichhardt, NSW: Federation Press, pp. 219–36.

5. Be careful what you wish for

John Uhr

Introduction

This chapter contrasts two competing models of an ethics of office suitable for democratic policy systems.[1] The one I favour is a model of dispersed ethical responsibilities where the precise ethical content varies with the nature of the public office. I label the model I oppose 'stealth ethics' because it promotes ethical public policy by subverting democratic ethics, which it sees as too conservative. Most conventional policy systems operate somewhere in-between, with mixtures of my favoured pluralism and my disfavoured paternalism. My aim is to nudge policy systems away from paternalism towards pluralism.

My chapter begins with a general warning about expecting too much from ethics in public policy and a more specific warning about the misguided ethical idealism I associate with the 'esoteric morality' promoted by influential utilitarian ethics theorists, of whom the model is British 19th century philosopher Henry Sidgwick. My recovery of a more realistic set of expectations for ethics is based on an artificial but I think productive distinction between 'ethics' and 'morality'. For policy purposes, I define 'ethics' in terms of right relationships among policy actors and 'morality' in terms of deeper value commitments that we each make as individuals, separate and distinct from our public roles. I conclude by contrasting the Sidgwick model of centralised ethical paternalism with my preferred model of dispersed ethical pluralism. I suggest that contemporary policy systems rely on ethics regimes that confer considerable regulatory power on political executives, which tilts them in the direction of paternalism rather than pluralism, at some cost to the ethics of sustainable democracy.

Great expectations

The idea behind the title of my chapter is a warning: be careful or beware of what you wish for. My argument is that we should not ask too much of ethics.

---

1   My thanks to Adrian Kay and Alec Mladenovic for comments on earlier drafts of this paper and to Don Locke and many other participants at the Ethical Foundations of Public Policy conference in Wellington, New Zealand, December 2009, for their welcome suggestions.

We should ask a lot of ethics, because it has a lot to offer: but we should not ask too much. I am confident that ethics is necessary, in public policy as in all aspects of our lives, and that we have better public policy when we construct policy on solid ethical foundations. My argument about not asking too much of ethics reflects my view that ethics, like so many good things, has its limits, which we should acknowledge. We respect ethics when we recognise its limits and do not call on it to do more than it is capable of: which is considerable, but not necessarily as far-reaching as some ethics enthusiasts want it to be. To respect the power of ethics means to accept the limits that define its integrity as an instrument of good public policy.

My warning is against inflated expectations of what ethics can contribute to public policy. Managing expectations is an important part of political and policy leadership, as we have seen over the last year of remarkable intergovernmental cooperation to deal with the global financial crisis. This involves raising expectations so that our political communities can strive to do more. This also involves moderating expectations so that our communities are protected against unrealistic expectations that policy makers can never meet. Moderating expectations can also protect communities against the impact of unforeseen and therefore uncontrollable shocks that policy makers fear are more likely than not to emerge out of the unknown. One of my aims is to help manage and moderate our expectations about what can be expected of ethics and public policy.

My tone might strike some as inappropriate or even offensive for a book on ethics. After all, what sort of friend of ethics is a person who talks ethics down? Where one might expect a visitor to be enthusiastic with helpful suggestions about strengthening the ethical foundations *for* public policy, here I come along with a cautionary tale about the ethical foundations *of* public policy. I risk disappointing those who are advocates of better ethical foundations for better public policy. I share that advocacy. My problem is that, having taught ethics and public policy for over 20 years, and having watched the remarkable growth of policies designed to encourage ethical conduct within governments, I fear that ethics may not be able to carry the load of our weighty expectations for 'better' government and 'better' public policy.

Ethical foundations

Analysts of public policy have long debated the precise place of ethics in theories and practices of public policy. One difficult question asks how useful ethics can be in both policy theories and policy practices. One really challenging answer comes from utilitarian policy analysts who take their inspiration from 19th century English moral philosopher Henry Sidgwick (1838–1900), revived for contemporary readers in John Rawls's *A Theory of Justice* (1971). This school of policy analysis takes its inspiration from Sidgwick's so-called doctrine of 'esotericism', which holds that policy elites can, under certain circumstances, have good moral reasons for hiding the practice of acting unethically. Sidgwick's model army of elite policy makers subscribes to the view that democracy is best ruled through policy arts that hide some of the hard truths from citizens, including the hard truth that policy elites will have to lie when exercising their policy responsibilities.

Against that background, I will try to help frame our discussion of ethics and public policy. My own view is that many of the strongest ethical foundations of public policy are matters of process rather than structure. Policy making works through process, and good policy making should be all about ethical processes. Ethics is particularly relevant to one type of process: managing the untidy but vital network of relationship processes – formal and informal, public and private. We recognise ethical relationships as those that measure up against processes of fairness. And how is fairness itself measured? In practical terms, ethical relationships are fair when they comply with agreed and acceptable standards.

Our general topic is 'ethical foundations'. The usual test of the quality of 'foundations' is whether the foundations are strong enough to 'carry weight', which is a test of structural strength. I think the better test of 'ethical foundations' is whether they are acceptable enough to 'carry conviction', which is a test of a different sort of strength: the strength that comes from shared purpose.[2] To promote ethical foundations, we need skills of advocacy and persuasion ('outreach') as much as knowledge of ethics ('insight'). The big test is this: can we persuade and convince the policy community to support a set of agreed ethical standards?

Given that there are so many legitimate policy communities, as there should be in a democracy, what manner of ethics will serve our common purposes? My answer is an ethics of due process seen as fair by as many policy participants as possible. The ethical foundations of public policy include agreement on standards of due process by those sharing the making and implementation of public policy. Getting these policy-making relationships right means stepping forward to acknowledge our shared public roles, so that we can then agree on what those involved in the policy process can reasonably expect of one another. Constructing ethical foundations is, thus, an exercise in community building.

One common test of the value of a public policy is whether it is democratic: produced by democratic processes for clearly democratic purposes. This test

---

2   See Toulmin (1976, p. 163).

of policy value seems a core test for many contemporary democracies, with its comforting assumption that the alignment of democratic form and substance is what is good about democracy. But what if a powerful school of ethics is or was convinced that democracy was not so much the solution but rather the main problem confronting ethical public policy? This question anticipates my examination of Sidgwick, which follows later in this chapter.

But the question at this early stage is more general: is it so easy to define the nature of ethical policy? It is easier to define ethical policy analysis (the means: laying out all relevant considerations) than to define ethical policy (the end: once all the hard decisions have been taken). Almost everyone agrees that ethics should be prominent in the study of public policy. But what about the place of ethics in the *practice* of public policy? Internationally, there is surprisingly little agreement on the precise place of ethics in the practical world of public policy. This chapter tries to promote fresh discussion about such matters by drawing critical attention to the often-unacknowledged limits of ethics as a guide for policy makers.

Esoteric ethics

Ethics has many dimensions. Shortly, I will provide my own policy-relevant definition of ethics as not simply individual 'right conduct' but 'right relationships' among those sharing policy responsibilities. But before I step forward with my own definition, I want to step back and take note of an alternative policy-relevant definition associated with utilitarianism: the philosophical doctrine associated with influential policy reforms in the 19th century, which contains a challenging alternative to my own approach to ethics and public policy. This influential ethics doctrine is also about relationships of public power, but not one that many contemporary democrats would call their own.

I will review the place of a fascinating school of 'esotericism' in democratic public policy, inspired by 19th century English utilitarian social theory, recently revived by Peter Singer.[3] This school of political thinking has influenced policy analysts not only in England but around the English-speaking world. Contemporary 'ethics entrepreneurs' who want lessons in how to 'make democracy more ethical' can find them in such classic utilitarian theorists as Sidgwick. Sidgwick stands out as an exemplary theorist of ethics and public policy who saw the importance of schooling policy elites in what he called 'esoteric' social doctrines that would strengthen emerging democracy by

---

3 See de Lazari-Radek and Singer (2010).

substituting a higher but hidden social morality for the lower social morality favoured by democrats. Critics have saddled Sidgwick with responsibility for championing 'Government House utilitarianism': a form of policy paternalism not unlike colonial rule where a ruling class does it best to advance the welfare of subject peoples, even to the point of disguising the underlying utilitarian logic of government programmes if that helps cement popular consent (Williams 1993, pp. 108–10).[4] John Rawls featured Sidgwick in his *A Theory of Justice* (1971) as a prominent representative of the (not unqualified) virtues of utilitarianism.[5] This chapter serves as a reminder about the role of policy elites in democratic policy systems and a warning about the recurrence of unethical use of 'ethics talk' in democratic public policy.

To some extent, I am examining a neglected but important feature of democratic ethics: the ethical role of policy elites. I am drawing on Sidgwick to generalise a portrait of ethics entrepreneurs who view democracy as a threat to ethics and whose solution involves a fascinating form of democratic deception: deception exercised by policy elites who fear that democracy tends to get in the way of ethical public policy. My critique of the Sidgwick framework is based on two core distinctions: generally between ethics and morality, in order to minimise opportunities for high-minded morality to justify unethical practice; and specifically between democratic ethics and esoteric morality, in order to minimise opportunities for esoteric doctrines to undermine democracy. Although democracy might well need policy elites, Sidgwick's 'esoteric ethics' eventually fails to show why policy elites need or even value democracy. I contend that some contemporary ethics advocates discount the ethical value of democracy. Those who value the conventional procedural ethics of democratic policy making should be on guard against the secret policy designs of utilitarian 'esotericism'.

Surprisingly, this conviction about the need for 'esoteric morality' remains a model for contemporary ethics advocates (or 'ethics entrepreneurs').[6] Many such advocates adopt a form of what I call 'stealth ethics' that hides their policy preferences behind what the original utilitarian theorists called an 'esoteric' social philosophy. As used in this sense, 'esotericism' refers to a disguised social doctrine that protects its anti-democratic ethics behind the façade of an 'exoteric' policy doctrine. Many advocates of ethics see democracy as one of the primary problems confronting ethical public policy: either we have ethical policy or democratic policy but we cannot have both. Democracy should give way to ethics. In practice, democracy should be regulated by an 'esoteric' social philosophy that hides or disguises its ethics: protecting its anti-democratic ethical

---

4   See also Williams (1981, p. 52).
5   See, for example, Rawls (1971, pp. 22, 26, 29, 32–3, 92, 400, 458, and especially 254–7 and 572–7).
6   See, for example, de Lazari-Radek and Singer (2010).

content beneath an 'exoteric' policy exterior that cause no harm to democracy. In fact, the hope is that the esoteric morality can strengthen democracy by importing ethical elements that democracy, if left to itself, would reject.

Esotericism is normally associated more with conservatives (think of recent debates over 'neo-conservatives') than social progressives like Sidgwick. What is remarkable is how infrequently debates over ethics and public policy pay any attention to the sort of 'stealth ethics' practised by Sidgwick and his followers, who illustrate many of the ways that friends of democracy can turn towards a form of democratic elitism to overcome what they see as democracy's fragile ethics infrastructure. Unfortunately, their remedy can become worse than the disease if the policy elite distance themselves too far from the democracy they disdain. Debates over ethics and public policy can benefit by paying closer attention to the sort of 'hidden hand' or 'stealth ethics' favoured by Sidgwick and followers and by holding policy elites to greater public accountability as one way of restraining their self-avowed elitism from straying too far from the conventional requirements of democratic ethics. Although democracy might well require policy elites, Sidgwick's school of 'esoteric ethics' fails to show why policy elites need or even value democracy. All the more reason for democracies to hold policy elites accountable for the power they exercise in the name of social utility.

Ethics defined

For simplicity's sake, let me define ethics as the agreed standards we expect of, say, public policy or even private policy if it comes to that. Thus, to have the right ethics means having the right standards: recognising the standards expected of us, and to the best of our ability living up to these standards. When we speak of the ethical foundations of public policy, we are speaking about our agreed standards we expect of public policy: standards appropriate to the various instruments of rule and regulation governments use to manage public affairs. Being ethical means doing the right thing consistent with our agreed standards. This is much more than compliance with the rules of the game. Being ethical typically means doing the right thing according to the spirit of the game. Hence, being ethical means doing what is expected according to the unwritten rules known to all who want to be regarded as 'a good sport', even in the competitive world of politics and public policy.

Ethics is thus about obligations or duties that we accept because we accept agreed standards. Almost always, doing the right thing means accepting our part in a relationship: doing what we owe others as part of a shared agreement. Of course, there are limits. Much depends on our bargaining power in such relationships: 'accepting our part' might cover many forms of acceptance that reflect unequal power relations, such as accepting our part as an instrument of convenience for power-holders. In this summary of an ethical relationship, I am highlighting the importance of voluntary cooperation as an ethical ideal. Acknowledging the inequalities of power is one thing, all too common in most government circumstances: less common is a situation of mutual respect among officials sharing public power, which helps point us toward a set of appropriate ethical standards.

As a regulatory ideal, doing the right thing more often than not means respecting the rights of others to be treated according to the standards we mutually acknowledge. As we can see, ethics and justice are closely related: ethics is accepting what others expect of us and justice is ethics at its fullest, when we act on ethical principle even when the law or the rules might not be so demanding. Doing the right thing more often than not means respecting the rights of others to be treated according to the standards we mutually acknowledge. My model of justice here is about basic fairness rather than any model of comprehensive social justice: in other words, my approach to justice as ethics-in-action is an admittedly 'thin' rather than 'thick' model, comprising norms of due process and fair procedure for all citizens, regardless of their claims to special treatment based on their self-confessed moral worth. My approach is standard fare in theories of liberal pluralism, which many communitarians will find too thin and spare an interpretation of ethics, with too formal an account of justice to promote moral public policy.

In explaining the reasons for my restraint, some readers will detect my reliance on Stuart Hampshire, the noted English philosopher and author of *Justice is Conflict* (1999), which provides a classic defence of the ethics of due process in politics and public policy. I am drawing from Hampshire the view that agreement about an ethics of fair procedure in public decision making is a top policy priority in liberal-democratic societies that tolerate extensive moral pluralism. That is, the greater the diversity of moral belief-systems, the greater the benefit from consensus on procedural ethics. Policy architects have to anticipate the need for reconciliation and instruct institutional designers to devise procedures that cause each of us to 'hear the other side'. This of course is easier to do in theory than in practice. But if ethics means anything, it means something practical. Being ethical means aligning the fair and the feasible.

Saving ethics from morality

Where does or should 'morality' feature in our analysis? Perhaps surprisingly, I propose that we make a distinction between the smaller topic of 'ethics' and the larger topic of 'morality'. I think we already distinguish in practice between the practical discourse of 'ethics', which can stimulate discussion over role relationships in the policy process, and the other-worldly discourse of 'morality', which has many virtues but lacks the pragmatic value of 'ethics' discourse. Where morality is intensely theoretical and speculative, ethics is quite practical. Talk of morality is talk about the meaning of fundamentals; ethics, as I am using that term here, is talk about action: what we do here and now in the social roles we occupy.[7]

I admit that the discourse of 'moral philosophy' frequently frames our approach to discussions of ethics and public policy. Prominent examples typically come from newly elected governments believing they have some sort of 'moral mandate' to steamroll opponents. The former Rudd Labor government in Australia is a good example where the prime minister has been explicit about his moral heroes, such as the anti-Nazi theologian Dietrich Bonhoeffer, in ways that his opponents protest as 'moralistic' (Rudd 2006).[8] The prime minister had a tendency to reach for the high moral ground, identifying climate change as 'the moral crisis of our times' and describing opponents of his border-protection policies as 'lacking a moral compass'. These are useful examples because they illustrate the way that public use of the discourse of morality often says 'no compromise', as though the stated public policy response is fundamentally right, with no room for alternative views. Bonhoeffer's uncompromising stand against Nazi policy and practice is truly admirable. Rudd deserves praise for bringing Bonhoeffer's religious commitments back into public consideration. But to what extent can we use this rare and valuable example of moral courage as a feasible model for the routines of policy making under less extreme circumstances?

The problem here is not morality but 'moralising'. There is nothing in ethical practice that quite matches 'moralising' ('sermonising' or being judgemental about others' lack of morals), and that is one very good reason to retain our focus on ethics. In fact, 'moralising' suggests why moral discourse is unhelpful for our purposes: moral discourse is more judgemental and exclusionary than ethics discourse, which suits the purposes of those uncompromising policy makers who want to take 'the high moral ground' and condemn, rather than converse with, their opponents who allegedly lack a 'moral compass'.

The deep and rich discourse of morality can be distinguished from the conventional and comparatively superficial discourse of ethics. This distinction between two related discourses is a useful way of separating out ethics and protecting it from too heavy a burden of moral expectation. My use of this distinction mimics the famous distinction between 'the right' and 'the good'

---

7 Consider Billington (2003, pp. 19–26).
8 Examples of anti-moralistic opposition include Uhlmann (2009) and Murphy (2009).

in English philosophical discourse, with ethics approximating the former and morality the latter. My claim is that policy analysis can benefit by distinguishing between issues of right and good, both of which are of fundamental importance, where 'the right' refers to right relationships among policy actors and 'the good' refers to the less visible world of deep personal value to which each of us as individuals are personally committed (Ross 1930, pp. 155–73).

My distinction is admittedly artificial but arguably a useful way of relating two realms that overlap. Think of morality as the social plant with deep roots and ethics as the social plant with shallow roots. Both are socially useful but in different ways. Our everyday language illustrates that the discourses of morality and ethics are frequently put to different social uses, with morality indicating the deeper realm of beliefs about conscience and personal identity (for example, belief systems), while ethics often, but not always, indicates a social realm of relationships based on the shared identity of interdependent roles (for example, public service roles).

Relating ethics to morality

All of this careful distinction between 'ethics' and 'morality' is nicely academic. The learned will tell us that the two terms *ethics* and *morality* are almost interchangeable. They will point out that the word ethics comes from the Greek language and that morality comes from the Latin language and that both terms refer to the same thing: in fact, the Latin term 'mores' was probably invented by Cicero when trying to translate the Greek term 'ethos' from Aristotle's classic treatise on ethics.

But I follow where others have been prepared to tread in adhering to this distinction of convenience between 'ethics' and 'morality'.[9] For example, Ricoeur's (1992) use of a similar distinction refers to 'the primacy of ethics over morality' where ethics refers to the internal character or characteristics we desire in order to do well in life and morality refers to the externally imposed obligations or norms expected of us by others. My rough and ready distinction is simpler than Ricoeur's grand theory, which seeks to promote Aristotle's school of virtue ethics over Kant's alternative school of strict compliance with duty. Our two approaches converge in thinking of ethics as having primacy over morality, even if our underlying justifications differ. Both approaches draw on Aristotle's virtue theory to spell out the ethical content of contemporary role ethics. Both approaches see moral theory as serving other purposes. Where we differ is that my approach is quite pragmatic. I see morality as the world

---

9   See Ricoeur (1992, pp. 169–239). See also Toulmin (2001, p. 168), arguing against those 'who want ethical theory to be moral'.

of *confessional* responsibilities (for the good things we value as fundamental, which we are reluctant to compromise). Accordingly, I see ethics as the world of *professional* responsibilities (for the right things we accept as part of our role or office or job).

This is an artificial but useful distinction about two realms that overlap. Ethics here refers to doing the right thing and morality here refers to our deepest beliefs about good and evil. Ethics relates to our duties and obligations in the roles we carve out for ourselves; morality relates to the concept of the good that shapes the inner individual. The term 'morality' often refers to unconditional value commitments that trump all other values. Here I am using the term morality much as it is often used in the policy process to designate the deepest reservoirs of our belief-system: the deepest springs of our value commitments that define who we are and what, at the end of the day, we stand for. The topic of ethics and public policy shifts away from an intractable wrangle over competing moral visions of different belief communities and becomes a debate over the important but limited role responsibilities we as a political community expect of one another in public life.

My point is that fruitful discussion over ethics and public policy can begin by separating ethics from morality in order to lessen the weight of value that ethics will be asked to carry. Devising agreed standards for public policy will be much harder if the task is approached in terms of an agreed morality informing the substance of public policy, compared with my suggested approach of an agreed ethics informing our roles in making and managing the processes of public policy. My distinction is between morality as a world of deep substance and ethics as a shallower world of process. We inhabit both worlds of course, but I am suggesting that ethics marks out the agreed social space we share when we play our allotted part in the public policy process; and morality marks out the personal space of individual conscience that I share with my belief community, however large or small that might be.

Ethics by example

An example will help. Think of the language we use around 'ethics committees' to refer to regulatory bodies that oversee communities (of employees or researchers or contractors) with shared and agreed expectations about the ethical norms expected of those carrying out the business of that community. We do not refer to 'morals committees'. Why is this? I think it is because we make a distinction between ethics as role-related (for example, my role as an employee of a hospital or healthcare facility) and morals as me-related, in my personal capacity when my professional or social role has been put to one side.

Ethics committees perform important functions in many organisations in the public and private sectors, helping clarify appropriate on-the-job conduct. For academic researchers, an important stage in the research process occurs when we get our ethics clearance, which means our employer or funding authority approves our research plan on the basis that we will comply with the relevant code of conduct for fair and honest dealing as researchers. But we do not have to undergo tests by a 'morals committee'. The reason for this is that we envisage a 'morals committee' as something quite different, potentially examining things much more deeply personal than our role-responsibilities.

I admit that the two spheres of ethics and morality are not separate and distinct but often overlap. Think only of the process called for by many professional associations when determining whether particular individuals measure up and deserve to be recognised as professionals: as medical professionals, legal professionals, or military professionals. One of the tests, not always made explicit, is whether particular persons are 'fit and proper persons' to take on the responsibilities of the profession: that is, whether they have the personal capacities to use and not abuse whatever responsibilities come with the professional office they seek. Such tests can drill down into the deeper layers of personal morality if there is reason to suspect that particular persons might hold or harbour deep value commitments that make them unlikely to honour the rights and privileges that go with professional standing. But most of the time, ethics committees and related ethics processes stay closer to the surface of our roles as employees or functionaries, making a rough and ready distinction between our deepest moral wells of personal meaning and our conventional worlds of on-the-job performance in the roles or offices expected of us.

What is the practical implication of this proposition about separating ethics from morality? Negatively, to accept that our task is not to arrive at a consensus about agreed moral belief-systems. Positively, to focus on the practical roles of those formulating and implementing public policy. Here we note the many networks of shared responsibility for public policy, in order to devise codes of practice to clarify the responsibilities of those exercising public power in the policy process.

Ethics entrepreneurs

In my view, some of the most committed ethics enthusiasts need to increase their commitment to democracy. Just as political executives can confuse their particular institutional interests with those of good government more generally, so too some influential ethics gurus are more impressed with their own school of ethics than they are with the norms and values of democracy. Until ethics experts make their peace with the messy realities of practical democracy, I think we should take their advice with a grain of salt. Again, this situation is not all bad. The welcome implication is that ethics has important political implications and we should judge ethics regimes as much by their political qualities as their moral qualities.

My example comes from utilitarianism: the same school of ethics ('consequentialism') identified in the *Stern Review* as the core of the ethical foundations of contemporary public policy (Stern 2006, pp. 31–4, 46–9).[10] This is the school of ethics that holds that the value of an action is judged by reference to its consequences, which seems a sane and sensible enough view. Much of utilitarian ethics is designed to undercut our tolerance for those well-intentioned blundering types who ask us to excuse them by claiming that the wrong they did was not all that bad, because after all, they meant well. Plenty of public policies come off the rails, even though the policy actors meant well. Many policy actors defend such policy failures on the basis that they did not intend any harm and, in fact, they meant well.[11]

The point of utilitarian ethics is to turn things around so that good intentions are no longer a sufficient reason for policy actions to be judged as right. Consequences also matter: results matter, perhaps even more than intentions. You can see where this is going: at a certain point, advocates of utilitarian ethics discount or undervalue both intentions and process, and privilege, or indeed overvalue, results. This approach has the air of worldly realism about it. I am all for realism. But I want to warn us against a downside risk of utilitarian realism, which is the link between thinking in utilitarian terms and acting with what are called 'dirty hands'. Most forms of the ethic of 'dirty hands' have to do with an embrace of the belief that the ends justify the means: valuable policy ends ('peace') can justify disreputable administrative means ('war').

I want to suggest that many of our contemporary ethics entrepreneurs walk in the shadow of this utilitarian cloud. In fact, the original ethics entrepreneur of this school went out of his way to justify why taking ethics seriously can mean not taking democracy seriously. My evidence comes from the first great policy publicist for utilitarian ethics: Henry Sidgwick, a truly remarkable example of the ethics entrepreneur who models the sort of 'stealth ethics' I want to highlight.[12]

Sidgwick is the very model of a theoretically informed policy innovator. But I want to identify a private 'moral' theory nested in the public 'ethical'

---

10 On consequentialism generally, see Hardin (1988).
11 See also Ward (2009, p. 5).
12 See Sidgwick (1907, especially pp. 484–495). Compare de Lazari-Radek and Singer (2010, pp. 37–42). See also Schultz (2004, especially pp. 18–20, 264–9, 507).

theory. The public doctrine is about using concepts of public (or social) utility to construct new ethical foundations for public policy: a classic and very influential advocacy of a progressive version of utilitarianism, designed to sweep away traditional public policies that served no clear public utility. What is most interesting about Sidgwick as policy reformer is his inner conviction that ethical reformation would require special political dedication by his core followers. They would have to work from within established systems and structures, steadily seeking to transform established society without publicly disclosing all of their reformist agenda.[13] Ethical reform might require a kind of high-minded ethical deceit where Sidgwick's followers would be called on to say one thing in public ('comply with social norms') and do another more important thing in private ('break social norms, but for the greater good of the public benefits this will produce').

If this is characteristic of ethics advocates generally, then those of us favouring democratic values of open public participation have a few problems. We have to look very closely at the elitist ethics being practised by well-intentioned but anti-democratic reformers, for whom the slow process of building public acceptance is reason enough to try an alternative reform strategy of what I call 'stealth ethics'. In two of his very influential works, Sidgwick (1898, 1907) draws his more attentive readers to the importance of what he terms the 'esoteric morality' (that is, the hidden or undisclosed morality) that utilitarian reformers should adopt.[14] In passages of quite cryptic prose, perhaps designed to deflect all but the most persistent of readers (the 'enlightened few'), Sidgwick teases out the example of lying for the greater good. He warns his readers that the people generally believe that lying is wrong, yet utilitarians know better: lying is not wrong if the public benefits outweigh the public losses. Trouble is, if utilitarians publicly admit to their inner conviction that lying is in principle beneficial, this would then cause significant public harm by weakening public confidence in the prevailing social morality prohibiting lying.[15]

Stealth ethics

Sidgwick's energetic 'stealth ethics' provides a standing example of a potential weakness in ethics advocacy. He is realist enough to acknowledge that many policy makers act unethically; for example, by lying. He is idealist enough to wish this were not so. Usually, lying politicians have no excuse for their wrong conduct. Sidgwick is also experienced enough in the practicalities of policy making to know that professional ethics confers special privileges on many

---

13 Consider Bok (1984, pp. 112–3).
14 See Sidgwick (1898, especially Essay 3, 'Public morality', pp. 52–82).
15 A convenient source is H. Sidgwick, 'The classification of duties: Veracity' in Bok (1978, pp. 272–5).

socially powerful groups to act in ways that are in tension with the rules of ordinary morality. For example, lawyers do their best to protect their client's interests by stretching the truth in ways that would be unacceptable according to the rules of everyday ethics, so too do leading opposition politicians when holding governments to account, and that rough and tumble activity is consistent with their socially useful ethics of role. Further, Sidgwick notes that many powerful groups in government are given authority to deny the truth that they are breaking the ordinary rules of ethics; for example, spies and military authorities and their political ministers deceive the enemy, even if this means deceiving friends as well. But Sidgwick takes this notion of professional political ethics one step further: he illustrates for us the temptation facing ethics advocates to devise a specialist form of professional ethics for ethics reformers. This warrant not only allows them to lie for the greater good but to lie about this practice of lying, and to deceive the public about the presence of the 'esoteric morality' that persuades the ethical elite of the justice of their covert practice.

Of course, the historical Sidgwick was not as bad or as troubling as I am making him out to be.[16] I am exaggerating and making the worst case for an otherwise good person. I concede that few ethics advocates fit the template I have constructed here. But my point is to identify a very real risk, which is that ethics advocates can be so keen to take ethics seriously that they forget to take the checks and balances of democracy just as seriously. My interest here is not in Sidgwick as such, but in Sidgwick as a type or exemplar of ethics reformer ('innovator' is his preferred term) who drills his followers in the importance of appearances. Policy innovators should manage publicity in ways that deflect public attention from their deviations from conventional social norms. The ethical reformer in this school of utilitarianism thus balances two truths: the general or popular truth about the wrongness of acting unethically (as in the case of lying); and the secret or esoteric truth known only to the committed reformers that acting unethically (for example, lying) is right under certain conditions. Appearances are everything because reformers such as Sidgwick appreciate that the ethical foundations of public policy rest in community sentiment, which disapproves of unethical conduct such as lying. But if reformers want to take ethics seriously, then they have to use every instrument, including well-calculated lying, to manage the policy process in ways that produce the social benefit that is the underlying measure of ethical policy.

What would be an example of such a policy deception that produces public benefits but only where the people generally remain ignorant of what is going on? Think of it in these very broad terms: any deception by anyone in a position of policy power that keeps the public ignorant about calculated wrongs done to produce right results. The systemic example is the very denial that such an

---

16   Consider Schultz (2004, pp. 703–13).

esoteric ethic of exceptionalism exists! Sidgwick knew the risks he was taking with his 'paradoxical' doctrine about esoteric or exceptional ethics. In *Practical Ethics* he noted that this warrant for public officials to manage their public duties in ways that are inconsistent with their private duties was 'not a proposition that a candidate for Parliament would affirm on a public platform' (Sidgwick 1898). But once elected, what becomes evident is the 'esoteric professional morality current among politicians, in which considerable relaxations are allowed of the ordinary rules of veracity, justice, and good faith' (Sidgwick 1898, p. 57). Building on this rather self-serving form of esotericism, Sidgwick constructs a marvelous edifice of public-serving esotericism, fit for the purpose of ethics reformers who can not afford to wait for democracy.

Does this make Sidgwick's account sound like special pleading: excusing certain policy agents of routine duties? There is something to Sidgwick's doctrine.[17] But it is a doctrine liable to misuse or abuse. At its best, Sidgwick's careful anatomy of ethical exceptionalism resembles traditional casuistry, as he himself noted when examining 'the esoteric morality of any particular profession or trade' (Sidgwick 1898, p. 19). At its worst, Sidgwick's doctrine about the ethical ends justifying the unethical means illustrates the disdain for the routines of democracy and popular government that well-intentioned but impatient ethics experts can display.

The practical implication of this discussion is that democracy is a core part of the ethical foundations of public policy. Negatively, this means we should downgrade the credit rating of those ethics advocates who want to short-circuit the slow but necessary processes of popular decision making. Positively, this means we should value democracy for the way it contributes to ethical foundations of public policy by holding ethics to public account, causing ethics advocates to demonstrate how their ethics schemes can strengthen rather than bypass or subvert democracy.

Contemporary ethics regimes

We can detect a distaste for democracy among some influential schools of ethics experts or ethics entrepreneurs. We forget that ethics advocates can pose risks to democratic policy making, particularly when their fervour for ethics outstrips their fondness for democracy. Some ethics advocates are quite elitist, with an impatience for the slow grind of democratic processes. This elitism often matches the concentrated ethics adopted by political executives seeking to

---

17   Consider Melzer (2007).

bolster the policy power of centralised government institutions. I think ethical public policy includes or presupposes democratic processes of public policy, in contrast to the anti-democratic sentiments of some influential ethics experts.

One practical suggestion I have about improving ethics and public policy is that, despite Singer's advocacy, we learn from the Sidgwick case study to be wary of policy elites bearing ethics (de Lazari-Radek and Singer 2010, pp. 51–8). The problem is not that policy elites generally do not take ethics seriously but that generally they do not take democracy seriously. Their dedication to their chosen school of ethics can mean they treat democracy as vulnerable to unethical tendencies. Their solution is to do what they can to prevent social or exoteric morality from disintegrating in ways traditionally feared of democracy, while devising an 'esoteric morality' to allow the policy elite to escape public distrust while engaged in their unrevealed but well-intentioned policy arts.

Contemporary democratic governance never quite lives up to Sidgwick's high expectations for stealth ethics. Instead, what we have is a preference by governing elites for ambitious ethics regimes devised by those in the political executive at the centre of government to regulate activities of those across the policy landscape. Such ethics regimes are prominent features of contemporary public policy. Nothing so bold as Sidgwick's stealth ethics seems to inspire the ethics regimes regulating contemporary policy systems. But one can detect a form of ethical zeal in the ambition that heads of governments have for taking responsibility for regulating official ethics, where ethical conduct in effect means acting responsively to implement government policies.

Democratic political executives are often tempted to use ethics as part of a credentialling package when searching for ways to increase public confidence and trust in government. Increasingly governments are attracted to ethics policies as a public relations exercise: that is, governments look to ethics not as an end in itself but as a means of strengthening public confidence in government. This is not all bad: the welcome implication here is that good government is wider and deeper than simply the good of 'the government' and that if the ethics initiatives of political executives stimulate ethics initiatives from other branches and components of our governments, then well and good. But it is mistaken to think that any one part of the system of government can take out a 'site licence' on ethics and claim that whatever use they make of ethics is proof that government has gone ethical. A bit of due diligence by other branches of government and a bit of auditing are in order to protect us from whole-of-government claims exercised by subordinate parts of the system of government.

If 'concentrated' ethics is the problem, one solution is along the lines of 'dispersed' ethics. My own approach (echoing F. H. Bradley's (1962) case against Sidgwick)[18] to dispersed ethics is the concept of the 'lattice of leadership', which emerged in my book *Terms of Trust* as a way of trying to explain the character of dispersed leadership in a democracy (Uhr 2005, pp. 78–81).[19] The concept derives from the theme of power-sharing across many different locations of authority. The lattice of leadership attempts to describe a style of dispersed public leadership based on a spread of locations where powers and influence intersect. In my view, ethical policy leadership in a democracy requires *dispersed* rather than *concentrated* foundations. Ethics as it emerges from the central structures of government is a classic case of concentrated ethics: ethics concentrated in the hands of executive officials, political and bureaucratic. However welcome might be the many ethics initiatives emerging from the central structures of government, the ethical footings of public policy require wider foundations than simply those of central agencies in executive government. Dispersal of policy power does not have to imply lack of energy or focus or impact: in fact, I argue that dispersed power can enrich the ethics of public policy by calling into play a richer blend of ethical viewpoints.[20]

Conclusion

My image of the 'lattice of leadership' is another way of conveying the message found in many traditional doctrines of 'ethics of office', where expectations about the right conduct of public figures derive from the nature of the specific office in question. One advantage of this type of so-called institutional or role ethics is that it helps officials avoid unnecessary abstraction in ethical thinking by keeping their focus on concrete circumstances and the practical responsibilities of role. Ethical responsibilities vary with role. Although general obligations to act honestly might be common, specific forms of honest ethical conduct can vary according to the role or office in question. This traditional orientation to public ethics undercuts expectations about a 'one size fits all' model of ethical conduct, deferring instead to a wide variety of clusters of ethical priorities varying with different types of public office. Theories of ethics of office have survived so long precisely because they match the living realities of the public realm, where what is considered appropriate public conduct for officials derives substantially from the nature of the offices being occupied: take the occupant into another public office and you probably change most of their official ethical obligations.

---

18   See, for example, Bradley (1962, pp. 126-9).
19   A more recent version is in Uhr (2008).
20   See more generally Kane et al. (2009).

The practical implication is that responsibility for maintaining the ethical foundations of public policy cannot and should not be left solely to executive government, which is the default position in most democratic systems. Negatively, this means there is no 'one size fits all' approach. Positively, this means a democratic ethic of dispersed public decision making. Democratic governance is much broader than the government of the day, and ethical policy systems rest on networks of dispersed public responsibility involving many types of public offices, each of which deserves to have its own distinctive code of practice reflecting its own particular ethical contribution.

References

Billington, R. 2003. *Living Philosophy: An introduction to moral thought*. 3rd edn. London: Routledge.

Bok, S. (ed.). 1978. *Lying: Moral choice in public and private life*. New York: Pantheon Books.

Bok, S. 1984. *Secrets: On the ethics of concealment and revelation*. Oxford: Oxford University Press.

Bradley, F. H. 1962. *Ethical Studies*. 2nd edn. London: Oxford University Press.

De Lazari-Radek, K., and P. Singer. 2010. 'Secrecy in consequentialism: A defence of esoteric morality.' *Ratio* (March): 34–68.

Hampshire, S. 1999. *Justice is Conflict*. London: Duckworth.

Hardin, R. 1988. *Morality within the Limits of Reason*. Chicago: University of Chicago Press.

Kane, J., H. Patapan, and P. 't Hart (eds). 2009. *Dispersed Democratic Leadership*. Oxford: Oxford University Press.

Melzer, A. 2007. 'On the pedagogical motive for esoteric writing.' *Journal of Politics* 69(4): 1015–31.

Murphy D. 2009. 'Rendering to Caesar, and a nod to God.' *Sydney Morning Herald*, 31 October – 1 November.

Rawls, J. 1971. *A Theory of Justice*. Cambridge, MA: Harvard University Press.

Ricoeur, P. 1992. *Oneself as Another*. Chicago: University of Chicago Press.

Ross, W. D. 1930. *The Right and the Good*. Oxford: Clarendon Press.

Rudd, K. 2006. 'Faith in politics.' *The Monthly Magazine*, October, no. 17. www.themonthly.com.au/print/300.

Schultz, B. 2004. *Henry Sidgwick: Eye of the universe. An intellectual biography.* Cambridge, UK: Cambridge University Press.

Sidgwick, H. 1898. *Practical Ethics: A collection of addresses and essays.* London: Swan Sonnenschein. www.archive.org/details/cu31924031432275.

Sidgwick, H. 1907. *The Methods of Ethics.* 7th edn. London: Macmillan.

Stern, N. 2006. *The Economics of Climate Change: The Stern Review.* Cambridge, UK: Cambridge University Press.

Toulmin, S. 1976. *Knowing and Acting.* New York: Macmillan.

Toulmin, S. 2001. *Return to Reason.* Cambridge, MA: Harvard University Press.

Uhlmann, C. 2009. 'St Kevin's halo may choke him.' *Weekend Australian*, 24–25 October.

Uhr, J. 2005. *Terms of Trust: Arguments over ethics in Australian government.* Sydney, NSW: University of New South Wales Press.

Uhr, J. 2008. 'Distributed authority in a democracy: The lattice of leadership revisited.' In P. 't Hart and J. Uhr (eds). *Public Leadership: Perspectives and practices.* Canberra: Australian National University E-Press, pp. 37–44. http://epress.anu.edu.au/anzsog/public_leadership/pdf_instructions.html.

Ward, T. 2009. 'Punishment and correctional practice: Ethical and rehabilitation implications.' *Policy Quarterly* 5(2): 3–8.

Williams, B. 1981. *Moral Luck.* Cambridge, UK: Cambridge University Press.

Williams, B. 1993. *Ethics and the Limits of Philosophy.* London: Fontana Press.

Part II
Ethics of climate change

6. The most important thing about climate change

John Broome

Ethics and climate change

The title of this volume – *Public Policy: Why ethics matters* – is highly significant. Among the protagonists in the debate about public policy in response to climate change, many think ethics is irrelevant. Most of the protagonists are scientists and economists, and they think they need no contribution from moral philosophy. They are wrong.

Take as an example a criticism directed by the economist Martin Weitzman against *The Stern Review* (Stern 2007). In comparing the well-being of future generations with our own well-being, Nicholas Stern uses a lower discount rate than many economists do. This means he attaches more value to the economic consumption of future generations. A consequence is that *The Stern Review* recommends strong and immediate action to diminish climate change. Stern justifies his lower discount rate on ethical grounds (Stern 2007, ch. 2A). Weitzman (2007, p. 712) says he justifies it by:

> relying mostly on a priori philosopher-king ethical judgements about the immorality of treating future generations differently from the current generation – instead of trying to back out what possibly more representative members of society … might be revealing from their behavior is *their* implicit rate of pure time preference. An enormously important part of the 'discipline' of economics is supposed to be that economists understand the difference between their own personal preferences for apples over oranges and the preferences of others for apples over oranges. Inferring society's revealed-preference value of [the discount rate] is not an easy task … but at least a good-faith effort at such an inference might have gone some way towards convincing the public that the economists doing the studies are not drawing conclusions primarily from imposing their own value judgements on the rest of the world.

Weitzman evidently thinks the discount rate used by governments when deciding their response to climate change ought to be derived from people's preferences about their private savings, as revealed in the money market. This judgement of Weitzman's is an ethical one, because it is about how governments ought to behave towards future generations. An enormously important part of the discipline of economics is supposed to be that economists understand the difference between ethical judgements and judgements of empirical fact – 'normative' and 'positive' judgements in the terminology of many text-books of economics. Especially as Weitzman's judgement, on the face of it, is so implausible, he could not possibly hope to justify it without recourse to the discipline that examines how people and other agents ought to behave. That discipline is ethics. Weitzman needs ethics.

Climate change raises a wide range of ethical issues. It raises issues of justice, for instance. Our emissions of greenhouse gases directly cause climate change, which is already harming other people. People are already losing their homes, their livelihoods, and even their lives as a result of the climate change we are causing. This is an injustice we are doing to those people.

Climate change also raises many issues of value. We are worsening the lives of future people by damaging the environment in which they will live. To help us decide how much we should reduce our emissions, we need to set a value on the badness of the harm we are doing to future people, and compare it with the badness of the sacrifices we could make to reduce it. Among the bad things future people will suffer is that many will die before their time, in floods and heat waves, in droughts and famines, and through increased poverty among the poorest. We need to set a value on the badness of those early deaths. We also need to assess the value of nature, which we are impoverishing. Those are some assessments of value we need to make, and there are many others too.

In this chapter, I concentrate on just one question of value to illustrate the need for moral philosophy. My question is whether the most important thing about climate change is the harm it is likely to cause or alternatively the utter catastrophe that it may possibly – though very improbably – cause. Weitzman argues that the small chance of catastrophe is the most important thing about climate change, and this view is gaining ground among economists. I shall consider whether it is right.

The very most important thing about climate change

However, since the 2009 Climate Change Conference in Copenhagen, I have come to the conclusion that the very most important thing about climate change is neither what is likely nor what is unlikely to result from it. The very most important thing is this fact: that the problem of climate change can be solved without anyone making any sacrifice.[1] At Copenhagen, many nations came together and failed to reach an agreement. They were asked to make sacrifices, and they declined to do so. But no sacrifice is necessary. The nations might have been more amenable if they had understood that point.

The fact no sacrifice is necessary is a consequence of elementary economics. Climate change is what economists call an *externality*. Many of our activities cause greenhouse gases to be emitted. In deciding how many of these activities to engage in, people weigh the benefits they gain from them against the costs of engaging in them. But most of the costs of emitting greenhouse gases are not borne by the people who emit them. Instead, they are distributed across the population of the world, through the damage the greenhouse gases do. When the costs of an activity are not fully borne by the person who decides to engage in it, that is an externality.

Elementary economics tells us that externalities cause *inefficiency*. When an economist says that a situation is inefficient, she means it would be possible to make someone better off without making anyone else worse off. More precisely, there is some alternative state such that someone prefers the alternative to the existing state and no one prefers the existing state to the alternative. To adopt economists' terminology, let us say this alternative is *Pareto superior* to the existing state. Moving to the Pareto superior state involves no sacrifice on anyone's part. Because climate change is an externality, there is a Pareto superior state we could move to. It will involve emitting less greenhouse gas. Moreover, there is a Pareto superior state that is *efficient*, which means no other state is Pareto superior to it. If we get to a state like that, the inefficiency caused by the externality will have been eliminated, and no one will have made any sacrifices.

The theory of externalities tells us that achieving a Pareto superior state will often require resources to be transferred from some people to others. In the case of climate change, it is obvious in broad terms what sorts of transfer are required. We the current generation benefit from emitting greenhouse gases as we do at present. Suppose we change our policies and emit less of them. That by itself would make us worse off. But the theory tells us that resources could be transferred to us from the beneficiaries of our reduction in emissions, in such a way that no one ends up worse off. In the case of greenhouse gases, most of the beneficiaries are people who will live in the future. Therefore, resources will need to be transferred from future people to present people.

How can that happen? We the current generation are set to bequeath a lot to future generations. We shall leave them artificial resources such as roads and museums. We shall also leave them natural resources, since this generation

---

1   I take this point from Foley (2007). It is widely recognised. For instance, it is mentioned by Stern (2010, p. 85).

will not exhaust all the natural resources the earth possesses. To compensate ourselves for reducing our emissions of greenhouse gases, we can use more of other resources for ourselves. We shall leave less of them for the future. By itself, that would be bad for future generations. However, those future generations will suffer less from climate change because we reduce our emissions. We know from the elementary economic theory that, if we do the transfer correctly, future generations will end up better off on balance, and we shall be no worse off.

The outcome I have described is not a nice one. It is Pareto superior to the existing state, but the existing state contains all the bad consequences of emitting greenhouse gases. For instance, it contains the injustices I mentioned: we are already harming some existing people by our emissions. If we reduce our emissions, we shall stop harming those people in that way. But it compounds the injustice to expect them to compensate us for reducing our emissions. Another example is that our emissions are damaging the conditions of life of future people. I have said it would be better if we reduced our emissions and compensated ourselves for doing so. But it would be even better if we reduced our emissions and did not compensate ourselves for doing so.

Compare three alternatives: *A*, we do nothing about the externality and continue to emit greenhouses gases profligately; *B*, we reduce our emissions to eliminate the externality, and compensate ourselves for doing so; *C*, we reduce our emissions to eliminate the externality, and do not compensate ourselves for doing so. *The Stern Review* in effect compares *C* with *A* by means of a cost–benefit analysis, and finds that *C* is much better than *A*. It recommends us to choose *C*. It does not compare *B* with *C*, but it is clear that Stern considers *C* better than *B*, or he would not have recommended *C*.

The difference between *B* and *C* is nothing to do with climate change. Moving from *A* to *B* eliminates the problem of climate change. To move from *B* to *C* is simply to redistribute wealth from present people towards future people. No doubt outcome *C* would be the best. But to reach *C* the current generation has to make sacrifices, and the experience in Copenhagen shows it is unwilling to do so.

I think we should try first to develop the institutional arrangements that will make the move from *A* to *B* possible. That will allow us to eliminate the problem of climate change. Then we should try going further to *C*. But we should not encumber the process of controlling climate change with the quite different matter of transferring resources to future people.

Expected utility theory and very bad possibilities

That very most important thing about climate change is a matter of economics alone; it has little to do with moral philosophy. But now I come to the real question of this chapter. It arises because the science of climate change is so uncertain. We do not know how much the world will warm, and we do not know what effects the warming will have. Fortunately, we have a well-established account of how we should take uncertainty into account in our planning. It is called expected utility theory.

Here is how expected utility theory works. Suppose you have several options to choose from. For instance, they might be alternative policies towards climate change. It is uncertain what outcome will result from each option. Each may lead to various different possible outcomes, depending on how the uncertain world develops.

Each possible *outcome* is good or bad to some degree. Each has a value, that is to say. We may also assign a value to each *option* on the basis of the values of the various outcomes it may lead to. The value of an option is the weighted average of the values of its possible outcomes, where each outcome is weighted by its probability. This weighted average is called the *expectation* of the value of the outcomes.

That is not a strictly accurate description of expected utility theory. Strictly, the value assigned to an option is the expectation of something called the 'utility' of its possible outcomes, rather than the expectation of value. The utility of an outcome is not exactly its value, but its value adjusted in a way that is designed to take account of the badness of risk. The difference between value and utility is important, but for the purposes of this chapter it is safe to ignore it.

Here is an example of the working of expected utility theory. Suppose you have a cold. Suppose a cold-cure pill is available that has a 95 per cent chance of curing your cold. In the terminology adopted by the Intergovernmental Panel on Climate Change, this means the pill is 'extremely likely' to cure your cold. But suppose that, in the extremely unlikely event – having 5 per cent probability – that the pill does not cure your cold, it will kill you. Should you take this pill?

You should not. The badness of the possible outcome of your death is so great that, even weighted by the small probability of its occurrence, it outweighs the goodness of curing your cold, even weighted by the large probability of its occurrence. The expected value of taking the pill is:

(value of having no cold) 95/100 + (value of dying) 5/100.

Your alternative option is not to take the pill, which I assume leaves you certain of continuing to have a cold. The expected value of this option is just:

(value of having a cold) 100/100.

This is far above the expected value of taking the pill.

When you make the choice I have described, the most important thing is the small chance of dying. That is a consequence of expected utility theory. What matters in making a choice is not the likelihood of outcomes but the expected value of outcomes. Consequently, the most important aspect of a choice is not necessarily what is likely to happen. It may be something that is very unlikely to happen, if it is extremely bad.

The small chance of a catastrophe

This is an elementary point, and the scientists of the Intergovernmental Panel on Climate Change (IPCC) surely know it very well. But you would not think so to read the IPCC's Fourth Assessment Report (IPCC 2007a–c). The uncertainty in the IPCC's report is presented almost entirely in terms of likelihood. The IPCC tells us what is likely to happen, what is very unlikely to happen, and so on. It does not tell us expectations.

If we take moderately strong steps to control climate change, the most likely outcome is 2°C or 3°C of warming. I shall call this 'likely climate change'. Its effects might be manageable. However, the Fourth Assessment Report also reveals a significant probability that the warming will be much greater. It is cautious about assigning probabilities to very high temperatures, but studies referred to in the report suggest there is as much as a 5 per cent probability of warming greater than about 8°C, and perhaps a 1–2 per cent probability of warming greater than 10°C (IPCC 2007a, section 9.6).

These temperatures are far beyond the experience of human beings. The world has not been as hot as that for tens of millions of years. For comparison, during the last ice age – only tens of thousands of years ago – ice-sheets kilometres thick covered Canada and northern Europe. A 10°C warming is likely to melt Antarctica, and that will raise the seas by 70 metres. The result of so much warming might be catastrophically bad. Consequently, even multiplied by its small probability, this possibility of extreme warming may be much more important in expected utility than all the predictions about what is most likely to happen.

This is the view that is being promulgated by Weitzman (2009). Weitzman claims that the most important thing about climate change is the small chance of what he calls a 'catastrophe'. In his argument, he adds to what I have been saying, another significant twist based on statistical theory. The IPCC's estimates of prospective temperatures are derived from observed data. But there is inevitably little data about unlikely events, because they happen only rarely. Therefore, the data we have do not allow us to set a limit on the probability of unlikely events. This gives us further reason to be concerned about them.

Is Weitzman right that the small chance of catastrophe is the most important thing about climate change? Should it dominate our calculations of expected utility? We cannot answer this question except by thinking about how bad a catastrophe it would be. To know whether it should dominate our calculations even when weighted by the very small probability that it will happen, we must have some quantitative idea of its badness. Weitzman does not try to estimate the badness of a catastrophe. He seems to assume it would obviously be so bad that an estimate would be otiose. But when we do try to make an estimate, it turns out not to be obvious that the small chance of catastrophe should dominate our calculations. An estimate is, therefore, not otiose.

In this chapter, I want to argue no more than that: the small chance of catastrophe does not obviously dominate. For this purpose, only the roughest preliminary estimate of the badness of the catastrophe is required. If my conclusion is right, the chance of catastrophe will have to be included in our expected utility calculations along with other, more likely, results of climate change. Far more precise calculations will be needed then, but here I can work with very rough figures.

Consequences of catastrophe

I shall try to make only a very rough, preliminary judgement of badness. I shall start by identifying the various sorts of harm that would result if we suffered extreme climate change of 8°C or more. For one thing, extreme climate change would be a disaster for the natural world. Millions of species would be lost and very many ecosystems destroyed. I do not wish to belittle these great harms, but I am going to set them aside in this chapter. I shall concentrate only on harms that would befall humanity specifically. I shall even set aside the harm that humans would suffer through having to live in a barren world, where nature has been impoverished. I shall consider only harms that afflict humanity more directly.

One thing is sure: if there is extreme warming, the earth will not be able to sustain anything approaching our present population. Our population would have to shrink by billions. We cannot even be confident that humanity will survive at all. Lots of species are already becoming extinct, and we cannot assume ours will not follow them. The possibility of extinction is one thing we shall have to consider in assessing the badness of a catastrophe.

How bad would extinction or a major population collapse be? It would be bad in various ways. If extinction were to occur, it would be the end of our species. It can be argued that this species has more value than others. For one thing, we are rational, and many philosophers think that is a property of special value. I shall not try to judge that claim.

A collapse of our population, even without extinction, would cause the loss of a great many valuable things. They include human cultures, with all their parts: their knowledge, their languages, their arts, and their ideas. Indeed, civilisation as a whole would go. These are great harms, but I am not going to concentrate on them because I do not how to judge the badness of their loss. Instead, I am going to concentrate on two other ways in which extinction or a population collapse would be bad. These are ways I can at least begin to evaluate.

The first of these more approachable sorts of badness is that billions of people would die early. A collapse of population, and even extinction, would not necessarily involve early deaths. Women could just stop having children for a while, or forever. But the collapse or extinction that climate change may cause will be brutal and violent. It will involve killing many people.

The second more approachable badness – or at least putative badness – that extinction or a population collapse would cause is that very many people who would have existed will not exist at all. An extinction would prevent the existence of all those human beings who would otherwise have lived. Even a collapse of population that falls short of an extinction would prevent very many existences, and an extinction would mean there will be no more people ever.

We are trying to judge whether the possibility of extreme climate change would be so bad that it should dominate our thinking about climate change, even when weighted by the very small chance it will occur. To make this judgement, we need only very rough, ball-park figures. For this purpose, we need only think about the numbers of people who will be killed or whose existence will be prevented. Numbers are enough; we do not need to think about the badness of all those deaths.

Since I shall conclude that Weitzman's case is dubious, I shall be generous to it in my calculations.

Deaths

Start with the first sort of approachable badness: the killing that extreme climate change would do. Out of generosity to Weitzman, let us assume the worst possibility, which is that everyone on earth is killed, at a time when our population is at its greatest. Our maximum population is predicted to be 9 billion in about 2050. Suppose extreme climate change kills 9 billion people. But extreme climate change is very unlikely. Suppose its probability is one in a thousand. Then the *expectation* of the number of deaths is 9 billion divided by a thousand, which is 9 million. If the probability is as high as one in a hundred, the expectation is 90 million. The expectation is, therefore, in the range of tens of millions of people killed.

These figures must be compared with the number of deaths we may expect from likely climate change of 2°C or 3°C. Likely climate change will kill in various ways. People will be killed in floods, droughts and famines, and other climate disasters. They will be killed by the increased range of tropical diseases, and they will be killed in heat waves. Also, they will be killed simply by impoverishment, since you die if you cannot afford enough to eat. Predictions about the numbers of deaths are hard to come by, but I have found a few relevant figures. The 1995 IPCC report offers a prediction that 215,000 people will be killed each year by heat waves alone, once the concentration of carbon dioxide in the atmosphere is effectively doubled (IPCC 1996, p. 198). A report of the World Health Organization attributed 150,000 deaths to climate change as long ago as 2000 (cited in IPCC 2007b, p. 407). The Food and Agriculture Organization reports that the world now contains more than 1 billion undernourished people (FAO 2009). A small increase in poverty can be expected to kill many of them. I think we might estimate that half a million people will be killed each year by likely climate change; that would be a conservative figure. As a check, about 60 million people die in the world each year. So this would amount to about a 1 per cent increase in the world's annual death rate. That increase seems plausible. No end is predicted to this killing; it will continue for decades. We must, therefore, expect likely climate change to kill tens of millions of people.

This puts the expected number of deaths that would result from likely climate change in the same ball-park – tens of millions – as the expected number that must be attributed to the small chance of the extinction of humanity. The first of two approachable badnesses I mentioned – killing – therefore, does not suggest that the small chance of catastrophe should dominate our calculations of expected value.

Absences and the intuition of neutrality

The second approachable badness of a catastrophe is that it will prevent the existence of a great many people who would otherwise have existed. In this case, the expected numbers of people involved are much bigger. The human species could exist for perhaps hundreds of thousands of years, renewing itself every century or so. All those future people amount to at least hundreds of times the world's present population. Extinction will prevent the existence of that number of people, and a population collapse may prevent the existence of many of them. Even multiplied by a small chance of one in a hundred or one in a thousand, the expected number of 'absences' – as I shall call them – associated with extinction is vastly greater than the number of deaths to be expected from likely climate change. The same may also be true of a population collapse. These numbers suggest we have a potentially dominating consideration here.

A first response is a point that was made to me by Lukas Wallrich. It is not just extinction or a population collapse that would cause absences. Likely climate change will do the same. Likely climate change will kill tens of millions of people, and many of those people would have had children had they survived. Indeed many would have started a long line of descendants. All their potential descendants will be absent because of likely climate change. The expected numbers of these absences may well be as great as the expected number associated with extinction. That depends on the details of human demography, which I shall not go into here.

This point by itself is enough to show that the chance of catastrophe from extreme climate change is not obviously a dominating consideration. But I shall go further. I shall consider whether absences are truly a bad thing in the first place. Is it bad if people who would have existed do not exist after all? To put the same question differently: is the existence of people a good thing? That is the question I come to now.

Many of us have conflicting intuitions about it. On the one hand, many of us are horrified at the thought of humanity's extinction; it strikes us as obviously a dreadfully bad thing. That seems to be Weitzman's reaction. But on the other hand, when we think of a particular person's existence, many of us think intuitively that it is neither good nor bad. We recognise that it may have good or bad effects on other people. The person may bring joy to her family, and she may detract from other people's well-being through the demands she makes on the earth's limited resources. But we do not think her existence is good or bad on its own account.

To illustrate this intuition: few of us think that the good a person would enjoy in her life constitutes a reason for creating this person. Suppose a couple who could have a child decide not to. We may think they are doing some good things: for instance, they are refraining from creating one more mouth to feed. We may also think they are doing some bad things: for instance, their own lives might be worse in the long run as a result of being childless. But few of us think they are doing a further bad thing in preventing the existence of a person just because the person herself would have enjoyed a good life.

I call the view I am describing 'the intuition of neutrality'. Put more exactly, it is this. Take a world A that has a number of people living in it, each with a particular level of lifetime well-being. Compare it with another world B that contains all the same people with the same levels of lifetime well-being, and also contains one more person. The intuition of neutrality is that neither A nor B is better than the other. Existence has neutral value, we might say.

This intuition is illustrated in Figure 1. The figure shows worlds A and B. Well-being is shown on the vertical dimension of the figure; better-off people are placed higher up. In this example, A contains four people. B contains those four at the same levels of well-being, and also one more person. The intuition of neutrality is that neither A nor B is better than the other.

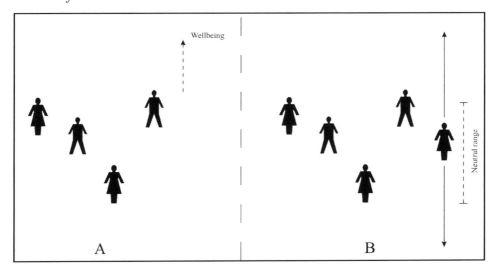

Figure 1: The intuition of neutrality

Plausibly, this common intuition has limits. Many people think that the existence of a person whose life is very bad is a bad thing. So if the extra person in B was very badly off, we might think B worse than A. Some people may think that the existence of an extremely well-off person is a good thing, so B would be better than A if the extra person was extremely well off. But at least for a range of qualities of life, which we may call 'the neutral range', we think that the existence of a person whose life is within that range is neither a good thing nor a bad thing. That is the limited version of the intuition of neutrality. It is shown in Figure 1.

I do not insist that there is a finite neutral range; I merely allow for the possibility that there is. Another possibility is that existence has neutral value, whatever the level of well-being of the extra person.

If the intuition of neutrality is correct, it tells us that extinction is neither good nor bad, provided the future people who will exist if humanity does not become extinct, live within the neutral range. So the intuition of neutrality conflicts with our other intuitive idea that extinction would be a dreadfully bad event. The intuition of neutrality threatens Weitzman's implicit view that extreme climate change would be catastrophically bad. We must, therefore, assess the truth of this intuition.

The intuition of neutrality is false

And actually, it is false. Unfortunately, the full demonstration of its falsity is too long for me to present in this chapter. It appears in my book *Weighing Lives* (Broome, 2004, chapters 10–12, summarised in Broome, 2005). Here, I shall set out only the first step, which demonstrates that one particular, strong version of the intuition is false.

The strong version is this. Compare the same two worlds A and B as before. The strong intuition is that they are equally good, at least if the extra person's well-being is within the neutral range. The weak version of the intuition is only that neither A nor B is better than the other. It leaves open the possibility that A and B are incommensurate in value. The strong version excludes this possibility.

The strong version is false for a reason that is illustrated in Figure 2. The worlds A and B in Figure 2 are the same as A and B in Figure 1. World C contains the same five people as B contains. The first four of them are equally as well off in C as in B, but the last person in C is worse off than she is in B. Obviously, B is better than C, since it is equally as good as C for four of the people and better for the fifth person. However, according to the strong version of the intuition of neutrality, B is equally as good as A, and A is equally as good as C. It follows, obviously, that B is equally as good as C. Yet we know already that this is not so: B is better than C. So the strong version of the intuition of neutrality entails a falsehood. Therefore, it is false itself.

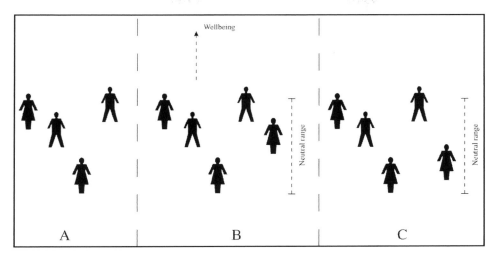

Figure 2: The strong version of the intuition of neutrality

This is a knock-down argument against the strong version. I think the weak version is also false, but the argument for that conclusion, presented in my *Weighing Lives*, is more open to debate (Rabinowicz, 2009). Still, in this chapter I shall take it for granted that the weak version is also false.

What follows? It follows that there is no such thing as a neutral range of well-beings of the sort shown in Figure 1. Compare the worlds A and B again. We have learnt that there can be at most one level of lifetime well-being such that, if B's extra person lives at that level, neither A nor B is better than the other. If the extra person lives above this level, B is better than A; if below, B is worse than A. I assume there is indeed such a level of well-being, and I call it the 'neutral level'. The only other possibilities are that B is worse than A whatever the extra person's well-being, or that B is better than A whatever the extra person's well-being. Neither of those possibilities is plausible.

So the neutral range collapses to a single neutral level. What does this tell us about the value of extinction? It tells us that extinction would almost certainly be either a good thing or a bad thing, and not a neutral thing. But it does not tell us whether it would be good or bad. That depends on how well off future people will be if humanity survives. If their well-being will on balance be above the neutral level, extinction would be a bad thing. If their well-being will on balance be below the neutral level, extinction would be a good thing.

To know whether extinction is a bad thing, we need to know what is the neutral level of well-being, and we also need to know what will be the levels of well-being of future people. The latter question is partly a matter for empirical prediction and partly a matter for moral philosophy. It is not entirely empirical, because to answer it we need first to know what a person's well-being consists in. That is one of the major topics of moral philosophy. On the other hand, the former question – what is the neutral level – is entirely a matter for moral philosophy.

Some existing philosophical views imply a conclusion about what the neutral level is. One is a version of the theory known as 'hedonism'. Hedonism is the theory that the only good thing is pleasure and the only bad thing pain. It can be interpreted as a theory about people's well-being. Under that interpretation, it tells us about the relative goodness for a person of different lives she might lead. It says that one life is better than another if and only if it contains a greater preponderance of pleasure over pain. I call this 'personal hedonism'. It does not tell us about the goodness or badness of a person's existence.

A different version of hedonism does. I call it 'general hedonism'. General hedonism is a theory about the goodness of worlds, rather than people's well-being. It says that one world is better than another if and only if it contains a greater preponderance of pleasure over pain. Think of a person who lives a life that contains no pleasure and no pain. According to general hedonism, this person's existence leaves the world equally as good as it would have been had she not existed. So her existence is neutral. According to general hedonism, the neutral level of well-being is therefore the level of a life that contains no pleasure and no pain.

I do not mention general hedonism to commend it, but to show that the neutral level is a matter for debate and discussion within ethics. There is work for moral philosophy to do in trying to figure out what the neutral level is. This work is a contribution towards assessing the badness of the catastrophe that might result from climate change.

Conclusion

What have we learnt? We have learnt, first, that we cannot just assume the small chance of catastrophe is the most important thing about climate change. It may or may not be. To know which, we must work out just how bad the catastrophe would be.

We have learnt, second, that working this out will be difficult. Extreme climate change will certainly cause a collapse of the human population. It may cause the extinction of humanity. Naively, we think of these as terrible disasters. Perhaps they are. But to know whether they are terrible, and if they are, how terrible, we must investigate how good or bad it is for a person to exist. This is a difficult task for moral philosophy.

One further lesson follows. Moral philosophers have worked on the value of existence for some decades, largely stimulated by the pioneering work of Derek Parfit (1984). The subject is extremely controversial, and we cannot expect any consensus to emerge soon. Yet the problem of climate change is very pressing; we must act soon. So we shall have to act while we remain very uncertain about what is the correct moral theory of the value of existence. We therefore need to know how we should act when our moral theory about how we should act is uncertain. This is in itself a problem for moral philosophy.

As yet, it has not been much explored by moral philosophers. But some interesting work has recently been appearing on this subject (for instance, Sepielli 2010). The problem of climate change makes it urgent.

References

Broome, J. 2004. *Weighing Lives*. Oxford: Oxford University Press.

Broome, J. 2005. 'Should we value population?' *Journal of Political Philosophy* 13: 399–413.

FAO. 2009. *The State of Food Insecurity in the World 2009*. Rome: Food and Agriculture Organization of the United Nations. www.fao.org/publications/sofi/en.

Foley, D. 2007. *The Economic Fundamentals of Global Warming*. Working paper 07-12-044. Santa Fe, New Mexico: Santa Fe Institute. www.santafe.edu/media/workingpapers/07-12-044.pdf.

IPCC (Intergovernmental Panel on Climate Change). 1996. *Climate Change 1995: Volume III: Economic and social dimensions of climate change*. Cambridge, UK: Cambridge University Press.

IPCC (Intergovernmental Panel on Climate Change). 2007a. *Climate Change 2007: The physical science basis. Contribution of Working Group I to the Fourth Assessment Report of the Intergovernmental Panel on Climate Change*. Cambridge, UK: Cambridge University Press.

IPCC (Intergovernmental Panel on Climate Change). 2007b. *Climate Change 2007: Impacts, adaptation and vulnerability. Contribution of Working Group II to the Fourth Assessment Report of the Intergovernmental Panel on Climate Change*. Cambridge, UK: Cambridge University Press.

IPCC (Intergovernmental Panel on Climate Change). 2007c. *Climate Change 2007: Mitigation of climate change. Contribution of Working Group III to the Fourth Assessment Report of the Intergovernmental Panel on Climate Change*. Cambridge, UK: Cambridge University Press.

Parfit, D. 1984. *Reasons and Persons*. Oxford: Oxford University Press.

Rabinowicz, W. 2009. 'Broome and the intuition of neutrality.' *Philosophical Issues* 19: 389–411.

Sepielli, A. 2010. 'Normative uncertainty and intertheoretic comparisons.' *PhilPapers: Online research in philosophy*. http://philpapers.org/rec/SEPNUA.

Stern, N. 2007. *The Economics of Climate Change: The Stern Review*. Cambridge, UK: Cambridge University Press.

Stern, N. 2010. *A Blueprint for a Safer Planet*. Vintage Books.

Weitzman, M. L. 2007. 'A review of *The Stern Review on the Economics of Climate Change*.' *Journal of Economic Literature* 55: 703–24.

Weitzman, M. L. 2009. 'On modeling and interpreting the economics of catastrophic climate change.' *Review of Economics and Statistics* 91: 1–19.

7. Recognising ethics to help a constructive climate change debate

Andy Reisinger and Howard Larsen

Too often, when we think we are arguing over scientific evidence for climate change, we are in fact disagreeing about our different political preferences, ethical principles and value systems. (Hulme 2009)

Introduction

The design and analysis of public policies related to climate change do not normally make explicit reference to ethical dimensions. Excluding explicit ethics from policy analysis could be seen to provide a more robust and objective basis for public policy, given that ethical principles generally require subjective judgements about which principles should guide decisions. This raises a dilemma in the context of climate change though, where one of the key challenges of public policy making is to achieve a framework that can endure beyond the electoral cycle and that can bridge the large temporal and geographical distances between greenhouse gas emissions and climate change impacts.

Surveys of public opinion indicate that the public takes the ethical dimensions of climate change seriously and regards them as one of the main reasons for actions to reduce greenhouse gas emissions and to support developing countries (Lorenzoni and Pidgeon 2006; Wardekker et al. 2009). Similarly, climate change policy advisers and negotiators appear to be guided in their judgements not only by country mandates but also by ethical considerations, even if their view of ethics tends to favour those ethical principles that would result in least-cost options for their country (Lange et al. 2007, 2010).

This suggests that in the case of climate change, a more explicit consideration of ethical dimensions that underpin policy decisions could be necessary to facilitate a public debate about these issues and provide a more direct and enduring mandate to implement climate policies. This would be the case especially if scientific, technological, and economic considerations alone were insufficient to determine optimal policy paths within a reasonably narrow range. This chapter analyses the extent to which ethical judgements are an intrinsic part of determining the limits of acceptable global climate change and sharing efforts to reduce greenhouse gas emissions between different countries. We conclude that the strong role for ethics in these issues suggests that an explicit recognition of ethical dimensions would be necessary, though not sufficient, to achieve a more enduring platform for public policies on climate change.

Ethical judgements underpinning global climate change targets

The overarching goal and challenge for any global climate agreement is stated in article 2 of the United Nations Framework Convention on Climate Change (UNFCCC, 2009):

> The ultimate objective of this Convention and any related legal instruments that the Conference of the Parties may adopt is to achieve, in accordance with the relevant provisions of the Convention, stabilization of greenhouse gas concentrations in the atmosphere at a level that would prevent dangerous anthropogenic interference with the climate system. Such a level should be achieved within a time-frame sufficient to allow ecosystems to adapt naturally to climate change, to ensure that food production is not threatened and to enable economic development to proceed in a sustainable manner.

The UNFCCC does not prescribe the specific level of greenhouse gas concentrations that would result in 'dangerous' climate change. Reaching agreement on this concentration level, therefore, is the continued subject of political debate. The debate often takes recourse to science in an effort to promote global agreement about the threshold to 'dangerous' climate change and the emissions reduction targets that avoiding such a threshold would require. For example, Europe's Commissioner for the Environment, Stavros Dimas, stated, '*Science tells us* what the goal [of reducing emissions] must be: to avoid dangerous climate change, we have to keep average global warming to less than 2° Celsius above the pre-industrial temperature. That is just 1.2°C higher than today' (Dimas 2009, emphasis added).

We argue that reliance on science alone to define the threshold of 'dangerous' or 'unacceptable' climate change ignores the fundamental ethical judgements that are necessary to arrive at such a conclusion. Relying on science alone removes the judgement about acceptable risks from the community and places it in the hands of (largely anonymous) scientific and technical experts who have no mandate, and may have no skill, in the ethical dimensions of the problem.

Importantly, relying on science limits the degree to which the wider community is able to take ownership of specific climate targets and of the policies to achieve them, and in turn limits the mandate of elected representatives to act on climate change in a way that is consistent with a risk management framework (IPCC 2007a; Yohe 2009). If climate policies and emissions targets are framed as being justified predominantly by science, the societal trade-offs between more or less stringent responses and accepting higher or lower risks from climate change will not have been fully presented to the electorate. This includes the transfer of risks between the current and future generations and between people living in different parts of the world.

Science dimension: Key vulnerabilities and 'reasons for concern'

The Intergovernmental Panel on Climate Change (IPCC) has recognised the inability of science alone to identify limits of acceptable climate change, and has instead pointed to a range of 'reasons for concern' or 'key vulnerabilities' about climate change. A clear assessment of these concerns is intended to help people to make their own determination of what constitutes acceptable risks and what climate changes might be deemed unacceptable. The latter would provide information on the long-term concentration targets that global mitigation policies should aim for to limit the probability that such changes in the climate system might occur (IPCC 2001, 2007a).

Key vulnerabilities can be identified using several criteria, including the magnitude of the impact, the impact's timing and persistence, the potential for adaptation, distributional aspects, the impact's likelihood, and the subjective 'importance' of the impact. These criteria are not sufficient to identify, let alone rank, all vulnerabilities to climate change that might be regarded as 'key', and they are not tied to specific thresholds. An assessment of key vulnerabilities is intended primarily to allow a more objective and hopefully constructive discussion about the amount of climate change that any given group of people may find unacceptable and unmanageable, and the reasons for such judgements (IPCC 2007a; Reisinger 2009).

This approach recognises that one cannot find a single, scientifically justified, optimal global balance between the costs of mitigation and damages from climate change given their very uneven distribution around the globe (Füssel 2009). The approach also highlights that the thresholds for unacceptable climate change not only depend on subjective judgements but also vary with different key vulnerabilities. For example, severe damage to and potential collapse of some ecosystems or individual species (such as some coral reefs, mountain cloud forests, or invertebrates) is expected to occur for almost any level of additional warming. On the other hand, collapse of the Gulf Stream is considered very unlikely for any of the best estimates of warming during the 21st century, though even a persistent slowing could have important consequences for marine ecosystems. Several hundred million people are expected to experience increased water stress for a global warming of 1.5°C above pre-industrial temperatures; this number is expected to climb to more than 1 billion for warming above 2.5°C and potentially more than 3 billion for warming above 3.5°C (IPCC 2007b).

Many of these projected impacts and risks could be seen individually as violations of article 2 of the UNFCCC and hence constitute 'dangerous' or 'unacceptable' climate change. However, it is also widely recognised that even the most stringent efforts to reduce greenhouse gas emissions currently thought as credible in the scientific literature would still lead to warming of about 2°C above pre-industrial temperatures. Hence, some level of local 'danger' is already unavoidable and can be responded to only by adaptation, no longer by mitigation. Figure 1 shows a range of potential impacts that will occur in different regions in the absence of adaptation, as identified by the IPCC, and their steady increase with the amount of warming.

The IPCC analysis shows that any global climate change target, whether it be defined through emissions reduction targets or a limit to temperature increase or greenhouse gas concentrations, is essentially a normative judgement. Such judgements must be informed by science, but any specific target is inevitably the result of an implicit or explicit ethical judgement about, first, the relevance that is accorded to particular impacts and, second, how uncertainties inherent in climate change projections are dealt with.

The assumption that a specific temperature threshold of, say, 2°C represents the beginning of 'dangerous' climate change implies that warming of less than 2°C is deemed 'acceptable' or 'safe'. However, as noted above, recent studies have identified significant impacts (for example, water stress) for many communities and ecosystems at or below this threshold (IPCC 2007b). The communities most vulnerable to these impacts are largely in developing countries, and many recent studies suggest that the cost of adapting to even limited warming in developing countries would lie in the order of tens of billions of US dollars per year by 2020 (see Parry et al. 2009 and references therein). By contrast, the public might interpret a scientifically defined threshold of 'dangerous' climate change as indicating that impacts below this threshold are not significant or at least can be managed well enough by the affected communities. This interpretation would be clearly incorrect but could result in reduced willingness by industrialised countries (and their voting public) to assist adaptation efforts in those of the most vulnerable developing countries, sectors, and populations who would be substantially negatively affected by warming below this normative global threshold.

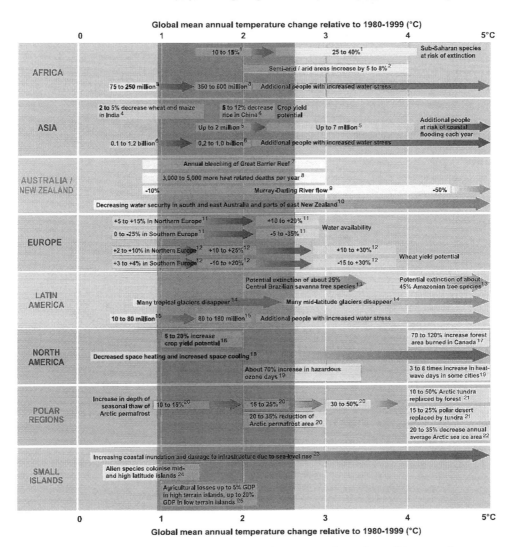

Figure 1: Potential impacts in various regions as a function of increasing global mean temperature

Notes: Impacts shown are in the absence of adaptation measures. Temperatures at the bottom of the figures are relative to global average temperatures in 1980–99. For temperatures relative to pre-industrial conditions, add 0.5°C. The grey band shows the likely range of warming if greenhouse gas concentrations were stabilised at 450 parts per million carbon dioxide equivalent, which would give as a best estimate a warming of about 2°C above pre-industrial levels or about 1.5°C above average temperatures in 1980–99.

Source: From IPCC (2007b, Technical Summary Table TS.3); grey band added by the authors based on IPCC (2007c, Table 10.8).

The second ethical judgement comes from the uncertainty of climate science. Science alone is unable to determine what resources should be expended to reduce the risk from events that are regarded as having a low or simply unknown probability, but which would have very severe consequences. Examples of such events might be the rapid disintegration of the Greenland ice sheet, collapse of the Amazon rainforest, or significant slowing of major ocean circulation patterns. Even if a generally 'acceptable' level of impacts from climate change could be agreed on, the uncertainties in the science mean a clearly 'non-risky' level of greenhouse gas emissions that would avoid those impacts with certainty cannot be identified. The uncertainty of climate science, therefore, requires an ethical judgement about the level of risk that society is prepared to accept. The IPCC highlighted that the inability to rule out severe consequences, even if they are not considered highly likely, is in itself a key 'reason for concern' about climate change that could justify more stringent emissions reductions than if impacts could be predicted with certainty (IPCC 2007a).

So-called 'tipping points' in the climate system have been studied in an attempt to resolve this gap between a scientific analysis of climate change and the normative judgement required to define the limit of acceptable change. Tipping points are generally defined as thresholds in the climate system that, when crossed, would result in a rapid and non-linear major change and significant impacts that could be regarded as 'unmanageable' for large numbers of people. The collapse of the Gulf Stream is one example of such a tipping point. Recent studies have summarised current knowledge about such large-scale tipping points (IPCC 2007c; Lenton et al. 2008; Smith et al. 2009), but have also highlighted that there is, as yet, little consensus about specific temperature thresholds in the scientific community (Kriegler et al. 2009).

This does not mean that such collapses cannot happen. In fact, they could even be quite likely, but we simply do not know how close to such collapses we might be, or could be in future. As a result, references to thresholds that would trigger such collapses are too qualitative to inform specific climate targets. Russill and Nyssa (2009) argue that the discourse on tipping points is in fact more strongly motivated by the explicit desire to create a public consensus for action, rather than a reaction to scientific evidence for the location of tipping points in the biophysical climate system. They suggest that a more careful separation of social and biophysical tipping points is warranted for a transparent and robust discussion.

Even if specific thresholds for large-scale tipping points could be identified with greater confidence than at present, translating such thresholds into limits for acceptable climate change would still require at least two ethical judgements. The first arises because scientific knowledge is never truly certain, so decisions about a specific limit for climate change would need to take into account our attitude to the risk of the tipping point occurring at a lower or higher temperature than the best scientific estimate. The second arises because even if a tipping point were known with near certainty, a collective ethical judgement is still required from society on whether it needs to be avoided and whether global society is prepared to pay the costs of avoidance. Major tipping points will have overwhelming damages associated with them, but these damages are still likely to be borne unevenly within and between societies. Therefore, they require collective moral judgements about their importance. Such judgements can be made: as an analogue, the decision by a country to go to war almost always implies the strong likelihood of death for some of its population but countries still make such judgements. They perceive that a greater goal is at stake that justifies such predictable sacrifices.

Judging which climate change tipping points are indeed unacceptable for global society and which ones might have to be borne for a greater goal of, for example, avoiding overly rapid emissions reductions and associated changes in current economic and social structures, remains an ethical decision that science alone cannot solve, even if science can make an important contribution to such decision-making processes.

Economic dimension: Cost–benefit analysis

An alternative approach to determining long-term climate change targets rests on traditional cost–benefit analysis. The most prominent example of this approach is by Stern (2006). Stern compared the damages from climate change with the costs of reducing emissions. This analysis concluded that the costs of climate change damages far outweighed the costs of even rapid emissions reductions to stabilise greenhouse gas concentrations at or below 500 parts per million (ppm) carbon dioxide equivalent (CO_2-eq).

The economic analysis underpinning this conclusion has attracted substantial scrutiny and debate, which it is beyond the scope of this chapter even to summarise (see, for example, Heal 2009; Weitzman 2007). The current discussion focuses on the ethical judgements that are implicit or explicit in Stern's analysis, but which are often not discussed when the results of his economic approach (and similar studies by others) are used to inform global climate policies or communicate the results and implications of these studies to the general public.

Stern used the so-called social cost of carbon as the basis by which to measure future damages from climate change. The social cost of carbon describes the damages that are created by the emission of an additional tonne of carbon dioxide over and above current emissions. It integrates those damages over time for as long as the carbon dioxide remains in the atmosphere; note that about 20 per cent will remain in the atmosphere for many thousands of years

(IPCC 2007c). This integration of damages requires the estimation of the cost of damages that occur only in the future, expressed relative to the value of the same damages were they to occur today. The relativity is described by a 'discount rate'.

The discount rate (r) incorporates three key parameters (equation 1): the pure rate of time preference (δ), the elasticity of the marginal utility of consumption (η), and the future growth rate of consumption (g; often, though somewhat misleadingly, described by gross domestic product).

[1] $r = \delta + \eta g$

Both the pure rate of time preference and the elasticity of the marginal utility of consumption embody crucial ethical judgements, even though they are often regarded as technical issues whose definition must appropriately be left to economists. The pure rate of time preference describes how much less future damages are valued simply because they occur in the future. Stern (2006) argued on ethical grounds that the pure rate of time preference for intergenerational problems must be set close to zero, because future generations have the right to be accorded the same consideration as the present generation. By contrast, most neoclassical economists argue that the market generally assumes a pure rate of time preference substantially greater than zero, and that economic analysis of climate policy must adhere to the judgements of the market since climate policy functions within, and aims to modify, a market system (Nordhaus 2009). The implications of either choice are significant. For example, a choice of 3 per cent for the pure rate of time preference (as a market approach might suggest) means the welfare of a person living 25 years from now (expressed through, for example, willingness to pay for environmental goods and services or for avoided health impacts) would be worth less than half the welfare of a person living today.[1]

Several studies have tried to reconcile the positions of Stern (2006) and Nordhaus (2009) by adopting different discount rates for different time horizons, where short-term rates (up to several decades) are aligned with revealed market discount rates, while long-term rates that reflect intergenerational equity over many decades to centuries use much lower rates (Weitzman 2007). Neumeyer (2007) argued that low discount rates were justified but that this justification arises primarily from the non-substitutability of natural capital: long-term climate change results in damages for which an increase in monetary wealth cannot compensate. An economic framework such as neoclassical economics that implicitly or explicitly assumes such substitutability underestimates

---

1   If V_0 is the current value and V_{25} the value in 25 years, then $V_{25} = V_0(1- \delta)25$.

the damages from climate change. This suggests an ethical dimension to intergenerational discounting that appears particularly relevant in the context of climate change.

Similar differences in view exist about the appropriate choice for the elasticity of the marginal utility of consumption, which describes the value that people of different wealth accord to gaining or loosing a set monetary amount. A value greater than zero for this parameter implies that a wealthier person (or community) will care less about the loss of some amount than a poorer person (or community) would care about the same loss. It is relevant here because future damages are discounted if the world on average is becoming wealthier over time; one cares less about impacts occurring in the wealthier future than in the (poorer) present.

This same parameter is also used to describe how impacts occurring in different parts of the planet should be weighted. An elasticity of the marginal utility of consumption greater than zero implies that the loss of say $1000 from a hypothetical climate change impact would be of less importance to a person in an industrialised country earning $100,000 per year than to a person in a poor developing country earning $500 per year.

However, there is no single answer to *how much less* the wealthier person will or should care about such a loss, and hence how climate change damages occurring in different parts of the world, or at different times, should equitably be aggregated into a global total.

Another interpretation of the parameter is that it reflects our aversion to loss compared with our desire for gain in wealth, or more generally, our risk aversion.

All three interpretations of the parameter have strong ethical foundations because they generalise and trade off the interests of different people against each other (in terms of income and attitudes to decreases or increases in income). However, most economic models lump the underlying ethical choices into a single parameter that has a crucial influence on the result of cost–benefit analyses (Dietz et al. 2009).

Anthoff et al. (2009) and Tol and Yohe (2009) undertook a sensitivity analysis of the approach underlying the analysis by Stern (2006). They found that the range of choices that can be or have been made for the pure rate of time preference and for the elasticity of the marginal utility of consumption in various contexts and different studies would allow such a wide range of values for the discount rate that almost any statement about the value of climate change damages compared with the costs of mitigation could be justified.

This finding is important because it implies that the question of how strongly greenhouse gas emissions should be reduced in order to limit climate change damages is irreducibly an ethical question. It cannot be replaced by recourse to economic or scientific arguments (Dietz et al. 2007). Pointing to market preferences in certain discount rates is insufficient to justify the use of market preferences in climate policy, without explicit considerations of its ethical implications. To do so would confuse a descriptive judgement ('markets do behave in a certain way') with a normative judgement ('everybody should behave in the same way that markets do').

The purpose of this chapter is not to argue for specific choices in either of these two economic parameters. The point is simply that no matter what the economic school of thought behind a particular choice, it has inescapable ethical implications and relies on assumptions about the underlying ethical frameworks that justify particular choices. Or looking at it the other way, different ethical judgements about economic parameters result in widely differing outcomes from cost–benefit analyses and, therefore, give rise to different answers about the urgency and stringency of actions to reduce greenhouse gas emissions.

Targets and the ethical implications of the risk of overshoot

Schlesinger (2009) argues that setting thresholds for any environmental pollution damage almost always has the effect of allowing damaging pollution right up to the stated threshold. Therefore, setting normative limits to any environmental degradation that increases steadily with increasing pollution levels can be counterproductive. This is particularly so where the infrastructure and economic incentives for the pollution to occur are difficult to halt or reverse. In this case overshooting the threshold is likely unless corrective action is taken well before the threshold is reached. Schlesinger's argument is consistent with the finding explored above that any long-term target for climate change requires a normative process that could result in a failure to recognise the damages that occur for some sectors and regions well below the target level.

The situation is exacerbated in the context of climate change by both the long lifetime of carbon dioxide in the atmosphere and the inertia of the climate system in responding fully to increasing greenhouse gas concentrations. Any long-term concentration or temperature target has an associated total emissions budget (Allen et al. 2009; Meinshausen et al. 2009). Delaying emissions reductions in the near term requires more rapid reductions in later decades to remain within the total emissions budget. Recent analyses have shown that if global greenhouse gas emissions continue to grow beyond about 2020, future emissions reductions would have to occur much quicker than the turn-over rate of capital infrastructure (IPCC 2007d; Meinshausen et al. 2009).

This implies that delays in near-term emissions reductions load an increasingly heavy and eventually impossible burden of action onto future generations, unless technologies are developed and implemented that allow the removal of carbon dioxide from the atmosphere after it has been emitted (Broecker 2007; Pielke Jr 2009; Read 2008). However, implementation of such technologies at the necessary scale may not be feasible (Boyd 2009; Dessler 2009; Marland and Obersteiner 2008).

The optimal timing of mitigation actions, of course, must be informed by economic analysis and assumptions about future technology development. However, whether to accept the risk that technology may not deliver the promised future solutions is inevitably an ethical decision, because the consequences of this decision are by and large not carried by the generation who makes the decision.

Ethical judgements underpinning burden-sharing arrangements

The preceding section considered ethical judgements that necessarily underpin any specific long-term global climate change target and intermediate global emissions targets. A subsequent question is how the global emissions that would be consistent with any such global target should be distributed amongst different countries. This question is generally more openly acknowledged as requiring not only technical information but necessarily also ethical judgements based on the concept of distributive justice (Gardiner 2004; IPCC 2007d; Ringius et al. 2000; Rose 1992). The UNFCCC includes the fundamental principle that all parties have 'common but differentiated' responsibilities (UNFCCC 2009, articles 3.1 and 3.2):

> The Parties should protect the climate system for the benefit of present and future generations of humankind, on the basis of equity and in accordance with their common but differentiated responsibilities and respective capabilities. Accordingly, the developed country Parties should take the lead in combating climate change and the adverse effects thereof.

> The specific needs and special circumstances of developing country Parties, especially those that are particularly vulnerable to the adverse

effects of climate change, and of those Parties, especially developing country Parties, that would have to bear a disproportionate or abnormal burden under the Convention, should be given full consideration.

Many different proposals for the sharing of efforts to reduce greenhouse gas emissions between different countries and groups of countries have been made that elaborate this generic principle (see Blok et al. 2005; Bodansky et al. 2004 for overviews). However few studies apply an explicit ethical analysis to specific burden-sharing (or, as some prefer to call them, effort-sharing) regimes. Most proposals build on a particular aspect of ethical principles, such as historical responsibilities, capacity to pay, or equal per capita entitlements to a common resource. Few check explicitly for internal consistency with the broader principles of distributive (or retributive) justice. An analysis of the internal consistency of the dominant approaches to burden sharing with ethical principles and their underlying logic is beyond scope of this chapter but has been attempted elsewhere (Boston et al. forthcoming). Instead, the following discussion focuses on the fundamental challenges that the concern for equity creates in the search for fairness in burden-sharing arrangements, and the interaction with the fundamental constraints imposed on any solutions by the climate system itself.

Trade-offs between ethical principles and physical constraints

A fundamental problem with burden-sharing arrangements is that they involve conflicts and trade-offs between different ethical principles. These trade-offs become more and more apparent the more stringent the global mitigation effort. Limiting global greenhouse gas emissions to levels that would be consistent with a long-term target of 450 ppm CO_2-eq concentrations (which as a best estimate is approximately equivalent to a global warming of 2°C above pre-industrial levels), requires global emissions to peak before 2020 and fall to about 50 per cent of 1990 levels by 2050, with carbon dioxide emissions reducing to close to zero (or potentially even below zero) by 2100 (IPCC 2007a). Such rapid emissions reductions can be achieved only if all major emitting countries or groups of countries implement policy actions, such as a universal price on greenhouse gas emissions. Delays in participation by major groups of countries would make reaching these long-term goals physically infeasible or prohibitively expensive (Bosetti et al. 2009; van Vliet et al. 2009; Vaughan et al. 2009).

Since the extent of climate change is determined by the total amount of greenhouse gas emissions entering the atmosphere, most international climate policy proposals focus on the largest emitters that collectively constitute the bulk of total global emissions. However, the countries or groups of countries that belong to the world's top 20 greenhouse gas emitters (by total amount of emissions) are at widely differing socioeconomic development levels. Some of these countries have very high per capita emissions, energy consumption, income, and general standards of living, while others rank much lower on all these counts but belong in the top emitting group largely as a result of large populations. Examples of some of these countries and their key greenhouse gas and socioeconomic development indicators are shown in Table 1. Proposals for burden sharing need to grapple with the question of what distribution of effort to reduce emissions is fair, given the significant differences in socioeconomic development evident in Table 1, but taking into account that without significant and rapid action by almost all major emitters, it will be impossible to stabilise greenhouse gas concentrations at low levels.

Table 1: Key greenhouse gas & development indicators for selected countries regions

Indicator	United States	European area	China	India	Nigeria
CO_2-eq emissions (total million tonnes, including land-use change)	6,561	3,406	7,172	1,813	491
Population, total (million)	296	321	1,304	1,095	141
CO_2-eq emissions per capita (tonnes, including land-use change)	23.5	10.5	5.5	1.7	2.1
Gross national income (international $ per capita)	42,040	29,507	4,100	2,220	1,530
Energy use (tonnes of oil-equivalent per capita)	7.9	4.0	1.3	0.5	0.7
Electric power consumption (MWh per capita)	13.7	6.9	1.8	0.5	0.1
Life expectancy at birth (years)	78	80	72	64	47
Mortality rate, children under five years (per 1,000 live births)	8	5	25	77	194
Improved sanitation facilities (% of urban population with access)	100	100 (est)	74	52	35
Malnutrition prevalence, weight for age (% of children under five years)	1	1 (est)	7	44	27
Internet users (per 100 people)	70	52	9	4	4

Notes: CO_2-eq = carbon dioxide equivalent; est = estimated; MWh = megawatt hour. All data are for 2005 or the closest year for which relevant data are available. Emissions data are from Climate Analysis Indicators Tool, World Resources Institute (cait.wri.org; gross emissions for year 2005 for all greenhouse gases in CO_2-eq, plus emissions from land-use change and forestry for 2000). European area comprises the countries in the European Union that have adopted the Euro as a common currency.

Source: World Bank Development Indicators (www.worldbank.org/data) and Reisinger (2009).

Alternative burden-sharing approaches

Some of the key ethical principles that underpin alternative burden-sharing arrangements consistent with a United Nations framework are outlined by

Boston et al. (forthcoming). These principles include sovereignty, equality (per capita entitlements), responsibility, need (including basic human-development rights), capacity (to reduce emissions and absorb costs), protection of the most vulnerable communities, and comparability (that is, similar countries should make similar efforts). No individual burden-sharing arrangement that uses a specific metric or quantitative methodology has been developed that satisfies all of these principles equitably. Most arrangements tend to emphasise just one particular aspect of ethical principles. They may be consistent with but not necessarily aim to satisfy other aspects or principles but may be inconsistent with yet other aspects or principles. As one example, the so-called 'Brazilian Proposal' calls for the setting of emissions targets for developed countries on the basis of their historical responsibility for climate change. This approach is strongly based on the principle of *retributive justice*, that is, holding countries to account for past actions, but it only weakly or accidentally correlates with most other ethical principles of *distributive justice* listed above (Boston et al. forthcoming).

Studies using a range of alternative burden-sharing proposals have suggested that to retain a 50–50 chance of limiting global warming to less than 2°C above pre-industrial levels, developed countries would need to reduce their aggregate emissions 25–40 per cent below 1990 levels by 2020 and 80–95 per cent below 1990 levels by 2050, while developing countries would need to reduce their collective emissions 15–30 per cent below business-as-usual trajectories by 2020 (den Elzen and Meinshausen 2005; IPCC 2007d; den Elzen and Höhne 2008; Höhne and Moltmann 2008). The breadth of these ranges reflects uncertainties in climate science and the global carbon cycle as well as differences in the ethical principles underpinning alternative burden-sharing arrangements.

Figure 2 shows the results for a range of burden-sharing proposals for Annex I (developed) countries as a group and some individual developing countries, based on data from Höhne and Moltmann (2008). Differences in emissions targets are large between developing countries, for example China and India, despite both being very large emitters, and these differences hold across the range of different burden-sharing proposals. The analysis shows the need to engage both China and India in future climate change agreements while at the same time differentiating between them. A failure to differentiate between these two key developing countries could be counterproductive, because India has much stronger ethical grounds to reject stringent emissions targets in the near term than China has. China could use the ethically justified concerns expressed by India about not imposing unfair mitigation requirements on developing countries to avoid accepting more stringent targets itself, even though on ethical grounds stronger mitigation action by China than for many other developing countries would appear to be justified.

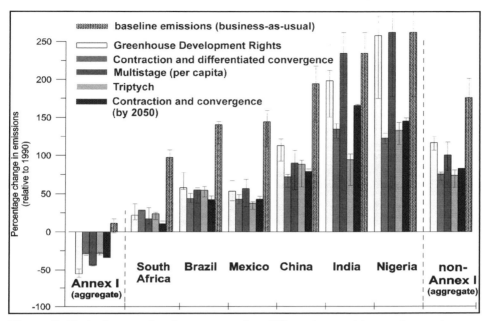

Figure 2: Emissions reduction targets for different countries and country groups, 2020

Notes: Reduction targets are given relative to 1990 emissions, aggregated for Annex I (developed) and non-Annex I (developing) countries and for individual developing countries under different burden-sharing proposals. The emissions reductions by 2020 under each scheme across developing and developed countries would be consistent with a long-term goal of stabilising greenhouse gas concentrations at 450 ppm CO_2-equivalent.

Source: Based on data from Höhne and Moltmann (2008, Table 10).

Burden-sharing approaches such as the Greenhouse Developments Rights approach would result in stronger aggregate emissions reductions for developed countries than other proposals, of the order of 50 per cent by 2020, and less stringent limits for developing countries. The Greenhouse Developments Rights approach is based on a combination of capacity to act (measured through per capita incomes) and responsibility for emissions since 1990, both above a minimum threshold. On the other hand, approaches that focus mainly on sector-specific technological mitigation options and potentials, and ignore per capita entitlements or income levels, such as the Global Triptych approach, would imply less stringent aggregate emissions reductions of around 25 per cent by 2020 for developed countries and require more rapid deviations from business as usual for developing countries (Höhne and Moltmann 2008). Targets for individual developed countries can deviate substantially from aggregate developed country targets but depend significantly on assumptions and the specific burden-sharing framework (den Elzen, Höhne, et al. 2009).

Most burden-sharing arrangements discussed in the literature to date focus on equity in mitigation efforts only and ignore the fact that developing countries are typically more vulnerable to the impacts of climate change. When the damages from climate change and costs of adaptation are taken into account, then the balance of equitable cost distribution shifts to place more on developed countries and less on developing countries (den Elzen, Hof, et al. 2009). This observation has been used to suggest that developed countries have a moral responsibility to support adaptation in developed countries *in addition to* undertaking significantly more ambitious emissions reductions (Füssel 2009). Estimates of different metrics to share the costs of adaptation in developing countries have been developed (Dellink et al. 2009). These approaches result in a range of estimates, consistent with the range of ethical principles that could be applied to determine what constitutes a 'fair' share for each country. Despite the range of figures that result from different approaches, such estimates could be used to broadly inform future negotiations and agreements on sharing the total cost of climate change in a way that might be more ethically sound than focusing on only mitigation aspects.

Public appreciation in developed countries of the degree of socioeconomic differences between developed and developing countries is likely to be limited. Television reports often show images from high-tech parts of commercial or political centres of developing countries (for example, Beijing or Shanghai), but much fewer images of the hundreds of millions of poor rural and urban dwellers that live well below Western living standards. Therefore, public appreciation in developed countries of the ethical foundations for burden-sharing arrangements in international climate policy is also likely to be limited, unless this information is explicitly made part of communications on the goals and rationale for international agreements on climate change.

Conversely, a departure from the broad range of emissions targets derived from the range of burden-sharing approaches implicitly or explicitly rejects the ethical principles of distributive justice that underpin these burden-sharing approaches. Surveys have shown that an appreciation of the ethical dimensions of climate change can alter perceptions of the urgency with which climate change needs to be addressed (Dannenerg et al. 2009; Lange et al. 2010; Lange et al. 2007; Lorenzoni and Pidgeon 2006). As a result, making the ethical implications of international negotiating positions explicit appears to be an important step if decision makers wish to find out the true level of public support for the degree and urgency of national climate change actions within a global agreement.

Conclusions

This chapter has provided a brief joint ethical and climate science analysis of global climate change targets and emissions targets between individual countries. Several lessons can be drawn.

Global climate change targets can be characterised through temperature limits, concentrations, or global emissions targets. Regardless of their specific form, scientific, technical, and economic analyses and assessments on their own cannot describe limits of 'safe' or 'dangerous' climate change. Climate change damages generally increase with the magnitude and rate of warming, but some damages occur for almost any level of warming for the most vulnerable sectors and communities. Even for warming of less than 2°C above pre-industrial levels, the potential impacts for some sectors and regions are projected to affect hundreds of millions of people and irreversibly alter many unique ecosystems.

The acceptability of any given amount of warming, or greenhouse gas concentrations giving rise to such warming, requires normative judgements about which impacts are deemed acceptable, but local perspectives will inevitably differ. Normative judgements are similarly required when weighing the need to reduce risks from unlikely (or simply uncertain) but highly damaging events. Attitudes to risk cannot be reduced to a scientific analysis, even though scientific analysis can be used to characterise and, ideally, quantify risks.

An economic comparison of damages from climate change and the costs of reducing emissions cannot produce an objective 'optimal' climate change target either, because choices in key parameters of the discount rate cannot be determined by objective criteria alone. A range of choices that can be justified by reference to particular aspects of the economic literature encompasses virtually arbitrary climate change damage costs. This implies that any given choice of a discount rate and economic framework for climate change inextricably requires ethical choices; claims that economic results regarding the costs and benefits of climate change mitigation are free from ethics cannot be justified, even if those ethical choices were not explicit in the economic and technical decisions that determine the conclusions.

Ensuring the ethical dimensions of global climate change targets are made transparent in public discussions is an important step in ensuring that the risks of low-level impacts, the risks to vulnerable regions, and the risks to future generations are adequately and appropriately considered in decision making. The failure to make the ethical dimensions transparent carries two key risks. One risk is that communities may not support climate policies aimed at providing adaptation assistance to developing countries as part of and in addition to an ambitious mitigation commitment, but regard this as an *either/or* choice. The second risk is that developed countries that generally regard themselves as relatively less affected by climate change than the global average could provide only a limited mandate for their governments to engage in ambitious international agreements that aim to reduce not only the well-understood impacts but also the uncertain risks arising from events that are unlikely but possibly globally catastrophic. Public support for participation in such global agreements is likely to be contingent on the risk dimensions of climate change and its essential irreversibility over many human generations and the intergenerational ethical judgements that dealing with such risk entails being made transparent.

Emissions targets for developed countries as a group fall within a reasonably robust range even if different principles of distributive justice are applied. This suggests that targets outside this broad range could violate established ethical principles, but this violation is not generally acknowledged or made explicit. A review of emissions targets for several developed and developing countries suggests that the simple formula of all major emitters having to accept binding targets in future agreements is not necessarily incorrect, but it may represent a dangerously shorthand description of a complex ethical issue. The failure to differentiate between the socioeconomic conditions of different major emitters in the developing world could contribute to a stalemate in international negotiations between developed and developing countries.

Based on these insights, we argue that the willingness of communities in Western democratic societies to accept strong and binding emissions targets (both global and national targets) depends on two factors. First, willingness might be greater or at least more durable if the ethical foundations of such targets were made more transparent. And secondly, willingness might be greater and less prone to erratic changes if the inevitable ethical foundations of targets that appear to be derived primarily from economic or scientific principles were made explicit.

Clearly, this hypothesis needs further testing. However, it appears to be supported by the strong concern that the New Zealand public tends to show towards climate change in Pacific Island countries, as well as the strong concern about ethical dimensions of climate change that surveys in other countries have shown. Surveys of public attitudes to climate change also point to an important moral dimension of perceiving and responding to risks (Lorenzoni and Pidgeon 2006; Rehmann-Sutter 1998; Sjöberg 2000).

Making ethical principles that underpin specific climate targets and goals explicit does not in itself guarantee the emergence of durable public support for specific climate policies. However, bringing ethics to the forefront of public debate on climate change appears to be a necessary condition to achieve an endurable public policy response, given the crucial role of ethics in constraining the range of climate policy choices that can otherwise be justified on scientific, economic, and technological grounds.

References

Allen, M. R., D. J. Frame, C. Huntingford, et al. 2009. 'Warming caused by cumulative carbon emissions towards the trillionth tonne.' *Nature* 458(7242): 1163–6.

Anthoff, D., R. S. J. Tol, and G. W. Yohe. 2009. 'Discounting for climate change.' *Economics: The open-access, open assessment e-journal* 2: 2009–276.

Blok, K., N. Höhne, A. Torvanger, et al. 2005. *Towards a Post-2012 Climate Change Regime*. Brussels, Belgium: 3E.

Bodansky, D., S. Chou, and C. Jorge-Tresolini. 2004. *International Climate Efforts beyond 2012: A survey of approaches*. Washington, DC: Pew Center on Global Climate Change.

Bosetti, V., C. Carraro, A. Sgobbi, et al. 2009. 'Delayed action and uncertain stabilisation targets. How much will the delay cost?' *Climatic Change* 96(3): 299–312.

Boston, J., F. Lemp, and L. Kengmana. Forthcoming. 'Considerations of distributive justice in the context of climate change mitigation.' *British Journal of Politics and International Relations*.

Boyd, P. W. 2009. 'Geopolitics of geoengineering.' *Nature Geoscience* 2(12): 812.

Broecker, W. S. 2007. 'Climate change: CO2 arithmetic.' *Science* 315(5817): 1371.

Dannenerg, A., B. Sturm, and C. Vogt. 2009. 'Do equity preferences matter for climate negotiators? An experimental investigation.' *IOP Conference Series: Earth and environmental science* 6(11): 112,002.

Dellink, R., M. den Elzen, H. Aiking, et al. 2009. 'Sharing the burden of financing adaptation to climate change.' *Global Environmental Change* 19(4): 411–21.

den Elzen, M., A. Hof, and D. P. Van Vuuren. 2009. 'Regional total climate change costs for different burden sharing regimes and concentration targets.' *IOP Conference Series: Earth and environmental science* 6(32): 322005.

den Elzen, M., and N. Höhne. 2008. 'Reductions of greenhouse gas emissions in Annex I and non-Annex I countries for meeting concentration stabilisation targets. An editorial comment.' *Climatic Change* 91: 249–74.

den Elzen, M., N. Höhne, M. Hagemann, et al. 2009. *Sharing Developed Countries' Post-2012 Greenhouse Gas Emission Reductions Based on Comparable Efforts*. The Netherlands: Netherlands Environmental Assessment Agency.

den Elzen, M., and M. Meinshausen. 2005. *Meeting the EU 2°C climate target: Global and regional emission implications*. The Netherlands: Netherlands Environmental Assessment Agency.

Dessler, A. 2009. 'Energy for air capture.' *Nature Geoscience* 2(12): 811.

Dietz, S., J. Helgeson, C. Hepburn, et al. 2009. 'Siblings, not triplets: Social preferences for risk, inequality and time in discounting climate change.' *Economics: The open-access, open assessment e-journal* 3: 2009–26.

Dietz, S., C. Hope, and N. Patmore. 2007. 'Some economics of "dangerous" climate change: Reflections on the Stern Review.' *Global Environmental Change* 17(3–4): 311–25.

Dimas, S. 2009. 'Act and adapt: Towards a new climate change deal.' Speech given at Green Week, Brussels, 23 June 2009.

Füssel, H.-M. 2009. 'The ethical dilemma of climate change: How unequal is the global distribution of responsibility for and vulnerability to climate change?' *IOP Conference Series: Earth and environmental science* 6(11): 112,013.

Gardiner, S. M. 2004. 'Ethics and global climate change.' *Ethics* 114(3): 555–600.

Heal, G. 2009. 'The economics of climate change: A post-Stern perspective.' *Climatic Change* 96(3): 275–97.

Höhne, N., and S. Moltmann. 2008. *Distribution of Emission Allowances under the Greenhouse Development Rights and Other Effort Sharing Approaches*. Germany: Heinrich-Böll-Stiftung.

Hulme, M. 2009. 'The science and politics of climate change.' *Wall Street Journal*, 2 December. http://online.wsj.com/article/SB100014240527487041 07104574571613215771336.html.

IPCC (Intergovernmental Panel on Climate Change). 2001. *Climate Change 2001: Synthesis report. Contribution of Working Groups I, II and III to the Third Assessment Report*. Cambridge, UK: Cambridge University Press.

IPCC. 2007a. *Climate Change 2007: Synthesis report. Contribution of Working Groups I, II and III to the Fourth Assessment Report.* Geneva, Switzerland: Intergovernmental Panel on Climate Change.

IPCC (Intergovernmental Panel on Climate Change). 2007b. *Climate Change 2007: Impacts, adaptation and vulnerability. Contribution of Working Group II to the Fourth Assessment Report of the Intergovernmental Panel on Climate Change.* Cambridge, UK: Cambridge University Press.

IPCC (Intergovernmental Panel on Climate Change). 2007c. *Climate Change 2007: The physical science basis. Contribution of Working Group I to the Fourth Assessment Report of the Intergovernmental Panel on Climate Change.* Cambridge, UK: Cambridge University Press.

IPCC (Intergovernmental Panel on Climate Change). 2007d. *Climate Change 2007: Mitigation of climate change. Contribution of Working Group III to the Fourth Assessment Report of the Intergovernmental Panel on Climate Change.* Cambridge, UK: Cambridge University Press.

Kriegler, E., J. W. Hall, H. Held, et al. 2009. 'Imprecise probability assessment of tipping points in the climate system.' *Proceedings of the National Academy of Sciences* 106(13): 5041–6.

Lange, A., A. Löschel, C. Vogt, et al. 2010. 'On the self-interested use of equity in international climate negotiations.' *European Economic Review* 54(3): 359–75.

Lange, A., C. Vogt, and A. Ziegler. 2007. 'On the importance of equity in international climate policy: An empirical analysis.' *Energy Economics* 29(3): 545–62.

Lenton, T. M., H. Held, E. Kriegler, et al. 2008. 'Tipping elements in the Earth's climate system.' *Proceedings of the National Academy of Sciences* 105(6): 1786–93.

Lorenzoni, I., and N. Pidgeon. 2006. 'Public views on climate change: European and USA perspectives.' *Climatic Change* 77(1): 73–95.

Marland, G., and M. Obersteiner. 2008. 'Large-scale biomass for energy, with considerations and cautions: An editorial comment.' *Climatic Change* 87: 335–42.

Meinshausen, M., N. Meinshausen, W. Hare, et al. 2009. 'Greenhouse-gas emission targets for limiting global warming to 2°C.' *Nature* 458(7242): 1158–62.

Neumayer, E. 2007. 'A missed opportunity: The Stern Review on climate change fails to tackle the issue of non-substitutable loss of natural capital.' *Global Environmental Change* 17(3–4): 297–301.

Nordhaus, W. D. 2009. 'Economic issues in a designing a global agreement on global warming.' Paper presented at Climate Change: Global risks, challenges, and decisions, Copenhagen, Denmark, 10–12 March 2009. http://climatecongress.ku.dk/speakers/professorwilliamnordhaus-plenaryspeaker-11march2009.pdf.

Parry, M., N. Arnell, P. Berry, et al. 2009. *Assessing the Costs of Adaptation to Climate Change.* London: International Institute for Environment and Development.

Pielke Jr, R. A. 2009. 'An idealized assessment of the economics of air capture of carbon dioxide in mitigation policy.' *Environmental Science & Policy* 12(3): 216–25.

Read, P. 2008. 'Biosphere carbon stock management: Addressing the threat of abrupt climate change in the next few decades – An editorial essay.' *Climatic Change* 87: 305–20.

Rehmann-Sutter, C. 1998. 'Involving others: Towards an ethical concept of risk.' *Risk: Health, Safety and Environment* 9(2): 119.

Reisinger, A. 2009. *Climate Change 101: An educational resource.* Wellington: Institute of Policy Studies and New Zealand Climate Change Research Institute, School of Government, Victoria University of Wellington.

Ringius, L., A. Torvanger, and A. Underdal. 2000. *Burden Differentiation: Fairness principles and proposals.* Working paper 1999:13. Oslo: Center for International Climate and Environmental Research and Netherlands Energy Research Foundation.

Rose, A. 1992. 'Equity considerations of tradable carbon emission entitlements.' In S. Barrett (ed.). *Combating Global Warming: Study on a global system of tradable carbon emission entitlements.* New York: United Nations Conference on Trade and Development.

Russill, C., and Z. Nyssa. 2009. 'The tipping point trend in climate change communication.' *Global Environmental Change* 19(3): 336–44.

Schlesinger, M. E. 2009. 'Planetary boundaries: Thresholds risk prolonged degradation.' *Nature Reports: Climate change* (September): 112–3.

Sjöberg, L. 2000. 'Factors in risk perception.' *Risk Analysis* 20: 1–12.

Smith, J. B., S. H. Schneider, M. Oppenheimer, et al. 2009. 'Assessing dangerous climate change through an update of the Intergovernmental Panel on Climate Change (IPCC) "reasons for concern".' *Proceedings of the National Academy of Sciences* 106(11): 4133–7.

Stern, N. 2006. *The Economics of Climate Change: The Stern Review*. Cambridge, UK: Cambridge University Press.

Tol, R. S. J., and G. W. Yohe. 2009. 'The Stern Review: A deconstruction.' *Energy Policy* 37(3): 1032–40.

UNFCCC. 2009. *The United Nations Framework Convention on Climate Change*. Bonn, Germany: Secretariat of the United Nations Framework Convention on Climate Change.

van Vliet, J., M. G. J. den Elzen, and D. P. van Vuuren. 2009. 'Meeting radiative forcing targets under delayed participation.' *Energy Economics* 31(Supplement 2): 152–62.

Vaughan, N., T. Lenton, and J. Shepherd. 2009. 'Climate change mitigation: Trade-offs between delay and strength of action required.' *Climatic Change* 96(1): 29–43.

Wardekker, J. A., A. C. Petersen, and J. P. van der Sluijs. 2009. 'Ethics and public perception of climate change: Exploring the Christian voices in the US public debate.' *Global Environmental Change* 19(4): 512–21.

Weitzman, M. L. 2007. 'A review of *The Stern Review on the Economics of Climate Change*.' *Journal of Economic Literature* 45: 703–24.

Yohe, G. 2009. 'Toward an integrated framework derived from a risk-management approach to climate change.' *Climatic Change* 95(3): 325–39.

8. Sharing the responsibility of dealing with climate change: Interpreting the principle of common but differentiated responsibilities

Dan Weijers, David Eng, and Ramon Das

Introduction

According to the 2007 Intergovernmental Panel on Climate Change report, unless global collective action on climate change can be achieved, the major threats posed by a rapidly changing climate are likely to have catastrophic effects for all life on Earth (IPCC 2007). Despite the fact all major governments have acknowledged the causal role of anthropogenic emissions in producing rapid global warming,[1] little action has yet been taken to reduce such emissions.

The best hope for reaching an effective international agreement on climate change is to base it on the widely agreed upon principle of common but differentiated responsibilities (CBDR), Principle 7 of the Rio Declaration on Environment and Development. This principle captures the international consensus that the ongoing responsibility to protect the global commons is to be shared, though not necessarily evenly. In particular, the principle of CBDR notes that developed states bear a greater responsibility to address climate change because of the pressure they have put on the global environment and their financial and technological ability to take action (Rio Declaration on Environment and Development 1992).[2] Unfortunately, serious disagreements remain about how the principle of CBDR is to be interpreted. At bottom, these interpretive disagreements are about justice: what is the most just way to decide what should be done about rapid climate change and who should do it? Insofar as this question hinges on matters of justice, philosophers have an important

---

1   United Nations Department of Public Information (1997).
2   Principle 7 of the Rio Declaration on Environment and Development provides the first formulation of the principle of CBDR, 'In view of the different contributions to global environmental degradation, States have common but differentiated responsibilities. The developed countries acknowledge the responsibility that they bear in the international pursuit of sustainable development in view of the pressures their societies place on the global environment and of the technologies and financial resources they command' (UNFCCC 1992).

role to play in answering this important question. This chapter is a contribution to the ongoing philosophical debate about how the principle of CBDR can be interpreted in a way that is both fair and amenable to the formation of policy.

Within the existing literature on how to fairly divide the responsibilities of dealing with climate change, several principles of justice have emerged as the main contenders.[3] As it turns out, the only current agreement on these principles of justice is that, considered individually, none distributes responsibilities in a way that is fair to all relevant parties (Page 2008). This has encouraged recent attempts to solve this problem by combining the main principles of justice into a hybrid account. The goal is to create a hybrid account that considers all of the main morally relevant considerations and distributes the responsibilities of dealing with climate change in a way that is fair to all parties and amenable to translation into policy.

In this chapter we follow the general approach just described. We first discuss the main principles of justice and note the standard objections to them, which we believe necessitate a hybrid approach. The hybrid account we defend is primarily based on the distributive principle of sufficientarianism, which we interpret as the idea that each country should have the means to provide a minimally decent quality of life for each of its citizens. We argue that sufficientarian considerations give good reason to think that what we call the 'ability to pay objection' should be taken much more seriously in this debate. Following this, our account emphasises what we believe are the two most important moral desiderata in any attempt to distribute responsibility for dealing with climate change: the *ability* to mitigate the problem and the making of *culpable contributions* to the problem. After noting that our proposal includes enough detail to be a useful start for policy makers, we defend our account against some potential objections.

Polluter pays principle

The polluter pays principle (PPP) identifies the parties who caused the pollution and apportions responsibility for paying the costs of dealing with climate change among those parties. Arguably, the PPP is the most intuitive way of thinking about the ethics of climate change. It is based on the widely shared idea that those who cause harm to others should be morally responsible for remedying that harm. As such, the PPP has the ability to provide the appropriate incentive to prevent polluting by directly linking moral responsibility, and the resulting accountability, to the kinds of actions that should be discouraged.

---

3   See, for example, Singer (2008), Caney (2005), Shue (1999), Neumayer (2000), Gardiner (2004), and Page (1999, 2008).

The 'polluting' to which the PPP refers should be taken to mean the emitting of greenhouse gases above some agreed upon quota. The quotas agreed upon in the Kyoto Protocol are all self-imposed and based on a reduction of their absolute per capita or per gross national product emissions relative to some past point in time.[4] These arbitrary quotas are patently unfair because they fail to acknowledge that there is no good *moral* reason for any distribution of a common global good, like the atmosphere, other than an equal share for everyone (Singer 2008, p. 671). There is a much fairer method of creating a quota (and one that would do more to reduce the likely catastrophic effects of climate change). This method would see the annual amount of total emissions considered safe by current United Nations Framework Convention on Climate Change (UNFCCC) estimates to be distributed to states based on their near-future population trajectory as compiled by the United Nations.[5] If this approach were adopted, then the per capita aspect of this method would plausibly result in current *and* future people receiving their fair share of the atmosphere. The use of near-future population trajectories instead of actual populations is meant to eliminate perverse incentives for population control.

The PPP fares well when applied to current and future polluting. However, when the PPP is applied to historical emitting a problem arises from the fact past polluters, for the most part, were not aware that their actions would have harmful consequences. This fact suggests two versions of the PPP. One version is an exacting version: the full liability PPP assigns moral responsibility to agents to redress all of the relevant harms they cause even when they are unaware their actions would lead to such harm. The other version is a weaker version: the conditional liability PPP (CPPP) assigns moral responsibility only to those who knowingly pollute or who should have known that their greenhouse gas emitting was likely to cause harm. We refer to such polluting as culpable polluting. Culpable polluting is to be distinguished from non-culpable polluting on the basis of whether the polluter can reasonably be held to have known that their polluting was likely to cause harm. We believe this distinction is morally significant, so adopt a version of the CPPP in our hybrid account.

Applying the CPPP to the current climate change debate requires a method to discern who can reasonably be held to have known that their polluting was likely to cause harm. We conservatively recommend taking 1992 (when the Rio Declaration on Environment and Development was signed) as the date past

---

4   Singer (2008 p. 671), references Claussen and McNeilly (1998) and says the targets agreed on at Kyoto 'were arrived at through negotiations with government leaders, and they were not based on any general principles of fairness, nor much else that can be defended on any terms other than the need to get an agreement'.

5   However, as Reisinger and Larsen (in this volume) argue, more thought needs to be given to what total amount of atmospheric greenhouse gas emissions is desirable because all amounts have different predicted outcomes for the various life forms on Earth. The setting of the 'safe' level of total atmospheric greenhouse gas emissions is a moral task that deserves greater attention than it has received.

which all states should be deemed as knowing that greenhouse gas emissions over a certain level are likely to cause harm. By using 1992 as the starting date for culpable polluting, the CPPP can satisfyingly deal with the problem of non-culpable polluting. However, Page (2008, p. 570) has criticised the use of this fairly recent date as the relevant starting date because he thinks it results in 'harsh treatment for the newly industrialised populations and lax treatment of those residing in countries of transition'. To move the starting date further back would decrease Page's fairness concerns but would exacerbate the unfairness to polluters who truly were not aware of the consequences of their actions. The combination of these two concerns makes it difficult to specify a fair date after which states should be deemed as knowing that greenhouse gas emissions over a certain level are likely to cause harm. And this difficulty, in turn, creates a problem for the PPP that it cannot easily solve by itself.

The main problem for the CPPP is that it fails to designate sufficient moral responsibility to address the problem given that a large portion of the polluting was caused before 1992 (Caney 2005). A common response to this sufficiency problem has been to argue that individuals currently residing in states that are primarily responsible for climate change should be held morally responsible for polluting that was caused by the previous generations of those states.[6] Closer inspection reveals that this response is unfair. Why should the mere fact someone lives in a country, whose previous citizens polluted, make them responsible for the polluting? A possible response to this intergenerational problem is to agree that current generations should have to pay only for their own polluting and not for the polluting of past generations. Although this would be a fair and consistent application of the PPP, it suffers from the same problem as the CPPP: it fails to designate enough moral responsibility to ensure adequate mitigation of and adaptation to the potentially catastrophic effects of rapid climate change.

It could be argued that the above intergenerational problem presupposes that the relevant moral agents are individuals as opposed to states. Against this, a collectivist approach to the PPP would view states as the relevant moral agents for the current climate change debate. Such an approach has initial intuitive plausibility given that any future agreement the UNFCCC reaches will distribute the responsibilities for dealing with climate change among states in the first instance. Applying this collectivist version of the PPP reveals that, because of their relatively long history of greenhouse gas emitting, the developed nations have the primary responsibility for mitigating and adapting to rapid climate

---

6 Applied to the current climate change debate, the full liability PPP receives the full force of this objection while the CPPP avoids it by pure luck – it just so happens that all greenhouse-gas emitting in the distant past (by previous generations) is unknowing pollution, so cannot incur responsibilities to pay for current generations. Theoretically, however, this objection applies equally to full liability PPP and CPPP. For example, imagine applying this objection to the CPPP in 100 years' time (when our distant descendants do not want to pay for our current knowingly polluting).

change. These states should pay, on this collectivist version of the PPP, because they have caused, and are likely to continue to cause, harms because of the high concentrations of greenhouse gases they have released through their historic polluting. Caney (2005) has argued against a collectivist approach to the PPP on the grounds that it would be unfair to the current citizens of an historically polluting state to have to pay for damages done by their forebears. He asks, 'individuals cannot inherit debts from parents or grandparents, so why should this be any different?' (Caney 2005, p. 760). Although we agree with the intuition that innocent individuals should not have a moral responsibility to remedy harms caused by others, we do not think Caney adequately engages with the rationale of collectivist views.

As a part of a collective, an individual is usually entitled to some benefits, but those benefits come at the cost of certain responsibilities. New citizens of New Zealand, by birth or grant, are entitled to, among other things, the benefits of social welfare, a public health system, and the freedom to live in a naturally beautiful country. However, these citizens also accrue several responsibilities, including abiding by the law and paying taxes. As a rule, the responsibilities of being a part of a collective come ineluctably hand in hand with the benefits. Therefore, individuals who did not vote for the creation of the benefits that they are now enjoying, as a part of a collective, should understand that with those benefits come responsibilities and that acceptance of the benefits entails acceptance of the whole package. Therefore, while citizens of industrialised countries are innocent of historic polluting, the collective of which they are a part is not. One may decide to opt out of the collective (of both the benefits and the responsibilities), but no one is entitled to opt out of the responsibilities only. In short, one can respond to Caney's worries about the unfairness of collective versions of PPP as follows. If individuals born into rich countries can make the case that it is unfair to require them to pay for harms they did not cause, then individuals born into poor, non-polluting countries can make an even stronger case that it is unfair that they lack so many benefits enjoyed by individuals of rich countries *solely* because of accidents of birth.

Therefore, a collectivist PPP, which views the relevant moral agents as states, can be defended against Caney's objections. However, as we argue later, both individual and collective versions of the PPP are susceptible to a different objection, which we call the 'ability to pay objection'.

Beneficiary pays principle

According to the beneficiary pays principle (BPP), agents who benefit from historic polluting should bear the moral responsibility for dealing with the problems caused by that polluting. One of the advantages of the BPP is that it easily avoids the intergenerational problem, since the BPP assigns moral responsibility to those who benefit regardless of whether they caused the pollution. According to the BPP, the response to Caney's innocent complainer should be, 'we agree that you are innocent of polluting, but you have benefited from the polluting, and *that* is why you have the moral responsibility to deal with it'.

The strongest ethical rationale for the BPP is based on the idea of minimising the unearned inequalities that have resulted from polluting. Unearned inequalities are welfare-affecting differences between agents that have come about because of circumstances beyond the agents' control. According to this rationale, because the benefits and costs associated with historic polluting are beyond current agents' control and are unequally distributed, the fairest way to rectify this is to assign the moral responsibility to deal with the problems caused by historic polluting to the agents who have benefited from it. On this view, the more an agent has benefited from greenhouse gas emissions, the more moral responsibility they have to pay for the mitigation of and adaptation to rapid climate change. On the face of it, this creates a fair result because it minimises the number of agents who, despite never having benefited from historic polluting, would nevertheless have to pay for the costs of it. Furthermore, by apportioning the costs of polluting in this way, the BPP moves everyone closer to a fair and equitable position in regards to the overall effects of the pollution.[7]

Ability to pay principle

The ability to pay principle (APP) regards states' per capita production capacity (or some other measure of welfare) as the only moral consideration in sharing the responsibilities of remedying the adverse effects of climate change. The APP requires that all and only those who can afford to pay for mitigating and adapting to climate change should pay and they should pay in proportion to their ability to pay. Adoption of the APP would result in the Annex I (developed) states paying for historic greenhouse gas emissions.[8] This allocation of responsibilities is in accordance with the element of the principle of CBDR that calls on developed states to bear more responsibility for dealing with climate change *because* they have the ability to do so.

---

7   Many contemporary writers have criticised the application of the BPP to historical polluting on different intergenerational grounds; namely, the non-identity problem. Although we think the BPP can be defended against the non-identity problem, we do not discuss the issue here. This is because we believe (as we argue below) that the BPP, like the PPP, is better rejected on the grounds of the ability to pay objection.
8   For a list of Annex I states, see UNFCCC (n. d.).

Several ways exist to discern a state's ability to pay, but the most promising method is morally justified by the notion of sufficientarianism. Sufficientarianism is the principle of distribution that benefits and burdens should be shared in such a way that as many people as possible (including future people) have sufficient resources to achieve a certain level of well-being (Page 2007).[9] A sufficientarian would argue that a government's primary moral responsibility is to ensure its citizens have a quality of life sufficient for a reasonable level of well-being. For practical purposes, a state's ability to provide this sufficient standard of living for its citizens should be measured by its per capita production because this is relatively easy to calculate and adequately reflects a state's ability to provide the goods that increase its citizens' quality of life.[10] The level of production considered sufficient should be based on international agreement, but should probably be somewhere close to the threshold where per capita real income begins to make little difference to subjective well-being.[11] Henceforth, we abbreviate 'sufficientarian-supported ability to pay principle' as 'APP'.

When a state has a sufficient level of production to provide this level of well-being for its own citizens, a sufficientarian would then argue that the state has a moral responsibility to ensure citizens of other states and future citizens of all states can also reach this level of well-being. As noted by Shue (1999, p. 542), this responsibility could be either weak or strong, where the strong version calls for positive action to assist others below the level of sufficiency and the weak version requires only that states are not interfered with in attempting to reach the level of sufficiency. For the APP, the strong version applies; the ability to pay for preventing the damage that rapid climate change is likely to cause creates a moral responsibility to do so. We propose that a state's ability to pay for helping other states deal with problems such as climate change be understood as the degree to which a state's per capita production exceeds the agreed level of sufficient per capita production. Of course, it could be the case that the government of a very wealthy state distributes its plentiful goods in

---

9   For more discussion of sufficientarianism, see Frankfurt (1987), Crisp (2003), Page (2008), and Shue (1992, 1999). Sufficientarianism might seem similar to egalitarianism and prioritarianism, but as elegantly discussed by Page (2007), the three views are not the same. An egalitarian views states of affairs as being increasingly just as they make individuals' well-being increasingly equal (and vice versa). A prioritarian sees changes in states of affairs as increasingly just as they improve the well-being of those increasingly worse off to begin with. A sufficientarian views states of affairs as being increasingly just as fewer people reside below a sufficient level of well-being. Therefore, in a situation of many unequally rich (but all very rich) agents, egalitarians and prioritarians would recommend redistributing the wealth, but a sufficientarian would not.

10   In the future, a state's ability to provide a sufficient quality of life might include consideration of its natural and cultural resources, such as pristine wilderness and celebrated heritage. The current difficulty quantifying the effects of such non-commercial goods on well-being prevents their inclusion in measures of sufficiency for now.

11   Of course, estimating the exact threshold for sufficient well-being is so fraught with difficulties that it is probably impossible to get right (Casal 2007, pp. 312–8; cf. Page 2008, p. 565). However, enough work has been done on this to create estimates that are reasonably well grounded to proceed with. For example, Baer et al. (2007) argue that the minimum should be US$9,000 (in 1995 dollars).

such a way that some or even many of its citizens are left without the resources required for a sufficiently good life. Although we do not wish to trivialise this issue, we set it aside here as a matter to be resolved between citizens and their governments. Thus, for present purposes, within-state distribution of income does not affect the objective assessment of whether a state has the ability to pay for protecting the global commons.

Using the idea of sufficientarianism as the moral justification for the APP, we can see that if the citizens of a poor state do not have a decent standard of living, then that state has no obligation to pay for helping citizens of other states. In contrast, if a rich country has the ability to provide *more* than a minimally decent life for its citizens, it is obliged to help pay for the prevention of harm to citizens of less fortunate states. A consequence of this sufficientarian justification for the APP is that a very poor country, such as Bhutan, could start polluting now without incurring any moral responsibility to mitigate its greenhouse gas emissions or pay to help others adapt to the rapidly changing climate. In fact, this view advocates that Bhutan's hypothetical polluting be paid for by all states that achieve above a certain level of production (and to the degree that their relative productions exceed this level). Although this consequence might seem unfair, and thereby pose a problem for the APP, it actually highlights a benefit of it. The current debate about climate change would never have come about if it were not for the potentially catastrophic consequences for humans, and the APP is designed to minimise the number of people living in appalling and thereby potentially catastrophic circumstances. The APP, as we define it here, ensures that people who are most likely to suffer as a result of rapid climate change are the central concern of any agreement on dealing with climate change.[12] Focusing on those who are suffering in this way reflects the moral desire to have as few people as possible suffer from the existence of 'radical inequalities'; situations in which there is enough of some good for everyone but some parties have much more than enough and others have less than enough (Nagel 1977).

Although the APP captures one vital moral consideration, it fails to address another. The APP fails to assign fair distributions of moral responsibility in the common case of rich states with an equal ability to pay but differing greenhouse gas emissions. According to the APP, richer states' ability to pay for the costs of mitigating and adapting to climate change justifies their doing so *regardless* of whether they knowingly contribute to the problem. The omission of this

---

12 This result nicely reflects several of the principles of the Rio Declaration on Environment and Development (UNFCCC 1992). Principle 1 states, 'Human beings are at the centre of concern for sustainable development'. Principle 5 states, 'All States and all people shall cooperate in the essential task of eradicating poverty as an indispensable requirement for sustainable development, in order to decrease the disparities in standards of living and better meet the needs of the majority of the people of the world'. Principle 6 states, 'The special situation and needs of developing countries, particularly the least developed and those most environmentally vulnerable, shall be given special priority. International actions in the field of environment and development should also address the interests and needs of all countries'.

consideration departs from the original text of the principle of CBDR, which ties developed nations' responsibilities for dealing with the costs of climate change to their greater role in producing it (as well as their greater ability to pay). More importantly, the failure to consider who knowingly created the climate-changing pollution creates unfair burdens on equally rich but non-polluting states.

Ability to pay objection to the polluter pays principle and beneficiary pays principle

Despite its own weaknesses, a sufficientarianism-based ability to pay constraint – the ability to pay objection – can be applied to the PPP and the BPP to highlight an important problem for both principles. The ability to pay objection has not been afforded much attention in the literature, especially as an objection to the BPP.[13] We argue that the ability to pay objection reveals how the PPP can unfairly assign moral responsibility to some agents without the ability to pay for it and that the BPP can fail to assign moral responsibility to some agents that do have the ability to pay for it.

If the notion of sufficientarianism is taken seriously, then very poor states should focus on their primary moral responsibility, the welfare of their citizens, and not the welfare of citizens belonging to other states. However, if we take either the individualist or collective version of the PPP seriously, then we allow for the possibility that some currently polluting, but still very poor, states will be morally obliged to help much richer states deal with the deleterious effects of climate change. According to the PPP, even if a state lacks the resources to provide a minimally decent quality of life for its citizens, it must pay for any polluting that it does; this remains the case even if the polluting is the result of efforts to raise the abysmal living conditions of the state's citizens. As a practical matter, no beneficent (or even self-interested, democratic) government would voluntarily deprive its own citizens of the basic goods of life to relieve some richer people from (what is to them) a tiny burden. And, more importantly, it would be unfair to obligate such a government to do so. Imagine a state that emits greenhouse gases in an attempt to rebuild its capacity to offer basic services to its citizens after being ravaged by famine and war. Even if it is currently polluting, it would be grossly unjust to require the government of such a state to give resources badly needed by its own citizens to some international fund so other citizens (most of whom already enjoy a comfortable life) do not have to contribute as much themselves.

---

13 For example, Caney (2005) uses a weaker version of this objection to argue that the PPP needs to be supplemented with the APP, but he does not use it to object to the BPP.

Another version of the ability to pay objection reveals how the BPP can also fail to assign moral responsibility to some culpable agents that do have the ability to pay for it. Imagine two states that have the same ability to pay, although one state has acquired its ability through historical non-polluting activities and the other from historical pollution-causing industrialisation. Let us further imagine that the latter state switched over to entirely renewable energy in the relatively recent past, and that none of its current citizens have ever produced any greenhouse gases. According to the BPP, the historically polluting state should bear moral responsibility for mitigating and adapting to climate change because it has benefited from greenhouse gas emitting, while the non-polluting state should bear none. It might be argued that it is fair for citizens of such non-polluting states to bear no responsibility to deal with climate change because they have neither caused nor benefited from it. However, a comparison of these citizens with the citizens of the benefiting state reveals that both are equally innocent of polluting and both enjoy unearned benefits. In both cases, the polluting and non-polluting actions that led to the benefits were beyond the current citizen's influence, so, in both cases, the benefits the current citizens enjoy are unearned. In the same way, neither generation of citizens caused the historic polluting (or non-polluting) that may have led to the current pollution, so they are equally (totally) innocent of causing the pollution. To assign more moral responsibility to the citizens of one state because the benefits that they have *just happen* to have come from historical greenhouse gas emitting instead of some other non-polluting actions is clearly unfair. Why should the citizens of an historically polluting state have to pay more for their unearned benefits when they had an equal (total) lack of ability to affect how those benefits came about?

The PPP and BPP both represent what appear to be important moral considerations for the climate change debate: both polluting and benefiting from polluting create some moral responsibility to deal with the harmful consequences of that polluting. However, we have argued here that the often-neglected ability to pay objection shows us two things. First, although polluters should generally pay, in some circumstances they should *not* have to pay (because they lack sufficient ability to do so). As a result of this, if the PPP were used to explain the principle of CBDR by itself, then the consequent apportionment of moral responsibility to deal with climate change might be unfair. And second, having benefited *from polluting* (as opposed to any other historical actions of our forebears) is not an important moral consideration because the sources of our benefits are generally out of our control. This finding reveals that the plausible moral justification for the BPP – that those who benefit *from polluting* have more responsibility to deal with the resulting pollution – does not reflect our considered judgements about what is really important in deciding who should have to bear the responsibility to deal with climate change.

Our hybrid account

So far, we have argued that none of the three one-dimensional principles of justice discussed in this paper is without major problems of unfairness. The most natural explanation for this is that more than one moral consideration is relevant to the issue of distributing the responsibilities of dealing with climate change. Thus, it is unsurprising that some authors have offered hybrid accounts that reflect what they believe to be the relevant combination of moral considerations for this issue (for example, Caney (2005); Page (2008)).

Our proposed hybrid account combines elements of the APP and CPPP. By combining these principles, our hybrid account fits nicely with the dual rationale behind the principle of CBDR. Specifically, it matches the only two reasons given in the principle of CBDR for why developed states should bear the lion's share of the responsibility to deal with climate change: developed states put greater pressure on the environment and they possess greater technological and financial abilities to facilitate the mitigation of and adaptation to rapid climate change. Our account bears similarities to that of Caney (2005), but it differs in specific details and, more importantly, it is justified differently. In contrast to Caney's rights-based approach, we use the distributive principle of sufficientarianism as the underlying moral justification for our inclusion of both the APP and CPPP. We consider the main potential problem of rapid climate change to be the increased numbers of people who will lead miserable lives as a result. Bearing this in mind, our hybrid account appeals to the APP to ensure those who already lack a minimally decent quality of life are not put under more pressure. For similar reasons, our hybrid account appeals to the CPPP to encourage much lower levels of emissions and, thereby, decrease the chances of catastrophic climactic changes that would plunge even more people into desperate poverty.

It is important to us that our hybrid account be useful to policy makers. Specifically, it should be useful as an aid to the fair assignment of responsibilities in current and possible future situations for both developed and developing states. To do this, first, the moral agents to which our hybrid account applies need to be states. Although applying the hybrid account directly to individuals is theoretically unproblematic, it suffers from obvious practical problems. Suffice it to say that arriving at a global agreement on climate change is difficult enough when the negotiators are hundreds of states, let alone billions of individuals.

Given that the relevant moral agents are states, we propose the following process for allocating the responsibilities of dealing with climate change. First, assess which states have the ability to pay. We propose that there should be three broad categories of ability to pay (no ability to pay, clear ability to pay, and unclear ability to pay) each of which corresponds to a state's ability to provide a minimally decent quality of life for its current citizens. States with no ability to pay should not be assigned any moral responsibility to deal with climate change because of their overriding responsibility to raise the standard of living of their own citizens to a sufficient level. States that have a clear ability to pay should have to pay for their own greenhouse gas emissions above their quota and their share of any remaining costs (based on how many other states are in this category and how much they exceed the lower limit of the band). States that have an unclear ability to pay should have to pay for their own greenhouse gas emissions above their quota, but they should not have to help the rich states pay to deal with any outstanding pollution. We propose that 4,000 international dollars of gross domestic product (purchasing power parity) per capita (GDP-PPP-PC) should be the upper limit of the no ability to pay band and 8,000 international dollars of GDP-PPP-PC should be the lower limit of the clear ability to pay category.[14] States with an unclear ability to pay would be those with 4,000–8,000 international dollars of GDP-PPP-PC. For perspective, in 2009, the United States's GDP-PPP-PC was 46,433 international dollars, China's was 6,546 international dollars, and India's was 2,932 international dollars (India's projected GDP-PPP-PC for 2014 is 4,285 international dollars).[15] Although we have set these thresholds according to what we believe roughly corresponds to what it takes to provide a minimally decent quality of life, a complete justification of these suggested figures would require much more research than is available and is certainly beyond the scope of this chapter.

After assessing which states have the ability to pay, the amount of existing pollution that has been 'culpably caused' (that is, caused after 1992) by each state with a 'clear' or an 'unclear' ability to pay should be gauged. Any agent with the ability to pay for dealing with the pollution it has caused must do so in full. Any remaining pollution that needs to be dealt with must have been created by past generations, the currently very poor, or rogue non-complying states. Since neither the dead people nor the poor states have the ability to pay for dealing with this pollution and the rogue states refuse to pay, the question arises of who should have to pay for it.

It might be suggested that no one should have the moral responsibility to pay for the outstanding pollution. However, if the precautionary principle and the right to development principle from the Rio Declaration on Environment and

---

14   The international dollar is a hypothetical currency that has purchasing power equivalent to the US dollar at a particular time. A state's purchasing power parity–adjusted annual gross domestic product is a measure of how many standardised baskets of goods that state could afford to buy at domestic prices if its total production output for the year were in money. Indexing this measure to international dollars allows for rough but meaningful across-state and across-time comparisons of how well a state can provide the basics of life.

15   These figures are from IMF (2009).

Development are adopted,[16] it must be concluded that someone has to pay for the outstanding pollution to avoid the risk of an environmental catastrophe that could have devastating effects for billions of future people. Assuming, then, that someone should bear the responsibility to pay for dealing with the outstanding pollution, a fair method for deciding *who* those bearers should be is required. Appealing once again to the idea of sufficientarianism, and more specifically to the idea that states that have fulfilled their responsibility to raise their own citizens' welfare to an acceptable standard then have a responsibility to ensure that all people (including future people) can reach this level of welfare, the distribution should be on an ability to pay basis. Therefore, after those who can pay for the costs of their own polluting have done so, the remaining costs should be distributed between those who can afford to pay them (states with a 'clear' ability to pay) and apportioned based on each state's degree of ability to pay. These costs should include the cost of creating institutions to encourage and, if necessary, enforce compliance of rogue states, as Caney (2005) recommends. This method of distribution is the fairest because any other method would result in the possibility of the governments of the worst-off states in the world having to forego their primary moral concern (their citizens' welfare) for the sake of generally much wealthier people elsewhere and in the future (the ability to pay objection from above).

In practical terms, our hybrid account results in the rich states paying for their own polluting and then sharing the costs associated with both the minor amounts of polluting caused by rogue states and very poor states and the historic pollution that was unknowingly caused by previous generations. Our sufficiency-based account gives primacy to the APP over the CPPP. This results in our hybrid account deeming it morally permissible for undeveloped and developing states to knowingly pollute, but only if that pollution is likely to result in higher well-being for their citizens. Because undeveloped countries can justifiably prioritise meeting the basic needs of their citizens over the less urgent needs of future people, they can knowingly pollute on our account without incurring the moral responsibility to deal with that pollution.

If we contrast our hybrid account of APP and CPPP with those that prioritise CPPP over APP, the main difference between them is that our hybrid account goes further to eliminate radical inequalities in the essentials of life between the very rich and the very poor. On the CPPP-prioritised hybrid account, very poor states do not get to fast-track themselves to a minimally good quality

---

16 Principle 15 of the Rio Declaration on Environment and Development states, 'In order to protect the environment, the precautionary approach shall be widely applied by States according to their capabilities. Where there are threats of serious or irreversible damage, lack of full scientific certainty shall not be used as a reason for postponing cost-effective measures to prevent environmental degradation'. Principle 3 states: 'The right to development must be fulfilled so as to equitably meet developmental and environmental needs of present and future generations' (UNFCCC 1992).

of life for their citizens through rapid industrialisation because that would entail polluting above their per capita quota for a time. Therefore, the CPPP-prioritised hybrid account goes against Principle 5 of the Rio Declaration on Environment and Development, which encapsulates the global agreement to try to eradicate poverty.[17] More importantly, though, denying poor states the benefits of rapid industrialisation is unfair because it robs their citizens of their chance to catch up with citizens of developed states (which were not prevented from industrialising in the past). Without the chance to rapidly industrialise, undeveloped states will remain economically insignificant and continue to be forced to draw the short straw on international trade agreements.

Furthermore, if our hybrid account is enacted, then developed states should help developing and undeveloped states adapt and develop so that they can meet the basic needs of their citizens without polluting. On our hybrid account, the wealthiest countries have the responsibility for dealing with all outstanding emissions, such as those created by states without the ability to provide a minimally good life for their citizens. Therefore, it is in their best interest to ensure that they fulfil that responsibility by giving enough technology and training to developing countries to provide a strong incentive for them to industrialise in a way that creates minimal greenhouse gas emissions. This plausible way to fulfil the moral responsibility to deal with historical emissions will help to ensure that very poor countries still get the welfare benefits of industrialisation and that few if any extra problems are created for future people.

Dealing with some potential objections

As discussed above, an implication of our hybrid account is that a very poor country could emit greenhouse gases above its per capita allowance and incur no moral responsibility to deal with the effects of that emitting. Shue (1999, p. 533) warns that, 'If whoever makes a mess receives the benefits and does not pay the costs, not only does he have no incentive to avoid making as many messes as he likes, but he is also unfair to whoever does pay the costs'. On the first point, our hybrid account allows poor states to make a mess only if it increases the well-being of their citizens. Furthermore, it encourages rich states to incentivise

---

17 Principle 5 of the Rio Declaration on Environment and Development states, 'All States and all people shall cooperate in the essential task of eradicating poverty as an indispensable requirement for sustainable development, in order to decrease the disparities in standards of living and better meet the needs of the majority of the people of the world'. However, Principle 2 would endorse a CPPP–APP hybrid account that prioritises CPPP over our account. Principle 2 states, 'States have, in accordance with the Charter of the United Nations and the principles of international law, the sovereign right to exploit their own resources pursuant to their own environmental and developmental policies, and the responsibility to ensure that activities within their jurisdiction or control do not cause damage to the environment of other States or of areas beyond the limits of national jurisdiction' (UNFCCC 1992).

low pollution-causing industrialisation for the poor states through technology transfer. The stipulation that poor states are permitted to emit greenhouse gases over the per capita limit only if no other means is available to increase their well-being for a similar cost could be added to enhance both of these points. Most importantly, poor states are permitted to pollute without incurring the responsibility to pay for the resulting damage only for a limited time (until they can provide a minimally good life for their citizens). On the second point, in the situations when the rich pay for the pollution of the very poor they do so (and do so *fairly*) because of their moral responsibility to the people of the world who do not have access to the basics for a minimally good life. This responsibility arises because the ability to secure the goods of a minimally decent life for ourselves and for others, which the citizens of rich states have, is mainly a product of chance, not deservedness. Moreover, these inequalities have been preserved and exacerbated to the further detriment of people who happen to be born into very poor countries.

Also mentioned above, Page (2008) has criticised the use of 1992 as the year after which states should have known that greenhouse gas emissions over a certain level create standing harms. According to Page (2008, p. 570), using 1992 results in 'harsh treatment for the newly industrialised populations and lax treatment of those residing in countries of transition'. Although this creates a problem for the PPP by itself, it is not a problem for our hybrid account. On our hybrid account, newly industrialised states are likely to have a low degree of ability to pay compared with states that industrialised over 100 years ago, so they will only have the responsibility to pay for a fraction of what the more established developed states have to pay. Furthermore, if a newly industrialised state happens to be as wealthy as the states that industrialised long ago, then they *should* have to pay as much as the more established states because they are all lucky enough to enjoy the benefits of wealth that came to them through the actions of previous generations (which were completely outside of their control).

As for the states in transition (those that are very close to the upper limit of not having the ability to pay), our hybrid account makes it morally permissible for them to pollute in order to complete the transition. However, they will incur the moral responsibility to pay for dealing with their own pollution as soon as they reach the threshold of sufficiency (when they will have an 'unclear' ability to pay – at 4,000 international dollars of GDP-PPP-PC). With this in mind, states in transition would be better off accepting technological assistance from developed states so they can complete the transition in a low pollution-causing manner and not have to undergo a comprehensive energy-production transition when they achieve the level of production that allows them to provide a minimally good quality of life for their citizens. Therefore, on our hybrid account, states in transition and very poor states are assigned less responsibility than developed states, because this distribution of responsibilities will help to reduce the most important inequalities between states, namely, the unequal distribution of the basic goods for a minimally decent life.

Conclusion

In this chapter, we have argued that a hybrid of the APP and the CPPP offers the best way of interpreting the principle of CBDR. More specifically, this hybrid provides the fairest guidance for sharing the responsibilities of dealing with climate change. Although our account bears interesting similarities to others in the literature, it is distinctive in prioritising the APP over the CPPP. This prioritisation stems from a distinctive rationale as to why the hybrid account on offer here should be preferred over each of the individual principles that have been discussed in the literature. We have argued that the most important moral consideration in the debate over climate change is that each government's primary responsibility is to raise its own citizens' welfare to a sufficient level for them to have a minimally good quality of life. The most important practical implication of our hybrid account is that undeveloped and developing states can continue to pollute without incurring any moral responsibility to deal with the effects of that pollution, as that polluting is the best way to achieve the agreed upon level of welfare for their citizens. This result is grounded in the conviction that the fundamental purpose of the current climate change debate is and should be to ensure that a minimally acceptable level of welfare is and will continue to be attainable for all people.

References

Baer, P., T. Athanasiou, and S. Kartha. 2007. *The Right to Development in a Climate Constrained World: The Greenhouse Development Rights Framework*. Berlin: Heinrich Böll Foundation.

Caney, S. 2005. 'Cosmopolitan justice, responsibility, and global climate change.' *Leiden Journal of International Law* 18: 747–75.

Casal, P. 2007. 'Why sufficiency is not enough.' *Ethics* 117(2): 296–326.

Claussen, E., and L. McNeilly. 1998. *Equity and Global Climate Change: The complex elements of global fairness*. Arlington, VA: PEW Center for Global Climate Change.

Crisp, R. 2003. 'Equality, priority, and compassion.' *Ethics* 113(4): 745–63.

Frankfurt, H. 1987. 'Equality as a moral ideal.' *Ethics* 98(1): 21–43.

Gardiner, S. M. 2004. 'Ethics and global climate change.' *Ethics* 114(3): 555–600.

IPCC (Intergovernmental Panel on Climate Change). 2007. *Climate Change 2007: The Physical Science Basis. Contribution of Working Group I to the Fourth Assessment Report of the Intergovernmental Panel on Climate Change.* Cambridge, UK: Cambridge University Press.

IMF. 2009. *World Economic Outlook, October 2009: Sustaining the recovery.* Washington, DC: International Monetary Fund. www.imf.org/external/pubs/cat/longres.cfm?sk=22576.0 (accessed April 2010).

Nagel, T. 1977. 'Poverty and food: Why charity is not enough.' In P. Brown and H. Shue (eds). *Food Policy: The responsibility of the United States in the life and death choices.* New York: Free Press, pp. 54–62.

Neumayer, E. 2000. 'In defence of historical accountability for greenhouse gas emissions.' *Ecological Economics* 33: 185–92.

Page, E. 1999. 'Intergenerational justice and climate change.' *Political Studies* 47: 53–66.

Page, E. 2007. 'Justice between generations: Investigating a sufficientarianism approach.' *Journal of Global Ethics* 3(1): 3–20.

Page, E. 2008. 'Distributing the burdens of climate change.' *Environmental Politics* 17(4): 556–75.

Shue, H. 1992. 'The unavoidability of justice.' In A. Hurrell and B. Kingsbury (eds). *The International Politics of the Environment.* Oxford: Oxford University Press, pp. 373–97.

Shue, H. 1999. 'Global environment and international inequality.' *International Affairs* 75(3): 531–45.

Singer, P. 2008. 'One atmosphere.' In T. Brooks (ed.). *The Global Justice Reader.* Oxford: Blackwell, pp. 667–88. (First published in P. Singer. 2002. *One World: The ethics of globalization.* New Haven: Yale University Press, pp. 14–50, 205–8.)

UN (United Nations) Department of Public Information. 1997. *UN Conference on Environment and Development (1992).* www.un.org/geninfo/bp/enviro.html (last revised 23 May 1997; accessed February 2010).

UNFCCC. 1992. *Report of the United Nations Conference on Environment and Development*. United Nations Framework Convention on Climate Change. A/CONF.151/26 (Vol. 1). www.poptel.org.uk/nssd/otherdocuments/Agenda21.doc (accessed February 2010).

UNFCCC. n. d. *List of Annex I Parties to the Convention*. United Nations Framework Convention on Climate Change. http://unfccc.int/parties_and_observers/parties/annex_i/items/2774.php (accessed February 2010).

9. Virtue and the commons

Xavier Márquez

Introduction

Many environmental problems have the familiar structure of the dilemmas of the commons (Gardner et al. 1990), where any given individual may have reason to act in ways that result in the group being collectively worse off when everyone else acts in similar ways, so that recognisably suboptimal outcomes are produced for all if each person acts in accord with their 'private' reasons.[1] The climate change problem (Gardiner 2001, 2004), the problems caused by rapid population growth (Hardin 1968), the problems of sustaining fisheries (Ludwig et al. 1993), some problems of agricultural and forest land use, and many other environmental problems have all been argued to have this structure (see also the examples discussed and literature cited in Gardner et al. 1990).[2]

At the same time, the broad outlines of any solutions to these dilemmas are well known. Three kinds of solutions are possible. We might call the first kind, following Hardin (1968), *technical* solutions. Here the dilemma is resolved by directly mitigating the harm done by the behaviour, without changing the motivational structure that gave rise to the harm-producing behaviour in the first place. If we take global climate change as our example of a commons dilemma, 'geoengineering' or carbon sequestration schemes fall into this category; if the problem is the depletion of commonly owned aquifers, the construction of desalination plants would be a technical solution.

The second kind of solution comprises what we might call *external* approaches. These approaches attempt to resolve the dilemma by changing the external incentives to which the agents respond, for instance by creating institutions that reliably provide either external sanctions for 'egoistic' behaviour or positive

---

1   An earlier version of this chapter was presented at the Ethical Foundations of Public Policy conference and at the Victoria University of Wellington Philosophy Programme research seminar. The final version benefited from comments by participants in both places. Thanks also to Ben Thirkell-White for useful comments on an earlier draft and to Marcus Frean for a stimulating discussion on the subject.

2   As Elinor Ostrom and her collaborators have noted (Gardner et al. 1990), however, not all common resource situations are commons dilemmas. Some problems that *appear* to have the structure of the commons dilemma may be best described in some other way; see, for example, Gardiner's criticism of Hardin's depiction of the 'population problem' (Gardiner 2001).

rewards for 'cooperative' behaviour.[3] The private reasons people might have to act in destructive ways are not changed, however; individuals are merely given potentially overriding reasons to act in a different way, so that if the institutions in question cease to operate, the individuals previously restrained by them may resume their previous (destructive) behaviour. Carbon taxes or cap-and-trade schemes fall into this category, as well as a wide variety of informal schemes that sanction some behaviours or incentivise others through social and peer pressure in different common resource situations.

Finally, the third category of solutions to commons dilemmas attempts to change the *internal* motivations of individuals so that they no longer engage in behaviour that is destructive of a commons, even in the absence of external sanctions or incentives. To use a relatively old-fashioned term, these approaches attempt to make the individuals *virtuous* rather than merely to discipline them. Any actions (for example, appeals to fair play or exemplary behaviour) or institutions whose aim (or one of whose aims) is to educate or build 'character' fall into this category.

These broad approaches are not necessarily independent of one another, and indeed one main purpose of this chapter is to explore how these approaches interact with one another. The other main purpose of this chapter is to examine the limits and possibilities of the *internal* approach to solving commons dilemmas, which a growing number of people, dissatisfied with external and technical approaches to these problems, have begun to promote. One needs more than incentives and sanctions or technical solutions, the claim goes; one needs a transformation of character, so that people are less likely to act in ways that harm the global commons to begin with; one needs a new ethical consciousness and new 'virtues' (Orr 2004; Barry 1999; Sandler 2007). Recent discussions about so-called 'environmental citizenship' or 'ecological citizenship' (Bell 2005; Dobson and Bell 2006; Hailwood 2005; Humphreys 2009; Mason 2009; Valencia Sáiz 2005; Barry 2006) also argue along similar lines that solutions to environmental commons dilemmas require specific forms of character, even if they do not always use the language of virtue. Here, the terminology of 'citizenship,' which denotes some bundle of rights and obligations possessed by the members of some community, is often paired, implicitly or explicitly, with a conception of the 'virtues' that articulate the appropriate dispositions and attitudes that the individual men and women who bear those rights and responsibilities should acquire. A common thread running through these discussions is that we can create political institutions that not only discipline our wayward (current)

3   These sanctions or incentives need not always be provided by external actors (for example, the state) in order to work, contrary to the 'Hobbesian' ideas of Hardin (1968) and Olson (1971); as Ostrom (2000, 1990) has argued over the years, communities can often develop rules and customary institutions that are quite capable of producing cooperation without the intervention of external agents. But the kinds of rules that Ostrom has described still represent a set of *external* incentives to behaviour in the sense described above.

dispositions (as corrupted and self-interested consumers, for example) but also (and more importantly) *educate* us and *transform* us into virtuous citizens. Instead of a politics that merely manages the deleterious effects on a particular commons of our (culturally created) dispositions, the rhetoric of virtue and citizenship strives for a politics that makes us *better* people, that is, more able to surmount our commons dilemmas without the constant use of explicit sanctions or incentives.

In this chapter, I suggest that the virtue–ethical approach to such problems, though not without merit, has important limitations. I begin by examining the meaning of 'virtue' in the context of commons dilemmas, and argue that we must understand such virtue as more than simply a disposition to restrain one's use of a common resource. The 'virtues' appropriate to commons dilemma situations are dispositions to *actively* contribute to the solution of the commons dilemma.

But, as I argue, there are two kinds of virtue, which I call 'robust' and 'conditional'. 'Robust' virtues are dispositions to contribute to the solution of the collective action problems presented by commons dilemmas that operate across a wide range of such dilemmas. On the other hand, 'conditional' virtues are dispositions to contribute to the solution of such dilemmas only under specific conditions, such as the fraction of other conditionally virtuous users of the common resource or the costs of contributing to the solution. Empirical evidence suggests that 'robust' virtues are rare, so cannot be relied on to solve the many commons dilemmas we confront today.

While conditional virtue is more common, I show that its 'supply' is an endogenous effect of the potential solutions to the commons dilemma that virtuous agents may promote. Moreover, since different potential solutions have opposed effects on this supply, virtuous agents must evaluate trade-offs between solutions that can deal with urgent commons dilemmas (which may over time decrease the supply of virtue) and solutions that increase the long-term supply of more robust virtue (which tend to be slow and unreliable).

Given plausible epistemic constraints on virtuous agents, this means that even virtuous agents will face severe collective action problems in deciding how to best contribute to a 'difficult' collective action problem (such as the problem of global climate change). This argument suggests there are sharp limits to any reliance on the inculcation of virtue for a solution to large-scale dilemmas of the commons. What virtue demands is not necessarily *more* virtue but more intelligent investment in various potential solutions to these dilemmas, including technical and external solutions.

Virtue in the context of commons dilemmas

The word 'virtue' has many meanings, not all of which are relevant to questions about the dilemmas of the commons. Moreover, as with any significant term in moral philosophy, the term is subject to a great deal of controversy. But we do not go far wrong if we define a virtue as a relatively stable affective and deliberative *disposition* or *character trait* (that is, an identifiable and consistent pattern of affective and deliberative responses to similar situations) that gives an agent *good reasons* to perform actions that systematically promote good ends in a variety of contexts. What is considered a good end (for example, the agent's natural flourishing) determines what counts as a good reason. A virtuous person is thus more *sensitive* or *practically responsive* to certain kinds of reasons for action than is a non-virtuous person, in the sense that a virtuous person will find certain kinds of (good-promoting) reasons more likely to motivate them to action than to motivate a non-virtuous person, and will be more likely to find such reasons *salient* in any given situation. A classic example is the virtue of courage. The courageous person, in contrast to the non-courageous person, has less sensitivity to *the potential for bodily harm* as a reason not to do something, and more sensitivity to *protecting the community* as a reason to do the same.[4]

Virtues thus have both 'cognitive' and 'affective' components that combine to enable an agent to 'respond appropriately' to a situation (Kamtekar 2004, p. 477), where 'appropriately' has a broad ethical meaning. Conversely, character traits are to be called virtues if by making the agent appropriately sensitive to certain kinds of reasons to perform actions in a variety of contexts, they systematically promote good ends (Sandler 2007; Driver 2001; Hursthouse 2001). We leave aside here the problem of the precise nature of those ends in general (for example, whether these ends are always agent-relative or should include 'noneudamonistic' ends). We simply assume that in any account of virtue character traits that systematically promote such ends can be called virtues, precisely in virtue of the fact that possessing a virtue makes a person sensitive to good reasons for acting.

From this point of view, a 'virtue' in the context of a commons dilemma can be defined as a stable character trait that provides an agent with good reasons to act in ways that systematically preserve the resource held in common. However, though such virtues will usually include such traditional traits as self-restraint or moderation (using only those resources that are sufficient for one's real needs) and justice (giving each what is due to them, and taking only what one is due), they cannot be restricted to them. In particular, given the structure of a typical

---

4 At the extreme, a virtuous person would be perfectly sensitive to *good* reasons for action (whatever those may be) and perfectly insensitive to *bad* reasons for action (whatever those may be). In this sense, virtue is a kind of knowledge, as in the Socratic formulation.

commons dilemma, mere self-restraint is often impotent to preserve a resource; the common resource is preserved only if others do the same. But the virtuous person would not be satisfied with restraining their consumption of a resource in the face of general indifference if they knew that more could be done to preserve the resource; in fact, the virtuous person would actively seek to *foster cooperation* (very broadly speaking) with others so as to preserve it. Mere self-restraint would seem to be *part* of what it means to have a virtuous disposition with respect to the commons, but not the whole of it. Thus, if a virtue in the context of a commons dilemma is a disposition to contribute (broadly speaking) to the solution of the commons dilemma, then a virtuous person should *invest resources* in finding and promoting the adoption of a solution to the dilemma. Hence, a virtuous person would decide whether they should support and promote a technical, an incentive-based, or an educational solution to the problem. In other words, the virtuous person is an *activist*; they are sensitive to reasons to act in ways that promote the solution of the dilemma, ways that will normally go beyond mere self-restraint on their part.

Robust and conditional virtues

It is also important to avoid understanding virtue as a sensitivity to reasons to cooperate in commons dilemmas that is *independent* of context. Virtue theorists assume, plausibly, that virtues can be produced, with greater or lesser reliability, through either intentional educational processes or as a by-product of other interactions (for example, formal schooling, participation in democratic institutions, or the other usual forms of socialisation). They also, less plausibly, tend to assume that these habits of character are not narrowly tailored to specific contexts (that is, are not merely 'local character traits') but are capable of furthering good ends in a variety of such contexts (that is, are 'global character traits', stable across multiple contexts). On this view, a virtuous person is not only sensitive to reasons for cooperation in some particular subset of commons dilemmas, but is well disposed to perform such actions in most of them, so long as such actions are not otherwise impossible or incoherent from the point of view of the person's ultimate goals or values. But it is an open question whether such character traits *can* exist (Kamtekar 2004; Doris 2002; Appiah 2008; Annas 2005; Arpaly 2005; Solomon 2005); people who perform virtuous actions in some contexts may not perform virtuous actions in other contexts that differ only in trivial respects. More to the point, people who are well disposed to cooperation in some commons dilemmas may not be well disposed to cooperate in trivially different situations. Indeed, research on cooperation in the commons shows that such cooperation, though much more easily achieved in some contexts than a standard rational choice model would lead us to expect, can just as easily be disrupted by relatively minor changes in incentives or beliefs (Camerer and Fehr 2006; Ostrom et al. 1999; Bicchieri 2008). Population growth, the introduction of new technologies, changes in sanctioning opportunities, framing effects that indicate which norm is operative, an inability to identify with other common resource users, all appear to easily turn responsible users of the resource into irresponsible ones, and 'virtuous' people into 'selfish' agents. This suggests that whatever character traits may underlie cooperation in commons dilemmas (or in general), they tend not to be 'robust' or 'global' but rather situation-specific. In other words, they are not 'virtues' in the strong sense of the term prominent in the work of some virtue ethicists (for example, Hursthouse 2001). Sensitivity to the right reasons for acting or not acting is *conditional*, not *global*, and *fragile*, not *robust*.

This 'situationist' challenge to virtue ethics (Harman 2009; Doris 2002) should be taken seriously, for it suggests that no solution to commons dilemmas can rely on the inculcation of 'global' virtues, be they green or otherwise; human beings do not appear to be well suited to the development of such 'robust' virtues. But this does not mean we cannot speak of virtue at all, or that the notion of virtue is useless for thinking about the solution of commons dilemmas. Instead, we should distinguish between the ethical ideal of 'robust' virtue, representing a (perhaps empirically impossible) consistent disposition to reason, feel, and act in ways that contribute to the solution of commons dilemmas *generally*, and more or less conditional virtues, representing dispositions to act in ways that promote the solution of *some* commons dilemmas in *some* circumstances. The virtues that are normally found among human beings are of the second kind, that is, they are 'conditional' or 'relative' virtues, which may of course be more or less robust (that is, they may approach the ideal for some individuals and some range of situations). Individuals may still look to the ideal of robust virtue as something that they should strive for even if they cannot quite achieve it, but we do not need to assume the possibility or actual existence of fully robust virtue in order to talk meaningfully about the many relatively virtuous dispositions that can be instilled in people with greater or lesser degrees of reliability.

On the other hand, we also need to be able to distinguish between actual virtue and the mere conditional willingness to cooperate that large numbers of people display in a wide variety of settings. As research on cooperation in the commons has shown, many people (somewhere between 40 per cent and 70 per cent of experimental subjects, with some variation due to cultural differences, learning, and the specific stakes involved) are 'conditional cooperators'. That is, they are disposed to cooperate (restrain their use of resources, contribute to the production of a common good, and so forth) even in the absence of purely external incentives (for example, in one-shot prisoner's dilemma or ultimatum games) but only if they understand well the consequences of general non-cooperation and estimate that enough others will cooperate as well (Camerer and Fehr 2006; Henrich et al. 2001; Ostrom 2000; Chuah et al. 2009; Dawes 1980; Roth et al. 1991; Kurzban and Houser 2005; Fischbacher et al. 2001). The mere presence of conditional cooperators is not enough to induce high levels of cooperation (indeed, it is compatible with very *low* levels of cooperation, if self-regarding individuals trigger a cascade of non-cooperation). However, high levels of cooperation can be sustained in experimental settings if subjects are given the opportunity to communicate and sometimes 'punish' non-cooperators even at some cost to themselves, an opportunity that some fraction of conditional cooperators usually take (Camerer and Fehr 2006; Ostrom et al. 1992; Bicchieri 2008). These altruistic punishers (or 'strong reciprocators'), that is, people who are willing to expend some of their own resources in sustaining cooperation, are essential to the maintenance of high levels of cooperation.

Yet though such 'altruistic punishers' display some of the features of virtuous individuals, it is clear that such people are not necessarily virtuous, even in the 'conditional' sense discussed above.[5] Altruistic punishers are not (always) appropriately sensitive to the effects of their actions on actual levels of cooperation, and they do not (always) adequately consider whether means other than punishment would sustain cooperation. A virtuous person, by contrast, is characterised by a sensitivity to reasons for punishing others when punishment is appropriate, or to invest resources in other potential solutions to the commons dilemma when other solutions are appropriate. Therefore, the virtuous person would be able to support or promote, when appropriate, not just schemes to discipline non-cooperators, but also schemes to mitigate the harm of non-cooperation or to increase the number of virtuous individuals. Virtue would involve here both a *motivational* component, disposing the virtuous individual to *want* to achieve collectively optimal outcomes and to react appropriately in emotional terms to the failure of cooperation (a component that is present among altruistic punishers), and an *epistemic* component, indicating that the virtuous individual has better than average understanding of *which* means can best resolve the common resource dilemma in question.

Investments in cooperation and the supply of virtue

But which means can best resolve commons dilemmas? As mentioned above, there are only three generic kinds of solutions to these dilemmas: technical,

---

5   Such a character trait can be likened to the 'natural virtue' that Aristotle opposes to genuine virtue on the grounds that the former is a mere tendency, uninformed by practical reason to a significant degree (*Nicomachean Ethics* 1144b5-22); see Kamtekar (2004, p. 480).

external (incentive schemes), and internal (educational interventions). Virtuous agents will have reason to invest resources in developing or promoting one or more of them, according to their social position, their personal resources, and their individual judgements of the relative feasibility of the particular options on the table. Virtuous agents may agitate for particular technical solutions or incentive schemes (for example, a particular legal regime or a particular irrigation technology) or directly provide incentives to others to engage in particular sorts of behaviour (for example, they may punish others for violating rules in small-scale settings). They may engage in 'exemplary' behaviour in the hopes that others may imitate them (for example, they may engage in conspicuous non-consumption or conspicuous recycling). They may promote the creation of certain institutions in the hopes that they will build certain kinds of character (for example, they may promote certain kinds of participative institutions). They may 'raise awareness' (providing information to others). From a *static* perspective, virtuous agents do not have an *a priori* reason to prefer one of these types of solutions to the others (for example, to prefer 'punishment' to 'education' or to the technical amelioration of the problem), since the effect of any of them is, considered in isolation (and assuming equal effectiveness), equivalent: a collective good is produced or a commons is preserved. In economic language, they are perfect 'substitutes' for each other. But because human virtue is not robust, each potential solution has different effects on the fraction of (conditionally) virtuous agents in the population (the 'supply' of virtue), at least relative to the particular commons dilemma in question, and these potential effects need to be considered by virtuous agents when deciding how best to respond to a commons dilemma. Let us examine this matter in more detail.

Technical solutions

Technical solutions have the effect of decreasing the collective costs of non-cooperation in a particular commons dilemma. For example, assume for the moment that there existed some technical solution to a commons dilemma: some geoengineering scheme for global warming, such as the (still fictional) 'carbon-eating super-trees' that Freeman Dyson has promoted (Dyson 2008), or some form of renewable, carbon-neutral, and cheap energy. Moreover, assume that such a scheme were generally effective and cheaper to implement than taxing carbon. The presence of this technology would make collective 'defection' (that is, continued used of fossil fuels at current levels) less costly than otherwise, and thus would make it possible to solve the problem by means of the same motivations that gave rise to it in the first place. For a more realistic example, we might point to the spread of technologies of drip irrigation or desalination plants, which might (under some circumstances) mitigate the harm involved in the overexploitation of aquifers in arid lands, allowing users to continue to consume water at levels that would have produced the overexploitation of the resource in the absence of the technology.[6]

The more effective a technical solution, the greater the incentives for non-cooperation regardless of any incentive or sanctioning schemes; indeed, under a sufficiently effective technology, even virtuous agents may 'defect,' since the dilemma may appear to be solved (the force of the reason to refrain for consumption being considerably weakened). Moreover, if virtue is a kind of habit, and thus a matter of *practice*, as virtue theorists have argued since Aristotle, then if an agent lacks consistent opportunity to practice virtue they will (slowly or quickly) lose it, at least for the particular common resource situation in question. Technical solutions will, thus, tend to decrease the existing supply of virtue in a particular commons dilemma through what economists sometimes call 'moral hazard', sometimes to such an extent that their effectiveness as solutions to these dilemmas may be undermined.[7]

A technical solution will also tend to affect negatively the *future* supply of virtue in the particular commons dilemma. For example, if a particular geoengineering scheme (for example, carbon-eating super-trees) mitigated the harm from carbon emissions, then there would be less incentive to *become* the kind of person who is spontaneously willing to adopt a less emissions-intensive lifestyle in the absence of external incentives. Similarly, by breaking the connection between harm and behaviour a technical solution may make it increasingly difficult to tell *what* exactly would constitute virtuous behaviour. In both cases the future supply of virtue decreases.

---

6   We ignore for the moment the possibility that in making defection less costly in some particular commons, a technical solution may create more problems in some other context or at some other time. It is clear, for example, that some geoengineering schemes (such as pumping sulphur into the atmosphere) would likely have bad side effects elsewhere (for example, disrupted rain patterns, a higher risk of fast warming if the scheme were stopped, increased risks of ocean acidification, not to mention various unwelcome political implications). See Rasch et al. (2008) for an overview of research into the possible climate effects of pumping sulphur into the stratosphere, and see Schneider (2008) and Keith (2000) for discussion of its political risks and moral hazard. Similarly, the use of desalination plants might accelerate the destruction of some marine ecosystems or, given their large energy use, contribute to global climate change.

7   For example, the use of biofuels, especially ethanol, in cars was initially conceived as a way to diminish the climate impact of the burning of gasoline, and indeed considered in isolation the burning of ethanol has less of an impact on the climate than the burning of gasoline. But the encouragement of ethanol production through legislative mandate in the United States seems to have induced an increase in land clearing for biofuel purposes, which *increases* the greenhouse gas emissions of ethanol production relative to the burning of gasoline (Searchinger et al. 2008). A (partial) technical solution to the climate problem was thus self-undermining when widely adopted.

Incentive schemes

Incentive schemes, by contrast with technical solutions, increase the benefits of individual cooperation and decrease the individual benefits of non-cooperation, making collective cooperation more likely. These incentives may be provided in a variety of ways: social and peer pressure, sanctions by specific users of the common resource (for example, altruistic punishment), sanctions by non-users of the resource (for example, the state), and explicit property regimes (for example, privatisation). An incentive scheme is not identical with *Leviathan*.

A perfectly efficient incentive scheme would be one that induces everyone (virtuous or not) to cooperate. Though the efficiency of an incentive scheme depends on many factors (for example, the monitoring technology available and material resources) it is worth noting such schemes tend to display 'increasing returns' to virtue, or at least have low virtue and high virtue equilibria. In other words, incentive schemes work better the greater the supply of virtue, since in that case fewer resources will need to be devoted to monitoring and sanctioning defectors. Moreover, such dependence may generate virtuous or vicious loops, where, for example, low-corruption equilibria may tend to induce more 'virtuous' behaviour (given the high costs of non-virtuous behaviour), which may reduce the need to monitor behaviour and sustain trust further. On the other hand, high-corruption equilibria may tend to induce less virtuous behaviour (given the low costs of non-virtuous behaviour), which may further reduce the amount of resources devoted to monitoring and punishing cheaters, leading to even more corruption.

Incentive schemes may have not only 'motivational' effects (affecting the payoffs for cooperation or non-cooperation of everyone, not only the virtuous), but may also have 'epistemic' effects (affecting the ability of the virtuous to do the right thing).[8] Consider the problems a person who wants to minimise their carbon emissions while retaining some of the comforts of civilisation faces today. Should they use paper or plastic bags? Buy frozen or fresh vegetables? Use dishwasher detergent? The 'right' decision under current circumstances here depends on a wide variety of highly controversial and technical judgements about energy use throughout the entire lifecycle of the product (Goleman 2009). But if there existed an incentive scheme that put an appropriate price on carbon, the decision might become straightforward, as the price of the item would already embody the appropriate signal regarding its carbon content. A well-designed incentive scheme, thus, aligns both motivation and information, making non-virtuous action (both intentional and unintentional) *harder* than virtuous action, though of course an ill-designed incentive scheme would do

---

8   I first became aware of this point by reading Matthew Yglesias's popular blog (http://yglesias.thinkprogress.org).

the opposite. Yet this very advantage of incentive schemes may induce a kind of 'epistemic' moral hazard. For example, a price on carbon may make it easier for the virtuous to act properly, but in the absence of appropriate price signals such behaviour may quickly go astray. By 'externalising' epistemic responsibility for the consequences of one's actions certain incentive schemes may make virtuous character *harder* rather than easier to achieve over time, reducing its future supply.

Incentive schemes might affect the supply of virtue in a given commons in two other ways. On the one hand, since virtue is partly a matter of habituation, practice in cooperation, though at first prompted by external incentives or sanctions, may, if sustained for long enough, become internalised.[9] We might call this the *socialisation* mechanism. Evidence from examples of successful management of commons dilemmas in small-scale settings (Gardner et al. 1990; Ostrom et al. 1992) suggests that a certain amount of socialisation is likely to occur when users of a common resource have a large role in designing the rules of their interaction and ample opportunity for communication. Moreover, there is good evidence that people do not like to be 'suckers': they may willingly cooperate in the solution of some commons dilemma only if they are assured (by some impartial mechanism, such as a law) that others will also cooperate. If people have evidence (for example, based on past rates of cooperation) that other people will cooperate, then they will be more sensitive to reasons to cooperate, or, in other words, reasons to cooperate will have more force for them.

On the other hand, a body of psychological literature on motivation (Frey 1994; Camerer and Hogarth 1999) suggests that the offer of external rewards can undermine internalised motivations under some circumstances. Virtuous people may become accustomed to cooperating primarily through external rewards, and so may over time lose their internal motivation (they may become *less* sensitive to the right reasons to cooperate in the absence of the 'external' reasons). Indeed, evidence from examples of failed management of commons dilemmas (also in Gardner et al. 1990) suggests that certain 'external' interventions (by the state, for example) can undermine 'internal' motivation (by shifting 'the locus of control') and lead to higher rates of opportunistic behaviour, especially in the absence of sufficient monitoring (see also Bowles 2008). We might call this the *corruption* mechanism. Whether socialisation or corruption dominates, however, cannot be determined *a priori*, since the net effect will depend on the specific details of the incentive scheme in question.

---

9   See Kuran (1997) who suggests a 'hidden' preference (in this case, the preference for defection, which incentive schemes make it appear as a preference for cooperation) can be transformed over time by social pressure into an internalised norm, that is, a true preference.

Educational interventions

Educational interventions counteract the corrosive effects of both technical solutions and incentive schemes by *directly* (rather than as a side effect) attempting to increase the supply of virtue (or rather, the number of virtuous individuals relative to a particular commons dilemma). We should understand such interventions very broadly. Exemplary behaviour, for example (consider the idea of 'living in truth' in Havel 1992), may enable other people to learn what virtue requires and to produce not only people who cooperate out of shame (that is, increase the number of cooperators) but people whose preferences shift towards cooperation (that is, increase the number of virtuous agents over time). People may become sensitive to the reasons for cooperation *made salient* by such exemplary behaviour. Certain institutions may also have long-term positive effects on the character of their users, and hence their creation would count as a kind of educational intervention. Thus, for example, some people advocate for the expansion of participatory and deliberative democratic institutions for their supposed benefits on the character of participants in them: such people, it is claimed, can take a broader, less selfish view of the problems confronting them and their communities (Warren 1992). That is, their participation in such institutions makes them more sensitive to the right sorts of reasons for action, though it is worth repeating that these benefits may exist only relative to the particular commons managed by those institutions, given the lack of robustness of human virtue.

In general, educational interventions can be usefully divided into interventions affecting the *motivation* of agents (turning some 'selfish' agents into 'cooperative' agents) and interventions affecting the *knowledge* of agents (increasing the availability of information about the right thing to do for individuals who are already motivated to act cooperatively), though of course some may do both at the same time. The second sort of intervention, which includes such activities as raising awareness of a problem and direct teaching about things to do to help, may not increase the proportion of genuinely virtuous individuals in the population, but may, nevertheless, encourage people disposed towards cooperation to do the right thing, so to speak. They may increase (or decrease) the *effectiveness* of virtue through their epistemic effects.

It seems plausible to think that this second sort of educational intervention (whose effects are mainly epistemic) may be generally more effective than the first. People can and do change their behaviour if they encounter new information in an unprejudiced way. However, they are also subject to all sorts of cognitive and other biases (for example, confirmation bias, cognitive dissonance reduction, and wishful thinking) that may lead them to discount information that, according to their own goals and values, may result in costly behaviour changes.[10] Moreover, though direct evidence on this point is scarce, the testimony of history and classical political thought suggest that enduring changes in motivation are difficult to accomplish quickly, intentionally, and on a large scale. Such changes are perhaps possible in the long term, on a small scale, or as unintended consequences of other changes, but may be less likely in the short term, on a large scale, or in a "planned" way. Directly increasing the number of (more or less robustly) virtuous individuals in entire societies, on any reasonable understanding of virtue, seems to be much harder to accomplish than making it easier for the less robustly 'virtuous' individuals to act on their unformed prosocial inclinations or enforcing overt compliance with 'virtuous' behaviour.

For example, direct 'indoctrination' seems not to work to produce virtuous individuals, though it may change some of their beliefs as to what should count as appropriate or inappropriate behaviour. But since virtuous activity is not merely a matter of 'correct' belief, requiring as well correct judgement and motivation, such belief changes may not have any impact on the actual proportion of virtuous individuals. For example, even if individuals come to believe that protecting the environment and acting to prevent anthropogenic climate change is an important thing (as polls suggest they do), this does not mean they will be motivated to invest many resources in solving the problem, especially if they perceive the immediate costs to be large and the benefits uncertain and small. Decades of 'prosocial' indoctrination in many Soviet countries and China seems to have failed rather spectacularly at increasing the supply of virtue relative to typical commons dilemmas. Furthermore, since beliefs induced by indoctrination are sustained merely by 'social proof' (rather than the everyday feedback given by the world for some of our other beliefs) they will at any rate tend to be rather fragile and subject to unexpected and unpredictable changes or intentional manipulation (Kuran 1997).

Even if intentional action by powerful agents (such as the state) can increase the number of relatively virtuous individuals relative to some set of commons dilemmas, this seems to be possible only in small-scale contexts. We find either large-scale cultural change that is not centrally planned (as in the 'civilising process' documented by Norbert Elias (1978)) or intentional cultural change that is only sustained through the creation of sharp exclusion boundaries in relatively small groups (as in many of the successful cases of common resource

---

10   For an overview of some of these biases, see Elster (2007, especially chapters 7, 11–12). For a discussion of how these biases may negatively affect responses to climate change, see Sunstein (2007). It should be noted that *misinformation* may be more destructive of virtuous behaviour than direct attempts to change the internal motivations of prosocial individuals. Many people do want to 'do the right thing,' as the phrase goes, and it may be difficult to convince them to act in ways they see as socially harmful unless the costs of not acting in selfish ways are large or they are ignorant of the consequences of their behaviour.

management documented by Gardner et al. (1990)).[11] The institutions of Sparta reliably produced 'courageous' warriors, and certain isolated communes can perhaps produce environmentally conscious individuals, but these achievements are exceedingly fragile, difficult to replicate, and dependent on the ability of the communities in question to exclude others. Overall, then, we may be justified in thinking that educational interventions have limited effectiveness to shift the balance of virtue in a large-scale society, though they may be more effective in smaller scale societies or over the (very) long term.

We should note that just as incentive schemes may have 'socialisation' effects, educational interventions may also have 'incentive' effects. The example of the educational activities of others may induce some cooperation in some individuals out of shame, conformism, or other mechanisms. Moreover, through the socialisation mechanism such cooperation, if sustained over time, may make some people internalise these cooperative norms. But since the effect is indirect, it will tend to happen slowly and unreliably, and it may be easily reversed.

Limits of virtue

This discussion of the effects on the supply of virtue of the different potential solutions to the commons dilemma should be sufficient to show that virtuous agents face real trade-offs when trying to decide which of these options to invest in to resolve a particular commons dilemma. This is so even before considering the effects of these options in the supply of virtue in other parts of society or the very large epistemic constraints under which they make their decisions. In particular, a virtuous agent may be willing to risk a decline in the supply of virtue if a particular commons dilemma seems especially pressing or alternative solutions especially intractable.

Consider again the example of geoengineering. Though the risks of geoengineering are large, and its 'technical' nature rewards irresponsible behaviour (after all, it seems not to address the 'root causes' of the problem of climate change), it may be that the potential for catastrophe implicit in global climate change and the difficulty of other solutions mean geoengineering proposals should be seriously considered.[12] This is not to say that the virtuous agent will in general look

---

11   It is not entirely clear *how* sharp exclusion boundaries work to increase the supply of virtue. On one understanding, what matters is consciousness of group membership, which makes individuals sensitive to reasons favouring group welfare over individual welfare; on another, what matters is the fact small groups make it easier to coordinate on expectations about operative norms, which makes individuals sensitive to reasons embodied in these particular norms (Bicchieri 2002).

12   For a technical discussion of the potential for catastrophe implicit in global climate change, see Weitzman (2009). Weitzman uses the standard utilitarian assumptions of economic analysis to argue that geoengineering proposals should be considered in any mix of potential solutions, but my point is that even from the point of view of virtue ethics one cannot escape such calculations entirely.

with favour to technical solutions, given their generally negative effects on the supply of virtue, but only that the virtuous agent may not entirely ignore such considerations, even if they remain sceptical.[13]

Effective technical solutions, incentive schemes, and educational interventions in the context of particular commons dilemmas are themselves *public goods* (Gardner et al. 1990), since benefits from their existence accrue to all users of the common resource. Hence, their production presents secondary collective action problems in addition to the primary collective action problem represented by the commons dilemma. This secondary collective action problem may not be of the same order as the primary one (indeed, to the extent that the primary collective action problem is solvable, it may be only because the secondary one is easier to resolve than the primary one), but it, nevertheless, exists as a problem *even for virtuous agents* who are disposed to cooperate. This is so because virtuous agents need to coordinate on beliefs; even if they all want to invest resources in solving the problem, they may not agree *which* solution will best deal with the problem.

To simplify greatly, imagine that the primary commons dilemma has the structure of an N-person prisoner's dilemma. Three solutions are possible: a technical scheme that increases the payoff to mutual defection, an incentive scheme that increases the payoffs to unilateral cooperation and decreases the payoffs to non-cooperation, and an educational intervention that turns some significant proportion of the players into altruists who will cooperate more or less unconditionally. Suppose now that any of these alternatives may be produced only if all virtuous individuals (who form only a fraction of the population) support them, and that all are equally effective and known to be so. Nevertheless, given their effects on the proportion of virtuous individuals over time and their assessments of the urgency of the primary problem, some virtuous agents prefer the technical solution, some the incentive scheme, and some the educational intervention. But if they do not agree on a *single* solution, no solution will be implemented, and the primary collective action problem (the commons dilemma) will not be solved. In game-theoretic terms, the solution of the prisoner's dilemma game depends here on the prior solution of a 'battle of the sexes'–type game (a pure coordination dilemma). Since pure coordination dilemmas are easier to resolve than prisoner's dilemmas (they sometimes have 'internal' solutions, or focal points, that may guide the choice of strategies), such a commons dilemma stands a good chance of being resolved. However, this

---

13 Ideally, the best policy for a virtuous agent from the point of view of the supply of virtue might be an incentive scheme with positive feedbacks from the supply of virtue, combined with an educational strategy. But such a policy might not exist, or it may not be known, or it may work only in the long run.

may not always be the case, especially in the face of significant uncertainties about the effectiveness of particular solutions and large disagreements about the urgency of the particular commons problem.

A more realistic depiction of the secondary collective action problem involved in producing a solution to a commons dilemma would recognise that sometimes partial solutions to commons dilemmas can be partially effective (that is, that unanimity may not be necessary, and full coordination may not be required). However, in general the production of solutions to commons dilemmas will be more effective the easier this secondary collective action problem is to resolve. On the other hand, different solutions to a commons dilemma may present different secondary collective action problems, a consideration that should affect the potential calculus of virtuous individuals wishing to resolve it. For example, one attraction of geoengineering schemes as a solution to global climate change is that they seem to present a far easier to resolve secondary collective action problem than the production of global incentive scheme to regulate carbon, even if this additional ease is purchased at the cost of creating *other* collective action problems elsewhere, in particular problems of governance (Schelling 1996; Barrett 2008; Schneider 2008; Victor 2008).[14]

There are several ready-made ways to resolve these secondary collective action problems to address the primary commons dilemma. In the context of a democratic state, one would expect that when the supply of virtue for some commons dilemma is low (and hence incentive schemes or technical solutions impossible to implement effectively), the virtuous should focus on educational interventions to increase their own number. They should do this until a threshold is reached that allows them to use the usual coordination opportunities provided by ordinary democratic politics to impose a particular incentive scheme that 'solves' the problem. This scheme would then be implemented through the action of a state (which itself may be conceived as an 'already solved' collective action problem for some range of issues).

This is the pattern found in many successful 'social movement' campaigns (Tilly 2006). A long 'education' campaign increases the number of people willing to sacrifice something for the sake of a social benefit, until a point is reached at which the 'virtuous' are numerous enough to impose their preferences on the rest of the population through legal regulation (consider here, for example, the 19th century campaigns against slavery or the 20th century campaigns against smoking). Such a pattern of collective action is more difficult where substantial disagreement exists among the virtuous regarding the appropriate forms of

---

14   It is also not entirely clear that the secondary collective action problems presented by geoengineering schemes really *are* easier to resolve than the secondary collective action problems presented by global incentive schemes.

education (since different forms of education may undercut one another) or where significant uncertainty exists about the problem (which may give rise to contradictory information about it) or where others deliberately attempt to use misinformation to protect their interests (which diminishes the effectiveness of educational interventions). Moreover, depending on how 'robust' such education is and on the specific characteristics of the incentive scheme eventually imposed through legal means, such a scheme may then prove self-reinforcing (through socialisation mechanisms) or it may be undermined in the short or long term, necessitating further campaigns.

Such ready-made solutions to the secondary collective action problems facing the virtuous are not, however, easily available in many large-scale commons dilemmas. The art of the 'virtuous' activist (indeed, the art of politics, if one wants to be grandiose about it) is instead an art of 'bootstrapping' – finding the right 'games' where collective action can be easily organised (for example, where the number of the virtuous is already large or can be easily increased) and using collective action there to affect collective action in other games and at other scales. This is usually not easy, given the complexity of modern societies; and the virtuous should not count on being able to resolve these problems by insisting on long-term educational schemes for the large-scale transformation of character.

References

Annas, J. 2005. 'Comments on John Doris's *Lack of Character.' Philosophy and Phenomenological Research* 71(3): 636–42.

Appiah, A. 2008. *Experiments in Ethics*. Cambridge, MA: Harvard University Press.

Arpaly, N. 2005. 'Comments on *Lack of Character* by John Doris.' *Philosophy and Phenomenological Research* 71(3): 643–7.

Barrett, S. 2008. 'The incredible economics of geoengineering.' *Environmental and Resource Economics* 39(1): 45–54.

Barry, J. 1999. *Rethinking Green Politics: Nature, virtue, and progress*. Thousand Oaks, CA: Sage.

Barry, J. 2006. 'Resistance is fertile: From environmental to sustainability citizenship.' In A. Dobson and D. Bell (eds). *Environmental Citizenship*. Cambridge, MA: MIT Press.

Bell, D. 2005. 'Liberal environmental citizenship.' *Environmental Politics* 14: 179–94.

Bicchieri, C. 2002. 'Covenants without swords: Group identity, norms, and communication in social dilemmas.' *Rationality and Society* 14(2): 192–228.

Bicchieri, C. 2008. 'The fragility of fairness: An experimental investigation on the conditional status of pro-social Norms.' *Nous (Philosophical Issues 18 Interdisciplinary Core Philosophy)* 18: 227–46.

Bowles, S. 2008. 'Policies designed for self-interested citizens may undermine "the moral sentiments": Evidence from economic experiments.' *Science* 320(5883): 1605–9.

Camerer, C. F., and E. Fehr. 2006. 'When does "economic man" dominate social behaviour?' *Science* 311(5757): 47–52.

Camerer, C. F., and R. M. Hogarth. 1999. 'The effects of financial incentives in experiments: A review and capital–labor–production framework.' *Journal of Risk and Uncertainty* 19(1): 7–42.

Chuah, S., R. Hoffmann, M. Jones, et al. 2009. 'An economic anatomy of culture: Attitudes and behaviour in inter- and intra-national ultimatum game experiments.' *Journal of Economic Psychology* 30(5): 732–44.

Dawes, R. M. 1980. 'Social dilemmas.' *Annual Review of Psychology* 31(1): 169–93.

Dobson, A., and D. Bell. 2006. *Environmental Citizenship*. London: MIT Press.

Doris, J. M. 2002. *Lack of Character: Personality and moral behaviour*. New York: Cambridge University Press.

Driver, J. 2001. *Uneasy Virtue*. Cambridge, UK: Cambridge University Press.

Dyson, F. 2008. 'The question of global warming.' *New York Review of Books* 55(10).

Elias, N. 1978. *The Civilizing Process*. 1st American edn. New York: Urizen Books.

Elster, J. 2007. *Explaining Social Behaviour: More nuts and bolts for the social sciences*. Cambridge: Cambridge University Press.

Fischbacher, U, S. Gächter, and E. Fehr. 2001. 'Are people conditionally cooperative? Evidence from a public goods experiment.' *Economics Letters* 71(3): 397–404.

Frey, B. S. 1994. 'How intrinsic motivation is crowded out and in.' *Rationality and Society* 6(3): 334–52.

Gardiner, S. M. 2001. 'The real tragedy of the commons.' *Philosophy and Public Affairs* 30(4): 387–416.

Gardiner, S. M. 2004. 'Ethics and global climate change.' *Ethics* 114(3): 555–600.

Gardner, R., E. Ostrom, and J. M. Walker. 1990. 'The nature of common-pool resource problems.' *Rationality and Society* 2(3): 335–58.

Goleman, D. 2009. *Ecological Intelligence: How knowing the hidden impacts of what we buy can change everything.* New York: Broadway Books.

Hailwood, S. 2005. 'Environmental citizenship as reasonable citizenship.' *Environmental Politics* 14: 195–210.

Hardin, G. 1968. 'The tragedy of the commons.' *Science* 162(3859): 1243–8.

Harman, G. 2009. 'Skepticism about character traits.' *Journal of Ethics* 13(2): 235–42.

Havel, V. 1992. *Open Letters: Selected writings, 1965–1990.* 1st Vintage Books edn. Edited by P. Wilson. New York: Vintage Books.

Henrich, J., R. Boyd, S. Bowles, et al. 2001. 'In search of homo economicus: Behavioural experiments in 15 small-scale societies.' Paper read at 113th Annual Meeting of the American Economic Association, New Orleans, Louisiana, 5–7 January.

Humphreys, D. 2009. 'Environmental and ecological citizenship in civil society.' *International Spectator* 44: 171–83.

Hursthouse, R. 2001. *On Virtue Ethics.* Oxford: Oxford University Press.

Kamtekar, R. 2004. 'Situationism and virtue ethics on the content of our character.' *Ethics* 114(3): 458–91.

Keith, D. W. 2000. 'Geoengineering the climate: History and prospect.' *Annual Review of Energy and the Environment* 25(1): 245–84.

Kuran, T. 1997. *Private Truths, Public Lies: The social consequences of preference falsification.* Cambridge, MA: Harvard University Press.

Kurzban, R., and D. Houser. 2005. 'Experiments investigating cooperative types in humans: A complement to evolutionary theory and simulations.' *Proceedings of the National Academy of Sciences of the United States of America* 102(5): 1803–7.

Ludwig, D., R. Hilborn, and C. Walters. 1993. 'Uncertainty, resource exploitation, and conservation: Lessons from history.' *Science* 260(5104): 17–36.

Mason, A. 2009. 'Environmental obligations and the limits of transnational citizenship.' *Political Studies* 57: 280–97.

Olson, M. 1971. *The Logic of Collective Action: Public goods and the theory of groups.* Rev. edn. New York: Schocken Books.

Orr, D. W. 2004. *Earth in Mind: On education, environment, and the human Prospect.* 10th anniversary edn. Washington, DC: Island Press.

Ostrom, E. 1990. *Governing the Commons: The evolution of institutions for collective action.* Cambridge: Cambridge University Press.

Ostrom, E. 2000. 'Collective action and the evolution of social norms.' *Journal of Economic Perspectives* 14(3): 137–58.

Ostrom, E., J. Burger, C. B. Field, et al. 1999. 'Revisiting the commons: Local lessons, global challenges.' *Science* 284(5412): 278–82.

Ostrom, E., J. Walker, and R. Gardner. 1992. 'Covenants with and without a sword: Self-governance is possible.' *American Political Science Review* 86(2): 404–17.

Rasch, P. J., S. Tilmes, R. P. Turco, et al. 2008. 'An overview of geoengineering of climate using stratospheric sulphate aerosols.' *Philosophical Transactions. Series A, Mathematical, Physical, and Engineering Sciences* 366(1882): 4007–37.

Roth, A. E., V. Prasnikar, M. Okunofujiwara, et al. 1991. 'Bargaining and market behaviour in Jerusalem, Ljubljana, Pittsburgh, and Tokyo: An experimental study.' *American Economic Review* 81(5): 1068–95.

Sandler, R. L. 2007. *Character and Environment: A virtue-oriented approach to environmental ethics.* New York: Columbia University Press.

Schelling, T. C. 1996. 'The economic diplomacy of geoengineering.' *Climatic Change* 33(3): 303–7.

Schneider, S. H. 2008. 'Geoengineering: Could we or should we make it work.' *Philosophical Transactions of the Royal Society* 18(08).

Searchinger, T., R. Heimlich, R. A. Houghton, et al. 2008. 'Use of US croplands for biofuels increases greenhouse gases through emissions from land-use change.' *Science* 319(5867): 1238–40.

Solomon, R. C. 2005. 'What's character got to do with it?' *Philosophy and Phenomenological Research* 71(3): 648–55.

Sunstein, C. R. 2007. 'On the divergent American reactions to terrorism and climate change.' *Columbia Law Review* 107(2): 503–58.

Tilly, C. 2006. *Regimes and Repertoires*. Chicago: University of Chicago Press.

Valencia Sáiz, A. 2005. 'Globalisation, cosmopolitanism and ecological citizenship.' *Environmental Politics* 14: 163–78.

Victor, D. G. 2008. 'On the regulation of geoengineering.' *Oxford Review of Economic Policy* 24(2): 322–36.

Warren, M. 1992. 'Democratic theory and self-transformation.' *American Political Science Review* 86(1): 8–23.

Weitzman, M. L. 2009. 'On modeling and interpreting the economics of catastrophic climate change.' *Review of Economics and Statistics* 91: 1–19.

Part III
Perspectives on ethics and the economy

10. Tackling economic inequality

Andrew Bradstock

Introduction

'Recession takes its toll on wealth of Kiwi rich list' ran a headline in the Business and Money section of the *Otago Daily Times* in July 2009 (Hartley 2009). It was a story unlikely to have pulled at readers' heartstrings, yet it listed how, according to figures compiled by the *National Business Review*, in the preceding 12 months $5.7 billion had been lost from the combined wealth of the 155 entrants on the rich list, a fall from $44.4 billion in 2008 to $38.7 billion for 2009. No one, it seems, managed to escape the ravages of the recession, not even New Zealand's richest person, Graeme Hart, who lost a cool $500 million in that 12-month period (though he remained well clear of the pack with assets in the region of $5.5 billion).

My purpose here is not to debate the rights and wrongs of individuals or families owning vast amounts of money per se – although writing from a theological perspective one could certainly mount an interesting critique using images of camels and eyes of needles, sycamore trees, and perhaps even Abraham's bosom. And no doubt this would be a timely challenge – as if the recession had not provided that already – not to lay up treasures on earth. Rather, I want to explore the implications for a society – in particular, New Zealand society – of such extreme levels of wealth existing alongside very serious levels of poverty. Does the rich–poor gap in New Zealand matter? Should it be a matter of concern if it continues to widen? What consequences does it have for the health and well-being of New Zealand communities? Ought Kiwis to look to their government, not just to reduce poverty, but to tackle inequality? Or is this simply to engage in the politics of envy, to show righteous indignation without achieving anything worthwhile?

After some preliminary ground-clearing I want to look at this question of inequality, first from a theological perspective – because the Bible has much of interest and relevance to say on the topic – and then at some recent research in the field of public health into the social implications of 'unequal' societies. Finally, I want to argue that, in any debate about the economy, the question of inequality should be central. But first, I need to back up my claim that New Zealand has an issue with 'inequality' that should concern us.

Identifying the issue

In their study published in 2009, *The Spirit Level: Why more equal societies almost always do better*, UK academics Richard Wilkinson and Kate Pickett produce data showing, for each of 23 developed countries, how much richer the richest 20 per cent of the population is than the poorest 20 per cent. Way out ahead is Singapore, whose top 20 per cent of citizens are nearly 10 times richer than its poorest 20 per cent, with the United States second with a figure of just over eight times. But New Zealand is tucked in there in sixth place, just behind Australia, the United Kingdom, and Portugal, with a figure of just under seven (Wilkinson and Pickett 2009, p. 17). At the other end are Japan and the four Scandinavian countries with figures around the 'four' mark. Therefore, New Zealand is among the most unequal developed countries in the world – a fact confirmed by a United Nations Development Programme report published in October 2009, the first since former New Zealand prime minister, Helen Clark, was appointed administrator (UNDP 2009). Recent data from the government also confirms New Zealand's record in terms of inequality. *The Social Report* for 2008 published by the Ministry of Social Development, for example, notes that New Zealand has a score of 34 on the Gini coefficient, ranking it 23rd equal (with the United Kingdom) among the 30 OECD countries (MSD 2008, p. 61). (Again, we might note that Denmark and Sweden have the lowest inequality, with scores of 23.) In 2007, Statistics New Zealand noted that the top 10 per cent of wealthy individuals own 51.8 per cent of New Zealand's total net worth while the bottom 50 per cent own 5.2 per cent (Cheung 2007, pp. 7–8).

Inequality in New Zealand rose most sharply between 1982 and 1998 when the mean household equivalent disposable income for the lowest group decile *decreased* 17 per cent, and *rose* for the top income group 36 per cent (Povey 2002, p. 22). This was a period when neoliberal market policies were initiated in New Zealand and when the move to greater inequality was seen by some 'as a badge of distinction' (Gould 2008, p. 36). It was a time when the minister of finance of the day could welcome a report describing how the bottom 80 per cent of income earners had suffered a reduction in income, and the top 5 per cent an increase, as proof that his economic reforms were rewarding those who had worked to up-skill themselves and contribute to the economy (Duncan 2007, pp. 259–60)! In 2009, the median income for wage and salary earners in New Zealand was around $35,000 per year, with the average salary of its 44 top chief executives somewhere above $1 million (which is not high by global standards, although in 2005 it rose 23 per cent while average wages rose 3.1 per cent, which is below the inflation rate). There is even more 'inequality' when income for Māori and Pacific peoples is considered: the average weekly income for Māori is around $200 less than that of European/Pākehā, with Pacific people a further $50 lower.

Let me define precisely the problem I propose to address, because there are many 'types' of inequality and discussions in this area often get bogged down in arguments over definitions. I want to argue two distinct but not unrelated points. First, that the Judaeo-Christian principle that all people are of equal value, because they are created in the divine image, places a responsibility on communities with respect to their social and economic arrangements — specifically, to ensure that none of their members are unable to meet their basic needs in terms of food, shelter, and security. And, second, that there are sound sociological as well as theological reasons for governments consciously to pursue policies aimed, not simply at relieving poverty, but at narrowing the differential between 'rich' and 'poor' in society.

Let me briefly defend theology's 'right' to engage with 'economic' issues, because it might seem an unusual conversation partner at first glance. First, there is the obvious point that people of faith represent a significant minority in society who, in any democracy, would expect to have their views heard along with everybody else. But more than this, the separation of theology and economics is relatively recent, dating, as R. H. Tawney notes, only from the development of capitalism in the 18th and 19th centuries. Until then 'economic thought had been understood as part of a hierarchy of values embracing all human interests and activities, of which the apex was religion' (Gorringe 1994, pp. 31–2).

Theology can bring us 'back to basics', reminding us of the roots of the case for equality and of the capacity of markets both to enhance and destroy 'community'. Theology can also challenge widespread assumptions — for example, that economic science is the 'disinterested pursuit of truth for truth's sake', when in fact it utilises just one account of what it means to be human — *homo economicus* — which holds precisely that a person's life *does* consist in the abundance of things they possess! As the 2009 Reith Lecturer, Michael Sandel, rightly says, how priorities are allocated for spending on health, education, defence, and so on is a moral as well as an economic matter (Sandel 2009). Markets are about values, and theology has something to say about those. Importantly, markets are about relationships, and theology has even more to say about those — as it does about some of the terms economics has borrowed from it such as 'credit' and 'trust'. And it is important to remember that Adam Smith, with whom the free market will ever be associated, was first and foremost a moralist, even if his *The Theory of Moral Sentiments* (1759) is less well known today than his *The Wealth of Nations* (1776). In his much acclaimed recent book *The Ascent of Money*, Niall Ferguson suggests that 'financial markets are like the mirror of mankind, revealing every hour of every working day the way we value ourselves and the resources of the world around us' (Ferguson, 2008, p. 358).

So what contribution might theology make to economic discourse? What can it usefully offer to a debate on economic equality? Let us first survey the Hebrew Scriptures, the books we usually call the Old Testament.[1]

A theological case for equality

A core theme in the Creation narratives in the book of Genesis is that people are endowed with an equality of worth and status by virtue of their being created by God. While all are subject to differences in terms of gender, ethnicity, size, or physical or intellectual ability – to be 'equal' is not to be the 'same', and we are to celebrate our differences – all have an inherent equality through creation. We are all 'a little lower than the angels' as the psalmist puts it, and bear to an equal extent the 'image of God'.

For the writers of Genesis, because all people are made in the image of God, all should reflect that by enjoying the basic gifts God bestows upon Creation. The land and its fruits are freely given to all to enjoy, with none being apportioned a greater share than any other. The old medieval saw, 'When Adam delved and Eve span, Who was then the gentleman?' sums it up perfectly (if we overlook the gender stereotyping). That *inequality* has been such a feature of human existence since the Creation is a consequence of human action, of the Fall, not the outworking of a divine plan: as the 4th century writer Pelagius rather tellingly put it, reflecting on 'natural' gifts we enjoy such as the sun and the air (in Bradstock and Rowland 2002, p. 18):

> we possess equally with others all the things which are not under our control but which we receive by God's dispensation, and on unjust and unequal terms only the things which are entrusted and subjected to our own rule ...

Affirmations of our inherent equality under God appear throughout the Hebrew Scriptures. While disparities of wealth and status are evident and acknowledged – the riches of certain patriarchs and kings are described uncritically or taken as a sign of divine blessing, and the existence of slaves is accepted – a concern that none should be denied their basic needs is constant. For the biblical writers, the fundamental equality of all people before God means that all must have their basic needs met, and many reserve their sharpest invective for rulers who act unjustly in this respect.

---

1 I limit myself in this paper to the Judaeo-Christian scriptures, but there are numerous relevant and stimulating insights into economic matters in Islamic teaching, which I have drawn on in other commentaries on the global economic crisis.

God is perceived to be against systems that institutionalise the exploitation of the poor. This is most clearly seen with respect to the distribution of that most basic commodity, land. In Numbers chapter 26, when Moses divides the land among the tribes in proportion to their size, he does it by lot to prevent the most powerful securing for themselves the best. The Jubilee laws stipulated that land was never to be sold in perpetuity, that those who benefited from the poverty of others by buying up their land should not retain it permanently. While these laws did not envisage a fully 'egalitarian' society, they did aim for a degree of equalisation through workable redistributive mechanisms. The prophets Isaiah, Micah, and Zechariah all envisage a time when everyone will enjoy the security that comes from having their own access to the necessities of life. Observing the Sabbath also had an equalising dimension, because in so far as it obliged rich and poor alike to abstain temporarily from work it provided a break in those patterns of relationships that sustain inequality.

Underpinning the concern that all should have equal access to land is the importance of community: in biblical terms, it is fundamental that no one is denied membership of their community on account of their economic circumstances. Where material aid is given it is to enable the impoverished person to live once again alongside their helpers. Community is predicated on an assumption that every person can maintain their own well-being: this seems to be the point of the prophets' depiction of 'all sitting beneath their own vine'. Where even one person becomes dependent on others the community is deficient, hence the importance of all having access to the land.

The New Testament also suggests that community exists only when all members are held to be equal. In his first letter to the Corinthians, chapter 12, Paul uses the metaphor of the body to describe the relationship between the followers of Christ, stressing that all limbs and organs are of equal value and equally vital to making the body function. As people join the fellowship of Christ, so their social status or standing diminishes in importance. True fellowship cannot exist where some members are held in higher esteem than others.

A striking example of equality among the early Christians appears in the Acts of the Apostles chapter 4, where the Jerusalem church preferred sharing goods to private ownership. Those who owned lands or houses sold them and the apostles distributed the proceeds to those in need. Again, the requirement that basic needs be met seems to have been fulfilled in that 'there was not a needy person among them' — an echo of the outcome when the people of Israel observed the Jubilee. Equality *between* churches was also important for Paul, as his call to the Corinthians to share their goods with a poorer fellowship suggests (II Corinthians chapter 8). This passage has echoes of the provision of manna in the wilderness, where 'those who gathered much had nothing over, and those who gathered little had no lack' (Exodus chapter 16).

The Mass or Communion also speaks of equality, anticipating powerfully the heavenly banquet when none shall be distinguishable by rank or status. It remembers the One who taught that, while in society people pull rank on one another, 'it shall not be so among you' (Mark chapter 10 verse 43). 'The last will be first and the first will be last' (Matthew chapter 20 verse 16).

At the beginning of Luke's account (chapter 4 verses 18, 19) Jesus affirms his call to proclaim the year of the Jubilee, and a leitmotif of his teaching was that, in the kingdom, the poor and humble are raised up and the rich and important brought down. Mary prefigured her son's mission by speaking of God filling the hungry with good things and sending the rich away empty, and Jesus challenged people to sell their possessions and give to the poor. Entry into the kingdom will not be possible without the abandonment of wealth – presumably, because there the categories of 'rich' and 'poor' do not exist.

Social consequences of inequality

In so far as the biblical writers are unequivocal in affirming (a) the fundamental equality of all people before God, (b) the social responsibilities placed on those with wealth, and (c) the duty of communities to ensure all members enjoy the basic needs of life, they speak a challenging word to Western societies. Confronting a culture characterised by a spirit of 'autonomy' and lack of communitarian connectedness – one that 'understands the market as a place for self-advancement at the expense of others, who are perceived either as rivals and competitors or as usable commodities' (Brueggemann, 2009, p. 5) – the Bible offers a radically different model. According to the Bible's writers, the whole point of economic arrangements is to build up and sustain communities. Therefore, they will incorporate measures to protect the interests of the most vulnerable and marginalised and ensure they can participate as fully in the community as everybody else. And while it would be a mistake to seek to 'apply' to our own context biblical economic models, there is much value in reflecting on how Scripture can help to foster the well-being of our own communities today, and discerning how its principles can most helpfully contribute to debates in the public square about the common good.

This is a singularly apposite time to be doing this, faced as we are with a global economic crisis crying out for fresh solutions. As we survey the fall-out from the present recession, and peer into an uncertain future, I believe our energies must be directed toward discerning, not so much how we can all get richer again, but how to improve the psychological and social well-being of our society as a whole. As surveys are continually showing, for those of us in the developed world who have reached the point where our worries for the future no longer centre around finding enough food, water, or shelter, becoming richer increases our quality of life hardly at all. Indeed, it can be demonstrated that as affluent societies have grown richer, so there have been long-term rises in rates of anxiety, depression, and other social problems. Hence, I believe it is time to expand the debate about how we achieve economic growth by seeking a shared vision of a better society.

For while New Zealand – like every other country in the developed world – has seen a significant increase in gross domestic product in recent decades, this has not led to a concomitant *decrease* in social problems. The media bring news every day of our 'need' for more prisons; of alarming rises in obesity, including among children; of growing alcohol consumption among the young, with a resultant rise in anti-social behaviour; of growing depression and other psychiatric problems; and of how we are rapidly bringing about the demise of our own and other species by our rapacious and unsustainable lifestyle. It is difficult to avoid the conclusion that New Zealand society, like many others in the Western world, is becoming increasingly dysfunctional, and that, rather than seeking out and addressing the root causes, we do little more than attempt to treat the symptoms. Surveys show that as citizens, we are more concerned about the quality of our lives than simply our wealth. However, politicians across almost all the main parties seem reluctant to take any new or imaginative steps (though it will be interesting to see if any will follow the lead of the French president, Nicolas Sarkozy, who said in September 2009 that his country will now include happiness and well-being in its measurement of economic progress) (Aldric 2009).

Therefore, I want to argue that (a) we need a debate now about how we renew our society and (b) central to this debate must be the thorny issue of economic inequality. I argue this, not just on the basis of the theological case I made earlier, but because we now have to face the extremely convincing claim, drawing on some 30 years of painstaking research, that one of the key factors – if not *the* key factor – behind dysfunctional societies is their level of economic inequality. In study after study it has been shown that countries with high levels of inequality – like New Zealand – will imprison a larger proportion of their population, have lower literacy scores, have more obesity, have more teenage pregnancies, have worse mental health, and have shorter average life-spans than those countries with much lower levels of income inequality. Richard Wilkinson and Kate Pickett have brought this research together in their book *The Spirit Level* (2009). They spell out their findings with a series of graphs disturbingly similar in appearance, and state that (2009, p. 181):

> across whole populations, rates of mental illness are five times higher in
> the most unequal compared to the least unequal societies. Similarly in

more unequal societies people are five times as likely to be imprisoned, six times as likely to be clinically obese, and murder rates may be many times higher.

And note that Wilkinson and Pickett say, 'across whole populations': it is not simply that in more equal societies there will be fewer poor people, that equality helps only those at the bottom: the effects of inequality affect everybody.[2]

Inequality, then, has a significant effect on all our lifestyles in wealthier countries. We often talk about being a consumer-oriented society, about how we buy lots of things yet end up being *less* happy: and scientific surveys into 'happiness' show that this is exactly the case. But the reason we buy things is less because we *need* them than that growing inequality has put pressure on us to maintain standards relative to others. Contentment has less to do with *actual* wealth than *relative* wealth, a factor that explains why we continue to pursue economic growth despite its apparent lack of benefits. In this connection it is interesting to note that spending on advertising also varies with inequality – in more unequal countries a larger proportion of gross domestic product is spent on advertising, with the United States and New Zealand spending twice as much as Norway and Denmark (Wilkinson and Pickett, 2009, p. 223).

Reducing inequality is also vital to our effort to help the environment. Instead of responding to constant pressure to devour ever more of the earth's resources, we need to focus on how to live *sustainably* – which will involve cutting back on our consumption and taking more seriously radical new ideas such as 'biomimicry' that explore technological changes to enable our resource use to *replenish* rather than destroy the ecosystem.[3] We might note, however, that doing this will not lead to any reduction in our real quality of life as measured in terms of health, happiness, and community life. Another interesting finding by Wilkinson and Pickett is that, because more equal countries manifest a greater sense of community spirit, their approach to environmental issues is more enlightened – so Japan and Sweden recycle a significantly larger proportion of their waste than do the United States and United Kingdom (Wilkinson and Pickett, 2009, p. 228).

Can we reduce inequality?

I have raised the possibility that we might want to break out of the spiral of consumption in which we find ourselves trapped, and rediscover ways in

---

2   For a useful, critical discussion of this point, see Runciman (2009).

3   For more on this see, for example, the Biomimicry website (www.biomimicry.net) and the website of Professor Dr Michael Braungart (www.braungart.com).

which the economy can benefit the whole of society. And I have argued that central to this task must be a commitment to reverse the trend that has seen economic inequality increase in the past few decades. At the risk of sounding like a religious or political fundamentalist who thinks there is one solution for all ills, I have argued that a mass of evidence suggests that across a wide range of social indices – from mental health to educational performance to rates of imprisonment to life expectancy – the more unequal a society, the less well it performs. But can anything be done about economic inequality, and if so, what?

The key to the kind of change I am advocating is political will, and there are few signs of that at present, whether in New Zealand or most other developed countries. Political will can, of course, be influenced by changes in the mood of voters, but given that popular concern in New Zealand about the level of inequality has *decreased* in the last 20 years, despite inequality itself having increased significantly during that period, signs of a change of thinking at governmental level are not immediately hopeful.[4] This, however, is in contrast to the situation in some other developed Western nations. Surveys in the United Kingdom over the last 20 years, for example, have shown that the proportion of people who think that income differences are too big is around 75 per cent to 80 per cent. Perhaps even more surprising is the 2005 Maxwell Poll on Civic Engagement in the United States that reported that over 80 per cent of the population thought that the extent of inequality was a problem, with 60 per cent believing the government should try to reduce it – figures that reinforced the findings of various Gallup polls between 1984 and 2003. These figures are even more remarkable given that most respondents underestimated how big the income differences were in their society.

In one sense there is a 'spiritual dimension' to this process, in that the kind of change necessary to make any significant difference in terms of reducing inequality would resemble that implied in the theological category of 'metanoia'. Metanoia speaks of a fundamental transformation of our vision of the world and ourselves, a radical change of mind or re-orientation linked to sorrow for the past. However, experiments have shown that we have a natural propensity, when confronted by limited resources, to share rather than seek to benefit at others' expense (Wilkinson and Pickett, 2009, pp. 199–200). As Marshall Sahlins pointed out in his study *Stone Age Economics*, for over 90 per cent of our time on this planet we lived, almost exclusively, in highly egalitarian societies where 'social and economic life was based on systems of gift exchange, food sharing, and on a very high degree of equality' and where 'forms of exchange involving

---

4   Data produced by the International Social Survey Programme in 2009 showed that 60 per cent of the population considered income differences in New Zealand were too large compared with 70 per cent in 1992 (Staff Writers 2010).

direct expressions of self-interest, such as buying and selling or barter, were usually regarded as socially unacceptable and outlawed' (cited in Wilkinson and Pickett, 2009, pp. 198–9).

Therefore, what measures might be adopted to reduce inequality in our society? It could be argued that it is not the business of 'theology' to offer concrete economic policies. However, it is rather a cop-out simply to critique a situation without offering alternatives, so let me try to outline possible issues to engage with if the business of tackling economic inequality is to be addressed. And note that these are simply 'issues' not solutions: my main concern is to promote debate and in so doing offer one or two pointers to what might be on the agenda.

A progressive role for the state

One issue we might as well confront head-on is the role of the state. When R. H. Tawney, arguably the most influential Christian advocate of economic equality in the 20th century, considered how the principle of equality that he discerned in Scripture could be reflected in social and economic structures, he assumed that the state would play a powerful role. For Tawney, the state had a duty to operate in the public interest and to use the levers of taxation and social security to ensure that differences of wealth and income were gradually narrowed – an assumption many of his readers in the 1920s and 1930s would have shared. Indeed, another great architect of the welfare state, Archbishop William Temple, argued that the state had a *duty* to ensure all families had an adequate income, good housing, and access to education, and the post-war Labour government in Britain (1945–51) enjoyed widespread public support when it nationalised key utilities and centrally administered a raft of services including education, health, and housing.

Today the issue is less clear-cut. While some still see the state as pivotal in the quest for equality, and taxation as a vital lever in the project, others argue that the greater freedom given to the market since the 1980s has raised living standards across the board and made the very notion of 'inequality' seem outdated. While government control of the 'commanding heights' of the economy in the public interest may have been welcomed by a people shattered by the ravages of war, today the idea that bureaucrats and politicians know best about providing services is seen as hopelessly outdated. It is true that Tawney – and for that matter his contemporary Beveridge – did not see the state as the *only* agency with the power to promote equality, arguing that local authorities, individual citizens, and what we would now call the 'third sector' (voluntary bodies and community groups) also had a crucial role. Now, however, the received wisdom on both the 'left' and 'right' is that the era of the 'big state' and government welfare as the 'institutional expression of altruism' has long passed, replaced by concepts like 'stakeholder welfare' and an emphasis on individual responsibility and the role of the voluntary sector. Yet attractive though these ideas are – and they have much to commend them from a theological perspective – the case for pressing toward greater equality, and for this to be a consciously shared project under government direction, still seems compelling.

Take the idea, which I have argued is central for the biblical writers, that everyone should receive an income sufficient to live on – an ideal also reflected in the 1948 Universal Declaration of Human Rights. While we will heed St Paul's injunction (in II Thessalonians chapter 3 verse 10) that anyone who will not work should not eat – noting that it says *will* not work, not *cannot* work – the mark of a good society must be its commitment to see that everyone receives sufficient to enable them to meet their basic needs. (And on this point, I believe we must challenge the 'distinction' often too readily drawn between the so-called 'deserving' and 'undeserving' poor.) The question then raised is, how is 'a society' to fulfil this function unless through some centrally administered apparatus?

Unlike 'relieving poverty', the business of ensuring that every person or family has the basic necessities for survival must involve some central coordination. To argue this is not to advocate a return to the heavily bureaucratic 'command economy' models of the old Soviet bloc, nor to rule out a vital role for the voluntary or business sectors or for local authorities or other agencies. But it is to rule *in* a 'managing' or 'co-ordinating' role for the state, rooted in a conscious commitment to achieve basic equality. While the historical argument for a 'direct' role for the state in providing for basic needs still has force, it is possible to conceive of government maintaining a 'mixed' approach to service provision, reflecting modern, progressive attitudes to the state, within a well-defined framework for tackling inequality. One lesson of history (we might take the latter half of the 19th century as a prime example) is that, for all its merits, voluntary charitable provision cannot *guarantee* a standard of living adequate for the health and well-being of all, so some degree of government intervention is required if this is to be achieved. The challenge for politicians is to set the balance between direct central provision and state-supported voluntary provision.

It is worth noting that societies with the greatest equality have followed different paths to that position. For example, while Sweden does it through redistributive taxes and benefits and a large welfare state, Japan has a greater equality of market incomes, of earnings *before* taxes and benefits. As a proportion of national income, public social expenditure in Japan is among the lowest of the major developed countries. How might things be approached in New Zealand?

One focus might be the minimum wage and welfare and pension levels and the methods used to set these levels. Should the merits of a *living* wage be considered, as well as welfare rates and pensions that take into account research into minimum income standards? Should incomes – especially those of people on the minimum wage – rise in line with average earnings (noting that an unemployed person receives less than 30 per cent of net average wages)? This would act as a brake on inequality and ensure the lowest earners do not get left even further behind. How about a return to a system of universal child support, since there is strong evidence to show this contributes to reducing inequality, is efficient (in terms of resources not being wasted by the logistics of targeting), and is unaffected by changes in the economic climate? Do people know to what they are entitled and how to get it? Can the benefit system be made more transparent – and less complex? Should we think outside the box on certain questions, for example, the value of a 'universal' approach to benefits and pensions? Are the Working for Families Tax Credits the best solution for everybody (for example, single parents)? Working for Families has been excellent in almost halving child poverty in the last seven years and leading to the first reduction in inequality for 20 years – but is it time for new initiatives focused on those with the lowest incomes?

A particular challenge New Zealand faces is that its fastest growing population groups are also those with least wealth and lowest incomes, namely Pacific peoples and, albeit to a slightly lesser extent, Māori. By 2026, approximately half of New Zealand's children will be growing up in its least wealthy households, which implies an entrenching of multigenerational poverty unless this is addressed now. And what about the other end of the scale: would caps or restrictions on upper salary levels lead to any more of the best brains in the country going offshore? Cleary, New Zealand must remain an attractive place to work and do business, but inequality is a factor to be included in that equation. Could there be measures to make housing more affordable – to make more houses 'homes' instead of investment opportunities – such as tax measures on capital gains on property and on rental property (perhaps balanced by tax incentives in other areas)? Can low-cost mortgages be made more available without fuelling speculation? Some of these ideas are deeply unpopular in political circles, of course, but it does depend how debates are framed and where they start from. Bringing all this together, how about a 'commission on inequality' to examine the costs and impacts of growing wealth inequality and identify remedies that would attract broad public support?

While we might think of measures to increase people's income, a related question is whether the extra revenue needed to ensure a decent standard of living for all should be raised through taxation – particularly taxation, at a higher level than at present, of the highest incomes. This could be one way of meeting the twin biblical imperatives of getting the rich to 'share' their wealth with the poor and achieving a greater level of economic equality within society. However, increasing taxation is now perceived to be deeply unpopular with voters and seldom advocated by mainstream parties. While in an opinion poll in 2008 a majority of New Zealanders said they did not want personal tax cuts at the expense of basic social services, tax is still seen largely in *negative* terms, as something punitive and freedom-restricting rather than serving a positive function. Therefore, is there scope for a fresh debate about the purpose of tax, involving a re-examination of its potential as a contributor to the promotion of 'social justice' and greater equality, to the well-being of the whole of society? As Wellington-based commentator Melanie Downer has argued (2008, p. 12):

> this is perhaps an argument that requires more explicit development in Christian circles: that the system of redistribution in the form of welfare benefits and Working for Families subsidies in New Zealand, constitutes a contemporary parallel to the jubilee ethic. In this matter, the task of Christians is to ensure that this mechanism – aimed at restoring the poor among us to a state in which they are able to participate in economic life – operates in a life-giving and sustaining way.

Perhaps even the language is important here for, as Downer says, the Jubilee system was not strictly 'redistributive' but 'restorative' (Downer, 2008, p. 6). The government's Tax Working Group, established to help it consider the key tax policy challenges facing the country, should think radically, not least because the tax cuts implemented on 1 April 2009 actually increased the gap between the highest and lowest earners because they were proportional – and even had a *negative* effect for those at the lower end, as they earned more in consequence and had their family tax credit reduced accordingly.

Critics of wealth redistribution to achieve social good claim that it stifles ambition and represents a loss of freedom. However, the relatively small reduction in the range of choices open to the richest 10 per cent of the population when subjected to, say, a higher level of personal taxation, compared with the enormous increase in 'freedoms' the redistribution of that wealth would mean for the very poor, makes that argument not wholly convincing. If, in the course of building an economy aimed at serving all, the choices open to the richest few diminish slightly, the 'freedom' enjoyed by society as a whole actually *increases* as it becomes more cohesive and the hitherto poor and disempowered have more chance to realise their God-given potential. This was a point recognised in 2009 by a group of 44 wealthy Germans, who petitioned their government to allow them to pay a 'wealth tax' to fund economic and social programmes to aid their country's economic recovery (*BBC News*, 2009).

Another creative approach to tackling inequality would be to stimulate a public debate around the values of generosity and giving. New Zealand does have a tradition of philanthropy – my post at the University of Otago is living proof of that – but it is still some way behind countries such as the United States in developing a 'giving culture', a sense of putting something back into the community. No society can legislate to make people generous, but there is value in highlighting the moral issues involved and seeking to change the culture. Encouraging (perhaps by tax breaks) wealthy individuals and institutions to be more publicly linked with poverty reduction, including through corporate social responsibility programmes, could well meet with a ready response at a time when these bodies are increasingly perceived to be 'part of the problem' on account of the high profits and bonuses attending their activities.

Another approach – one suggested by Wilkinson and Pickett (2009) – could be for the government to encourage, through tax concessions, democratic employee ownership. When combined with participative management this can enable a business to become more obviously a 'working community', while also bringing the fixing of earning differentials ultimately under democratic control. It can also involve a substantial redistribution of wealth from external shareholders to employees and a simultaneous redistribution of the income from that wealth (Wilkinson and Pickett, 2009, pp. 248–56).

Conclusion

So, does it matter that some in New Zealand earn more in a month than most 'average' workers will see in a lifetime? In one sense no, for a degree of inequality of income will always exist in society. Economic equality – what we might define as 'equalised after-tax real income' – is neither practically nor politically possible, and a society with *no* inequality, with a Gini coefficient of 0, would provide no incentive to advancement. Yet where conspicuous wealth exists alongside material poverty there are grounds for concern, both about the fact of that poverty and the structures that allow such gross inequality to exist. This is at the heart of what the biblical writers argue, and much of the empirical data available today confirms the continuing relevance and applicability of their concerns.

Therefore, I argue that in New Zealand, where even without this recession (which is hitting the poorest hardest) thousands of people struggle to keep warm, pay their bills, feed themselves and their families, cope with debt and ill health, and be heard in their interactions with government agencies, action is needed to bring about a greater 'levelling' of income and ensure the basic needs of all are met. And this action, as well as realising a more economically just society, will reap benefits across society in terms of greater cohesion, higher levels of trust, and a better quality of life.

Much of what I have been arguing is not new. In 1993, the Social Justice Statement issued by the New Zealand churches called for 'fairness in the distribution of incomes, wealth and power in our society' (Boston, 1994, p. 16). Their calls were not heeded – but this is a different time. Can all sections of society – politicians, business, trades unions, faith communities – work together to tackle inequality? I hope I have shown that this has to do, not with the 'politics of envy', but with recognising that the quality of our social relations is related to the material foundations of our society, that the scale of our income differences has a powerful effect on how we relate to each other, and that we need a society that materially acknowledges that all of us are made in God's image and should live in ways that reflect that status.

We do not talk much about a 'vision' for society – politics seems much more 'managerial' these days. And while this chapter does promote a vision, it is not an impossible one, for even small decreases in inequality, such as have occurred in some developed countries, can make an important difference to quality of life across society. As Wilkinson and Pickett (2009, p. 264) say:

> there is a better society to be won: a more equal society in which people are less divided by status and hierarchy … in which we regain a sense of community, in which we overcome the threat of global warming, in which we own and control our work democratically as part of a community of colleagues, and share in the benefits of a growing non-monetized sector of the economy.

I hope that we can begin to generate a new debate about how we achieve this 'better society'.

References

Aldrick, P. 2009. 'Nicolas Sarkozy wants "well-being" measure to replace GDP.' *Daily Telegraph*, 14 September. www.telegraph.co.uk/finance/economics/6189582/Nicolas-Sarkozy-wants-well-being-measure-to-replace-GDP.html.

BBC News. 2009. 'Rich Germans demand higher taxes.' 23 October. news.bbc.co.uk/go/pr/fr/-/2/hi/europe/8321967.stm.

Boston, J. 1994. 'Christianity in the public square: The churches and social justice.' In J. Boston and A. Cameron (eds). *Voices for Justice: Church, law and state in New Zealand*. Palmerston North: Dunmore.

Bradstock, A., and C. Rowland (eds). 2002. *Radical Christian Writings: A reader*. Oxford: Blackwell.

Brueggemann, W. 2009. 'From anxiety and greed to milk and honey.' *Faith and Finance: Christians and the economic crisis – Discussion guide*. Washington DC: Sojourners.

Cheung, J. 2007. *Wealth Disparities in New Zealand*. Wellington: Statistics New Zealand.

Downer, M. 2008. 'Wealth, ownership, and social care: Towards a consideration of jubilee in New Zealand's contemporary political context.' *Stimulus* 16(3): 2–15.

Duncan, G. 2007. *Society and Politics: New Zealand social policy*. 2nd edn. Auckland: Pearson Education.

Ferguson, N. 2008. *The Ascent of Money: A financial history of the world*. New York: Penguin.

Gorringe, T. J. 1994. *Capital and the Kingdom: Theological ethics and economic order*. Maryknoll, NY: Orbis.

Gould, B. 2008. *Rescuing the New Zealand Economy: What went wrong and how we can fix it*. Nelson: Craig Potton.

Hartley, S. 2009. 'Recession takes its toll on wealth of Kiwi rich list.' *Otago Daily Times*, 25 July, p. 25.

MSD. 2008. *The Social Report: Te Pūrongo Oranga Tangata 2008*. Wellington: Ministry of Social Development.

Povey, D. M. 2002. *How Much is Enough? Life below the poverty line in Dunedin*. Dunedin: Presbyterian Support Otago.

Runciman, D. 2009. 'How messy it all is.' [Review of *The Spirit Level*.] *London Review of Books* 31(20): 3–6.

Sandel, M. 2009. 'Markets and morals.' First 2009 Reith Lecture. www.bbc.co.uk/programmes/b00kt7sh.

Smith, A. [1759] 1790. *The Theory of Moral Sentiments*. 6th edn. London: A. Millar.

Smith, A. 1776. *An Inquiry into the Nature and Causes of the Wealth of Nations.* 5th edn. Edited by E Cannan. 1904. London: Methuen.

Staff Writers. 2010. 'All things being equal.' *The Listener* 223(3651). www.listener.co.nz/issue/3651/features/15346/all_things_being_equal.html.

UNDP (United Nations Development Programme). 2009. *Human Development Report 2009: Overcoming barriers – Human mobility and development.* Houndmills, Basingstoke, Hampshire: Palgrave Macmillan. http://hdr.undp.org/en/reports/global/hdr2009.

Wilkinson, R., and Pickett, K. 2009. *The Spirit Level: Why more equal societies almost always do better.* London: Allen Lane.

11. Is ethics important for economic growth?

David Rea

Introduction

> Over the last four decades, living standards in New Zealand have fallen far behind those in Australia. … The Prime Minister has articulated his vision of closing the gap with Australia by 2025. We share that vision. New Zealand has vast potential: strong institutions, hardworking and creative people, *a degree of trust and integrity second to none in the world*, and abundant natural resources. So of course the gap can be closed. But it won't close of its own accord. And if nothing is done the gap could get worse, with increasingly serious long-term implications for our country's future. Starting from here, closing the gap will require far-reaching policy reforms. That will take bold courageous leadership over at least the next decade. (2025 Taskforce 2009, p. 3, emphasis added)

In its first report, the 2025 Taskforce (2009) observed that trust and integrity are important factors determining economic growth. However, despite this observation, the taskforce did not recommend that government should encourage business, workers, or consumers to be more ethical or trustworthy. The taskforce seems to have been of the view that because New Zealand already had the world's highest levels of trust and integrity, no major change in economic policy in this area was needed.

The aim of this chapter is to look more closely at this intriguing and somewhat unusual area of economic policy. The chapter first looks at indicators of ethical behaviour in New Zealand, and then reviews the theory and evidence about the extent to which 'ethical behaviour' might be important for the economy. Lastly, the chapter considers the public policy implications of the finding that ethical behaviour might be important for economic growth.

This chapter is organised around the following questions.

- How should we conceptualise ethical behaviour in an economic context?

- How ethical or trustworthy are New Zealanders?

- Is ethical behaviour important for economic efficiency and economic growth?

- Is there any evidence that New Zealand's economic performance would improve if we were more ethical?

- Should economic policy aim to foster ethical or trustworthy behaviour?

The focus of this chapter is the relationship between ethical behaviour and economic efficiency. This focus is rather narrow and neglects other important reasons why such behaviour might be important. Ethical behaviour in particular might lead to a 'fairer' distribution of resources, and trustworthy behaviour might improve the quality of relationships between people in the community. This chapter is not an argument that these outcomes are unimportant. Instead, the chapter asks whether, in addition to these issues, we should also be concerned about ethical behaviour because it might enhance economic performance.

The rest of the chapter is structured as follows. The next section defines ethical behaviour in an economic context. The third section looks at the prevalence of ethical behaviour in the New Zealand. The fourth section summarises advances in economic theory that suggest that ethical behaviour is important for the economy. The fifth section looks at whether there is any evidence to suggest that improving ethical behaviour would enhance New Zealand's economic performance. The sixth section looks at the public policy implications of these findings. The final section provides concluding comments.

What is ethical behaviour in an economic context?

The key to the nature of ethical behaviour is that it involves an individual or organisation acting in a manner that is considerate of others. An agent acts ethically where they choose a course of action where the welfare of others is given some appropriate moral consideration. In a descriptive sense, ethical behaviour typically involves using some moral principles as a guide for decision making.

Ethical behaviour stands in contrast to the behaviour that is traditionally assumed in economics. Traditionally, economists have assumed individuals are almost entirely selfish and frequently act in a way that benefits only themselves. It is typically assumed that most individuals are unethical and – if they can get away with it – will lie, cheat, or steal for their own personal gain.

However, in contrast to the theory, in the real world many people seem to act in trustworthy or ethical ways. For example:

- it is not uncommon to observe customers who have been undercharged for goods volunteering this information to shop assistants

- many individual and firms pay the expected amount of tax on their income, despite opportunities to use tax loopholes and avoidance mechanisms

- many people go beyond what is strictly required in their employment contracts because they want to do a good job.

Actual behaviour occurs for a variety of reasons, and it is important to distinguish between 'good' behaviour that occurs because of a motivation 'to do the right thing' and 'good' behaviour that occurs for more selfish reasons. Consider, for example, observing the speed limit in a car. For some people obeying this law is the 'right thing to do'. Others might act lawfully, but only because of the risk of penalties if they are caught and prosecuted. In this chapter, I am particularly interested in 'ethically motivated behaviour' because it is a low cost means of ensuring people do the right thing, and avoids the need to create private or public systems of incentives to ensure appropriate behaviour.

How much ethical behaviour is there in New Zealand?

Measuring the extent to which individuals are ethical is somewhat problematic for several reasons. Defining ethical behaviour in any particular situation is difficult, and it is not something amendable to straightforward measurement.

However, notwithstanding these difficulties, I have identified eight indicators that provide information about levels of ethical behaviour in New Zealand. These indicators also provide the same information for 25 other countries, so comparisons can be made. The indicators are as follows.

The level of perceived corruption among politicians and public officials in different countries: This indicator is an index that Transparency International developed based on a range of expert and business surveys. The data is drawn from the Corruption Perceptions Index 2008 (Transparency International 2009).

Ethical behaviour indicators drawn from the fifth wave of the World Values Survey: These four indicators are the extent to which people believe it is not justifiable to cheat on their taxes, accept a bribe, claim government benefits to which they are not entitled, and avoid a fare on public transport. The surveys were conducted over 2004 to 2008. The New Zealand survey was conducted in 2004 and had responses from 894–902 people, depending on the question.

'Trust' drawn from the fifth wave of the World Values Survey: This indicator is drawn from the World Values Survey question about the extent to which survey respondents believe 'most people can be trusted'. The surveys were conducted over 2004 to 2008. The New Zealand survey was conducted in 2004 and had 905 responses to the question.

Accounting standards: This indicator is drawn from an International Monetary Fund working paper. It measures the quality of accounts of leading companies in each country (De Nicolò et al. 2006).

Deaths by violence: This indicator is reported by the World Health Organization (WHO 2004). It provides the most recent estimates of age-specific rates of death by violent causes in different countries.

More details about each indicator, the criteria used for selecting the indicators, and an assessment of the quality of the data are set out in Rea (2010). Taken as a whole, the indicators measure both normative views, as well as actual behaviour. An analysis of the eight indicators suggests there is a high level of ethically motivated behaviour in New Zealand. In particular:

- compared with other countries, New Zealand has the lowest level of perceived corruption among politicians and public officials (Transparency International 2009)

- approximately 60 per cent of respondents to the New Zealand component of the fifth wave of the World Values Survey said it was never justifiable to cheat on taxes

- over 80 per cent of respondents to the New Zealand component of the fifth wave of the World Values Survey said it was never justifiable to accept a bribe

- over 70 per cent of respondents to the New Zealand component of the fifth wave of the World Values Survey said it was never justifiable to falsely claim government benefits

- slightly more than 60 per cent of respondents to the New Zealand component of the fifth wave of the World Values Survey said it was never justifiable to avoid a fare on public transport

- just over 50 per cent of respondents to the New Zealand component of the fifth wave of the World Values Survey said most people could be trusted

- the accounts of the top 10 manufacturing companies in New Zealand achieved an 83 per cent level of compliance with best practice reporting in an International Monetary Fund study that compared accounting standards across countries (De Nicolò et al. 2006)

- the extent of criminal offending, as measured by deaths by violence, is relatively low with an average of 1.2 deaths per 100,000 from violence (WHO 2004).

How do New Zealanders compare with the citizens of other countries on these measures? Is the extent of trust and integrity 'second to none' as claimed by the 2025 Taskforce (2009). Among the sample of 26 countries, New Zealand ranks highly on many but not all measures. For example, New Zealand ranks highest in terms of the absence of perceived corruption of politicians and public servants, but only roughly average in terms of attitudes towards cheating on tax.

Figure 1 shows a simple composite index of the eight indicators to give some insight into how overall ethical behaviour might vary across the 26 nations in the sample. The index is the average of each country's ranking on each of the eight indicators. As can be seen, New Zealand scores relatively highly, but Japan and Switzerland record higher overall levels of ethical behaviour. Interestingly, Australia also scores higher than New Zealand. However, given the high level of measurement error, it is important not to place too much weight on this small difference. The index also shows a group of countries (Brazil, Mexico Malaysia, Thailand, and India) for which the overall level of ethical behaviour is low. More information on how the index was constructed is set out in Rea (2010).

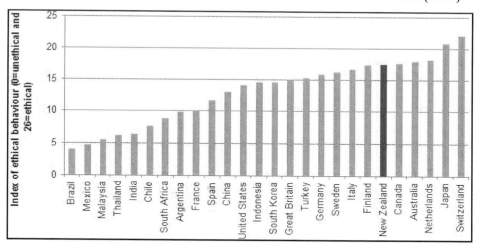

Figure 1: Index of ethical behaviour across 26 selected nations

Note: The index is the average of the rank of each country using all eight indicators. The results for China, Italy, Indonesia, and Turkey seem at odds with popular perceptions. However, they have been retained in the sample in the interests of transparency.

Source: Rea (2010).

Is ethical or trustworthy behaviour important for markets?

In *The Economics of Integrity*, Anna Bernasek (2010) provides compelling evidence of the extent to which markets require integrity or ethical behaviour in order to function effectively. Bernasek's description of the workings of real world markets reveals an economy that is very different to that traditionally assumed by many economists.

The traditional economic approach generally assumes that most people are selfish. Therefore, while people might say that accepting a bribe is wrong, it is assumed most people will act unethically if they can get away with it.

The traditional approach also assumes that markets work effectively with selfish rather than ethically motivated individuals. It is assumed that penalty clauses within contracts and wider market-based reputation mechanisms mean that people generally do what they had agreed. The incentive structure of the market protects against any natural inclination towards dishonesty, duplicity, misleading claims, or poor performance.

The traditional economic approach comes to a conclusion that seems paradoxical. Despite individuals being almost pathologically self-interested and lacking in any motivation to behave in an ethical or trustworthy manner – the process of contracting within competitive markets is the best means of ensuring that people act in each other's best interest. In fact, voluntary market exchange between purely self-interested individuals is argued to provide better outcomes than exchange based on more worthy motives. This point is often made with reference to Adam Smith's ([1776] 1904, Book 1, ch. 2) famous statement:

> It is not from the benevolence of the butcher, the brewer, or the baker that we expect our dinner, but from their regard to their own interest. We address ourselves, not to their humanity but to their self-love, and never talk to them of our own necessities but of their advantages.

The alluring paradox of self-interest within markets has often led economists to argue that selfish behaviour should be encouraged within markets, and even that ethical behaviour should be discouraged. However, in recent decades evidence has emerged to suggest that many of the basic assumptions of the traditional economic approach are misleading. In particular, the evidence suggests that many people behave ethically and that ethical behaviour is necessary to allow markets to operate effectively.

Are individuals selfish or ethical?

Everyday behaviour provides compelling evidence of the prevalence of non-selfish behaviour. The existence of volunteering, charitable giving, voting, and mass collaboration projects on the internet all suggest individuals act in ways that benefit others.

'Laboratory' experiments provide evidence from more controlled conditions about the extent to which people are selfish. One of the widely replicated 'laboratory' experiments has used the ultimatum game (Güth et al. 1982). This game consists of a proposer and a responder. The proposer is given an endowment of money and the task of proposing a division of the endowment between the proposer and the responder. The responder then has two choices. They can either accept the proposed division, whereupon both parties receive what was proposed, or they can reject it, and both players receive nothing. These experiments are conducted anonymously and as one-shot encounters to isolate pure effects.

Experiments using the ultimatum game test the hypothesis that people are selfish. Where 1 per cent is the smallest possible division of the endowment, a purely selfish proposer should offer only 1 per cent of the endowment to the responder. A purely self-interested responder should also accept the 1 per cent they are offered. The evidence from experiments is that this does not occur. Most offers are between 30 per cent and 50 per cent when the game is played by university students. There is more diversity of offers when the experiments are conducted among people from small-scale, less-developed societies. Where offers are low, responders tend to reject offers. For example, about half the time offers less than 20 per cent are rejected (Camerer and Fehr 2004).

Other experimental games provide evidence about the extent of selfish behaviour. Another widely replicated experiment uses the structure of the public goods game (Ledyard 1995). In this experiment, participants can choose to contribute their endowment to a public good or free-ride on the contributions of others. The hypothesis that all individuals are selfish is rejected in experiments based on one-shot public goods games. Instead of free-riding on others, players typically contribute 50 per cent of their endowment to the public good (Carmerer and Fehr 2004).

There is also good evidence from field experiments about the extent to which people are selfish. In natural experiments such as those that occur with anonymous giving, there is considerable evidence that a proportion of people do not behave strictly selfishly (Frey and Meier 2004; List 2004; DellaVigna 2009).

Overall, the evidence suggests that many people behave in a non-selfish manner. However, the experiments also reveal considerable heterogeneity. Most experiments find that a minority of people are consistently selfish. The size of this minority differs when experiments are repeated in different communities (Gintis et al. 2005).

One possible reason for non-selfish behaviour might be that people care about others. Another possible reason might be that people have preferences to do 'the right thing'. While the evidence seems to be that both forms of social preferences exist, behaviour based on doing what is right seems to be an important motivation. The finding that many people expect others to behave fairly, and that many people are willing to invest resources in punishing those who do not behave fairly, seems to suggest that norms of ethical behaviour play an important role (Bicchieri 2006).

As an aside, it is interesting to note that the recent findings about selfish behaviour have also led to a more careful interpretation of Adam Smith's work. As well as the *Wealth of Nations* (1776), Smith also wrote *The Theory of Moral Sentiments* (1759). In that later work, Smith argued that people have a natural sympathy towards others. Smith argued that this natural sympathy led to the motivation of benevolence. A careful reading of the famous quotation about buying dinner (above) shows that Smith was contrasting 'benevolence' with 'self-interest' (Alvey 1999).

Do markets require selfish behaviour?

In direct contrast to the traditional economic assumption, recent evidence suggests that selfish behaviour is actually a problem in real world markets.

Selfish behaviour is not a problem in the traditional economic approach because it is assumed there are no transactions costs. It is assumed individuals are fully rational and have perfect information, and no costs are associated with writing, monitoring, or enforcing contracts. However, studies of the actual nature of market exchange show that transactions costs are very important, and individuals invest significant resources in the process of contracting (Williamson 1985).

In the real world of transactions costs, selfish behaviour or 'opportunism' becomes a problem. Classic examples of markets where this occurs include:

- the markets for used vehicles where the costs of determining quality leads to some sellers representing 'lemons' as good quality cars (Akerlof 1970)

- the employment of chief executives where contracts are incompletely specified and there are costs to the company of terminating a contract (in these instances shareholders need to trust that the company manager is going to act reasonably in the performance of their duties) (Williamson 1985)

- insurance markets where monitoring costs create a risk of moral hazard (Arrow 1963).

A key finding is that markets sometimes fail or function poorly because of selfish behaviour. As a result, individuals spend a great deal of time constructing governance arrangements to reduce their risks from selfish behaviour. In some instances, they completely avoid transactions where the probable costs of selfish behaviour are high.

New Institutional Economics identifies three stages in the contracting process: search and screening, the specification of contracts, and monitoring and enforcement. Each stage has the same structure. At each stage, the parties face some level of uncertainty. Where a transaction requires the parties to invest significant resources in overcoming uncertainty, it is often not economic to completely undertake that stage of the contracting process. This then leaves the parties open to the risk of losses from selfish behaviour.

Consider for example the first stage of contracting – search and screening. Many transactions are conducted despite search and screening activities being incompletely performed. As a result, there is residual uncertainty about quality, and parties face a risk of adverse selection – a risk that the quality of products or services may turn out to be less than promised or expected.

There is a similar problem when writing contracts. The process of writing and specifying contracts is also often incompletely performed. This tends to occur where there are complex or long-term transactions. Because of incomplete specification, parties are exposed to a risk of losses from selfish behaviour. This occurs where one party attempts to amend an incomplete contract in a manner that 'unfairly' changes the distribution of the surplus from the exchange. In short-term incomplete contracts – such as contracts involving medical professionals and their patients – therez is a risk of opportunistic behaviour because one party needs to trust the other to determine some of the details of the contract. In longer-term relational contracts, the risk of opportunism is referred to as 'hold up'. This occurs where one party attempts to force an unfair amendment to an incomplete contract where there are sunk costs (Williamson 1985).

Where monitoring and enforcement of contracts is costly, these activities also tend to be incompletely performed. In this instance, parties are exposed to the risk of selfish behaviour in the form of contractual non-performance or moral hazard. For example, where it is difficult to observe agreed performance, one party runs the risk that the other will not fulfil their side of the bargain.

When faced with the risk of opportunism arising from incompleteness, parties to contracts can create contractual governance arrangements called safeguards. These are protections against the risk of selfish behaviour or opportunism. Safeguards may include writing more detailed provisions such as guarantees (for example, where parties are exposed to the risk of adverse selection); creating self-enforcing mechanisms through the use of bonds (for example, where parties are exposed to the risk of hold up); contracting only with individuals who have a good reputation (for example, where there is a risk of moral hazard); structuring repeated interactions, so that selfish behaviour in one instance can be punished in a subsequent trade; or trading only with family and friends who are less likely to be opportunistic. Critically, the construction of contractual safeguards is costly and not always fail-safe.

Role of ethical or trustworthy behaviour in markets

Contracting is a costly process and often undertaken in an incomplete manner. As a result, market participants frequently need to trust that others will act in a trustworthy or ethical manner.

This can work well where most individuals are ethical and trustworthy. In such an environment, parties to contracts do not have to invest much in ensuring that every stage of the contracting process is complete, and they do not have to invest as much in creating safeguards against opportunism. They are also more likely to undertake risky transactions.

However, this approach becomes difficult where only a small proportion of individuals are ethical or trustworthy. Individuals will avoid risky transactions, and those that are undertaken will require costly investments in governance to protect against cheating and other forms of opportunism.

It is easy to identify examples of what occurs in markets where ethical behaviour becomes less prevalent. Consider, for example, car and appliance repair where purchasers find it difficult to verify the quality of work. If a large proportion of firms are ethical and trustworthy, then the overall costs and risks of purchasing repairs will be low. However, if there is a large proportion of 'dodgy' firms, then consumers will have higher search costs, they will spend more time negotiating detailed contracts, and they will probably incur higher costs in disputes about defective repairs. Competition within the market will also be hindered, as individuals will want to remain with the firm they know.

It is important to note that where there are significant transactions costs, unethical behaviour can be tolerated or even encouraged by the incentive structure of the market. Where there is considerable uncertainty and a large proportion of untrustworthy participants, the market will function poorly or even fail completely. In this case, a version of Gresham's law can apply as 'bad companies drive out the good'. In such an environment, the market becomes dominated by selfish rather than ethical participants.

Consider as an example the market for non-bank savings. A saver in this market faces an adverse selection problem because of uncertainty about the risks of investing. Finance companies in the market may differ in the extent to which they inform potential customers of the risks associated with their products. Some companies might, in the interests of higher profits, fail to fully disclose the risks in their balance sheet. Other companies might be of the view that it is ethical to fully disclose such risks. In some circumstances, finance companies that are more ethical will find it hard to compete against firms with lower standards. If the industry becomes dominated by unethical firms, then savers will, in the end, save less because they face a market that offers only poor-quality, risky products. Conversely, if ethical behaviour is widespread, then this allows an efficient market. Savers are not surprised by unexpected losses, there is less need to invest in due diligence, and savers will save more.

Ethical behaviour where markets fail

As well as providing an important foundation for markets to operate effectively, ethical or trustworthy behaviour is important for another important economic reason. Because of transactions costs, not everything is traded in markets, and ethical behaviour is an important means of allocation where markets fail or work imperfectly. Where there are externalities, public goods, or common pool resources ethical behaviour often provides an important means of regulating behaviour. Doing what is 'right' is important in circumstances such as recreational fishing, driving in a car, or polluting the atmosphere (Ostrom 2000).

Is there any evidence to suggest a link between ethical behaviour and New Zealand's economic performance?

The theory suggests ethical behaviour is important for the economy, because it both reduces the costs of contracting and provides a means of guiding behaviour when markets are absent. However, although the theory is persuasive, the critical question is whether there is any empirical evidence to support or refute the notion that ethics are important for economic performance.

To assess whether ethical behaviour plays a meaningful role in economic growth, it is possible to use the variation in ethics between countries. Countries that have higher ethical standards should, other things being equal, have higher growth rates and higher levels of per capita economic output.

Zak and Knack (2001) looked at this question using the 'trust' indicator. They analysed growth and investment rates in 41 countries over 1970 to 1992, and found that the level of reported trust in a country had an important influence over the level of growth and investment. Zak and Knack found that after controlling for a variety of other influences on growth, a 15 percentage point increase in the level of reported trust raised the level of annual economic growth in a country by 1 per cent per year.

A less sophisticated approach is to look at the relationship between gross domestic product per capita and the index of ethical behaviour described previously. This is shown graphically in Figure 2. As can be seen, a reasonable correlation exists between a country's ethical ranking and gross domestic product per capita. Countries with high levels of ethics tend to be richer, and those with lower levels of ethics tend to be poorer

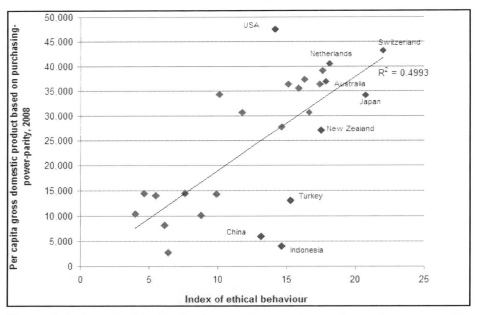

Figure 2: Index of ethical behaviour and gross domestic product per capita across 26 selected nations

Note: The index of ethical behaviour is the average of each country's ranking on eight indicators of ethics.

Source: Gross domestic product per capita data is from IMF (2003b), otherwise Rea (2010).

Of course, the correlation may be a statistical artefact. Gross domestic product per capita is influenced by many factors, and it might be that not controlling for these other influences gives rise to a false relationship where some of these other factors are correlated with ethical behaviour. The evidence suggests that good institutions – well-defined and enforceable property rights, effective and fair justice systems, and controls over public corruption are critically important for economic growth (Acemoglu and Johnson 2005; Glaeser et al. 2004; IMF 2003a; World Bank 2001). It is possible that these institutions also engender a high level of ethical behaviour, and so give rise to a spurious relationship between economic output and ethical behaviour.

It could also be that there is a causal relationship, but occurring in a reverse direction. It is possible that higher levels of economic output create higher levels of ethical behaviour. This is a proposition advanced by Adam Smith. In his lectures on jurisprudence, Smith (1762, p. 458) argued:

> Whenever commerce is introduced into any country, probity and punctuality always accompany it. These virtues in a rude and barbarous country are almost unknown. Of all the nations in Europe, the Dutch, the most commercial, are the most faithfull to their word. The English are more so than the Scotch, but much inferiour to the Dutch, and in the remote parts of this country they [are] far less so than in the commercial parts of it. This is not at all to be imputed to national character, as some pretend. There is no natural reason why an Englishman or a Scotchman should not be as punctual in performing agreements as a Dutchman. It is far more reduceable to self interest, that general principle which regulates the actions of every man, and which leads men to act in a certain manner from views of advantage, and is as deeply implanted in an Englishman as a Dutchman. A dealer is afraid of losing his character, and is scrupulous in observing every engagement. When a person makes perhaps 20 contracts in a day, he cannot gain so much by endeavouring to impose on his neighbours, as the very appearance of a cheat would make him lose.

Smith argued that commerce increased the prevalence of ethical behaviour because there were incentives to behave ethically. However, this view, while undoubtedly containing some element of truth, crucially depends on the nature of the markets in question. Where ethical conduct is highly visible, market incentives will encourage ethical behaviour. However, where markets are characterised by uncertainty and it is hard to detect cheating, then the strong incentives of the market may in fact encourage unethical conduct.

It is also possible that the observed correlation between ethics and economic output in Figure 2 occurs because of a causal relationship from ethics to economic performance. If this were the case, it would mean New Zealand – despite already having a relatively high ranking – might be able to reach the income levels of Australia if we had levels of ethical behaviour similar to Switzerland.

The empirical question about the relationship between ethical standards and economic performance can also be assessed in other ways. One approach is to look at particular industries. If there is a causal relationship between higher levels of ethical behaviour and economic performance, then it should be relatively easy to point to examples where ethics and integrity play an important role in the effective working of a market. Bernasek (2010) provides several such case studies. Conversely, it should also be possible to point to industries where poor ethical standards have adversely affected particular industries. Table 1 presents brief examples of industries where ethical standards seem to have been a problem. The table attempts to identify the nature of the failing in ethical standards, and the scale and economic consequences of the failure.

Table 1: Impact of ethical standards on particular industries in New Zealand

Example	Nature of the failure of ethical standards	Potential scale of issue
Collapse of the finance company sector, 2004–09	About 27 finance company failed between 2006 and 2008. The Registrar of Companies reported 'that a number of the failed finance companies were in the end acting in a similar manner to ponzi schemes'.[1] Many firms misled investors about the performance of loans, and some auditors failed in their duty to issue qualified audits.	The Reserve Bank of New Zealand estimated that the direct loss to creditors of the finance companies in receivership at that time ranged from $0.6 billion to $1 billion.[2]
Investment advisors	Evidence of poor information disclosure, poor training and management of advisors, inappropriate selling practices, and perverse incentive payments.[3]	In 2001, there were 7,836 'financial advisers', 2,817 'financial dealers or brokers' and 3,840 'insurance representatives'.[4]
Leaky homes	The Hunn Report suggests that one of the reasons for the construction of leaky homes was a lack of care and responsibility in the design, construction, and certification of buildings following the repeal of the Building Act.[5] This seems to have been particularly prevalent in developer driven construction projects.	The Hunn Report suggested the costs of repairing leaky homes would be between $0.12 billion and $0.24 billion. More recent reports are suggesting $11.5 billion.[6]
Tax avoidance by major banks using structured finance transactions	Over the last decade several banks used structured finance transactions to minimise their tax liabilities. The High Court found that the BNZ and Westpac's use of these transactions constituted illegal tax avoidance.[7] These cases represent unethical behaviour in that the banks took advantage of legal uncertainty and aggressively minimised their tax liabilities, rather than complying with the intent of the legislation.	Treasury provisioned $1.4 billion of income in the financial year to 30 June 2009 to represent lost tax revenue. The Inland Revenue Department has invested significant resources in prosecuting the cases so far.[8]

Sources: (1) Harris (2009, p. 10). (2) RBNZ (2008). (3) Consumer (2009); Grimes (2005); Securities Commission (2002). (4) MED (2007). (5) Hunn et al. (2002); Parliamentary Library (2002). (6) Hunn et al. (2002); NZPA (2009). (7) *BNZ Investments Ltd v. Commissioner of Inland Revenue* 15 July 2009, Wild J, HC Wellington CIV 2004-485-1059; *Westpac Banking Corp. v. Commissioner of Inland Revenue* 7 October 2009, Harrison J, HC Auckland CIV 2005-404-2843. (8) Treasury (2009).

The collapse of finance companies, the related problem with financial advisers, the widespread construction of leaky buildings, and tax avoidance by major banks all point to the relationship between ethical standards and economic performance.

In a similar manner, the global financial crisis also provides insights into the relationship between ethical standards and economic performance. One view is that an important cause of the global financial crisis was a failure of ethics and integrity within large multinational financial institutions. This point was made succinctly in early 2009 by the secretary-general of the OECD when he stated (Gurría 2009):

> The current global economic crisis is costing the world trillions of dollars, a protracted recession, millions of lost jobs, a huge loss of confidence in financial markets and a reversal in our efforts to cure global poverty. It is the result of the combination of several failures. A failure of business ethics is one of them; one that lies at the epicenter of this financial and economic earthquake.
>
> ...
>
> Business ethics should be at the center of any new road-map for the global economy. Markets should not only be more stable, but morally acceptable as well. It is time to reunite ethics and economics.

Similar sentiments were also expressed by the chair of New Zealand's Securities Commission (Diplock 2009):

> There is no question in my mind that a major factor precipitating the global crisis was the eventual overwhelming by unregulated market forces of traditional, centuries-old standards of conduct.
>
> We are now transitioning from a time when ethics in business – at any level – tended to be seen more as an optional add-on than an essential operating principle.

Lack of ethical standards varied from illegal fraud (as in the case of Bernie Madoff) to the selling of mortgages to individuals who could not afford them to the misleading ratings of the resulting bundles of mortgages by ratings agencies. An important cause of the erosion of traditional prudential standards seems to have been payment systems that provided incentives for behaviour that was at variance to traditional standards of behaviour (Blinder 2010). If this analysis is correct, it provides a significant example of the importance of ethical standards for the operation of markets.

Therefore, returning to the overall question, it does appears there is reasonable evidence of a causal relationship between levels of ethical behaviour and overall economic performance. This evidence arises when comparing countries, as well as when looking more closely at the performance of particular industries.

How should public policy support ethical behaviour?

Theory and evidence suggest ethical behaviour plays an important role in allowing markets to operate effectively. However, despite this evidence, ethical or trustworthy behaviour is not a major focus of economic policy in New Zealand. The Treasury's (2008) post-election briefing on medium-term economic policy makes no mention of ethics, and among academic and private sector economists there is little research on ethics and economic growth.[1]

One reason for this lack of focus seems to be the view that New Zealand already has a high degree of ethical and trustworthy behaviour. The evidence in this paper suggests that the level of ethical and trustworthy behaviour, although high, is not as high as in some other countries, and across many indicators there is, of course, room for improvement.

Another reason for a lack of focus is the view that while trust and integrity might be important, the government cannot directly influence such behaviour. Instead, it is argued that the best means of fostering ethical or trustworthy behaviour is to deregulate markets. Competitive markets are assumed to punish cheating, so removing barriers to competition is often argued to be the only route to a more trustworthy and ethical economy. Market-based mechanisms – including contractual guarantees, reputation effects, and the internalisation of risky transactions within firms – are argued to be the best means by which ethical behaviour can be encouraged. By way of contrast, it is argued that attempts by the government to require people to be ethical or trustworthy will tend to backfire because of poor information or incentives.

The typical view of economic policy makers in New Zealand is that the government does not have the ability to regulate for ethical or trustworthy behaviour with any 'delicacy' or 'judgement'. However, an alternative view recognises the importance of clear legal rights and competitive markets, but points out that there are particular areas in which the government can improve the level of ethics, trust, and integrity. In this wider pro-ethical approach to market regulation, it is argued that in some areas (such as education), the

---

1   Murray Petrie's work on social norms and institutions is an important exception to this (Petrie 2002).

government can influence the extent to which economic actors are motivated to behave in an ethical manner. It is also argued that in some markets – where there is very high uncertainty and high costs of unethical behaviour – direct government regulation should be used to avoid the sometime significant consequences of unethical behaviour. In the discussion that follows, I look at specific elements of this wider pro-ethical approach.

Legal regulation

In all countries, legal rules are used to require or encourage ethical or trustworthy behaviour in particular circumstances. For example, many countries have legal rules that ban the sale of certain dangerous goods, outlaw deceptive advertising, or impose fiduciary requirements in certain contracts.

Importantly, as with all legal regulation, these restrictions can come in different forms. One dimension is that the legal rules may be mandatory or default provisions. Defaults can be contracted out of, but encourage ethical behaviour because they establish good behaviour as the norm. Mandatory provisions on the other hand cannot be contracted out of, and are often argued for when there are particularly significant risks such as death (for example, vehicle safety standards).

A further dimension of legal regulation is that rules can be specific (for example, you cannot sell fireworks to people aged under 18) or constructed as general duties (for example, sellers owe a duty of care to consumers). The advantage of general duties is that they are flexible and respond to changing circumstances. However, the trade-off is that they also create a degree of legal uncertainty.

From an economic policy perspective, the question is whether legislative restrictions on economic freedom aimed at improving ethical or trustworthy behaviour will enhance the functioning of markets. One circumstance where, on the face of it, it might appear possible, is in a particular market characterised by a high level of uncertainty and where the consequences of unethical or untrustworthy behaviour are significant.

For example, where the quality of a good or service is difficult to determine and dangerous, it is often argued that statutory safety regulation will lower the costs of trading and ensure fewer consumers are harmed. The general law of negligence and specific product regulation (such as around the sale of alcohol or cigarettes to children) are common examples.

A further example is the laws governing a relationship of trust where the risk and consequences of unethical behaviour are significant. Fiduciary duties create requirements for ethical conduct in contracts where one party has to rely on another to act in good faith. In this area, statutory requirements may also be more specific. As well as general fiduciary duties, some countries have specific bans on self-dealing and related-lending by directors and senior managers (Djankov et al. 2008; La Porta et al. 2003).

Quasi-legal and informal regulation

It is also common to observe quasi-legal rules aimed at promoting ethical or trustworthy behaviour within markets. One example is occupational self-regulation. As part of the training in some traditional apprenticeships (for example, doctors, plumbers, hairdressers, carpenters, and lawyers) an emphasis is on ensuring apprentices learn standards that are the professions rules about ethical conduct. In many occupations there are also written codes of behaviour that define and promote ethical behaviour. Such quasi-legal and informal regulation helps to guarantee a minimum level of quality within these markets.

Social norms

The prevalence of ethical or trustworthy behaviour also depends on social norms and culture. The role of these is well recognised within firms. For example, an important issue for firms is creating a workplace culture that minimises fraud. Other workplace standards (for example, hygiene practices in fast-food outlets) can also be viewed as attempts by firms to create norms about ethical behaviour.

Bicchieri (2006) is of the view that social norms are a collection of rules, preferences to follow rules, and expectations. A key feature of these norms is the general expectation that they ought to be followed, but this is conditional on other people also following these norms. Ethical social norms will be effective where principles of ethical conduct are clearly articulated, where behaviour is transparent, and where people can be informally punished (Harms and Skyrms 2008).

There is increasing evidence that social norms can be influenced (Cialdini 2006). One way is though the use of descriptive norms (informing people of what others are doing) and another through injunctive norms (identifying the ethical course of action).

To test the notion that ethical behaviour might be open to influence about 'descriptive norms', I recently conducted a small experiment with a class of public policy students. The experiment involved randomly assigning students to two groups, and asking the students (in individual questionnaires) to identify how they would behave when confronted by five different ethical dilemmas.

The ethical dilemmas were identical for both groups, except for a small amount of information in each question about how other people behaved. For example, one of the ethical dilemmas was expressed as follows in the two questionnaires:

> A very small number of tertiary students use accounting firms to file their tax returns. They do this to access a soon to be closed legal loophole that gives them a refund of $1000 on their student fees. Would you pay $40 to an accounting firm to access this refund?

> Almost all tertiary students use accounting firms to file their tax returns. They do this to access a soon to be closed legal loophole that gives them a refund of $1000 on their student fees. Would you pay $40 to an accounting firm to access this refund?

It appears that information about the behaviour of other people affected how students responded to the ethical dilemma questions. The group that was told other people behaved in an ethical fashion indicated that they would make ethical choices 58 per cent of the time. The group that was told people behaved unethically made ethical choices only 38 per cent of the time. Although a small sample (n=28), the difference was statistically significant. See Rea (2010) for more detail on the nature of this experiment.

The finding that behaviour is influenced by descriptive norms about the behaviour of others has also been found in a variety of field and laboratory experiments. In a famous early experiment, individuals seeing other people place rubbish in a bin reduced the likelihood of littering (Cialdini et al. 1990). The statement that 'other people reuse their towels' also seems to be a very effective means of ensuring guests in hotels reuse their towels (Cialdini, 2006).

To some extent, it seems that social norms are amenable to influence by the government. Examples where there seems to have been some success include smoking, the payment of tax, the use of condoms, recreational fishing limits, littering, safe driving, and domestic violence. Another public policy implication is that ethical leadership – a clear articulation and modelling of ethical standards – is important for maintaining social norms of integrity.

Socialisation and education

Another important area of public policy to consider relates to the education and socialisation of children and young people.

The evidence seems to suggest that ethical behaviour is apparent very early in a child's life and progressively develops. Crucially, ethical behaviour seems influenced by early environments. Traditionally, a focus of the study of moral development was an analysis of moral reasoning. However, it now appears that other factors such as personality are also very important. The formation of ethical dispositions in children and young people focuses attention on the role of early childhood experiences, parenting, and schooling (Killen and Smetana 2006; Narvaez and Lapsley 2009). Parenting programmes, early intervention programmes, and civics education and experiences for young people seem important to foster ethical behaviour.

Transparency mechanisms

Lastly, mechanisms that promote transparency of behaviour are also important for fostering ethical and trustworthy behaviour. Consumer organisations and investigative reporting play an important role in exposing organisations that act unethically. Mandating public reporting of behaviour (for example, requiring corporate disclosure of a company code of ethics) is another means by which the government can encourage ethical or trustworthy behaviour.

Conclusion

Traditionally, economists have not worried about unethical or untrustworthy behaviour. It was assumed that even though individuals were almost entirely selfish, market incentives would punish cheating and untrustworthy behaviour.

However, recent evidence suggests quite a different conclusion. First, people are not as self-seeking or selfish as traditionally assumed. Second, markets need people to act with a degree of trust and integrity. The existence of transaction costs means contracting within markets is a costly and difficult exercise, and in most markets trust is needed.

Without high levels of ethical behaviour, the costs and risks of contracting are greatly increased. In markets where ethical behaviour is absent, some risky transactions will be avoided, and individuals and firms will waste considerable time and resources on the process of contracting.

It is highly likely that the general prevalence of ethical behaviour is an important influence over a country's overall economic performance. A comparison of the relative economic prosperity of different nations shows a positive relationship between indicators of ethics and economic output. It is also not hard to find examples of industries in New Zealand where poor ethical standards have had adverse economic consequences.

The relationship between ethical behaviour and economic performance means that economists have to carefully examine their policy prescriptions. There is some evidence that ethical behaviour can be influenced positively by public policy. At times, this might involve increased legal regulation to ban particular unethical practices, as well as a more general focus on encouraging a climate of ethical behaviour.

Ethical behaviour should also be an important focus of New Zealand's economic policy agenda because it represents an area where the country potentially has a comparative advantage. Indicators suggest that New Zealand, although not the highest, is a good performer compared with many other countries in terms of measured ethical behaviour. In future decades, our rankings in this area should make New Zealand an attractive destination for investment, if our regulatory regime can adequately foster ethical and trustworthy behaviour.

References

Acemoglu, D., and S. Johnson. 2005 'Unbundling institutions.' *Journal of Political Economy* 113(5): 949–95.

Akerlof, A. 1970. 'The market for "lemons": Quality uncertainty and the market mechanism.' *Quarterly Journal of Economics* 84(3): 488–500.

Alvey, J. 1999. *An Introduction to Economics as a Moral Science*. Working paper 15. Independent Institute. www.independent.org/pdf/working_papers/15_introduction.pdf (accessed 13 November 2009).

Arrow, K. 1963. 'Uncertainty and the welfare economics of medical care.' *American Economic Review* 53(5): 941–73.

Bernasek, A. 2010. *The Economics of Integrity*. New York: Harperstudio.

Bicchieri, C. 2006. *The Grammar of Society: The nature and dynamics of social norms*. Cambridge: Cambridge University Press.

Blinder, A. 2010. 'When greed is not good.' *Wall Street Journal*, 11 January. www://online.wsj.com/article/SB10001424052748703652104574652242436408008.html.

BNZ Investments Ltd v. Commissioner of Inland Revenue 15 July 2009, Wild J, HC Wellington CIV 2004-485-1059. http://jdo.justice.govt.nz/jdo.

Camerer, C., and E. Fehr. 2004. 'Measuring social norms and preferences using experimental games: A guide for social scientists.' In J. Henrich, E. Fehr, and H. Gintis (eds). *Foundations of Human Sociality: Economic experiments and ethnographic evidence from fifteen small-scale societies*. Oxford: Oxford University Press.

Cialdini, R. 2006. *Influence: The psychology of persuasion* Rev. edn. New York: Harper Paperbacks.

Cialdini, R., R. Reno, and C. Kallgren. 1990. 'A focus theory of normative conduct: Recycling the concept of norms to reduce littering in public places.' *Journal of Personality and Social Psychology* 58: 1015–26.

Consumer. 2009. 'Financial advisers: Getting good advice.' www.consumer.org. nz/reports/financial-advisers/getting-good-advice (accessed 25 February 2010).

De Nicolò, G., L. Laeven, and K. Ueda. 2006. *Corporate Governance Quality: Trends and real effects.* Working paper WP/06/293. International Monetary Fund. www.imf.org/external/pubs/ft/wp/2006/wp06293.pdf.

DellaVigna, S. 2009. 'Psychology and economics: Evidence from the field.' *Journal of Economic Literature* 47(2): 315–72.

Diplock, J. 2009. 'The financial crisis and corporate governance.' Speech to Auckland Rotary. www.seccom.govt.nz/speeches/2009/220609.shtml.

Djankov, D., D. La Porta, F. López-de-Silanes, et al. 2008. 'The law and economics of self-dealing.' *Journal of Financial Economics* 88(3): 430–65.

Frey, B. S., and S. Meier. 2004. 'Social comparisons and pro-social behavior: Testing "conditional cooperation" in a field experiment.' *American Economic Review* 94(5): 1717–22.

Gintis, H., S. Bowles, R. Boyd, et al. 2005. *Moral Sentiments and Material Interests: The foundations of cooperation in economic life.* Cambridge MA: MIT Press.

Glaeser, E., R. La Porta, F. López-de-Silanes, et al. 2004. 'Do institutions cause growth?' *Journal of Economic Growth* 9(3): 271–303.

Grimes, A. 2005. 'Improving consumer trust in the retail savings industry.' Paper prepared for the Retirement Commission. www.retirement.org.nz/ files/retirement-files/research-library/improving-consumer-trust-in-the-retail-savings-industry.pdf.

Gurría, A. 2009. 'Business ethics and OECD principles: What can be done to avoid another crisis?' Remarks by OECD secretary-general at the European Business Ethics Forum, Paris, 22 January 2009. www.oecd.org/document/3/ 0,3343,en_2649_201185_42033219_1_1_1_1,00.html.

Güth, W., R. Schmittberger, and B. Schwarze. 1982. 'An experimental analysis of ultimatum bargaining.' *Journal of Economic Behavior and Organization* 3(4): 367–88.

Harms, W., and B. Skyrms. 2008. 'Evolution of moral norms.' In M. Ruse (ed.). *The Oxford Handbook of Philosophy of Biology*. Oxford: Oxford University Press, ch. 18.

Harris, N. 2009. 'Finance company failures: Observations of the Registrar of Companies.' In Commerce Committee. *2007/08 Financial review of the Ministry of Economic Development: Report of the Commerce Committee*. Wellington: Ministry of Economic Development, Appendix B. www.parliament.nz/ NR/rdonlyres/16F22058-8DD8-4541-B9A9-064848076239/100892/DBSCH_ SCR_4272_6521.pdf.

Hunn, D., I. Bond, and D. Kernohan. 2002. *Report of the Overview Group on the Weathertightness of Buildings to the Building Industry Authority*. Wellington: Building Industry Authority. www.dbh.govt.nz/whrs-publications-reports.

IMF. 2003a. 'Growth and institutions.' In *World Economic Outlook: April 2003*. Washington: International Monetary Fund, ch. 3. www.imf.org/external/ pubs/ft/weo/2003/01.

IMF. 2003b. *The World Economic Outlook (WEO) Database April 2003*. Washington: International Monetary Fund. www.imf.org/external/pubs/ft/ weo/2003/01/data/index.htm (acessed October 2009).

Killen, M., and J. Smetana. 2006. *Handbook of Moral Development*. New Jersey: Lawrence Erlbaum Associates.

La Porta, R., F. López-de-Silanes, and G. Zamarripa. 2003. 'Related lending.' *Quarterly Journal of Economics* 118(1): 231–68.

Ledyard, J. 1995. 'Public goods: A survey of experimental research.' In J. Kagel and A. E. Roth (eds). *Handbook of Experimental Economics*. Princeton: Princeton University Press.

List, J. 2004, 'Young, selfish and male: Field evidence of social preferences.' *Economic Journal* 114(492): 121–49.

MED. 2007. *Financial Advisers: A new regulatory framework*. Regulatory Impact Statement. Wellington: Ministry of Economic Development. www.med.govt. nz/upload/47854/financial-advisors-ris.pdf.

Narvaez, M., and D. Lapsley. 2009. *Personality, Identity and Character: Explorations in moral psychology*. Cambridge: Cambridge University Press.

NZPA (New Zealand Press Association). 2009. 'Leaky homes bill likely to top $11.5 billion.' *NZ Herald*, 18 August. www.nzherald.co.nz/nz/news/article. cfm?c_id=1&objectid=10591520.

Ostrom, E. 2000. 'Collective action and the evolution of social norms.' *Journal of Economic Perspectives* 14(3): 137–58.

Parliamentary Library 2002. 'Leaky buildings.' *Background Note* 2002/10, 6 November. www.parliament.nz/NR/rdonlyres/464AB9F9-B197-4B53-BE9F-4F411CB67877/360/0210LeakyBuildings1.pdf.

Petrie, M. 2002. *Institutions, Social Norms and Well-Being*. Working paper 02/12. Wellington: The Treasury. www.treasury.govt.nz/publications/research-policy/wp/2002/02-12.

RBNZ. 2008. *Financial Stability Report*. Wellington: Reserve Bank of New Zealand. www.rbnz.govt.nz/finstab/fsreport/3311557.pdf.

Rea, D. 2010. *Would New Zealand's Economic Performance Improve if We Were More Ethical?* Working paper 10/05. Wellington: Institute of Policy Studies, School of Government, Victoria University of Wellington. http://ips.ac.nz/publications/publications/list/7.

Securities Commission. 2002. *Investment Advisers: A case study. Gideon Investments Pty Limited – Morison Guildford & Associates Limited*. www.sec-com.govt.nz/publications/documents/morison_guildford/index.shtml.

Smith, A. [1759] 1790. *The Theory of Moral Sentiments*. 6th edn. London: A. Millar. Available from the Library of Economics and Liberty, www.econlib.org (accessed 1 November 2009).

Smith, A. 1762. 'Lectures on jurisprudence'. In R. L. Meek, D. D. Raphael, and P. G. Stein (eds). 1982. *The Glasgow Edition of the Works and Correspondence of Adam Smith*. Vol. 5. Indianapolis: Liberty Fund.

Smith, A. 1776. *An Inquiry into the Nature and Causes of the Wealth of Nations*. 5th edn. Edited by E. Cannan. 1904. London: Methuen. Available from the Library of Economics and Liberty, www.econlib.org/library/Smith/smWN.html (accessed 17 October 2009).

Transparency International. 2009. *Corruption Perceptions Index 2008*. www.transparency.org/policy_research/surveys_indices/cpi (accessed 24 October 2009).

Treasury. 2008. *Briefing to the Incoming Minister of Finance: Medium-term economic challenges*. Wellington: The Treasury. www.treasury.govt.nz/publications/briefings/2008/big08.pdf.

Treasury. 2009. *Financial Statements of the Government of New Zealand for the Year Ended 30 June 2009*. Wellington: The Treasury. www.treasury.govt.nz/government/financialstatements/yearend/jun09/05.htm.

2025 Taskforce. 2009. *Answering the $64,000 Question: Closing the income gap with Australia by 2025 – First report of the 2025 Taskforce*. Wellington: New Zealand Government. http://purl.oclc.org/nzt/r-1252.

Westpac Banking Corp. v. Commissioner of Inland Revenue 7 October 2009, Harrison J, HC Auckland CIV 2005-404-2843.

WHO. 2004. 'Causes of death.' *Data and Statistics*. World Health Organization. www.who.int/research/en (accessed 1 October 2009).

Williamson, O. 1985. *The Economic Institutions of Capitalism: Firms, markets, relational contracting*. New York: Free Press.

World Bank. 2001. *World Development Report 2002: Building institutions for markets*. New York: Oxford University Press. econ.worldbank.org/external/default/main?pagePK=64165259&theSitePK=469372&piPK=64165421&menuPK=64166093&entityID=000094946_01092204010635.

World Values Survey (n. d.) Online data analysis. www.wvsevsdb.com/wvs/WVSAnalize.jsp.

Zak, P., and S. Knack. 2001. 'Trust and growth.' *Economic Journal* 111(470): 295–321.

12. Regulation of financial markets: Panics, moral hazard, and the long-term good

Simon Smelt

Introduction

Much of the research relating to the recent events discussed in this chapter is – in academic terms – at an early stage and relatively untested. Hence, this chapter is both provisional and tentative.

Greed and morality

Debate over the causes of the recent financial tsunami and the policies to deal with it will probably continue for decades. There is still considerable disagreement over such matters in relation to the Great Depression.[1] By contrast, the key moral point from recent events – the devastating effects of 'greed' – might seem self-evident: greed of financiers, greed of investors, perhaps greed of US consumers. Bankers have been a favourite target. This is understandable given the huge public bailouts they have received. In Britain, the chancellor has referred to 'kamikaze bankers' damaging the economy (presumably he did not mean they intended to wreak havoc).[2] The chief executive of the British Financial Services Authority tried to sound like a tough cop warning the criminals on his patch, 'a principles-based approach does not work with individuals who have no principles ... People should be very frightened of the [Financial Services Authority]' (Townsend 2009). An industry spokesperson responded that they were not drug dealers at the school gates (Monaghan 2009).

Alan Greenspan, previous governor of the US Federal Reserve, spoke of financiers having 'got greedy' (Goodman 2008), and widespread accusations of out-of-control greed suggest the return of the character Gordon Gecko from the

---

1 Interpretations of the Great Depression have been a central source of contention between Keynesians and Monetarists. See, for example, Friedman (1994) and Galbraith (1961).
2 See '"Kamikaze" bankers damaged economy, says Alistair Darling' (2009).

1987 film *Wall Street*, with his mantra 'greed is good'. The Australian prime minister, Kevin Rudd (2008), gave a speech entitled 'The children of Gordon Gekko'.

But is this new? As US President Hoover is said to have remarked, 'The trouble with capitalism is capitalists; they're too damn greedy'. Condemning bankers is reminiscent of traditional attitudes to moneylenders who were sought after for credit but otherwise were treated with disdain and got the blame and worse when things went wrong. A current film version of Shakespeare's *Merchant of Venice* (2004) nicely captures this.

In probably the most nuanced and carefully considered moral commentary on the crisis, the Vatican goes much beyond such blame games. To quote Benedict XVI (2009, p. 35):

> The market is subject to the principles of so-called commutative justice, which regulates the relations of giving and receiving between parties to a transaction. But the social doctrine of the Church has unceasingly highlighted the importance of distributive justice and social justice for the market economy, not only because it belongs within a broader social and political context, but also because of the wider network of relations within which it operates. ... Without internal forms of solidarity and mutual trust, the market cannot completely fulfill its proper economic function. And today it is this trust that has ceased to exist, and the loss of trust is a grave loss.

Thus, the Vatican sees the need to connect the marketplace to distributive and social justice and the wider community. It identifies the financial failure as stemming from moral factors – solidarity and mutual trust – and without simplistic labelling.

This chapter argues that there is indeed a moral dimension underlying the recent financial havoc, but that it stems from a weakness in the commutative justice that underpins the marketplace, rather than from a lack of distributive or social justice. (That is not to say that distributive justice and social justice are not vital concerns.) Examination of the evidence shows solidarity and trust to be central issues but not in the way one might expect. Attempts at distributive justice may have worsened the situation. The moral questions raised and lessons to be learned are both surprising and generic for policy makers. In the extreme furnace of the financial meltdown, broader principles emerge. The form in which morality is applied turns out to be critical – as both part of the problem and part of the solution.

Warning signs

Consider a key presenting problem: the inability or insouciance of both government authorities and those governing and managing the great commercial financial institutions to spot or act early on impending disaster. We find a seeming weakness in decision making at the micro level, institution by institution, by those who were supposed to be – and paid very well to be – smart at reading market signals.

There was no shortage of warning comments: aside from various commentators and economists, Warren Buffet (2003, p. 15) spoke of 'financial weapons of mass destruction', the Federal Bureau of Investigation warned of massive mortgage fraud (Frieden 2004), the Mortgage Insurance Companies of America (2006, p. 15, fn. 32) referred to an apocalyptic paper *This Powder Keg Is Going To Blow*,[3] and the annual reports of the central bankers' central bank made grim reading (Bank for International Settlements 2007, 2008). There was no shortage of warning signs; out of many signs consider those shown in Figure 1 for the United States.

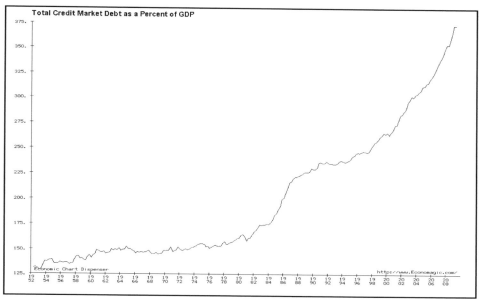

Figure 1: United States total credit market debt as percentage of gross domestic product, 1952–2009

Source: Economagic, www.economagic.com/em-cgi/data.exe/var/togdp-totalcreditdebt.

---

3   Mortgage Insurance Companies of America (2006) was commenting on proposed guidance to lenders on 'non-traditional' mortgages.

Figure 1 shows the US economy in this decade fuelled by rapid growth in debt. The predominant view of financial and macro-economic managers was that other variables were more critical. New levels of financial sophistication and economic management were overcoming the old boom–bust cycle. Phrases such as the 'great moderation' and the 'Goldilocks economy' ('not too hot; not too cold') were deployed.[4] Increasing levels of debt were facilitated by improvements in financial markets and financial products, and it was assumed the marketplace should be left to sort out acceptable levels of debt.

The market did sort out acceptable levels of debt, but through a handbrake turn! We should not be surprised. *This Time is Different*, by Reinhart and Rogoff (2009), brings out a recurrent pattern over eight centuries of debt-fuelled asset price bubbles leading to the inevitable crash.[5] Before each crash, there were strident claims that 'this time is different' – whether it was about South Sea islands, South American silver mines, canals, railways, dotcoms, or – the last manifestation – housing and new financial techniques.

This crash was no different, and Charles Mackay's 1841 classic *Extraordinary Popular Delusions and the Madness of Crowds* still rings true (Mackay 1996). Are we unable to escape the madness of crowds? The economist Hyman Minsky outlines a cycle of economic boom leading to an appetite for increased risk and looser regulation, culminating in the 'Minsky moment', when the bubble bursts, leading to reaction in the opposite direction, and so forth (Minsky 2008).

The basic picture is of a behavioural cycle driven by greed and fear. In July 2007, before the big meltdown in 2008 but when the financial markets were already severely disturbed, the then president of Citibank said, 'As long as the music is playing, you've got to get up and dance. We're still dancing'.[6] Is it hubris by the policy makers and financial leaders in thinking that a combination of new technology and market forces could provide escape from cyclical forces or hopelessness in seeing little chance of escape and so just going with the crowd?

Greed as new or greed as a constant

Compare two quotations from Alan Greenspan, the first from 1998, and the second – which we have already glanced at from 2008 (in Goodman 2008):

---

4   The former term may have originated from Stock and Watson (2002). It was favoured by both Mervyn King, the governor of the Bank of England, and Ben Bernanke. See, for example, Bernanke (2004). The latter term is attributed to David Shulman of Salomon Brothers by wikipedia.org.
5   The most well-known economic text on the recurring nature of financial bubbles is Kindleberger and Aliber (2005).
6   Charles Prince quoted in *Financial Times* interview, 9 July 2007. www.ft.com/cms/s/0/80e2987a-2e50-11dc-821c-0000779fd2ac.html.

Regulation of derivatives transactions that are privately negotiated by professionals is unnecessary.

The problem is not that the contracts failed. Rather, the people using them got greedy. A lack of integrity spawned the crisis.

Between 1998 and 2008 we move from a picture of consenting adults – they know what they are doing and will experience the consequences, so leave them to it – to one of excessive greed: they 'got greedy'. The verb 'got' is the giveaway: imagine the shock headline in the *Wall Street Journal*, 'Greed found in Wall Street'.

In fact, a whole series of revelations and commentaries by denizens of Wall Street going back to the 1920s show a remarkably consistent picture: downstairs brutal deal room managers bully their staff and ignore the rules whilst upstairs in the boardroom the grey heads reminisce over a more gentlemanly, golden age.[7] Sociological workplace studies explain why deal room managers behave so badly (Godechot 2008a, 2008b). History is littered with large financial entities that went bust or were damaged due to outrageous greed.[8]

Greed and bad behaviour are not new and the 'got' in Greenspan's 'got greedy' does not belong there. This time was not different in terms of greed either. Therefore, why did the new technology fail to deal with greed, if greed were indeed the problem?

We can use the work of Oliver Williamson – who belatedly received the Nobel Prize in 2009 – to unpack the concept of 'greed'. Williamson puts together five factors:

- asymmetric information (when you and I contract, we each know pertinent things that the other does not know)

- incomplete contracting (it is neither feasible nor economic for a contract to specify every possible circumstance)

- myopia (undue weight given to the short term)

---

7   For the 1920s, see Lefèvre (2006). See also Brooks (1999). For the 1960s, see Brooks (1998). For the 1980s, see Stewart (1992), Mayer (1990), and Lewis (1990). For the 1990s and early 21st century, see Knee (2006) and Cramer (2002). And no doubt many more.

8   In the last quarter century before the most recent crisis, examples are (a key year indicated in brackets): United States – Continental Illinois (1984), Lehmans (previous incarnation, 1984), E. F. Hutton (1988), Drexel Burnham Lambert (1990), Citicorp (1991), Salomon (1991), Kidder Peabody (1994), LTCM (1997), Arthur Anderson (2002); United Kingdom – Barings (2005), Lloyds of London (1993), Equitable Life (2000); Ireland – Allied Irish Bank (1985, 2002); France – Lyonnaise (1993), Societe Generale (2008); The Middle East – BCCI (1991); Japan – Industrial Bank of Japan (1991), Daiwa (1995), Sumitoto (1998), Bank of Japan (1998), Sanwa (1998). The problems in Australasia with Westpac, the State Bank of South Australia, and the Bank of New Zealand were probably due mainly to poor management.

- opportunism (taking advantage of circumstances)

- satisficing (people economise effort – they are lazy).[9]

Thus, in a world of imperfect information and incomplete contracting, greed is expressed through myopia, opportunism, and laziness. The picture is of bounded rationality, with contracting (whether formal or informal) defining the bounds of both greed and risk.

Williamson's work is widely cited in contemporary economics and received considerable attention in designing contracts to deal with those five issues and solve the 'agency problem'. Greed cannot be eliminated but we know a lot about how to deal with and harness it. In Williamson's terms, adequate contracting serves to contain the adverse impact of greed on a contractual relationship. Weak or inappropriate contracting or enforcement of contracts is liable to lead to failure to contain problems with greed. This perspective is opposite to Greenspan's view that greed undermined contracts that were otherwise satisfactory.

Greed is scarcely new and we have a fair idea how to harness it. Similarly, and as I will discuss shortly, much work has gone into a better understanding of risk and how to handle it. Yet, along with greed, this was a point of failure in the crisis. As with previous bubbles, risk was underestimated, despite the sophisticated tools for assessing and handling it.

Governance and regulatory failure

One might expect that the best available technology for dealing with greed and risk would provide some shelter in the most recent crisis.

A 2009 international study of the crisis uses some well-established OECD metrics to assess the quality of banks' governance and the regulatory regimes to which they were subject (Beltratti and Stulz 2009). The study found an inverse relationship between the quality of governance and regulation on the one hand and the likelihood that the bank had run into difficulties on the other. The *better* governed and regulated the bank, the *more* likely it was to be in trouble. This seems counterintuitive until you put it the other way round: laggard banks were less likely to be in trouble. In other words, the industry leaders were heading over a cliff, with the ones at the back furthest from the edge. The best-available technology failed.

This pattern is illustrated in Figure 2. The figure shows, for the United States, the surge into issuing asset backed securities and then the even stronger move

---

9   Notably in Williamson (1985).

away from issuing this innovative type of security as the crisis began to build. Regulation and governance forms did not restrain the pursuit of profits through asset backed securities.

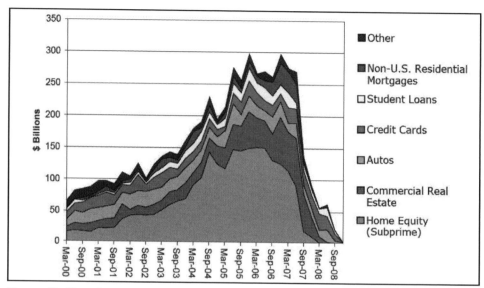

Figure 2: New issuance of asset backed securities, six monthly, 2000–2008

Source: J. P. Morgan from the International Monetary Fund website http://imf.org/external/np/res/seminars/2009/arc/pdf/ashcraft1.pdf.

As much of the problem originated in the United States, it could be argued that aspects of it originated from the deregulation in the financial sector that has been under way there since the late 1990s. However, the international nature of the problem and the extent of international effort put into developing the Basel I and Basel II banking accords show that the best regulatory practice (in terms of the prevailing wisdom at the time) may not achieve its goals and can be counterproductive. After 2008, Basel II is widely viewed as being deeply flawed and possibly inferior to its simpler predecessor, Basel I.[10] However, this does not seem to have been a common view before the crash.

Nor can the problems be explained by the size or direction of international capital flows (for example, into the United States and United Kingdom). A new study finds no correlation between the size of the trade deficit or surplus and the extent of dealing in fancy debt instruments (Acharya and Schnabl 2009).

---

10   Each of the three pillars of Basel II – minimum capital requirements, supervisory review, and market discipline – requires a high degree of analytical precision and validation to achieve the aims of enhanced risk management and capital adequacy. Basel II gives banks more discretion in some areas than Basel I. As there are lower capital requirements for off-balance sheet items than for on-balance sheet items, the accord sets up perverse incentives for banks to shift liabilities off balance sheet.

For example, German and Icelandic banks were enthusiastic players. Nor is it a matter of big financial entities conning the innocent consumer or small Norwegian town council. The fancy debt instruments were almost entirely dealt between large financial entities (Acharya and Schnabl 2009). If anybody should have understood what was involved, they should have.

The best regulatory and governance endeavours failed and Greenspan's picture of consenting adults failed. With hindsight, it may well be possible to identify certain specific forms of regulation and governance that could have helped counter the crisis and much work is under way. But it would be foolish to say, 'This time is (or will be) different'.

Some of the tough-sounding proposals for regulating the financial sector in fact replicate what is already there. Here is the US Federal Deposit Insurance Corporation (2002, section 4.4–1(II)) on the responsibilities of bank boards:

> bank directors are held to the highest fiduciary standards. They are responsible not only to the stockholders who elected them but [also for] the safety of depositors' funds and the pervasive influence the bank exercises on the community it serves.

This sounds both tough and wide-ranging. What about legislation to restrain greedy bankers' pay? Try this:

> Compensation Standards – Each appropriate Federal banking agency shall, for all insured depository institutions, prescribe—
>
> (1) standards prohibiting as an unsafe and unsound practice any employment contract, compensation or benefit agreement, fee arrangement, perquisite, stock option plan, postemployment benefit, or other compensatory arrangement [etc.].

The previous quotation is from section 39 of the Federal Deposit Insurance Corporation Improvement Act 1991. It has been in force for some 18 years.

In the United States, in the wake of the 'Savings and Loans' crisis of the 1980s and then in the wake of the Enron fraud and collapse at the beginning of this decade, requirements on banks in particular and corporates more generally have been toughened up in some areas, even as they have been relaxed in others.[11] Compliance costs from numerous law changes have been significant and unresolved issues of complexity arise from the interaction of different bodies of

---

11   The most notable piece of new regulation is the Sarbanes Oxley Act 2002, which imposed new reporting requirements. In terms of deregulation, the Gramm-Leach-Bliley Act 1999 allowed commercial, investment, and insurance activities within a single bank while the Commodity Futures Modernization Act 2000 exempted much trading in futures from regulation by federal or state agencies.

legislation.[12] Current efforts (as of early December 2009) in the US Congress to draft the Wall Street Reform and Consumer Protection Act and, in particular, the Over-the-Counter Derivatives Markets Act, have produced much lobbying, debate, and confusion about phraseology and alleged loopholes, amendments that appear, disappear, and then reappear, and so forth. Starting with a good, clear intention is not enough.

This leads us to the familiar issue of regulatory failure and regulatory capture.[13] If these were problems before the crisis, they will unavoidably be worse now. High stakes games played under intense pressure are liable to be ugly and destructive of high-minded principles, ivory tower theories, political undertakings, and legislative parameters alike. Previous regulatory bursts responding to financial crises or misdemeanors may have made matters worse.[14]

With footloose international capital, there is also the much-discussed problem of regulatory arbitrage: business gravitating towards regimes that have the softest touch.[15] We are left seeking some robust but flexible rules and mechanisms for enforcement that can have international purchase. The G20 and other forums have yet to yield this.[16]

Moral hazard

The nature of the game and of the financial sector brings us to the issue of moral hazard. One aspect of moral hazard has been well known since Adam Smith: the problem of banks drifting toward high-risk investments because others will

---

12   Here are two examples. (1) The Due Diligence Repository was launched by Bankersalmanac.com in 2004. By 2009 it contained over '64,500 documents against 16,800 financial institutions, comprising licenses, corporate governance documents, anti-money laundering policies, USA Patriot Act/Foreign Bank Certification and the Wolfsberg Group Anti-Money Laundering Questionnaire' (American Bankers Association 2009). (2) In September 2009, the US law firm Davis Polk produced a 260-page guide entitled *A Guide to the Laws, Regulations and Contracts of the Financial Crisis* for 'anyone who wants to understand the flurry of new legislation, old law used in new ways, contracts with Treasury, press releases, frequently asked questions, guidelines and other rulemaking that has occurred at a dizzying speed over the last year and a half' (Davis Polk 2009, p. 1).

13   One recent report – *In Praise of Unlevel Playing Fields* – is particularly critical of this aspect. See Warwick Commission on International Financial Reform (2009).

14   State-by-state research shows that strong regulatory responses to the 1929 crash tended to worsen subsequent bank failures (Mitchener 2007). Similarly, it can be argued that the main solutions to the savings and loans crisis of the 1980s – securitization, risk-based capital, and market value accounting – contributed to the present crisis. See White (1991). Regulatory missteps may also have played a part in creating the Savings and Loans crisis. See Barth et al. (2004).

15   Regulatory competition between financial centres was an argument advanced for deregulation in, for example, the report by the Presidential Working Group on Financial Markets (1999).

16   The G20 is a group representing 19 leading economies and the European monetary union. Collectively, they account for 85 per cent of the world economy.

share in the costs of failure to a greater extent than in the benefits of such investments (Smith [1776] 1994, pp. 290–340). One might expect that robust solutions would be in place by now.

The intrinsic moral hazard with banks – the government may have to step in and rescue large ones due to their economic importance – is precisely why they are subject to distinct and generally tight regulatory regimes and why for the past 20 years massive international effort has been put into the Basel I and Basel II banking accords. The first two banks to require bailing out in the present debacle were two German *landesbanks* – both with full underwriting by their unfortunate state governments (Acharya and Schnabl 2009).

Even with such generous backing, moral hazard does not mean bankers are indifferent to risk. Part of the costs of the downside is liable to be borne by the stakeholders in the entity concerned. Managers and board members risk prosecution for breach of fiduciary or other duties.[17] Bailouts and a smooth ride for management are not guaranteed. Accounts of the Lehmans and AIG collapses illustrate the highly uncertain future at the time for even the biggest of the commercial financial institutions. As the chief executive of Morgan Chase put it, 'There aren't enough lifeboats. Someone is going to die'.[18] Among the major firms, Bear Stearns, Lehmans, Merrill Lynch, Wachovia, and Washington Mutual did not survive 2008 as independent entities. In 2009, to the end of November, over 120 US banks failed, 5 with assets of over $10 billion (Federal Deposit Insurance Corporation 2009). There are other kinds of risk for financial leaders. The board and chief executive of Royal Bank of Scotland, for example, can scarcely have been indifferent to becoming figures of derision and hate. Iceland's banking leaders have found themselves repudiated by their fellow citizens.

Obviously, such outcomes were not expected, which illustrates the underestimation of risk that we shall turn to shortly. However, another source of moral hazard lies behind the current crisis and arises from outside financial markets. In the United States, two 'government-sponsored' housing agencies, Fannie and Freddie, and a succession of legislation under both Democrats and Republicans – notably the Community Reinvestment Act 1977, the Housing and Community Development Act of 1992, and the American Dream Downpayment Act 2003 – sought to make mortgages, and thus house ownership, more accessible to the poor. Regulators instructed banks to consider alternatives to traditional credit histories because borrowers targeted by the Community Reinvestment Act

---

17   Following the Savings and Loans crisis of the 1980s, several leading financiers – notably Charles Keating – were indicted.

18   The most well known account so far is Sorkin (2009). See also, for example, the Bloomberg series of articles in *Bloombergs* magazine of 8–10 September 2009 on the Lehmans collapse: Ivry et al. (2009a, 2009b) and Pittman and Ivry (2009). The quotation is on the back cover of Sorkin (2009).

often lacked traditional credit histories. The banks were expected to be creative and consider other indicators of reliability. Similarly, regulators expected banks to relax income requirements (see Litan et al. 2000; Meyer 1998; Comptroller of the Currency Administrator of National Banks 1996). Thus, in pursuing social justice aims, successive governments encouraged loose lending practices for housing. Fannie and Freddie were not federally guaranteed but became the two biggest recipients of federal rescue money.

In pursuing social justice in this way, not only was the housing bubble fed, but the commutative justice of marketplace contracting was undermined. The usual lender's considerations of a borrower's ability to repay and of ensuring the borrower had shown the ability to save and had 'skin in the game' through a down payment were removed. A contract might be signed between lender and borrower but the driver was public policy and the hidden guarantor was Freddie or Fannie and thus, as it turned out, the taxpayer. Neither borrower nor lender was liable to face the full consequences of their actions, so the bilateral contract in many cases became a sham, held in place by moral hazard. With the downturn in house prices, the sham was revealed. The pursuit of social justice by making mortgage funding more accessible, expanded the moral hazard in the financial sector. US housing policy was a destabilising factor in the financial sector.

Risk

Government guarantees and bailouts in the financial sector may shift risk appetites but the core puzzle is the huge underestimation of risk by the financial sector before the crisis. My appetite for investment risk may rise if I (the investor) think I can shed much of the downside onto you, but I still need to evaluate the risks being run before deciding to make an investment: how likely are the downsides and upsides to occur, and how much downside risk can I really shed?

Broadly, the role of financial markets is to match those who have capital with those who want capital and discover a price for the deal. That means pricing the risk involved. The under-pricing of risk revealed in the 2008 bust was a major malfunction by financial markets and the financial institutions. They got it wrong.

Against the Gods: The remarkable story of risk was written in 1998 and describes how humanity has, over the ages, got better at estimating and handling risk and thus discovering business opportunities (Bernstein 1998). It discusses the history of an investment firm called Long Term Capital Management (LTCM) in the 1990s. Two economists, Black and Schoels, received the Nobel Prize for their pioneering work on modelling risk. LTCM was set up to operationalise their model, which worked extremely well in the real world and made vast sums of money, until it didn't. LTCM went bust and to prevent contagion was bailed out by other Wall Street firms (Lowenstein 2000). *Against the Gods* sees that as a blip on the upward path of risk analysis. Since LTCM-leading Wall Street firms have hired many quantitative analysts or 'quants' – typically with postgraduate qualifications in maths and science from MIT (the Massachusetts Institute of Technology) – to undertake more and more sophisticated risk analysis for them. This worked well, until it didn't.[19] One hedge fund is said to have given its clients a chess set inscribed with the words of a chess grandmaster, 'It often happens that a player carries out a deep and complicated calculation, but fails to spot something elementary right at the first move'.[20]

The extensive use of quants in the financial sector shows the concern there to measure risk. Sophisticated approaches to measuring 'value at risk' and for 'stress testing' were developed so managers could assess and control the exposure of their company to risk. But the vulnerability to mundane human failure remains. Faced with complex situations, people use computational shortcuts (Tversky and Kahneman 1992). For example, in 2000, the market for collateralised debt obligations was revolutionised by David X. Li, working at J. P. Morgan. Rather than requiring vast amounts of data analysis, Li developed a simple formula for correlating the default rates between different securities. He appeared to have found a convenient law of correlation. His approach was rapidly adopted throughout the industry and it worked well, until it didn't. The years 2007 and 2008 proved his approach to be completely inadequate; the shortcut was illusory.[21] To quote G. K. Chesterton, 'the world's exactitude is obvious, but its inexactitude is hidden; its wildness lies in wait' (quoted in Bernstein 1998, p. 331).

In *Black Swan*, Nassim Taleb (2007) argues that the quant approach is unable to allow for rare, outlier events. If you have only seen white swans, you are not expecting, and do not allow for, a black one. Thus, quant analysis provides only spurious accuracy. But, as *This Time is Different* (Reinhart and Rogoff 2009) shows, there is no shortage of historical black swans – if one is prepared to look. Analysts have long been aware of the problem of so-called 'fat tails': financial markets do not show anything like a statistically normal distribution of outlier events – such events are more common, so more dangerous, than that.[22]

Yet risk modelling in the financial sector was very poor at allowing for outlier events. There appear to be at least three aspects to this.

---

19 Discussed in Haldane (2009b).
20 Amaranth Hedge Fund, which went bust in 2006 in one of the largest hedge fund collapses to that date.
21 See Salmon (2009). A more favourable view is taken by Tett (2009).
22 See, for example, Mandelbrot and Hudson (2006). The work by Tversky and Kahneman (1992) is seminal.

- Incentives were weak to look at worst-case scenarios; as in most large institutions, why undermine day-to-day practices by looking for trouble.

- There was genuine – even extraordinary – belief in the effectiveness of the risk modelling undertaken and thus in the extreme unlikelihood of events unfolding as harshly as they did.[23]

- Increasing complexity and inter-linkages of markets – partially fostered by the risk modelling and new financial products themselves – increased interdependency and reduced the ability to comprehend the exposures to other parties involved.[24]

The tendency to underestimate risk appears embedded. A November 2009 report to G20 finance ministers and governors found that self-assessments by 20 large financial institutions were 'too positive and that much stronger ongoing management commitment to risk control' as well as greater resources were required to 'close gaps between actual and recommended practices' (Financial Stability Board 2009, p. 4).[25] The expectations embodied in 'recommended practices' may well appear to banks as an exogenously imposed extra cost to doing business that is best minimised under competitive pressure: management 'buy-in' is needed.[26] However, this leaves unresolved the issue of assessing and allowing for risk from outlier scenarios.

To summarise so far, we find a clear impending disaster that was ignored, the implementation of prevailing wisdom on governance and regulation that failed and may have been counterproductive, US government housing policies that added fuel to the fire, the use of best available risk analysis that failed and failed predictably, and an industry unwilling fully to address risk issues in the ways that regulators seek.

Systemic risk and network management

The alternative to blaming particular groups or entities for the meltdown has been to look at systemic risk and see the need for coordinated action at a systemic level. One writer states that the 'wizardry' of recent financial innovations is 'increasing complexity, and by forging tighter links between various markets and securities, making them dangerously interdependent' (Bookstaber 2008). If

---

23   Examples of both are given by Haldane (2009a). See also Guttentag and Herring (1986).
24   See, for example, Bookstaber (2008). The role of financial modelling in shaping the markets it seeks to model is discussed in MacKenzie (2006).
25   The Financial Stability Board was referring to a 'Senior Supervisors Group report' of October 2009.
26   The Basel Committee on Banking Supervision found that the viability and usefulness of a bank's economic capital processes – as required by Basel II – depended critically on the existence of a credible commitment or 'buy-in' on the part of senior management (Bank for International Settlements 2009).

crowd mentality or systemic risk is the driving force, then policy needs to deal with the crowd or systemic level; network externalities need to be addressed at the network level (see, for example, Kern et al. 2005; Morris and Shin 2008). The whole is greater than the sum of its parts.

Models of infection (whether for the spread of disease or of ideas) are well established in the social sciences. Patterns of usage on websites such as Facebook, YouTube and Twitter demonstrate network behaviour, how things go viral, and so forth, so can help in the design of control mechanisms as can analysis of ecosystems (see Sornette 2009; Crane 2009).

A well-received paper by Andrew Haldane at the Bank of England puts forward several network management solutions on this basis (Haldane 2009a, pp. 16–7). His approach is insightful and some of the solutions may well be valid. However, there is a non-trivial flaw with his and similar approaches. It parallels the flaws with many of the approaches to macro-management and financial supervision and governance that recently failed.

The efficient market hypothesis assumes that enough people are sufficiently rational and sufficiently well informed for a sufficient amount of the time so that markets will work quite smoothly to discover market-clearing prices and allocate scarce resources. The market largely looks after itself, provided the right framework of rules is provided. The granularity of actual deals and behaviours in the market place vanishes. The network management approach recognises the clumpiness around 'nodes' and the risks of infections and surges through the network. But, in a similar fashion to the efficient market hypothesis, the graininess of real-life deals vanishes. The market may no longer quite look after itself because of network effects, but a big spider sitting in the middle of the network (such as the Bank of England) can provide control.

The managerial approach to networking makes no reference to trust or integrity or pursuing value for money through the efficient use of resources. The distinguishing characteristics of the marketplace vanish. Instead, analysis of ecosystems or the use of websites such as YouTube is used to provide examples and test beds for network management. This is revealing. Interaction in such cases is largely or entirely non-contractual. The flows of information and network behaviours are consequent on that. Hence, the contractual problem and the way its solutions shape economic institutions are irrelevant. Consequently, the solutions that contracting can provide to opportunism, myopia, and so forth do not apply. Yet, based on Williamson, these contractual solutions are why financial institutions are the way they are and why they rarely show the same patterns of behaviour as ecosystems or YouTube. Market behaviour most resembles such patterns when contracting is superficial or momentary.

The network approach removes itself even further from the details of the marketplace than the efficient market hypothesis. Rather than seeking a higher and higher overview, maybe, as with the boss figure in the current Auckland Savings Bank advertisement, we need to be brought down about 20 storeys so we can 'almost see people' from our office window. Then we can discover that 'markets are as personal as the people in them'.[27] Looking at the dynamics of bilateral contracting and the bounded rationality of those involved brings people back into the picture. It also brings ethics back into the picture at the person-to-person level, for contract law is based on a system of moral precepts.

Contracting

The financial innovations of recent years have greatly modified and stretched the nature of contracting.[28] It is a commonplace that, over the last quarter century, banks have moved from relational lending – based on personal contacts and knowledge at the bank manager level – to more wholesale and transactional approaches to lending, where transaction costs are lower but competition is more open (see, for example, the discussion in Rajan 1998). Recent innovations have further shifted the locus of contracting.

To gain flexibility and to respond to global opportunities and changes, financial markets seek liquidity; that is, ready saleability of an asset.[29] For the individual investor, more liquidity is also generally preferable. The other side of liquidity is less commitment: if I can readily cash up my investment, I am not committed to it. The search for liquidity creates pressure to reduce commitments and hence to loosen up or find ways round contracts that otherwise would bind or limit the actions of the parties concerned. Hence, the move to greater liquidity and flexibility has also been a move to looser contracting and lower levels of mutual commitment by parties.

This has consequences for the way greed and risk are framed and constrained by contracting. Take the remark by Greenspan (1998) quoted earlier:

> Regulation of derivatives transactions that are privately negotiated by professionals is unnecessary.

---

27   A phrase ascribed to the economist and social commentator Thomas Sowell.
28   For example, Haldane (2009a, p. 7) states, 'Diversification came care of two complementary business strategies. The first was "originate and distribute". Risk became a commodity. As such it could be bundled, sliced, diced, and then re-bundled for onward sale. Credit became, in the jargon, structured. Securitization was one vehicle for achieving this. Derivatives, such as [credit default swaps], were another. As these marketable instruments passed between participants, the network chain lengthened'. Talking of AIG, Haldane (2009a, p. 16) remarks, 'The network chain was so complex that spotting the weakest link became impossible'.
29   The concept of liquidity in economics is considerably more complex than this!

Behind this are assumptions both about the capabilities of the professionals involved and the meaningfulness of their contracting. Without the latter, the former fails. If risk and greed are not well bounded, then they cannot be factored in accurately. Greed may not have changed but the vessel to contain it has. If Williamson's approach is accepted, the institutional forms to undertake and enforce such contracting have either changed or need to change if they are to cope with the new high liquidity, global environment.

We have seen how the pursuit of social justice through housing finance riddled the contractual relationship between borrower and lender with moral hazard, because government policies and agencies were effectively a third party to the deal. Competition and innovation have also shifted the nature of contracting. Two instances can be used to illustrate the weakening of contractual relationships occurring in consequence of the financial innovations of recent years.

First consider Mortgage Electronic Registration Systems Inc (MERS), which the big banks set up to facilitate the transfer and recording of mortgages. MERS is vital to the 'slicing and dicing' of mortgages used to construct some of the new debt instruments that fuelled the financial boom. Without MERS, mortgages could not have been so packaged and transferred in financial market dealings. Most US mortgages now reside on the MERS system. But MERS and the trading of mortgages it facilitates create numerous contractual problems. MERS is not a mere register; it actually holds the mortgages. As mortgagee of record, MERS is both agent and principal to lenders and banks. The original holder of the mortgage is rarely the party servicing the mortgage, and modifications and changes of ownership made through MERS will be unknown to the real owner of the promissory note. When a payoff is made, MERS records the release, although it never held a financial interest and the real owner files no release of the mortgage.

These may seem like technicalities but there is a real effect. By making mortgages into mere data points that can be readily aggregated, packaged, sold, and resold, MERS undermines the original contractual relationship between lender and borrower. The borrower may find they are negotiating with an unknown or unexpected party.[30] MERS has been widely criticised in courts and its legal standing is in doubt. As one court judgment put it, 'The relationship that MERS has to (the holder of a loan) is more akin to that of a straw man than to a party possessing all the rights given a buyer'.[31]

---

30   Though not posing the same legal issues, in New Zealand in 1991 the mortgage portfolio of the Crown-owned Housing Corporation was sold to a private company owned by an investment bank. Mortgagees soon found their mortgage payments substantially increased. See *Hansard: Parliamentary Debate* for 5 October 1994 at http://vdig.net/hansard/content.jsp?id=43766.

31   Kansas Supreme Court in *Landmark National Bank v. Kesler* 2009 Kan. LEXIS 834 (28 August 2009). It was also stated, 'The relationship that MERS has to [the holder of a loan] is more akin to that of a straw man than to a party possessing all the rights given a buyer ... The law generally understands that a mortgagee is

At the same time, the financial packages assembled together by 'slicing and dicing' huge numbers of separate mortgages cannot be assessed by any conventional means, with the 'due diligence' documentation estimated to run to over 1 billion pages for some collateralised debt obligation packages (see Haldane 2009a). Hence, the relationship between both borrower and lender and between those selling and buying financial assets has, in the last 10 years or so, been stretched by financial innovations.

The second instance of weakened contractual relations can be drawn from another notorious form of financial instrument: derivatives that enable positions to be taken out against specified future movements in prices. As a farmer or exporter I may wish to insure against unexpected future movements in crop prices or exchange rates or to lock in a current price. Derivatives enable me to take out such insurance and have been around since at least the 17th century.[32] However, as a speculator I may also wish to bet on the direction of future price movements. Broadly speaking, the difference is between insurance and gambling. In one case, I am seeking to reduce risk from something I have exposure to. In the other, I am seeking exposure to risk where otherwise I would have none. Of course, in real life it gets more complicated than that. Historically, common law cases have developed sophisticated criteria for distinguishing between insurance and gambling and different procedures for dealing with the relevant contracts. As derivatives developed, so did the common law dealing with them (see Stout 1999). But in the United States, futures were removed from common law coverage and subject to specific 'black letter' law, notably the Commodity Exchange Act 1936, which banned some forms of financial speculation, with various attempts to strengthen market oversight of futures since.[33]

Since then, derivatives have been used not only for insurance and gambling but to launch hostile attacks on companies by driving down the price of their options or to overinsure a company against failure of its own product so it has been able to bet against both its own product and customers.[34] Again, the

---

not distinct from a lender: a mortgagee is "[o]ne to whom property is mortgaged: the mortgage creditor, or lender." ... What stake in the outcome of an independent action for foreclosure could MERS have? It did not lend the money ... MERS is not an economic "beneficiary" under the Deed of Trust. It is owed and will collect no money from Debtors under the Note, nor will it realize the value of the Property through foreclosure.' See also Commonwealth of Massachusetts Trial Court in *US Bank National Association v. Ibanez* and *Wells Fargo Bank v. Larace* 29 October 2009 (www.boston.com/business/articles/2009/10/15/ibanezruling) and New York Court of Appeals *Merscorp v. Romaine* NY Int 167 (2006).

32 See the 17th century writer Joseph De la Vega (1688).

33 The Commodities Futures Trading Commission was set up in 1975 and deals with financial as well as commodity futures. It has struggled with its task and its remit has been extended or reduced on various occasions, for example, by the Commodity Futures Modernization Act 2000. Recently, President Obama has criticised its effectiveness with respect to energy futures (Obama for America n. d.).

34 Goldman Sachs sold subprime-mortgage investments but in 2006 began using derivatives to trade against its own product and clients, without informing them. Chief financial officer David Viniar boasted that their risk bias in the mortgage was short and their net short position profitable (Goldman Sachs 2007).

relationship between the buyer and seller of financial assets is undermined. Application of the common law to this area is now hypothetical but it is noteworthy that historically courts were sensitive to drawing the boundaries of legally enforceable derivative contracts so as to preserve the sanctity of bilateral contracting for the provision of specific goods or services from being undermined by speculative activities (Stout 1999).

These examples show how financial innovations can weaken the basis of contractual relations, with the consequent danger of greed leaking out.[35] Previous approaches to, and understandings of, commutative justice no longer apply and solidarity and mutual trust are undermined. Both examples also show how, conversely, the application of common law principles has the potential to return focus to the underlying contract, the parties to that contract, and those parties' responsibilities.

Trust and liquidity

These examples bring out a further consequence of moving away from traditional forms of contracting and commitment: the problem of trust. With the erosion of tight bilateral forms of contracting and their enforceability through a well-understood pattern of contract law, in whom can we trust?

In the complex 'slice and dice' of MERS-based packages, the individual mortgage vanished from sight. Trust was placed in risk modelling and the ratings agencies that provided the label on the package. Liquidity may reduce the need for trust in others but rests on the assumption of a readily accessible market and that the party concerned will know when to utilise that liquidity. Rather than trust in others, liquidity rests on trust in one's own ability to reach the exit quicker than others. The financial crisis showed that this was an unwise assumption. When many parties simultaneously try to exit specific assets, that market becomes illiquid and the assets devalue rapidly, if they can be sold at all. In the 2008 crisis, insurance purchased by major financial entities to cover various exposures they held also proved illusory because the main insurer, AIG, failed. Liquidity and trust in counterparties vanished, and the market teetered on collapse.

Surprisingly, it was not that trust was too low in the build up to the crisis but that trust was far too high or was misplaced. The basis of mutual trust built through clear bilateral contracting occurring within a well-understood, predictable, and relevant legal framework had been lost. In the new era, trust did not prove well founded, whether it resided in the ability to be first to the exit, the reliability

---

35   Some examples from the 18th century can be found in Dale (2004).

of counterparties to each trade (that is, reputation and labelling), or in risk analysis. In addition, otherwise sound bilateral contracts were inter-locked with those that were not sound. The slowness of financial firms to address risk issues after the 2008 crash may in part stem from the difficulty and implications of not being able to assume reasonably high levels of trust in the business from which they draw their living. Without some level of trust, there can be no music to dance to.

In the wake of the crisis, suggested solutions are focusing on better regulation and on methods to control network or systemic risk. Whatever the value of such solutions, for the most part they do not deal with the issue of the erosion of contractual relations and of commutative justice in the financial marketplace and thus of finding a basis for substantive, mutual trust. Without a well-developed and understood framework to determine what is in and what is out of bounds, players in the marketplace can place little trust in bilateral contracting with each other; it lacks foundation.

The most notable exception to this lacuna in current approaches is the proposal to anchor various types of over-the-counter transactions in specific exchange bodies. This is an attempt to tie down and systematise bilateral contracting in over-the-counter transactions by making the exchange body the counterparty to each deal, rather than over-the-counter transactions involving myriad counterparties in a complex web.[36] The experience of MERS suggests a critical challenge will be to ensure the central counterparty for such dealings has legal substance and is not a straw man.

Morality and the law as foundation for change

There are no magic solutions to the problems faced with financial markets; nor can we wind back the clock to the era when traditional commercial banking dominated. However, reference points for navigation can be provided through basic legal precepts and frameworks relating to contract. These provide a platform for fair dealing in bilateral contracts in the marketplace; that is, they provide commutative justice.

Evidence for this possibility is shown in major commercial contracts. Internationally, wherever they originate, such contracts usually include a 'choice of law' clause, and the law chosen is a common law jurisdiction where there is depth of judicial practice.[37] The reason for this preference is that the contracting

---

36   Progress is discussed in Financial Stability Board (2009).
37   For example, corporations are often formed subject to the jurisdiction of the State of Delaware and commercial contracts made subject to the jurisdiction of the State of New York.

parties know broadly what they are getting in terms of the legal framework and its implications. The effect is to make their contracting less incomplete, as the principles and procedures applied by courts should there be a dispute between the parties are predictable. Even for those wishing to proceed dishonestly, the wrong signals are sent to potential partners if a weak or obscure legal regime is sought instead. In this way, the quality of legal regime preferred is driven up rather than being driven down, as with regulatory arbitrage.

Research from the 1990s showed that both capital markets and investor protections were strongest in those countries applying common law (La Porta et al. 1997, 1998). By contrast, pre-crash research found little evidence for the superiority of one form of financial market regulation over another (for example, centralised as against decentralised regulation) (Barth et al. 2002). As we have noted, post-crash research has found the quality of regulation to be inversely related to the adverse impact of the crash. All this points to the legal framework for contracting, rather than financial regulation, as providing the basis for sound financial markets.

Both greed and risk – and the need to handle them in order to undertake commerce – are as old as civilisation. For many countries, basic legal precepts reflect a shared derivation of underlying concepts from the great monotheistic religions and subsequent Christian, Jewish, and Islamic understandings of justice and jurisprudence. These interpretations have been set out most notably through Halachaic (Jewish) law, Sharia (Islamic) law, and Anglo–Saxon common law.[38] Of course, the extent and working out of their origins are much debated but one can detect common moral foundations and rules of thumb built upon them.

An interesting comparison can be made. The reach of common law is enormous. Its framework is there to achieve commutative justice for the parties to the contract and make contracting workable. Its jurisdiction is sought after internationally and some underlying precepts are held in common across Western and Middle Eastern societies, and former European colonies beyond that. By contrast, specific regulation of financial markets is typically 'top down', very recent in origin, specific to a locality, subject to major shifts, and mostly pursuing broader

---

[38] The seminal work of John Selden (1679), *De Synedriis & Praefecturis Juridicis Veterum Ebraeorum*, traces the relationship between ancient Jewish legal structures and procedures and those of the Classical and Arab worlds and Christianity. Selden was co-participant with Hugo Grotius in the founding debates for modern international law and was chosen by Oliver Cromwell to draft England's constitution. See Berkowitz (1993). Selden appears to have influenced the views of key legal interpreters and experts on jurisprudence such as William Blackstone ([1763] 1983, cf Vol. 4, p. 59) and Lord Mansfield who in *Chamberlain of London v. Evans* (1767) states, 'The essential principles of revealed religion are part of the common law' (speech to the House of Lords, 4 February 1767, see Cobbett 1813, col. 319). Similarly, the impact of Hebrew Scripture on Puritanism was a core resource for developing republican practices and civic norms in the American colonies. See, for example, Cherry (1998).

ends than fairness and predictability for the contracting parties. Consequently, problems arise with regulatory arbitrage and with achieving the necessary degree of buy-in to new regulations by those subject to them, in addition to questions of regulatory failure.

Because common law is the most well-developed and widely accepted basis for commercial practice, it can provide a reference point or platform for the development of real-world contracting practice. Within the bounds set by its framework, it is highly adaptive by means of case law. One example, already noted, is the development of US case law on derivatives in the 19th century. Another example can be drawn from Britain. Before the collapse of Northern Rock in 2007, the last major bank bust in Britain was Overend Guerney in 1866. Overend Guerney was the 'bankers' bank' and its collapse caused significant economic damage. It was occasioned by the bank's misuse of the new vehicle of limited liability companies to over-leverage its bets on a railway boom. After much recrimination and debate, the government left the legislation little changed, taking the view that investors would learn their lesson and that the courts should be left to work through the implications of the new corporate form (Taylor 2006). This appears to be what happened.

Amidst the rubble of the most recent financial bust, we can find some clear reference points and deep-seated rules of thumb provided by an inherited legal and moral framework. Take two specific illustrations of how this might work.

The first illustration is in terms of improving *oversight*. In Basel II and elsewhere much attention has been given to developing sophisticated criteria to distinguish between banks' on- and off-balance sheet items and then to apply different liquidity tests based on such distinctions. Metrics for the tightness and enforceability of bilateral contracting through accepted jurisdictions could probably be as easily developed and would be less liable to produce perverse incentives on banks than the on- and off-balance sheet approach. Minimum capital requirements on banks could be set higher where banks entered into more remote contracting and/or placed contracts outside the most well-known common law, or equivalent, jurisdictions for the type of contract concerned.

The second illustration is in terms of improving *industry practice*. Risk analysis could usefully analyse risks arising from the contractual form itself as well as exogenous events and default risks. Thus, metrics for the degree of stretch in contracting and for the quality and predictability of jurisdiction(s) applying could be developed that would, for example, capture the risks inherent to MERS or be consequent upon the removal of common law coverage of an area.

Such approaches would neither have prohibited recent developments in financial instruments nor applied additional sets of regulations. Instead, these kinds of approach can identify and internalise (or at least price) the likely costs of innovations or other moves that shift activities away from familiar forms of contracting anchored in a reliable framework for financial transactions. They aid transparency both for the financial sector and for those responsible for its oversight.

Using existent legal frameworks and principles as the reference point moves the focus away from attempting to constrain risky competition and innovation through regulation. Such constraints necessarily struggle with market forces and, if successful, incur unknown costs from innovations forgone. Instead, the suggested focus is on developing the framework for commutative justice so it can continue to provide the basis for fair contracting. Such contracting, when based on a sound framework of law, is the front-line defence and most viable means of constraining greed and contractual risk.

Conclusion

The resources that have been invested during the past decade in governance, regulation, and risk analysis in the financial sector probably far exceed such investment in other sectors. The failure in the financial sector is, therefore, sobering and suggests great caution about how much we know and can deliver through new policy technology. Rather than pursuing lofty goals or solving problems through the top-down application of sophisticated techniques, the moral of the story points toward the practice of ethical policy and governance through established principles of day-to-day fairness applied so as to build and earn trust.

The commutative justice necessary to smooth functioning of contracting in the marketplace does indeed rest on what the Vatican calls 'internal forms of solidarity and mutual trust'. However, the foundations for these lie in the framework of law that provides a basis for determining day-to-day fairness and for adapting past criteria and decisions in the light of new technologies and circumstances. Commutative justice does not flow from the pursuit of distributive justice or social justice by means of market mechanisms. Its requirements are not the same. Pursuing distributive justice or social justice through the market can weaken rather than strengthen the workings of the marketplace, as shown by the impact of the housing boom that led into the financial crisis.

There is a high price to be paid for weakening commutative justice. This chapter suggests the erosion of common law principles and their application in the financial developments of recent years undermined the basis for sound bilateral contracting and mutual trust. In consequence, the ability to harness – set the boundaries for – greed and risk through contracting was diminished.

Trust in sophisticated risk analysis, macro-management and new financial and regulatory techniques has proved to be misplaced. The precise dynamics of how that occurred and who is to blame are beyond our scope. Blaming 'greed' does not help to elucidate matters.

A focus on sound bilateral contracting, along with fairness and predictability in legal procedures and enforcement, provides a humble building block and reference point. It does not exclude other approaches to the regulation and governance of financial institutions and markets. Rather, by drawing on the well-tested foundation of common law–based approaches and principles, it can provide fresh ways of thinking about how to contain the problems that recently devastated global finances.

References

Acharya, V. V., and P. Schnabl. 2009. 'Do global banks spread global imbalances? The case of asset-backed commercial paper during the financial crisis of 2007–2009.' Paper presented at the 10th Jacques Polak Annual Research Conference, Washington, DC, 5–6 November.

American Bankers Association. 2009. *BAFT Welcomes Re-Launch of Due Diligence Repository*. News release, 17 February. www.aba.com/Press+Room /021709DueDiligenceRepository.htm.

Bank for International Settlements. 2007. *77th Annual Report 1 April 2006 – 31 March 2007*. www.bis.org/publ/arpdf/ar2007e.htm.

Bank for International Settlements. 2008. *78th Annual Report 1 April 2007 – 31 March 2008*. www.bis.org/publ/arpdf/ar2008e.htm.

Bank for International Settlements. 2009. *Range of Practices and Issues in Economic Capital Frameworks*. Basel, Switzerland: Basel Committee on Banking Supervision. www.bis.org/publ/bcbs152.pdf.

Barth, J. R., D. E. Nolle, T. Phumiwasana, et al. 2002. *A Cross-Country Analysis of the Bank Supervisory Framework and Bank Performance*. Economics Working paper 2002–2. Washington, DC: Office of the Comptroller of the Currency.

Barth J. R., S. Trimbath, and G. Yago (eds). 2004. *The Savings and Loan Crisis: Lessons from a regulatory failure*. Norwell, MA: Kluwer Academic Publishers.

Beltratti, A., and R. M. Stulz. 2009. *Why Did Some Banks Perform Better During the Credit Crisis? A cross-country study of the impact of governance and regulation.* Working paper 2009-12. Columbus, Ohio: Ohio State University, Charles A. Dice Center for Research in Financial Economics. http://econpapers.repec.org/paper/eclohidic/2009-12.htm.

Benedict XVI. 2009. *Encyclical Letter: Caritas in Veritate.* Rome: The Vatican.

Berkowitz, A. 1993. 'John Selden and the biblical origins of the modern international political system.' *Jewish Political Studies Review* 6(1–2): 27–47.

Bernanke, B. S. 2004. 'The great moderation.' Remarks at meetings of the Eastern Economic Association, Washington, DC, 20 February.

Bernstein, P. 1998. *Against the Gods: A remarkable story of risk.* New York: Wiley.

Blackstone, W. [1763] 1983. *Commentaries on the Laws of England.* Birmingham, Alabama: Legal Classics Library.

Bookstaber, R. M. 2008. *A Demon of Our Own Design: Markets, hedge funds, and the perils of financial innovation.* Hoboken, NJ: John Wiley & Sons.

Brooks, J. 1998. *The Go-Go Years: The drama and crashing finale of Wall Street's bullish 60s.* New York: Allworth Press.

Brooks, J. 1999. *Once in Golconda: A true drama of Wall Street 1920–1938.* New York: John Wiley & Sons.

Buffet, W. 2003. Chairman's letter to the shareholders of Berkshire Hathaway Inc., 21 February. In *Berkshire Hathaway Inc, 2002 Annual Report*, pp. 3–23. www.berkshirehathaway.com/2002ar/2002ar.pdf.

Cherry, C. 1998. *God's New Israel.* Chapel Hill: University of North Carolina.

Cobbett, W. (ed.) 1813. *The Parliamentary History of England.* vol 16. London: T. C. Hansard. (Available from the Oxford Digital Library, www2.odl.ox.ac.uk/gsdl/cgi-bin/library?e=d-000-00---0modhis06--00-0-0-0prompt-10---4------0-1l--1-en-50---20-about---00001-001-1-1isoZz-8859Zz-1-0&a=d&c=modhis06&cl=CL1&d=modhis006-aap.)

Comptroller of the Currency Administrator of National Banks. 1996. *New Opportunities to Excel Outstanding CRA Actions for Community Banks.* www.occ.treas.gov/cra/excel.htm.

Cramer, J. 2002. *Confessions of a Street Addict.* New York: Simon & Schuster.

Crane, R. 2009. 'Network effects and risks.' Unpublished presentation. Swiss Federal Institute of Technology.

Dale, R. 2004. *The First Crash: Lessons from the South Sea bubble*. Princeton, NJ: Princeton University Press.

Davis Polk. 2009. *A Guide to the Laws, Regulations and Contracts of the Financial Crisis: Financial crisis manual*. www.davispolk.com/files/News/7f041304-9785-4433-aa90-153d69b92104/Presentation/NewsAttachment/3c9302c0-409f-4dd1-9413-24e8cd60cd93/Financial_Crisis_Manual.pdf.

De la Vega, J. 1688. *Confusións de Confusiones*. Reprint edn. In M. S. Frisdon. 1996. *Confusions and Delusions: Tulipmania, the South Sea bubble and the madness of crowds*. Hoboken, NJ: John Wiley & Sons.

Economagic. n. d. *Economic Time Series*. www.economagic.com/em-cgi/data.

Federal Deposit Insurance Corporation. 2002. *Manual of Examination Policies (Safety and Soundness)*. Washington, DC: Federal Deposit Insurance Corporation.

Federal Deposit Insurance Corporation. 2009. *Bank Failures in Brief: 2009*. Washington, DC: Federal Deposit Insurance Corporation. www.fdic.gov/BANK/HISTORICAL/BANK/2009/index.html.

Financial Stability Board. 2009. *Progress since the Pittsburgh Summit in Implementing the G20 Recommendations for Strengthening Financial Stability: Report of the Financial Stability Board to G20 finance ministers and governors*. Basel, Switzerland: Financial Stability Board.

Frieden, T. 2004. 'FBI warns of mortgage fraud "epidemic": Seeks to head off "next S&L crisis".' *Cable News Network*, 17 September. http://edition.cnn.com/2004/LAW/09/17/mortgage.fraud.

Friedman, M. 1994. *Money Mischief: Episodes in monetary history*. 1st Harvest edn. San Diego: Mariner Books.

Galbraith, J. K. 1961. *The Great Crash, 1929*. Boston; New York: Houghton Mifflin.

Godechot, O. 2008a. '"Hold-up" in finance: The conditions of possibility for high bonuses in the financial industry.' *Revue Française de Sociologie*, (Supplement Annual English edn) 49: 95–123.

Godechot, O. 2008b. 'What do heads of dealing rooms do? The social capital of internal entrepreneurs.' In M. Savage and K. Williams (eds). *Remembering Elites*. Malden, MA: Wiley-Blackwell.

Goldman Sachs. 2007. *Goldman Sachs Reports Third Quarter Earnings Per Common Share of $6.13*. New York: Goldman Sachs Group, Inc. www2.goldmansachs.com/our-firm/investors/financials/archived/quarterly-earnings-releases/attachments/2007-third-quarter-earnings.pdf.

Goodman, P. 2008. 'Taking hard new look at a Greenspan legacy.' *New York Times*, 8 October. www.nytimes.com/2008/10/09/business/economy/09greenspan.html.

Greenspan, A. 1998. Testimony by Alan Greenspan, chair of the Board of Governors of the Federal Reserves System, to United States Senate Committee on Agriculture, Nutrition and Forestry, 30 July. http://agriculture.senate.gov/Hearings/Hearings_1998/gspan.htm.

Guttentag, J. M., and R. J. Herring. 1986. *Disaster Myopia in International Banking*. Princeton University Essays in International Finance 164. Princeton, NJ: International Finance Section, Department of Economics, Princeton University.

Haldane, A. G. 2009a. 'Rethinking the financial network.' Speech delivered at the Financial Student Association, Amsterdam, 28 April. www.cnbv.gob.mx/recursos/Combasdr176.pdf.

Haldane, A. G. 2009b. *Why Banks Failed the Stress Test*. Basis for a speech given at the Marcus–Evans Conference on Stress-Testing, 9–10 February 2009. www.bankofengland.co.uk/publications/speeches/2009/speech374.pdf.

Hansard: Parliamentary Debate for 5 October 1994. http://vdig.net/hansard/content.jsp?id=43766.

Ivry, B., C. Harper, and M. Pittman. 2009a. 'Missing Lehman lesson of shakeout means too big banks may fail.' *Bloomberg*, 7 September. www.bloomberg.com/apps/news?pid=newsarchive&sid=aX8D5utKFuGA.

Ivry, B., M. Pittman, and C. Harper. 2009b. 'Sleep-at-night-money lost in Lehman lesson missing $63 billion.' *Bloomberg*, 8 September. www.bloomberg.com/apps/news?pid=newsarchive&sid=aLhi.S5xkemY.

J. P. Morgan. n. d. 'ABS issuance: Growth and collapse by asset class.' [Chart.] In A. B. Ashcraft. *Credit,Investment, and Payment Risk:Discussion of 'do global banks spread global imbalances'?* http://imf.org/external/np/res/seminars/2009/arc/pdf/ashcraft1.pdf.

'"Kamikaze" bankers damaged economy, says Alistair Darling.' 2009. *Daily Telegraph*, 5 July. www.telegraph.co.uk/finance/newsbysector/banksandfinance/5747952/Kamikaze-bankers-damaged-economy-says-Alistair-Darling.html.

Kern, A., R. Dhumale, and J. Eatwell. 2005. *Global Governance of Financial Systems: The international regulation of systemic risk*. New York: Oxford University Press.

Kindleberger, C. P., and R. Z. Aliber. 2005. *Manias, Panics, and Crashes: A history of financial crises*. 5th edn. Hoboken, NJ: John Wiley & Sons.

Knee, J. A. 2006. *The Accidental Investment Banker: Inside the decade that transformed Wall Street*. Hoboken, NJ: Wiley.

La Porta, R., F. López-de-Silanes, A. Shleifer, et al. 1997. 'Legal determinants of external finance.' *Journal of Finance* 52(3): 1131–50.

La Porta, R., F. López-de-Silanes, A. Shleifer, et al. 1998. 'Law and finance.' *Journal of Political Economy* 106(6): 1113–55.

Landmark National Bank v. Kesler 2009 Kan. LEXIS 834 (28 August 2009, Kansas Supreme Court).

Lefèvre, E. 2006. *Reminiscences of a Stock Operator*. Hoboken, NJ: John Wiley & Sons.

Lewis, M. 1990. *Liar's Poker: Rising through the wreckage on Wall Street*. New York: Penguin Books.

Litan, R. E., N. P. Retsinas, E. S. Belsky, et al. 2000. *The Community Reinvestment Act after Financial Modernization: A baseline report*. Washington, DC: US Department of the Treasury.

Lowenstein, R. 2000. *When Genius Failed: The rise and fall of long-term capital management*. New York: Random House.

Mackay, C. 1841. *Extraordinary Popular Delusions and the Madness of Crowds*. Reprinted in M. S. Frisdon. 1996. *Confusions and Delusions: Tulipmania, the South Sea Bubble and the Madness of Crowds*. Hoboken, NJ: John Wiley & Sons.

MacKenzie, D. 2006. *An Engine, Not a Camera: How financial models shape markets*. Cambridge, MA: MIT Press.

Mandelbrot, B., and R. L. Hudson. 2006. *The Misbehavior of Markets: A fractal view of financial turbulence*. New York: Basic Books.

Mayer, M. 1990. *The Greatest Ever Bank Robbery: The collapse of the savings and loan industry*. New York: Collier Books.

Merscorp v. Romaine NY Int 167 (2006, New York Court of Appeals).

Meyer, L. H. 1998. 'Community Reinvestment Act in an era of bank consolidation and deregulation.' Remarks before the 1998 Community Reinvestment Act Conference of the Consumer Bankers Association, Arlington, Virginia, 12 May. www.federalreserve.gov/Boarddocs/Speeches/1998/19980512.htm.

Minsky, H. P. 2008. *Stabilizing an Unstable Economy*. New York: McGraw-Hill.

Mitchener, K. J. 2007. 'Are prudential supervision and regulation pillars of financial stability? Evidence from the Great Depression.' *Journal of Law & Economics* 50(1): 273–302.

Monaghan, A. 2009. 'FSA treats mortgage lenders like "drug dealers", says CML chief.' *Daily Telegraph*, 13 November. www.telegraph.co.uk/finance/newsbysector/banksandfinance/6562111/FSA-treats-mortgage-lenders-like-drug-dealers-says-CML-chief.html.

Morris, S., and H. S. Shin. 2008. 'Financial regulation in a system context.' Paper prepared for the Brookings Panel meeting, 11–12 September 2008 (version dated 7 September 2008). www.brookings.edu/economics/bpea/~/media/Files/Programs/ES/BPEA/2008_fall_bpea_papers/2008_fall_bpea_morris_shin.pdf.

Mortgage Insurance Companies of America. 2006. Letter addressed to the Board of Governors of the Federal Reserve System, the Federal Deposit Insurance Corporation, and two others, 29 March. www.fdic.gov/regulations/laws/federal/2005/05c45guide.pdf.

Obama for America. n. d. *Barack Obama and Joe Biden: New energy for America*. www.barackobama.com/pdf/factsheet_energy_speech_080308.pdf.

Pittman, M., and B. Ivry. 2009. 'London suicide connects Lehman lesson missed by Hong Kong woman.' *Bloomberg,* 9 September. www.bloomberg.com/apps/news?pid=newsarchive&sid=aNFuVRL73wJc.

Presidential Working Group on Financial Markets. 1999. *Over-the-Counter Derivatives and the Commodity Exchange Act*. Washington, DC: US House of Representatives. www.ustreas.gov/press/releases/reports/otcact.pdf.

Rajan, R. G. 1998. 'The past and future of commercial banking viewed through an incomplete contract lens.' *Journal of Money, Credit & Banking* 30(3): 524–50.

Reinhart, C. M., and K. S. Rogoff. 2009. *This Time is Different: Eight centuries of financial folly*. Princeton, NJ: Princeton University Press.

Rudd, K. 2008. 'The children of Gordon Gekko.' Extract from speech by the prime minister in Sydney, 3 October. *The Australian*, 6 October. www.theaustralian.com.au/news/the-children-of-gordon-gekko/story-e6frg7b6-1111117670209.

Salmon, F. 2009. 'Recipe for disaster: The formula that killed Wall Street.' *Wired Magazine,* 17 March. www.wired.com/techbiz/it/magazine/17-03/wp_quant.

Selden, J. 1679. *De Synedriis & Praefecturis Juridicis Veterum Ebraeorum*. Three volumes. Amstelædami: Ex officina Henrici & Theodori Boom, & viduæ Joannis à Someren, 1679.

Smith, A. 1776. *The Wealth of Nations*. Edited with an introduction and notes by E. Cannan. 1994. New York: Random House.

Sorkin, A. R. 2009. *Too Big to Fail: The inside story of how Wall Street and Washington fought to save the financial system – and themselves*. New York: Viking.

Sornette, D. 2009. *Dragon-Kings, Black Swans and the Prediction of Crises*. Research paper 09–36. Geneva: Swiss Finance Institute.

Stewart, J. B. 1992. *Den of Thieves*. New York: Simon and Shuster.

Stock, J., and M. Watson. 2002. *Has the Business Cycle Changed and Why?* Working paper W9127. National Bureau of Economic Research.

Stout, L. A. 1999. 'Why the law hates speculators: Regulation and private ordering in the market for OTC derivatives.' *Duke Law Journal* 48: 701–86.

Taleb, N. N. 2007. *The Black Swan*. New York: Random House.

Taylor, J. 2006. *Creating Capitalism: Joint-stock enterprise in British politics and culture, 1800–1870*. London: Boydell Press.

Tett, G. 2009. *Fool's Gold: How the bold dream of a small tribe at J. P. Morgan was corrupted by Wall Street greed and unleased a catastrophe*. New York: Free Press.

The Merchant of Venice. 2004. Directed by M. Radford. Culver City, CA: Sony Pictures Classics.

Townsend. A. 2009. 'Hector Sants says bankers should be "very frightened" by the FSA.' *Daily Telegraph*, 12 March. www.telegraph.co.uk/finance/newsbysector/banksandfinance/4978496/Hector-Sants-says-bankers-should-be-very-frightened-of-the-FSA.html.

Tversky, A., and Kahneman, D. 1992. 'Advances in prospect theory: Cumulative representation of uncertainty.' *Journal of Risk and Uncertainty* 5: 297–323.

US Bank National Association v. Ibanez 29 October 2009, Commonwealth of Massachusetts Trial Court, Misc. Case No. 08-384283 (KCL). www.boston.com/business/articles/2009/10/15/ibanezruling.

Wall Street. 1987. Directed by O. Stone. Beverly Hills: Twentieth Century Fox.

Warwick Commission on International Financial Reform. 2009. *In Praise of Unlevel Playing Fields*. Coventry: University of Warwick. www2.warwick.ac.uk/research/warwickcommission/report.

Wells Fargo Bank v. Larace 29 October 2009, Commonwealth of Massachusetts Trial Court, Misc. Case No. 08-386755 (KCL). www.boston.com/business/articles/2009/10/15/ibanezruling.

White, L. J. 1991. *The S&L Debacle: Public policy lessons for bank and thrift regulation*. New York: Oxford University Press.

Williamson, O. 1985. *The Economic Institutions of Capitalism: Firms, markets, relational contracting*. New York: Free Press.

13. An alternative reply to the free-rider objection against unconditional citizenship grants

Julia Maskivker

Introduction

A powerful objection against unconditional welfare benefits is the so-called 'free-rider argument'. This objection is based on considerations of justice. It tells us that it is unjust that some people benefit from the efforts of others without contributing to the common enterprise from which all stand to gain (Elster 1986). This line of accusation is usually directed to left-libertarian defences of stake-holding proposals such as the basic income scheme, which, if sufficiently generous, could substantially relax the necessity to work for a livelihood through a universal, non-means-tested grant. The free-rider objection against unconditional welfare provisions reads like this: why should people who work devote part of the fruits of their efforts to paying taxes to finance the unconditional welfare benefits of those who opt not to work when they perfectly could? Allowing for this possibility, the argument goes, amounts to exploitation, understanding the latter as taking advantage of someone else's efforts without contributing to the creation of common benefits.[1] The objection conveys the idea that free-riders breach an important principle of reciprocity by obtaining the fruits of the efforts of others and contributing nothing themselves in return.

Defenders of the basic income scheme have responded that insofar as the option to exit cooperation is equally available to everybody, there are no reasons to suspect injustice. One reply to the view that living off other people's work is a case of injustice is to deny that living off other people's work is unjust when *everybody* is given the same possibility (Van der Veen 1991, p. 200). In this sense, equal distribution of the free-riding option is sufficient to consider free-riding just. When all face the same possibility, defenders of the basic income scheme say (Van der Veen and Van Parijs 1986, p. 726):

---

1 'Exploitation' is understood in a non-technical way, that is, not as the unequal exchange between employer (or capitalist) and employee (or worker) but more generally as a benefit produced by illegitimately taking advantage of someone's efforts.

some will choose little or no paid work, while others will want to work a lot, whether for the additional money or for the fun of working, thereby financing everyone's universal grant. If the latter envy the former's idleness, why don't they follow suit?

The preceding argument has been viewed as flawed because it does not speak to the fundamental concern that motivates the exploitation objection, namely, that free-riding is by nature unjust regardless of how many individuals are in a position to engage in it. It cannot always be enough, in assessing the justness of a given state of affairs, to evoke a distributive criterion as the primordial index of fairness. When defenders of the exploitation objection against the basic income scheme, or unconditional welfare goods in general, argue that escaping cooperation while receiving the benefits of it is unjust, they point to the nature of this injustice irrespective of how extended the injustice is. They wish to condemn what they understand to be an illegitimate advantage based on the violation of fairness considerations; they do not criticise the actual allocation of opportunities. They think that the individual who gains from a common practice without making a contribution in return when he or she is physically able to is arrogating to himself or herself unjustified preferential treatment (Cullity 1995).[2]

However, defenders of the basic income scheme have provided a more 'principled' response to the free-rider objection. In particular, Philippe Van Parijs offers a powerful argument to counteract the claim that non-conditionality is unfair: the argument of a fair share to natural resources.[3] Defenders of the exploitation objection, nevertheless, still press their objections of fairness against Van Parijs's line of reasoning. Considerations of fair reciprocity, they argue, trump rights to initially unowned natural resources that require labour and already developed technologies to be made use of in any meaningful way.[4]

In the framework of this heated debate, this chapter aims to provide an alternative response to the free-rider argument; one that has been consistently under-explored in discussions about social reciprocity and fairness. Drawing significantly on H. L. A. Hart's and John Rawls's thinking on cooperative obligations, in this chapter I claim that freedom from cooperation in the generation of social benefits is justified on the basis of two considerations,

---

2   Cullity alludes to this line of reasoning, although he defends the idea that free-riding can be moral under certain circumstances.

3   The argument is that people have basic entitlements, and among these entitlements is an entitlement of each member of society, or of humankind, to an equal share in the natural resources. The claim is that this leads to the justification of a basic income at a level that would match the competitive value of an equal share of these resources. This view of justice is based on these equal entitlements in land plus the ownership of each person by that person. See Van Parijs (1995), and his later work more generally, for a complete account of this perspective.

4   See, paradigmatically, White (2004).

namely, injustice in the design of the cooperative scheme and the non-voluntary nature of that scheme. The latter is explained by the fact it is impossible to abandon employment on pain of deprivation. The former relates to the claim that access to self-realisation through the use of human talents and dispositions is unequally distributed in society. I claim that society's failure to provide minimal opportunities for self-realisation imposes a non-voluntary – hence, morally arbitrary – limitation on the individual. This arbitrariness arises from the market heavily rewarding those talents and pursuits that happen to be economically profitable while disdaining the non-profitable ones that are nevertheless worthy according to non-market criteria (under the assumption that the value attributed to any individual's talents is not a reflection of his or her own actions or conceptions).

Grounds for the duty to cooperate: a challenge

At this point, a fundamental question arises as to how to establish the basis for an obligation to cooperate in the framework of a cooperative scheme of which we form part. Hart (1955, p. 185) provides a principle of mutual restriction as a source of such obligation:

> when a number of persons conduct any joint enterprise according to rules and thus restrict their liberty, those who have submitted to these restrictions have a right to a similar submission from those who have benefited by their submission.

Hart's principle has been fiercely criticised by Robert Nozick, who argues that only explicit consent grounds duties of cooperation. The fact you left a book on my doorstep inviting me to form part of your reading club, says Nozick, does not put me in an obligation to reciprocate and give you another book (or payment) in turn, since I did not ask to be a member of your club. This holds even if I truly enjoy, and would therefore benefit from, reading. Thus, 'you may not decide to give me something, for example, a book, and then grab money from me to pay for it even if I have nothing better to spend the money on', claims Nozick (1975, p. 95). 'One cannot, whatever one's purposes, just act so as to give people benefits and then demand (or seize) payment. Nor can a group of persons do this' (ibid.). It is clear from this example that unasked-for benefits, no matter how desirable, cannot be grounds for reciprocation.

Nozick, however, disregards the fact his arguments apply only to certain types of benefits, namely, excludable benefits. Excludable benefits are benefits that the provider can choose to whom to provide them. You can choose whether or not to include me in your reading club. Therefore, the benefits you distribute can be taken away from me at your will. In this scenario, it makes sense to demand explicit adherence to the scheme as a condition for reciprocation. If I decline to be part of your club, you have the means to cease the provision of benefits to me. But the situation is different when the benefits in question are non-excludable. When a cooperative scheme distributes non-excludable goods that means it is impossible or prohibitively costly to exclude those who do not contribute to their expense from enjoying those goods. Pure public goods are of this sort.[5] Definitions of public goods vary widely, but they usually involve, at least:

- jointness in supply: if a public good is available for one member of the group for which it is public, then it is available to every other member at no cost to that other member

- non-excludability: if anyone is enjoying the good, no one else can be prevented from doing so without excessive cost to the would-be excluders[6]

- jointness in consumption: one person's consumption of the good does not diminish the amount available for consumption by anyone else

- equality: if everyone receives the good, everyone receives the same amount.[7]

The public goods literature tells us that when regulating cooperative schemes that distribute pure public goods, individuals are under a reciprocal obligation to contribute irrespective of consent (Arneson 1982; Klosko 1987). This obligation is an obligation of *fair play* and it is fundamentally informed by Hart's principle of mutual restriction. In situations of non-excludability, since it is impossible to direct the benefits only to those who contribute, it would be unfair not to demand that all contribute since *all* benefit. The duty of fair play typically applies to public goods *because* they are non-excludable. It is precisely because they are non-excludable that gives rise, in the first place, to the automatic moral duty to contribute (Arneson 1982; Maphai 1987).

Situations where the benefits are non-excludable and membership is non-voluntary have motivated a wealth of philosophical thinking on the nature of cooperative obligations. Political obligation is the paradigmatic example: we do

5 Sea travellers benefiting from a lighthouse (the quintessential example of a moral good) have a moral duty to contribute towards its construction and maintenance precisely because its light is non-excludable. A lighthouse projecting an excludable right (suppose it beams an infrared light that only seafarers with special night-vision equipment can see, the sale of which the lighthouse operator controls) produces no duty of fair play. Instead, an explicit contract would be applied here, and a toll levied. See Segall (2005, p. 339).
6 Non-excludability does not entail jointness of supply, necessarily. Consider a pile of newspapers made freely available to all bystanders in the street. In practice, it is possible to exclude some from getting a newspaper, in which case the benefit is jointly supplied but non-excludability does not follow. See Cullity (1995, pp. 3–4).
7 This condition should be qualified, however, since it may be too strong. A public good may be of no use to people lacking the capacities necessary to enjoy it. For example, a public park is of no use to someone who cannot get around; and public lighting is of no use to someone who cannot see. However, we can say that public goods are worth supporting on grounds of broader public utility.

not choose to be born in a given country (and it is significantly costly to leave that country). How can we account for the obligation to cooperate – by abiding with the law – if we have not explicitly chosen to be members of the scheme? Social contract theories have resorted to the notion of *tacit consent* in order to ground political obligation but the public goods literature saves us from using such a dubious concept. The public goods literature tells us that (Arneson 1982, p. 623) where a scheme of cooperation:

> is established that supplies a collective benefit that is worth the cost to each recipient, the burdens of cooperation are fairly divided, and were voluntary acceptance of the benefits is impossible, those who contribute their assigned fair share of the costs of the scheme have a right against the remaining beneficiaries that they should also pay their fair share.

This revised formulation of Hart's principle preserves the idea that accepting or even simply receiving the benefits of a cooperative scheme can sometimes obligate an individual to contribute to the support of the scheme, even though the individual has not consented to such scheme. The source of the obligation is the fact the benefits produced are non-excludable (all receive them) and desirable (all need them).[8] It follows that cooperative schemes the fruits of which are excludable do not justify an automatic duty of reciprocity; they simply give rise to an acquired obligation.

In justifying a duty to work in return for welfare benefits, many thinkers argue that social wealth should be seen as a non-excludable (public) good. The idea that the creation of social surplus from which all individuals in society benefit justifies a duty to cooperate is espoused by Stuart White when he argues for the idea of 'normative non-excludability' (White 2003, p. 61). This idea draws from a technical concept common in the economic public goods literature, that is, the concept of excludability. At this point, it is worth quoting White (ibid.):

> in egalitarian pictures of the good society, the tendency is to view the whole social product as having a quality of normative non-excludability that is analogous to the non-excludability characteristic of public goods. The social product is, if not a public good, what we might call a shared good: a good that everyone is presumptively entitled to share in to a more or less equal (or more or less equally needs-satisfying) extent. Every output is supposed to be in the collective pot (or to follow Winstanley, warehouse) for all to share equally in. When the social product is viewed in this light, however, worries analogous to those of public goods free-riders arise. The thought arises that, as with public goods, if the benefits of collective effort are going to be shared, so too should be this effort.

---

8   Assuming that desirability springs from need.

In the same vein, Joseph Carens, another defender of the ethics of social duty, writes (Carens 1986, p. 37):

> [t]he high level of production created if all or most citizens make good use of their talents and skills may be regarded as a collective good in an egalitarian society. People may desire the affluence that will be created if all contribute, but in the absence of shared and effective sense of social duty, each might be inclined to be a freerider and shirk.

There is something fishy about the line of reasoning espoused by White and Carens. If we reflect on the nature of the so-called 'social product' in market societies such as the ones in the Western developed world, we will realise that White's and Carens's descriptions are faulty. The non-excludability arguments that apply to public goods arise out of a fact of reality, namely, that it is impossible to exclude people from benefiting from that type of goods. Is this the case with social wealth more generally? It is not, unless we live in a kibbutz or a similar communal arrangement that is based on egalitarian distribution *after* production.[9] In other words, in our society, people have to earn their living through work, and what they receive in return will be proportional to how much, and which type of, work they do. In societies of the sort we are used to living in there is no common pool or warehouse that guarantees to each of us a share of the social product. With the only exception of those public goods that flow to all irrespective of contribution (for example, national defence, clean streets, and public parks), the individual is not free-riding if he or she does not participate in the productive activities of society (being perfectly able to do so). By not participating, the individual will not be able to buy the food he or she needs to suppress hunger, nor to afford the housing he or she needs to protect himself or herself from the inclemency of climate.

In the framework of a kibbutz-like arrangement of the sort White is (allegedly) presupposing, there is, in actuality, a process of common accumulation and posterior distribution. But such communal process does not take place in market capitalistic systems. People are certainly going to demand that each member of the kibbutz cooperates, but if the individual immorally decides to disobey that duty (and nobody else realises this), the individual will receive the benefits produced by the effort of others at the end of the day, not only public goods-wise, but also in terms of food and other basic supplies. This is not likely to occur in larger societies not ruled by the common pool logic. In those societies,

---

9   It has been suggested to me that my interpretation of White is wrong because he should be taken to say that *if* we had a society in which all wealth was treated as a common pool and divided equally, that would generate a duty to contribute. This observation is mistaken, however. If White's words are read carefully, it is clear he says that society as it is now should be seen in the light of the common pool interpretation. White argues that the tendency is to view the *actual* social product as a common pool resource. This is logical since White's aim is to justify a duty to cooperate in actual society, not in a hypothetical scenario.

if you decide (for no impairing reason related to disability) to withdraw from economic cooperation there is little you can do to avoid deprivation eventually, even if nobody in the whole world becomes aware of your change of lifestyle.[10] Furthermore, private property alones impedes the common pool logic from becoming a reality: Property rights serve as a means of excluding some from enjoyment of social wealth since these rights establish rules of appropriation – and sanctions – that give rise to claims of ownership – and reparation – in the eyes of the law, and separate the 'haves' from the 'have-nots'. Indeed, there is no more clear example of an institutional mechanism that literally bars some from *directly* accessing wealth created in society. This means social wealth is not fully comparable to a public good in real life: It does not accrue equally to all after being generated (equality requirement specified above). The idle rich exemplify this. Their cooperation is close to null but their share of benefits is proportionally larger than their cooperative burden.

Social wealth is neither characterised by jointness in consumption, for a person's consumption of social wealth does leave less social wealth for others, on many occasions. If I preclude you from entering my property, for example, you will have less space in which to be and develop. Additionally, although money makes the finitude of land and the spoilage of natural resources less of a relevant constraint, as John Locke (1967) argued in his classical *Second Treatise of Government*, money does not confer on the dispossessed the type of control that ownership confers on the propertied. This is so because there is no title to money, so no rights associated to it as a possession.

The compulsoriness characteristic of traditional pure public goods is neither present in the case of social wealth. Benefits of social cooperation largely accrue to oneself by means of one's work. Receipt of the good produced by the scheme of cooperation is not automatic and is independent from other people's situation as to the good: the fact others receive the benefits does not mean I cannot avoid doing so at high cost. If I do not work, I will not receive the benefits.[11] Therefore, we have established that, real public goods aside, the social product *is* excludable. The fair play duty (Hart's principle of mutual restriction) cannot be invoked to justify an obligation to work in societies of the sort with which we are most familiar. This does not mean that no reprimand can be justified for non-cooperators, but the sanction cannot include denying individuals the means necessary for economic survival, namely, an income. It does not follow from all this that conditionality in the provision of welfare goods is ever unjustified, but it does follow that it cannot be justified on the basis of a civic duty to work.

---

10 Assuming the absence of independent wealth.

11 White's claims about normative non-excludability apply to society as we know it, not to society as it should be in an ideal world. I argue that his account of how distribution takes place is flawed. In this sense, the duty to work is not justified as long as society's product continues to be distributed as it currently is, that is, on the basis of one's employment situation, primordially.

The foregoing conclusion is very important to understand why free-riding on those who work is not necessarily in tension with justice. In the context of our discussion on work, there are no ethical grounds to consider that reciprocation is required since the individual does not automatically benefit from the work of others regardless of the individual's efforts. If the individual does not work, he or she does not eat. Social wealth is largely excludable. Thus, the case at hand is one in which membership to a given scheme is non-voluntary but benefits are excludable. Social wealth, broadly understood as the collective production of the means to livelihood, is not like national defence (a pure public good) because it is not conferred on us *regardless* of whether we cooperate. That social wealth is excludable challenges the idea that an automatic obligation to cooperate in its making is due to society.

Justifying financial support when not cooperating, however, requires a more complex argument than the reasoning in the previous paragraphs offers. Such support constitutes a positive requirement on others, not a negative claim to freedom from cooperation. It is one thing to say that I am not required to cooperate because the benefits in question are excludable, but it is quite another thing to demand that cooperators support me. Why should individuals who contribute to the creation of social wealth actively pay for my non-cooperation? To answering this question I now turn.

A positive duty of support

My answer builds on basic principles of liberal egalitarianism. Specifically, it is based on a principle of rectification for morally arbitrary disadvantage. In discussions about social justice, compensation for this type of disadvantage motivates elegant and complex theories of distributive equality. In different ways, egalitarian theorists are concerned with limiting the effects of moral arbitrariness by minimising the advantage gaps that the latter causes. They may not all agree on what it is that should be equalised to attain that goal, but they all concur in the thought that morally arbitrary disadvantage is one source of unjustified inequalities.

Morally arbitrary disadvantage is triggered by factors that, one could say, it is reasonably to suppose the individual has no control of, such as gender, place of birth, ethnicity, and family's social background, to name a few. This lack of control has been referred to as 'brute luck' (Dworkin 1981). The occurrence of an event, or attribute, is due to brute luck to the extent that the agent could not have (reasonably) influenced the possibility or probability of its occurrence. This of course raises questions about what 'reasonably' exactly amounts to. However, the general intuition is that the presence of a capacity to exert control legitimises holding the individual to some degree responsible for a certain result. In this sense, distributions and states of affairs are just only when they result from decisions people make under 'controllable' conditions.

A preoccupation with morally arbitrary factors reflects how Rawls, most prominently, views the distribution of natural talents and luck more generally in his 'original position', an ideal hypothetical situation evoked to legitimise impartial and acceptable to all principles of justice (Rawls 1971). Parties to the original position know nothing about their particular social and personal circumstances, so acting rationally they will choose principles of justice that will not allow the most fortunate among them to take advantage of their special situation (for example, their superior wealth, intelligence, better health, and more convenient geographical location). This idea is a cornerstone of Rawls's egalitarianism, and, although it has given room to endless interpretation and debate, it is clear that it is rooted in a concern with alleviating disadvantages that are traced to factors the individual as a moral agent has done nothing to deserve or not deserve, because they lie beyond the scope of moral responsibility. This means that attaching blame or praise for their existence is senseless, philosophically. One can discuss the extent to which particular situations are uncontrollable, but the truth is that it is not hard to think of examples that confirm Rawls's concern: People usually may not be held responsible for their gender, socioeconomic familial background, place of birth, or innate talents, insofar as they have done nothing to enjoy or suffer the social consequences of these characteristics. Rawls objects to social arrangements and their underlying principles of justice that allow people to compete for available positions and advantages making no attempt to compensate for deprivations that some individuals suffer due to social contingency and natural chance, that is, due to factors attributable to moral luck, beyond the responsibility of the agent.

That society facilitates the exercise of certain activities and not others is a matter of moral arbitrariness from the individual's point of view. It is arbitrary that the system in which I live does not reward the type of talents I enjoy practising while it rewards the talents that other people enjoy practising. Nobody has done anything to deserve or not deserve this type of fortune – just as nobody has done anything to deserve being born a citizen of Norway instead of Somalia. And this arbitrariness is unfortunate because most people enjoy developing and exercising skills and abilities they possess or want to possess. It is not far-fetched to think that most people, regardless of culture and political leaning, will desire to have those higher-order needs fulfilled to some important degree. Rawls's reference to the Aristotelian principle, a psychological law of motivation, reflects this assumption. The principle reads, 'other things equal, human beings enjoy the exercise of their realized capacities (their innate or trained abilities) and this enjoyment increases the more the capacity is realized, or the greater its complexity' (Rawls 1971, p. 426). The free-riding possibility that refusing cooperation in the creation of social wealth implies does not necessarily have to be seen in the light of an intention to minimise effort and retain gain, but as an opportunity to transit the road of self-realisation understood as a developmental human need.[12]

Many societies of today offer great opportunities for self-realisation in the form of meaningful work. Those opportunities are characteristic for being highly rewarding (materially, psychologically, or both) and for being socially necessary and appreciated by the public. It is this very fact that invites reflection on the situation of individuals who will not, through no fault of their own, have an opportunity to contribute to society while achieving self-realisation. The manner in which current societies are organised represents a morally arbitrary disadvantage for people whose self-definition hinges on the practice of talents and skills for which the market, or society more generally, finds little or no appreciation. To see this clearly, think of the following example.

John is a surfer who lives in Malibu and surfs all day long because he finds the exercise of his surfing talent extremely fulfilling. His surfing skills are so amazing that he regularly manages to attract a crowd of spectators who would be willing to pay to see John display his marvellous talent. Since the beach John surfs at is a private beach (which belongs to his dear friend Paul) John decides, with Paul's approval, that he will start charging spectators a small fee and devote the proceeds to charity after retaining some of the money to pay for food and board. John is generating economic gain that clearly contributes to society's general wealth. Now picture Matt, an experienced and passionate trumpet player who desires to live off his talent and help others, as John does. He mounts performance shows in his garden but nobody shows up to listen to him play. In Matt and John's society people are averse to trumpet playing, they find it boring.

These trivial examples illustrate one non-trivial normative conundrum: the specific type of social arrangement in which John and Matt live is favourable to John's self-realisation because it couples it with satisfaction of other people's (legitimate) preferences, which allows John to create wealth. But it is not equally favourable to Matt's self-realisation because Matt has an unappreciated skill. How arbitrary is to deny Matt a fair opportunity to exercise his talent and subsist because his abilities are not as acclaimed as John's? Differently put, how

---

12 For a pluralist, non-metaphysical, view of self-realisation, from which I draw, see Dewey (1893). The conception of self-realisation through the use of talents, understood as a higher-order developmental need is inspired by the widely accepted psychological theory of Abraham Maslow. See Maslow (1943).

morally responsible for his contributive inclinations is John compared with Matt? It seems as if the social system made it much easier for John to comply with duty; and this rings unfair.[13]

Being able to exercise one's talents while contributing to society is relative to a cooperative framework (Buchanan 1990). And cooperative frameworks are chosen, reformed, and built by humans. Thus, it makes sense to say that it is a matter of collective choice what type of cooperative arrangement is established in a society. Therefore, the nature of such cooperative arrangements – whether they are biased in favour or against certain practices and talents – is a matter of justice, not nature. Different cooperative arrangements demand different skills, and make certain skills appreciated and needed in comparison with other abilities and predispositions that may not be considered equally useful for cooperation. For example, a penchant for artistic pursuits may imperil self-fulfilling contribution under a market system highly focused on industrialised and technological progress in which more humanistic skills are usually unappreciated. However, artistic abilities may flourish in tandem with cooperation in societies where education and economic production are more diversified in their goals. If human development is an important social goal, however diversely understood such a concept is, we must acknowledge that the ways in which society facilitates or truncates the exercise of our skills and talents are philosophically (and by implication politically) important.

The arbitrariness of a cooperative scheme that is biased against certain talent-holders is accentuated if we add to the picture the fact that membership to the scheme is not voluntary. We are born under a given socioeconomic system, and it is extremely difficult to exit it without risking survival: we have to feed ourselves and fulfil our basic needs. We cannot afford to exit under normal circumstances in the absence of independent wealth to sustain our withdrawal. Because of the high costs of leaving the scheme, it makes sense to say that membership is involuntary in a substantial sense. My claim is that it is the co-existence of this non-voluntariness and the bias of the scheme in favour of certain talents and dispositions that call for a positive duty of support. To elaborate on this claim, I have to go back to Hart.

In his reflections on contributive obligations, Hart is oblivious to the nature of the scheme of cooperation. The formulation of his principle makes no reference

---

13   It may be objected that Matt's disadvantage is only due to the random fact that preferences are aligned such way that his talent is not appreciated, but that is a question of luck, not justice. To this I reply that an economic system which permits the distribution of self-realisation to hinge on randomness is unfair. Thus, I am not criticising preferences as unfair, but that which the system makes of those preferences. A parallel reasoning can be found in Rawls's reference to a social system that compensates for natural and social contingencies. He says that people's natural endowments are 'neither just nor unjust; nor is it unjust that men are born into society at any particular position. These are simply natural facts. What is just or unjust is the way that institutions deal with these facts' (Rawls 1971, p. 102).

to the *aim* of the scheme, only the distribution of burdens and benefits *within* the scheme are the object of fairness. To reiterate, Hart's principle reads (Hart 1955, p. 185):

> When a number of persons conduct any joint enterprise according to rules and thus restrict their liberty, those who have submitted to these restrictions have a right to a similar submission from those who have benefited by their submission.

Hart emphasises the importance of a fair distribution of cooperative burdens and gains, but refrains from making mention of any justice requirement beyond the allocation of effort and benefits among the members of any scheme. A fair distribution of cooperative burdens, one would think, consists of a proportionate relationship between effort and gain for each individual cooperator. This means free-riding should be condemned because it violates this rule: it brings a larger share of benefits than the effort realised justifies. It does not constitute 'a similar submission' to the 'restrictions' imposed by the scheme, in Hart's terminology.

Rawls, in his reflections on fair cooperation, includes new features not developed by Hart in his principle of mutual restriction. According to Rawls, the benefit-conferring scheme must be a just one, as interpreted under the logic of his two principles of justice. Rawls calls this qualified Hartian principle 'the principle of fairness'. In advocating this principle of fairness, Rawls, in *A Theory of Justice,* refers to the following argument (1971, pp. 111–2):

> a person is required to do his part as defined by the rules of an institution when two conditions are met: fist, the institution is just (or fair), that is, it satisfies the two principles of justice; and second, one has voluntarily accepted the benefits of the arrangement or taken advantage of the opportunities it offers to further one's interests.

Building directly on the Hartian principle of restriction, Rawls's principle of fairness reads (1971, p. 108):

> when a number of persons engage in a just, mutually advantageous, cooperative venture according to rules and thus restrain their liberty in ways necessary to yield advantages for all, those who have submitted to these restrictions have a right to similar acquiescence on the part of those who have benefited from their submission.

Rawls seems to suggest that injustice in the rules of cooperation weakens the moral obligation to contribute to the cooperative scheme. Note that this type of injustice is content-based, not procedural. This is to say that a scheme is unjust if its *goals* are detrimental, unfairly, to the interests of a certain group of people. The injustice would be procedural, on this stipulation of the terms, if the scheme's allocative rules were unfair to some individuals because they imposed a greater burden on them but did not grant a benefit commensurate with those individuals' greater efforts, even if the ultimate goals of the arrangement were overall just. (Think, for example, that the scheme of cooperation is a non-governmental organisation whose mission is the alleviation of poverty in disadvantaged urban areas, but the employees with more responsibilities are paid less than those with smaller responsibilities.) The justice that Rawls's principle of fairness refers to is concerned with the goals of the rules themselves even if the allocation of benefits among the cooperators is fair. For example, one would be hard-pressed to think that a band of bank robbers constitutes a just cooperative enterprise only because each member of the group is in charge of an equally hard and effort-demanding task. The group's *objectives* are at odds with norms of justice because robbery generally is.

Taking society as a cooperative scheme, it is possible to identify injustice if rules of cooperation prejudice certain individuals for no ethically valid reasons. Biased rules of cooperation, unlike an unfair allocation of the burdens of cooperation, direct the efforts of contributors towards ends that some would-be cooperators have legitimate grounds to find objectionable. Their objections may be of two kinds, in broad terms: comprehensive or contextual, I stipulate. The former applies to the nature of a given encompassing goal or character associated with a scheme of cooperation. The person objects to this goal, or rationale, because he or she finds it morally repulsive with independence of its effects on his or her individual life-situation. Someone may find racism morally repulsive even if, in strictly self-interested terms, that institution is beneficial for him or her (because it excludes a sizable portion of the population from the pool of competitors for certain coveted posts and social stations, for example).

A contextual-type of objection, in turn, does not necessarily imply moral condemnation, but the realisation that a given goal is relevantly detrimental to one's interests in such way that accepting it impedes the attainment of goods one has a moral claim to enjoy, under normal circumstances. For this reason, the contextual objector does not object to the existence of the scheme as such (on the basis of its overall immoral or unjust goals) but to the lack of alternatives to the scheme, that is, to the absence of freedom to refrain from (fully) participating in it.

If it is possible that a cooperative scheme is associated with unjust overall goals and rationales (at least from a contextual perspective), it is also reasonable to raise a moral objection against the obligatoriness of contribution. Whichever conceptualisation of social justice we hold, we do not need to completely adhere to Rawls's theory of justice in order to rely on his intuition that the *goals* of the cooperative scheme are important in assessing the morality of non-cooperation. It is important that we show concern for the substantive justness of the rules of cooperation (that is, the nature of its goals). This justness is surely a question of degree. In relation to this, the following question arises: what types of injustices, and what degrees thereof, loosen the force of the obligatoriness of cooperation in the creation of societal wealth? Rawls does not directly deal with this question because he stays at the level of generality. Anything that falls short of his two principles of justice is supposed to be unjust and grounds for reluctance to cooperate, in principle.

This chapter develops the argument that it is conceivable that a society that does not guarantee equal opportunities for the exercise of meaningful talents be regarded as unacceptably unjust, all things considered. I rest my claim on the idea that any institutional arrangement that truncates equal distribution of opportunities to fulfil central human interests looks suspicious from a substantive justice viewpoint. We have already established that the exercise of talents may be regarded as one such type of interest, founded on a higher-order human need, namely, the need to use our human potentialities, as Rawls's Aristotelian principle suggests.[14]

Rawls's principle of fairness seemingly leaves the individual free to refuse cooperation when the scheme to which the individual belongs is unjust, or when it presents elements of injustice that cannot be accepted. However, nowhere in his principle of fairness does Rawls explicitly offer grounding for a positive duty on the part of contributors to finance non-contributors. In what follows, however, I argue that Rawls's principle of fairness can be invoked to justify financial support for those who desire to enjoy freedom from social cooperation through the receipt of unconditional welfare goods (of which the basic income scheme is an example).

Under a system that rewards certain skills but not others, some people will find it easy to make a livelihood while others will have to forsake self-realisation to secure the means necessary for survival. This disadvantage is due to no fault of their own, it is 'morally arbitrary'. If this moral arbitrariness could be amended by relaxing the obligation to cooperate, we would end this discussion here. However, relaxing cooperation is not sufficient since the cooperative scheme guarantees survival *only* through work. This means that subjection to the rules of cooperation is non-voluntary. It is extremely costly to exit the cooperative scheme owing to a lack of other acceptable alternatives.[15] Thus, we are faced with

---

14 The relationship between 'interests' and 'needs' is not self-evident, and calls for specification. It is reasonable to think that needs and interests may not always imply each other, for someone may have interests that are not supported by needs (in the sense of fundamental and universally recognizable necessities). However, one would be hard-pressed to deny the idea that needs give rise to a concomitant interest in their fulfillment under normal circumstances (assuming minimal rationality and absence of conflicting considerations).

15 For the notion of 'acceptable alternative', see Cohen (1988).

the problem of how to compensate for the moral arbitrariness of a cooperative scheme that is biased in favour of certain talent-holders when mere freedom to abstain from cooperating *does not suffice* as a means to redress.

In view of this difficulty, the only way to compensate for the bias is to award the material means that will preclude slavery to the system. Because of the particular nature of the inequality, the negative liberty to abstain from cooperating must be complemented by a positive duty of support. This positive duty is grounded on the non-voluntary nature of the (unjust) scheme. Insofar as survival can be secured only by cooperating, nothing short of a positive compensation for having talents the scheme does not reward can serve justice. Limiting any principle of rectification to freedom from cooperation would address only half of the moral arbitrariness in question: it would relieve individuals from the burden of contribution, but it would also leave them to die while free. The point of conceiving of self-realisation as a central human interest is to highlight the desirability of full human development. It is dubious that this goal can be attained when others refrain from imposing on us certain activities if such refraining does not go hand in hand with effective opportunities to *make use of* our freedom. The excludability of social wealth grounds our freedom not to cooperate, but since the scheme is non-voluntary, in the sense that it is unacceptably costly to exit it, a positive duty of support to make that freedom *real as opposed to merely formal* is called for.

Thus, to recapitulate, let me summarise the argument based on Rawls's principle of fairness: a concrete policy that relaxes the centrality of employment as a social duty of reciprocity is justified on the basis of two elements. The first element is the injustice given by unequal access to self-realisation opportunities in society (in tension with Rawls's requirement of justice applied to the cooperative scheme). The second element is the fact that membership in the scheme of cooperation is non-voluntary. Therefore, permission to refrain from cooperation does not suffice to mend the above-mentioned injustice (this reflects my principle of active support).

At this juncture, the question whether the exercise of 'expensive talents' should be given room arises. If equality of access to self-realisation through the use of talents is a legitimate social goal (as Rawls's allusion to the Aristotelian principle seems to suggest), one may wonder how society is to accommodate all the different ways in which people will want to reach self-realisation. Some of those ways are going to be expensive in comparison with others. Should society make them all possible? If individuals are going to be treated with equal respect, it follows that their specific claims to self-realisation have to be taken into consideration on an equal footing. But how can this be possible if, in the context of budgetary limitations, some people will need many more resources than others to achieve self-realisation? (Some will want to be writers, while others will want to be epic film directors, for instance.)

The funding that society offers to its members should allow them, if desired, to pursue activities and projects that require the active exercise of an ability or skill that is normally enjoyed and relatively challenging to use (in keeping with the spirit of Rawls's Aristotelian principle). But this does not mean that society should necessarily fund any particular pursuits that individuals desire to engage in. It is crucial to justice that the agent, being free to choose which talent to develop, be in a position to enjoy the *background capabilities* that are necessary for self-realisation. The latter include, among others, a certain degree of autonomy, space for creativity, non-repetitiveness, and a sense of responsibility for the final product of using one's talents. The individual should be free from market constraints so that he or she has the opportunity to experience the meaningful exercise of his or her powers if her self-realisation entails, in some way, the use of non-marketable skills. To honour equality of respect on the part of society towards its members, the individual's capacity to exercise his or her talents should be decoupled from other people's conceptions of that which is of value or desirable, at least partially. However, this justice requirement does not permit funding for any one particular activity or plan that is a vehicle to self-realisation. It is a human interest to be able to exercise one's talents minimally autonomously and with independence of their popularity, but it is not a human interest to exercise one's talents in *one and only one* way. Justice warrants equal access to the conditions of self-realisation, but it also warrants that such access be equally distributed among all members of society. These two potentially conflicting requisites justify limitations on the claims to self-realisation. Not all particular paths to self-realisation can, or should, be guaranteed to the individual. However, society should see to it that minimal conditions favourable to the attainment of self-realisation for all exist.

Since my views reject the idea that individuals with more expensive self-realisation needs should get more resources, they are not archetypically 'welfarist'.[16] This rejection is rooted in a philosophical premise, not in circumstantial considerations of costs. The premise is that only fundamental interests should be the primary focus of distributive justice.[17] Those interests have an objective aspect that in the case of self-realisation is given by the universally recognised human need to exercise one's talents autonomously and in a challenging way. It is a human interest to be able to exercise one's talents

---

16 Welfarist conceptions of equality take preference formation or subjective desire as the yardsticks of dsitribution. For an overview of these views, see Dworkin (1981)

17 For a non-subjective approach to distributive justice based on the concept of 'fundamental human interests', see Scanlon (1975).

minimally autonomously but it cannot be thought that every particular pursuit constitutes a fundamental human interest that all individuals could reasonably be said to share *qua* human beings.

Admittedly, the moral arbitrariness argument evoked to justify society's positive duty to make freedom from marketable work possible does not apply to individuals who have the option to engage in intrinsically satisfying work (that is, work that is conducive to self-realisation) but nevertheless prefer not to work because they are lazy. For the lazy, it is not at all clear that society has a positive duty of financial support to make their negative freedom from the obligation to cooperate sustainable, simply because a bias against laziness on the part of collective social arrangements does not count as creating morally arbitrary disadvantage that is relevant from the standpoint of justice. In keeping with the argument that self-realisation constitutes a generally recognised developmental need, I must say that it is not clear that laziness can contribute to fulfilling this need, since it does not imply the use of talents but rather the exact opposite. This conclusion is in stark contradiction with traditional left-libertarian defences of unconditional welfare provisions – such as Van Parijs's – that are ethically neutral among work and non-work preferences. However, in the absence of a consistent-with-autonomy way to identify the non-deserving beneficiaries of unconditional welfare provisions, it makes sense to extend the policy to everybody, under the (quite realistic assumption, I believe) that a sizable part of the population will still desire to form part of the workforce.

Conclusion

My reply to the free-rider objection against unconditional welfare policies (such as the basic income scheme) revolved around the idea that if we take society as a cooperative scheme, its excludable benefits justify freedom to exit cooperation. Additionally, the scheme's non-voluntary nature gives rise to a positive duty, on the part of society, to fund such freedom. Rawls's principle of fairness, inspired by Hart's principle of restriction, is the philosophical building block for this view. To further ground a right to freedom from cooperation, I developed the argument that equality of opportunity for self-realisation through the use of talents is necessary to offset slavery to the 'marketability logic', which renders fulfillment of a higher-order developmental need impossible for many. That self-realisation is partly associated with subjective preference – since there are many different ways in which it can be attained – does not mean that distributive justice should be concerned with all particular interests and desires, especially if they are unacceptably expensive.

Finally, my arguments for self-realisation are not meant to obviate considerations of feasibility and conflicting social needs. Fulfillment of basic human needs such as nourishment, medical care, and shelter, to name a few, should always count as prior to any higher-order developmental needs such as self-realisation, if only for reasons of fundamental justice as well as humanity. Nevertheless, acknowledging some type of lexicographic ordering of human needs does not detract from the importance of self-realisation in a context in which (some) attention to it can legitimately be paid.

References

Arneson, R. 1982. 'The principle of fairness and free-rider problems.' *Ethics* 92(4): 616–33.

Buchanan, A. 1990. 'Justice as reciprocity versus subject-centered justice.' *Philosophy and Public Affairs* 19(3): 227–52.

Carens, J. 1986. 'Rights and duties in an egalitarian society.' *Political Theory* 14(1): 311–49.

Cohen, G. 1988. *History, Labour and Freedom*. Oxford: Oxford Clarendon Press.

Cullity, G. 1995. 'Moral free-riding.' *Philosophy and Public Affairs* 24(1): 3–34.

Dewey, J. 1893. 'Self-realization as the moral ideal.' *Philosophical Review* 2(6): 652–64.

Dworkin, R. 1981. 'What is equality? Part II: Equality of resources.' *Philosophy and Public Affairs* 10(4): 283–345.

Elster, J. 1986. 'Comment on Van der Veen and Van Parijs.' *Theory and Society* 15(5): 709–21.

Hart, H. L. A. 1955. 'Are there any natural rights?' *Philosophical Review* 64(2): 175–91.

Klosko, G. 1987. 'Presumptive benefit, fairness and political obligation.' *Philosophy and Public Affairs* 16(3): 241–59.

Locke, J. 1967. *Second Treatise of Government*. Cambridge: Cambridge University Press.

Maphai, V. 1987. 'The principle of fairness.' *South African Journal of Philosophy* 6(3): 73–80.

Maslow, A. 1943. 'A theory of human motivation.' *Psychological Review* 50(4): 370–96.

Nozick, R. 1975. *Anarchy, State and Utopia.* Cambridge: Harvard University Press.

Rawls, J. 1971. *A Theory of Justice.* Cambridge: Harvard University Press.

Scanlon, T. 1975. 'Preference and urgency.' *Journal of Philosophy* 72(19): 655–69.

Segall, S. 2005. 'Unconditional welfare benefits and the principle of reciprocity.' *Politics, Philosophy and Economics* 4(3): 331–54.

Van der Veen, R. 1991. *Between Exploitation and Communism: Explorations in the Marxian theory of justice and freedom.* Amsterdam: Groningen.

Van der Veen, R., and P. Van Parijs. 1986. 'Universal grants versus socialism: A reply to six critics.' *Theory and Society* 15(5): 723–57.

Van Parijs, P. 1995. *Real Freedom for All: What (if anything) can justify capitalism?* Oxford: Oxford University Press.

White, S. 2004. *The Civic Minimum: Rights and obligations of economic citizenship.* Oxford: Oxford University Press.

References

Acemoglu, D., and S. Johnson. 2005 'Unbundling institutions.' *Journal of Political Economy* 113(5): 949–95.

Acharya, V. V., and P. Schnabl. 2009. 'Do global banks spread global imbalances? The case of asset-backed commercial paper during the financial crisis of 2007–2009.' Paper presented at the 10th Jacques Polak Annual Research Conference, Washington, DC, 5–6 November.

Akerlof, A. 1970. 'The market for "lemons": Quality uncertainty and the market mechanism.' *Quarterly Journal of Economics* 84(3): 488–500.

Aldrick, P. 2009. 'Nicolas Sarkozy wants "well-being" measure to replace GDP.' *Daily Telegraph*, 14 September. www.telegraph.co.uk/finance/economics/6189582/Nicolas-Sarkozy-wants-well-being-measure-to-replace-GDP.html.

Alford, J. 2009. *Engaging Public Sector Clients: From service delivery to co-production.* Basingstoke, Hampshire: Palgrave Macmillan.

Alford, J. 2009. *Public Value from Co-production by Clients.* Working paper. Australia and New Zealand School of Government. http://ips.ac.nz/events/downloads/2009/Building%20the%20Public%20-%20Spring%20Series (accessed May 2010). (Forthcoming in J. Benington and M. Moore (eds). *In Search of Public Value.* London: Palgrave Macmillan.)

Allen, M. R., D. J. Frame, C. Huntingford, et al. 2009. 'Warming caused by cumulative carbon emissions towards the trillionth tonne.' *Nature* 458(7242): 1163–6.

Alvey, J. 1999. *An Introduction to Economics as a Moral Science.* Working paper 15. Independent Institute. www.independent.org/pdf/working_papers/15_introduction.pdf (accessed 13 November 2009).

American Bankers Association. 2009. *BAFT Welcomes Re-Launch of Due Diligence Repository.* News release, 17 February. www.aba.com/Press+Room/021709DueDiligenceRepository.htm.

Amy, D. J. 1984. 'Why policy analysis and ethics are incompatible.' *Journal of Policy Analysis and Management* 3(4): 573–91.

Annas, J. 2005. 'Comments on John Doris's *Lack of Character*.' *Philosophy and Phenomenological Research* 71(3): 636–42.

Anthoff, D., R. S. J. Tol, and G. W. Yohe. 2009. 'Discounting for climate change.' *Economics: The open-access, open assessment e-journal* 2: 2009–276.

Appiah, A. 2008. *Experiments in Ethics*. Cambridge, MA: Harvard University Press.

Arneson, R. 1982. 'The principle of fairness and free-rider problems.' *Ethics* 92(4): 616–33.

Arpaly, N. 2005. 'Comments on *Lack of Character* by John Doris.' *Philosophy and Phenomenological Research* 71(3): 643–7.

Arrow, K. 1963. 'Uncertainty and the welfare economics of medical care.' *American Economic Review* 53(5): 941–73.

Arts, B., and J. Van Tatenhove. 2004. 'Policy and power: A conceptual framework between the 'old' and 'new' policy idioms.' *Policy Sciences* 37: 339–56.

Australian Public Service Commission. 2007. *Tackling Wicked Problems: A public policy perspective*. Barton, ACT: Commonwealth of Australia. www. apsc.gov.au/publications07/wickedproblems.htm (accessed May 2010).

Baehler, K. 2005. 'What are the limits to public service advising? The "public argument" test.' *Policy Quarterly* 1(3): 3–8.

Baehler, K., and J. Bryson. 2009. 'Behind the Beehive buzz: Sources of occupational stress for New Zealand policy officials.' *Kōtuitui: Journal of Social Sciences Online* 4: 5–23. www.royalsociety.org.nz/site/publish/journals/kotuitui/ default.aspx (accessed May 2010).

Baer, P., T. Athanasiou, and S. Kartha. 2007. *The Right to Development in a Climate Constrained World: The Greenhouse Development Rights Framework*. Berlin: Heinrich Böll Foundation.

Bank for International Settlements. 2007. *77th Annual Report 1 April 2006 – 31 March 2007*. www.bis.org/publ/arpdf/ar2007e.htm.

Bank for International Settlements. 2008. *78th Annual Report 1 April 2007 – 31 March 2008*. www.bis.org/publ/arpdf/ar2008e.htm.

Bank for International Settlements. 2009. *Range of Practices and Issues in Economic Capital Frameworks*. Basel, Switzerland: Basel Committee on Banking Supervision. www.bis.org/publ/bcbs152.pdf.

Bardach, E. 2000. *A Practical Guide for Policy Analysis: The eightfold path to more effective problem solving*. New York and London: Chatham House Publishers.

Bardach, E. 2008. *A Practical Guide for Policy Analysis: The eightfold path to more effective problem solving.* 3rd edn. Washington, DC: CQ Press.

Barrett, S. 2008. 'The incredible economics of geoengineering.' *Environmental and Resource Economics* 39(1): 45–54.

Barry, J. 1999. *Rethinking Green Politics: Nature, virtue, and progress.* Thousand Oaks, CA: Sage.

Barry, J. 2006. 'Resistance is fertile: From environmental to sustainability citizenship.' In A. Dobson and D. Bell (eds). *Environmental Citizenship.* Cambridge, MA: MIT Press.

Barth, J. R., D. E. Nolle, T. Phumiwasana, et al. 2002. *A Cross-Country Analysis of the Bank Supervisory Framework and Bank Performance.* Economics Working paper 2002–2. Washington, DC: Office of the Comptroller of the Currency.

Barth J. R., S. Trimbath, and G. Yago (eds). 2004. *The Savings and Loan Crisis: Lessons from a regulatory failure.* Norwell, MA: Kluwer Academic Publishers.

BBC News. 2009. 'Rich Germans demand higher taxes.' 23 October. news.bbc.co.uk/go/pr/fr/-/2/hi/europe/8321967.stm.

Bell, D. 2005. 'Liberal environmental citizenship.' *Environmental Politics* 14: 179–94.

Bellah, R. 1983. 'Social science as practical reason.' In D. Callahan and B. Jennings (eds). *Ethics, the Social Sciences, and Policy Analysis.* New York and London: Plenum Press, pp. 37–64.

Beltratti, A., and R. M. Stulz. 2009. *Why Did Some Banks Perform Better During the Credit Crisis? A cross-country study of the impact of governance and regulation.* Working paper 2009-12. Columbus, Ohio: Ohio State University, Charles A. Dice Center for Research in Financial Economics. http://econpapers.repec.org/paper/eclohidic/2009-12.htm.

Benedict XVI. 2009. *Encyclical Letter: Caritas in Veritate.* Rome: The Vatican.

Bennis, W. 2003. *On Becoming a Leader.* 3rd edn. New York: Basic Books.

Benveniste, G. 1984. 'On a code of ethics for policy experts.' *Journal of Policy Analysis and Management* 3(4): 561–72.

Berkowitz, A. 1993. 'John Selden and the biblical origins of the modern international political system.' *Jewish Political Studies Review* 6(1–2): 27–47.

Bernanke, B. S. 2004. 'The great moderation.' Remarks at meetings of the Eastern Economic Association, Washington, DC, 20 February.

Bernasek, A. 2010. *The Economics of Integrity*. New York: Harperstudio.

Bernstein, P. 1998. *Against the Gods: A remarkable story of risk*. New York: Wiley.

Bicchieri, C. 2002. 'Covenants without swords: Group identity, norms, and communication in social dilemmas.' *Rationality and Society* 14(2): 192–228.

Bicchieri, C. 2006. *The Grammar of Society: The nature and dynamics of social norms*. Cambridge: Cambridge University Press.

Bicchieri, C. 2008. 'The fragility of fairness: An experimental investigation on the conditional status of pro-social Norms.' *Nous (Philosophical Issues 18 Interdisciplinary Core Philosophy)* 18: 227–46.

Billington, R. 2003. *Living Philosophy: An introduction to moral thought*. 3rd edn. London and New York: Routledge.

Blackstone, W. [1763] 1983. *Commentaries on the Laws of England*. Birmingham, Alabama: Legal Classics Library.

Blinder, A. 2010. 'When greed is not good.' *Wall Street Journal*, 11 January. www://online.wsj.com/article/SB10001424052748703652104574652242436 408008.html.

Blok, K., N. Höhne, A. Torvanger, et al. 2005. *Towards a Post-2012 Climate Change Regime*. Brussels, Belgium: 3E.

BNZ Investments Ltd v. Commissioner of Inland Revenue 15 July 2009, Wild J, HC Wellington CIV 2004-485-1059. http://jdo.justice.govt.nz/jdo.

Bodansky, D., S. Chou, and C. Jorge-Tresolini. 2004. *International Climate Efforts beyond 2012: A survey of approaches*. Washington, DC: Pew Center on Global Climate Change.

Bok, S. (ed.). 1978. *Lying: Moral choice in public and private life*. New York: Pantheon Books.

Bok, S. 1984. *Secrets: On the ethics of concealment and revelation*. Oxford; New York: Oxford University Press.

Bookstaber, R. M. 2008. *A Demon of Our Own Design: Markets, hedge funds, and the perils of financial innovation*. Hoboken, NJ: John Wiley & Sons.

Bosetti, V., C. Carraro, A. Sgobbi, et al. 2009. 'Delayed action and uncertain stabilisation targets. How much will the delay cost?' *Climatic Change* 96(3): 299–312.

Boston, J. 1994. 'Christianity in the public square: The churches and social justice.' In J. Boston and A. Cameron (eds). *Voices for Justice: Church, law and state in New Zealand*. Palmerston North: Dunmore.

Boston, J., F. Lemp, and L. Kengmana. Forthcoming. 'Considerations of distributive justice in the context of climate change mitigation.' *British Journal of Politics and International Relations*.

Bowles, S. 2008. 'Policies designed for self-interested citizens may undermine "the moral sentiments": Evidence from economic experiments.' *Science* 320(5883): 1605–9.

Boyd, P. W. 2009. 'Geopolitics of geoengineering.' *Nature Geoscience* 2(12): 812.

Bradley, F. H. 1962. *Ethical Studies*. 2nd edn. London: Oxford University Press.

Bradstock, A., and C. Rowland (eds). 2002. *Radical Christian Writings: A reader*. Oxford: Blackwell.

Brock, G. 2009. *Global Justice: A cosmopolitan account*. Oxford: Oxford University Press.

Broecker, W. S. 2007. 'Climate change: CO2 arithmetic.' *Science* 315(5817): 1371.

Bromell, D. 2008. *Ethnicity, Identity and Public Policy: Critical perspectives on multiculturalism*. Wellington: Institute of Policy Studies, Victoria University of Wellington.

Bromell, D. 2009. 'Diversity and democracy.' *Policy Quarterly* 5(4): 29–35.

Bromell, D. 2009. 'Recognition, redistribution and democratic inclusion.' In R. Openshaw and E. Rata (eds). *The Politics of Conformity in New Zealand*. North Shore City: Pearson, pp. 231–55.

Brooks, J. 1998. *The Go-Go Years: The drama and crashing finale of Wall Street's bullish 60s*. New York: Allworth Press.

Brooks, J. 1999. *Once in Golconda: A true drama of Wall Street 1920–1938*. New York: John Wiley & Sons.

Broome, J. 2004. *Weighing Lives*. Oxford: Oxford University Press.

Broome, J. 2005. 'Should we value population?' *Journal of Political Philosophy* 13: 399–413.

Brown, G., and K. Rudd. 2009. 'Speech and Q&A at St Paul's Cathedral.' London, 31 March. http://webarchive.nationalarchives.gov.uk/+/number10.gov.uk/news/speeches-and-transcripts/2009/03/pms-speech-at-st-pauls-cathedral-18858.

Brueggemann, W. 2009. 'From anxiety and greed to milk and honey.' *Faith and Finance: Christians and the economic crisis – Discussion guide*. Washington DC: Sojourners.

Buchanan, A. 1990. 'Justice as reciprocity versus subject-centered justice.' *Philosophy and Public Affairs* 19(3): 227–52.

Buffet, W. 2003. Chairman's letter to the shareholders of Berkshire Hathaway Inc., 21 February. In *Berkshire Hathaway Inc, 2002 Annual Report*, pp. 3–23. www.berkshirehathaway.com/2002ar/2002ar.pdf.

Callahan, D., and B. Jennings (eds). 1983. *Ethics, the Social Sciences, and Policy Analysis*. New York and London: Plenum Press.

Camerer, C., and E. Fehr. 2004. 'Measuring social norms and preferences using experimental games: A guide for social scientists.' In J. Henrich, E. Fehr, and H. Gintis (eds). *Foundations of Human Sociality: Economic experiments and ethnographic evidence from fifteen small-scale societies*. Oxford: Oxford University Press.

Camerer, C., and E. Fehr. 2006. 'When does "economic man" dominate social behaviour?' *Science* 311(5757): 47–52.

Camerer, C., and R. M. Hogarth. 1999. 'The effects of financial incentives in experiments: A review and capital–labor–production framework.' *Journal of Risk and Uncertainty* 19(1): 7–42.

Campbell, T. 1974. 'Humanity before justice.' *British Journal of Political Science,* 4: 1–16.

Campbell, T. 2010. *Justice*. 3rd edn. London: Macmillan.

Caney, S. 2005. 'Cosmopolitan justice, responsibility, and global climate change.' *Leiden Journal of International Law* 18: 747–75.

Caney, S. 2005. *Justice beyond Borders: A global political theory*. Oxford: Oxford University Press.

Carens, J. 1986. 'Rights and duties in an egalitarian society.' *Political Theory* 14(1): 311–49.

Casal, P. 2007. 'Why sufficiency is not enough.' *Ethics* 117(2): 296–326.

Chapman, B. 1959. *The Profession of Government*. London: George Allen & Unwin.

Cherry, C. 1998. *God's New Israel*. Chapel Hill: University of North Carolina.

Cheung, J. 2007. *Wealth Disparities in New Zealand*. Wellington: Statistics New Zealand.

Chuah, S., R. Hoffmann, M. Jones, et al. 2009. 'An economic anatomy of culture: Attitudes and behaviour in inter- and intra-national ultimatum game experiments.' *Journal of Economic Psychology* 30(5): 732–44.

Cialdini, R. 2006. *Influence: The psychology of persuasion* Rev. edn. New York: Harper Paperbacks.

Cialdini, R., R. Reno, and C. Kallgren. 1990. 'A focus theory of normative conduct: Recycling the concept of norms to reduce littering in public places.' *Journal of Personality and Social Psychology* 58: 1015–26.

Claussen, E., and L. McNeilly. 1998. *Equity and Global Climate Change: The complex elements of global fairness*. Arlington, VA: PEW Center for Global Climate Change.

Cobbett, W. (ed.) 1813. *The Parliamentary History of England*. vol 16. London: T. C. Hansard. (Available from the Oxford Digital Library, www2.odl. ox.ac.uk/gsdl/cgi-bin/library?e=d-000-00---0modhis06--00-0-0-0prompt-10---4------0-1l--1-en-50---20-about---00001-001-1-1isoZz-8859Zz-1-0&a=d&c=modhis06&cl=CL1&d=modhis006-aap.)

Cohen, G. 1988. *History, Labour and Freedom*. Oxford: Oxford Clarendon Press.

Comptroller of the Currency Administrator of National Banks. 1996. *New Opportunities to Excel Outstanding CRA Actions for Community Banks*. www. occ.treas.gov/cra/excel.htm.

Considine, M. 1994. *Public Policy: A critical approach*. South Melbourne: Macmillan.

Consumer. 2009. 'Financial advisers: Getting good advice.' www.consumer.org. nz/reports/financial-advisers/getting-good-advice (accessed 25 February 2010).

Covey, S. M. R. 2006. *The Speed of Trust: The one thing that changes everything*. New York: Simon and Schuster.

Covey, S. R. 1991. *Principle-Centered Leadership*. New York: Free Press.

Cramer, J. 2002. *Confessions of a Street Addict*. New York: Simon & Schuster.

Crane, R. 2009. 'Network effects and risks.' Unpublished presentation. Swiss Federal Institute of Technology.

Crisp, R. 2003. 'Equality, priority, and compassion.' *Ethics* 113(4): 745–63.

Cullity, G. 1995. 'Moral free-riding.' *Philosophy and Public Affairs* 24(1): 3–34.

Cyert, R. M., and J. G March. 1963. *A Behavioral Theory of the Firm*. Englewood Cliffs, NJ: Prentice-Hall.

Dale, R. 2004. *The First Crash: Lessons from the South Sea bubble*. Princeton, NJ: Princeton University Press.

Dannenerg, A., B. Sturm, and C. Vogt. 2009. 'Do equity preferences matter for climate negotiators? An experimental investigation.' *IOP Conference Series: Earth and environmental science* 6(11): 112,002.

Davis Polk. 2009. *A Guide to the Laws, Regulations and Contracts of the Financial Crisis: Financial crisis manual*. www.davispolk.com/files/News/7f041304-9785-4433-aa90-153d69b92104/Presentation/NewsAttachment/3c9302c0-409f-4dd1-9413-24e8cd60cd93/Financial_Crisis_Manual.pdf.

Dawes, R. M. 1980. 'Social dilemmas.' *Annual Review of Psychology* 31(1): 169–93.

De la Vega, J. 1688. *Confusións de Confusiones*. Reprint edn. In M. S. Frisdon. 1996. *Confusions and Delusions: Tulipmania, the South Sea bubble and the madness of crowds*. Hoboken, NJ: John Wiley & Sons.

De Lazari-Radek, K., and P. Singer. 2010. 'Secrecy in consequentialism: A defence of esoteric morality.' *Ratio* (March): 34–68.

De Nicolò, G., L. Laeven, and K. Ueda. 2006. *Corporate Governance Quality: Trends and real effects*. Working paper WP/06/293. International Monetary Fund. www.imf.org/external/pubs/ft/wp/2006/wp06293.pdf.

deLeon, P. 1994. 'Democracy and the policy sciences: Aspirations and operations.' *Policy Studies Journal* 22(2): 200–12.

DellaVigna, S. 2009. 'Psychology and economics: Evidence from the field.' *Journal of Economic Literature* 47(2): 315–72.

Dellink, R., M. den Elzen, H. Aiking, et al. 2009. 'Sharing the burden of financing adaptation to climate change.' *Global Environmental Change* 19(4): 411–21.

den Elzen, M., A. Hof, and D. P. Van Vuuren. 2009. 'Regional total climate change costs for different burden sharing regimes and concentration targets.' *IOP Conference Series: Earth and environmental science* 6(32): 322005.

den Elzen, M., and N. Höhne. 2008. 'Reductions of greenhouse gas emissions in Annex I and non-Annex I countries for meeting concentration stabilisation targets. An editorial comment.' *Climatic Change* 91: 249–74.

den Elzen, M., N. Höhne, M. Hagemann, et al. 2009. *Sharing Developed Countries' Post-2012 Greenhouse Gas Emission Reductions Based on Comparable Efforts.* The Netherlands: Netherlands Environmental Assessment Agency.

den Elzen, M., and M. Meinshausen. 2005. *Meeting the EU 2°C climate target: Global and regional emission implications.* The Netherlands: Netherlands Environmental Assessment Agency.

Dessler, A. 2009. 'Energy for air capture.' *Nature Geoscience* 2(12): 811.

Dewey, J. 1893. 'Self-realization as the moral ideal.' *Philosophical Review* 2(6): 652–64.

Dewey, J. 1927. *The Public and its Problems.* New York: Holt.

Dewey, J. 1939. *Freedom and Culture.* New York: Putnam.

Dietz, S., J. Helgeson, C. Hepburn, et al. 2009. 'Siblings, not triplets: Social preferences for risk, inequality and time in discounting climate change.' *Economics: The open-access, open assessment e-journal* 3: 2009–26.

Dietz, S., C. Hope, and N. Patmore. 2007. 'Some economics of "dangerous" climate change: Reflections on the Stern Review.' *Global Environmental Change* 17(3–4): 311–25.

Dimas, S. 2009. 'Act and adapt: Towards a new climate change deal.' Speech given at Green Week, Brussels, 23 June 2009.

Diplock, J. 2009. 'The financial crisis and corporate governance.' Speech to Auckland Rotary. www.seccom.govt.nz/speeches/2009/220609.shtml.

Djankov, D., D. La Porta, F. López-de-Silanes, et al. 2008. 'The law and economics of self-dealing.' *Journal of Financial Economics* 88(3): 430–65.

Dobson, A., and D. Bell. 2006. *Environmental Citizenship.* London: MIT Press.

Doris, J. M. 2002. *Lack of Character: Personality and moral behaviour.* New York: Cambridge University Press.

Downer, M. 2008. 'Wealth, ownership, and social care: Towards a consideration of jubilee in New Zealand's contemporary political context.' *Stimulus* 16(3): 2–15.

Driver, J. 2001. *Uneasy Virtue.* Cambridge, UK: Cambridge University Press.

Duncan, G. 2007. *Society and Politics: New Zealand social policy*. 2nd edn. Auckland: Pearson Education.

Dworkin, R. 1977. *Taking Rights Seriously*. Cambridge, MA: Harvard University Press.

Dworkin, R. 1981. 'What is equality? Part II: Equality of resources.' *Philosophy and Public Affairs* 10(4): 283–345.

Dyson, F. 2008. 'The question of global warming.' *New York Review of Books* 55(10).

Economagic. n. d. *Economic Time Series*. www.economagic.com/em-cgi/data.

Eichbaum, C., and R. Shaw. 2005. 'Why we should all be nicer to ministerial advisers.' *Policy Quarterly* 1(4): 18–25.

Eichbaum, C., and R. Shaw. 2007. 'Minding the minister? Ministerial advisers in New Zealand government.' *Kōtuitui: Journal of Social Sciences Online* 2: 95–113. www.royalsociety.org.nz/site/publish/journals/kotuitui/default. aspx (accessed May 2010).

Eichbaum, C., and R. Shaw (eds). 2010. *Partisan Appointees and Public Servants: An international analysis of the role of the political advisor*. Cheltenham, UK: Edward Elgar Publishing.

Elias, N. 1978. *The Civilizing Process*. 1st American edn. New York: Urizen Books.

Elster, J. 1986. 'Comment on Van der Veen and Van Parijs.' *Theory and Society* 15(5): 709–21.

Elster, J. 2007. *Explaining Social Behaviour: More nuts and bolts for the social sciences*. Cambridge: Cambridge University Press.

Epictetus. c. AD 55–135. *The Art of Living*. New interpretation by S. Lebell, 1994. New York: HarperCollins.

Ethics Resource Center. 2007. *New Zealand State Services Integrity and Conduct Survey: August 2007*. Ethics Resource Centre: Washington, DC. www.ssc. govt.nz/display/document.asp?DocID=6276 (accessed May 2010). Results of a follow-up survey conducted in March 2010 are on the State Services Commission's website (www.ssc.govt.nz/display/home.asp).

FAO. 2009. *The State of Food Insecurity in the World 2009*. Rome: Food and Agriculture Organization of the United Nations. www.fao.org/publications/ sofi/en.

Federal Deposit Insurance Corporation. 2002. *Manual of Examination Policies (Safety and Soundness)*. Washington, DC: Federal Deposit Insurance Corporation.

Federal Deposit Insurance Corporation. 2009. *Bank Failures in Brief: 2009*. Washington, DC: Federal Deposit Insurance Corporation. www.fdic.gov/ BANK/HISTORICAL/BANK/2009/index.html.

Ferguson, N. 2008. *The Ascent of Money: A financial history of the world*. New York: Penguin.

Financial Stability Board. 2009. *Progress since the Pittsburgh Summit in Implementing the G20 Recommendations for Strengthening Financial Stability: Report of the Financial Stability Board to G20 finance ministers and governors*. Basel, Switzerland: Financial Stability Board.

Fischbacher, U, S. Gächter, and E. Fehr. 2001. 'Are people conditionally cooperative? Evidence from a public goods experiment.' *Economics Letters* 71(3): 397–404.

Foley, D. 2007. *The Economic Fundamentals of Global Warming*. Working paper 07-12-044. Santa Fe, New Mexico: Santa Fe Institute. www.santafe.edu/ media/workingpapers/07-12-044.pdf.

Fox, J. J. 2002. *How to Become a Great Boss*. New York: Hyperion.

Frankfort-Nachmias, C., and D. Nachmias. 1996. *Research Methods in the Social Sciences*. 5th edn. New York: St. Martin's Press.

Frankfurt, H. 1987. 'Equality as a moral ideal.' *Ethics* 98(1): 21–43.

Frey, B. S. 1994. 'How intrinsic motivation is crowded out and in.' *Rationality and Society* 6(3): 334–52.

Frey, B. S., and S. Meier. 2004. 'Social comparisons and pro-social behavior: Testing "conditional cooperation" in a field experiment.' *American Economic Review* 94(5): 1717–22.

Frieden, T. 2004. 'FBI warns of mortgage fraud "epidemic": Seeks to head off "next S&L crisis".' *Cable News Network*, 17 September. http://edition.cnn. com/2004/LAW/09/17/mortgage.fraud.

Friedman, M. 1994. *Money Mischief: Episodes in monetary history*. 1st Harvest edn. San Diego: Mariner Books.

Füssel, H.-M. 2009. 'The ethical dilemma of climate change: How unequal is the global distribution of responsibility for and vulnerability to climate change?' *IOP Conference Series: Earth and environmental science* 6(11): 112,013.

Galbraith, J. K. 1961. *The Great Crash, 1929*. Boston; New York: Houghton Mifflin.

Gallagher, J. 1981. 'Models for policy analysis: Child and family policy.' In R. Haskins and J. Gallagher (eds). *Models for Analysis of Social Policy: An introduction*. Norwood, NJ: Ablex Publishing Corporation, pp. 37–77.

Gardiner, S. M. 2001. 'The real tragedy of the commons.' *Philosophy and Public Affairs* 30(4): 387–416.

Gardiner, S. M. 2004. 'Ethics and global climate change.' *Ethics* 114(3): 555–600.

Gardner, R., E. Ostrom, and J. M. Walker. 1990. 'The nature of common-pool resource problems.' *Rationality and Society* 2(3): 335–58.

Gawthrop, L. 1984. *Public Sector Management, Systems, and Ethics*. Bloomington: Indiana University Press.

Geva-May, I. 1997. *An Operational Approach to Policy Analysis: The craft – Prescriptions for better analysis*. Boston: Kluwer Academic Publishers.

Gewirth, A. 1982. *Human Rights: Essays on justification and adjudication*. Chicago: University of Chicago Press.

Gintis, H., S. Bowles, R. Boyd, et al. 2005. *Moral Sentiments and Material Interests: The foundations of cooperation in economic life*. Cambridge MA: MIT Press.

Glaeser, E., R. La Porta, F. López-de-Silanes, et al. 2004. 'Do institutions cause growth?' *Journal of Economic Growth* 9(3): 271–303.

Godechot, O. 2008. '"Hold-up" in finance: The conditions of possibility for high bonuses in the financial industry.' *Revue Française de Sociologie*, (Supplement Annual English edn) 49: 95–123.

Godechot, O. 2008. 'What do heads of dealing rooms do? The social capital of internal entrepreneurs.' In M. Savage and K. Williams (eds). *Remembering Elites*. Malden, MA: Wiley-Blackwell.

Goldman Sachs. 2007. *Goldman Sachs Reports Third Quarter Earnings Per Common Share of $6.13*. New York: Goldman Sachs Group, Inc. www2.goldmansachs. com/our-firm/investors/financials/archived/quarterly-earnings-releases/ attachments/2007-third-quarter-earnings.pdf.

Goleman, D. 2009. *Ecological Intelligence: How knowing the hidden impacts of what we buy can change everything*. New York: Broadway Books.

Goodman, P. 2008. 'Taking hard new look at a Greenspan legacy.' *New York Times*, 8 October. www.nytimes.com/2008/10/09/business/economy/09greenspan. html.

Gorringe, T. J. 1994. *Capital and the Kingdom: Theological ethics and economic order*. Maryknoll, NY: Orbis.

Gould, B. 2008. *Rescuing the New Zealand Economy: What went wrong and how we can fix it*. Nelson: Craig Potton.

Greenspan, A. 1998. Testimony by Alan Greenspan, chair of the Board of Governors of the Federal Reserves System, to United States Senate Committee on Agriculture, Nutrition and Forestry, 30 July. http://agriculture.senate. gov/Hearings/Hearings_1998/gspan.htm.

Gregory, R. 2005. 'Politics, power and public policy-making: A response to Karen Baehler.' *Policy Quarterly* 1(4): 26–32.

Grimes, A. 2005. 'Improving consumer trust in the retail savings industry.' Paper prepared for the Retirement Commission. www.retirement.org.nz/ files/retirement-files/research-library/improving-consumer-trust-in-the-retail-savings-industry.pdf.

Gurría, A. 2009. 'Business ethics and OECD principles: What can be done to avoid another crisis?' Remarks by OECD secretary-general at the European Business Ethics Forum, Paris, 22 January 2009. www.oecd.org/document/3/ 0,3343,en_2649_201185_42033219_1_1_1_1,00.html.

Güth, W., R. Schmittberger, and B. Schwarze. 1982. 'An experimental analysis of ultimatum bargaining.' *Journal of Economic Behavior and Organization* 3(4): 367–88.

Guttentag, J. M., and R. J. Herring. 1986. *Disaster Myopia in International Banking*. Princeton University Essays in International Finance 164. Princeton, NJ: International Finance Section, Department of Economics, Princeton University.

Habermas, J. 1974. *Theory and Practice*. London: Heinemann.

Habermas, J. 1984. *The Theory of Communicative Action, Vol. 1: Reason and the rationalization of society*. London: Heinemann Education.

Hailwood, S. 2005. 'Environmental citizenship as reasonable citizenship.' *Environmental Politics* 14: 195–210.

Haldane, A. G. 2009. 'Rethinking the financial network.' Speech delivered at the Financial Student Association, Amsterdam, 28 April. www.cnbv.gob.mx/recursos/Combasdr176.pdf.

Haldane, A. G. 2009. *Why Banks Failed the Stress Test*. Basis for a speech given at the Marcus–Evans Conference on Stress-Testing, 9–10 February 2009. www.bankofengland.co.uk/publications/speeches/2009/speech374.pdf.

Hampshire, S. 1999. *Justice is Conflict*. London: Duckworth.

Hansard: Parliamentary Debate for 5 October 1994. http://vdig.net/hansard/content.jsp?id=43766.

Hanson, K. 2006. 'Perspectives on global moral leadership.' In D. Rhode (ed.). *Moral Leadership: The theory and practice of power, judgment, and policy.* Hoboken: Jossey-Bass, pp. 291–300.

Hardin, G. 1968. 'The tragedy of the commons.' *Science* 162(3859): 1243–8.

Hardin, R. 1988. *Morality within the Limits of Reason*. Chicago: University of Chicago Press.

Hardin, R. 2006. 'Morals for public officials.' In D. Rhode (ed.). *Moral Leadership: The theory and practice of power, judgment, and policy.* Hoboken: Jossey-Bass, pp. 111–25.

Harman, G. 2009. 'Skepticism about character traits.' *Journal of Ethics* 13(2): 235–42.

Harms, W., and B. Skyrms. 2008. 'Evolution of moral norms.' In M. Ruse (ed.). *The Oxford Handbook of Philosophy of Biology*. Oxford: Oxford University Press, ch. 18.

Harris, N. 2009. 'Finance company failures: Observations of the Registrar of Companies.' In Commerce Committee. *2007/08 Financial review of the Ministry of Economic Development: Report of the Commerce Committee.* Wellington: Ministry of Economic Development, Appendix B. www.parliament.nz/NR/rdonlyres/16F22058-8DD8-4541-B9A9-064848076239/100892/DBSCH_SCR_4272_6521.pdf.

Hart, H. L. A. 1955. 'Are there any natural rights?' *Philosophical Review* 64(2): 175–91.

Hartley, S. 2009. 'Recession takes its toll on wealth of Kiwi rich list.' *Otago Daily Times*, 25 July, p. 25.

Havel, V. 1992. *Open Letters: Selected writings, 1965–1990*. 1st Vintage Books edn. Edited by P. Wilson. New York: Vintage Books.

Hawke, G. 1993. *Improving Policy Advice*. Wellington: Institute of Policy Studies, School of Government, Victoria University of Wellington.

Heal, G. 2009. 'The economics of climate change: A post-Stern perspective.' *Climatic Change* 96(3): 275–97.

Henrich, J., R. Boyd, S. Bowles, et al. 2001. 'In search of homo economicus: Behavioural experiments in 15 small-scale societies.' Paper read at 113th Annual Meeting of the American Economic Association, New Orleans, Louisiana, 5–7 January.

Henry, K. 2009. 'Fiscal policy: More than just a national budget.' Address to the 2009 Whitlam Institute Symposium, 30 November. www.treasury.gov.au/documents/1678/HTML/docshell.asp?URL=Whitlam_Institute_Speech.htm.

Hibbs, T. 2001. *Virtue's Splendour: Wisdom, prudence and the human good*. New York: Fordham University Press.

Hicks, C. 2007. 'A case for public sector ethics.' *Policy Quarterly* 3(3): 11–15.

Höhne, N., and S. Moltmann. 2008. *Distribution of Emission Allowances under the Greenhouse Development Rights and Other Effort Sharing Approaches*. Germany: Heinrich-Böll-Stiftung.

Hood, C., and M. Lodge. 2006. *The Politics of Public Service Bargains: Reward, competency, loyalty – and blame*. Oxford and New York: Oxford University Press.

Hulme, M. 2009. 'The science and politics of climate change.' *Wall Street Journal*, 2 December. http://online.wsj.com/article/SB10001424052748704107104574571613215771336.html.

Humphreys, D. 2009. 'Environmental and ecological citizenship in civil society.' *International Spectator* 44: 171–83.

Hunn, D., I. Bond, and D. Kernohan. 2002. *Report of the Overview Group on the Weathertightness of Buildings to the Building Industry Authority*. Wellington: Building Industry Authority. www.dbh.govt.nz/whrs-publications-reports.

Hursthouse, R. 2001. *On Virtue Ethics*. Oxford: Oxford University Press.

IMF. 2003. 'Growth and institutions.' In *World Economic Outlook: April 2003*. Washington: International Monetary Fund, ch. 3. www.imf.org/external/ pubs/ft/weo/2003/01.

IMF. 2003. *The World Economic Outlook (WEO) Database April 2003*. Washington: International Monetary Fund. www.imf.org/external/pubs/ft/ weo/2003/01/data/index.htm (acessed October 2009).

IMF. 2009. *World Economic Outlook, October 2009: Sustaining the recovery*. Washington, DC: International Monetary Fund. www.imf.org/external/ pubs/cat/longres.cfm?sk=22576.0 (accessed April 2010).

IPCC (Intergovernmental Panel on Climate Change). 1996. *Climate Change 1995: Volume III: Economic and social dimensions of climate change*. Cambridge, UK: Cambridge University Press.

IPCC (Intergovernmental Panel on Climate Change). 2001. *Climate Change 2001: Synthesis report. Contribution of Working Groups I, II and III to the Third Assessment Report*. Cambridge, UK: Cambridge University Press.

IPCC (Intergovernmental Panel on Climate Change). 2007. *Climate Change 2007: The Physical Science Basis. Contribution of Working Group I to the Fourth Assessment Report of the Intergovernmental Panel on Climate Change*. Cambridge, UK: Cambridge University Press.

IPCC (Intergovernmental Panel on Climate Change). 2007. *Climate Change 2007: Impacts, adaptation and vulnerability. Contribution of Working Group II to the Fourth Assessment Report of the Intergovernmental Panel on Climate Change*. Cambridge, UK: Cambridge University Press.

IPCC (Intergovernmental Panel on Climate Change). 2007. *Climate Change 2007: Mitigation of climate change. Contribution of Working Group III to the Fourth Assessment Report of the Intergovernmental Panel on Climate Change*. Cambridge, UK: Cambridge University Press.

IPCC. 2007. *Climate Change 2007: Synthesis report. Contribution of Working Groups I, II and III to the Fourth Assessment Report*. Geneva, Switzerland: Intergovernmental Panel on Climate Change.

Ivry, B., C. Harper, and M. Pittman. 2009. 'Missing Lehman lesson of shakeout means too big banks may fail.' *Bloomberg*, 7 September. www.bloomberg. com/apps/news?pid=newsarchive&sid=aX8D5utKFuGA.

Ivry, B., M. Pittman, and C. Harper. 2009. 'Sleep-at-night-money lost in Lehman lesson missing $63 billion.' *Bloomberg*, 8 September. www.bloomberg.com/ apps/news?pid=newsarchive&sid=aLhi.S5xkemY.

J. P. Morgan. n. d. 'ABS issuance: Growth and collapse by asset class.' [Chart.] In A. B. Ashcraft. *Credit, Investment, and Payment Risk: Discussion of 'do global banks spread global imbalances'?* http://imf.org/external/np/res/seminars/2009/arc/pdf/ashcraft1.pdf.

Jamieson, D. 1992. 'Ethics, public policy, and global warming.' *Science Technology and Human Values* 17(2): 139–53.

Jones, B. D. 2001. *Politics and the Architecture of Choice: Bounded rationality and governance.* Chicago: University of Chicago Press.

Jones, L. B. 1995. *Jesus, CEO: Using ancient wisdom for visionary leadership.* New York: Hyperion.

'"Kamikaze" bankers damaged economy, says Alistair Darling.' 2009. *Daily Telegraph*, 5 July. www.telegraph.co.uk/finance/newsbysector/banksandfinance/5747952/Kamikaze-bankers-damaged-economy-says-Alistair-Darling.html.

Kamtekar, R. 2004. 'Situationism and virtue ethics on the content of our character.' *Ethics* 114(3): 458–91.

Kane, J., H. Patapan, and P. 't Hart (eds). 2009. *Dispersed Democratic Leadership.* Oxford and New York: Oxford University Press.

Kant, I. 1797. 'Groundwork of the metaphysics of morals.' Translated by H. J. Paton. Reproduced in L. Pasternack (ed.). 2002. *Immanuel Kant: Groundwork of the metaphysics of morals, in focus.* London: Routledge, ch. 11.

Keith, D. W. 2000. 'Geoengineering the climate: History and prospect.' *Annual Review of Energy and the Environment* 25(1): 245–84.

Keith, K. 1990. 'On the constitution of New Zealand: An introduction to the foundations of the current form of government.' *Cabinet Manual 2008.* Wellington: Cabinet Office, pp. 1–6. www.cabinetmanual.cabinetoffice.govt.nz/introduction (updated 2008; accessed May 2010).

Kelman, S. 1988. *Making Public Policy: A hopeful view of American government.* New York: Basic Books.

Kern, A., R. Dhumale, and J. Eatwell. 2005. *Global Governance of Financial Systems: The international regulation of systemic risk.* New York: Oxford University Press.

Kernaghan, K. 1995. 'The emerging public service culture: Values, ethics, and reforms.' *Canadian Public Administration* 37(4): 614–30.

Killen, M., and J. Smetana. 2006. *Handbook of Moral Development*. New Jersey: Lawrence Erlbaum Associates.

Kindleberger, C. P., and R. Z. Aliber. 2005. *Manias, Panics, and Crashes: A history of financial crises*. 5th edn. Hoboken, NJ: John Wiley & Sons.

Kingdon, J. 1995. *Agendas, Alternatives, and Public Policies*. 2nd edn. Boston, MA: Little, Brown.

Klosko, G. 1987. 'Presumptive benefit, fairness and political obligation.' *Philosophy and Public Affairs* 16(3): 241–59.

Knee, J. A. 2006. *The Accidental Investment Banker: Inside the decade that transformed Wall Street*. Hoboken, NJ: Wiley.

Kotter, J. P. 1996. *Leading Change*. Boston, MA: Harvard Business School Press.

Kraft, M. E., and S. R. Furlong. c. 2007. *Public policy: Politics, analysis, and alternatives*. 2nd edn. Washington, DC: CQ Press.

Kramer, R. M. 1999. 'Trust and distrust in organizations: Emerging perspectives, enduring questions.' *Annual Review of Psychology* 50: 569–98.

Kriegler, E., J. W. Hall, H. Held, et al. 2009. 'Imprecise probability assessment of tipping points in the climate system.' *Proceedings of the National Academy of Sciences* 106(13): 5041–6.

Kuran, T. 1997. *Private Truths, Public Lies: The social consequences of preference falsification*. Cambridge, MA: Harvard University Press.

Kurzban, R., and D. Houser. 2005. 'Experiments investigating cooperative types in humans: A complement to evolutionary theory and simulations.' *Proceedings of the National Academy of Sciences of the United States of America* 102(5): 1803–7.

La Porta, R., F. López-de-Silanes, A. Shleifer, et al. 1997. 'Legal determinants of external finance.' *Journal of Finance* 52(3): 1131–50.

La Porta, R., F. López-de-Silanes, A. Shleifer, et al. 1998. 'Law and finance.' *Journal of Political Economy* 106(6): 1113–55.

La Porta, R., F. López-de-Silanes, and G. Zamarripa. 2003. 'Related lending.' *Quarterly Journal of Economics* 118(1): 231–68.

Landmark National Bank v. Kesler 2009 Kan. LEXIS 834 (28 August 2009, Kansas Supreme Court).

Lange, A., A. Löschel, C. Vogt, et al. 2010. 'On the self-interested use of equity in international climate negotiations.' *European Economic Review* 54(3): 359–75.

Lange, A., C. Vogt, and A. Ziegler. 2007. 'On the importance of equity in international climate policy: An empirical analysis.' *Energy Economics* 29(3): 545–62.

Le Grand, J. 2003. *Motivation, Agency, and Public Policy: Of knights and knaves, pawns and queens.* Oxford: Oxford University Press.

Ledyard, J. 1995. 'Public goods: A survey of experimental research.' In J. Kagel and A. E. Roth (eds). *Handbook of Experimental Economics.* Princeton: Princeton University Press.

Lefèvre, E. 2006. *Reminiscences of a Stock Operator.* Hoboken, NJ: John Wiley & Sons.

Lenton, T. M., H. Held, E. Kriegler, et al. 2008. 'Tipping elements in the Earth's climate system.' *Proceedings of the National Academy of Sciences* 105(6): 1786–93.

Lewis, M. 1990. *Liar's Poker: Rising through the wreckage on Wall Street.* New York: Penguin Books.

Lindquist, E. 2009. *There's More to Policy than Alignment.* CPRN Research Report, Canadian Policy Research Networks. www.cprn.org/doc.cfm?doc=2040&l=en (accessed May 2010).

List, J. 2004, 'Young, selfish and male: Field evidence of social preferences.' *Economic Journal* 114(492): 121–49.

Litan, R. E., N. P. Retsinas, E. S. Belsky, et al. 2000. *The Community Reinvestment Act after Financial Modernization: A baseline report.* Washington, DC: US Department of the Treasury.

Locke, J. 1967. *Second Treatise of Government.* Cambridge: Cambridge University Press.

Lodge. M. 2009. 'Strained or broken? The future(s) of the public service bargain.' *Policy Quarterly* 5(1): 53–7.

Longstaff, S. 1994. 'What is ethics education and training?' In N. Preston (ed.). *Ethics for the Public Sector: Education and training.* Leichhardt, NSW: Federation Press, pp. 138–60.

Lorenzoni, I., and N. Pidgeon. 2006. 'Public views on climate change: European and USA perspectives.' *Climatic Change* 77(1): 73–95.

Lowenstein, R. 2000. *When Genius Failed: The rise and fall of long-term capital management*. New York: Random House.

Ludwig, D., R. Hilborn, and C. Walters. 1993. 'Uncertainty, resource exploitation, and conservation: Lessons from history.' *Science* 260(5104): 17–36.

Machan, T. R. 2009. 'The virtue of prudence as the moral basis of commerce.' *Reason Papers* 3: 49–61.

Mackay, C. 1841. *Extraordinary Popular Delusions and the Madness of Crowds*. Reprinted in M. S. Frisdon. 1996. *Confusions and Delusions: Tulipmania, the South Sea Bubble and the Madness of Crowds*. Hoboken, NJ: John Wiley & Sons.

MacKenzie, D. 2006. *An Engine, Not a Camera: How financial models shape markets*. Cambridge, MA: MIT Press.

Majone, G. 1989. *Evidence, Argument, and Persuasion in the Policy Process*. New Haven: Yale University Press.

Mandelbrot, B., and R. L. Hudson. 2006. *The Misbehavior of Markets: A fractal view of financial turbulence*. New York: Basic Books.

Maphai, V. 1987. 'The principle of fairness.' *South African Journal of Philosophy* 6(3): 73–80.

Marland, G., and M. Obersteiner. 2008. 'Large-scale biomass for energy, with considerations and cautions: An editorial comment.' *Climatic Change* 87: 335–42.

Martin, J. 1994. 'Ethics in public service: The New Zealand experience.' In N. Preston (ed.). *Ethics for the Public Sector: Education and training*. Leichhardt, NSW: Federation Press, pp. 91–114.

Maslow, A. 1943. 'A theory of human motivation.' *Psychological Review* 50(4): 370–96.

Mason, A. 2009. 'Environmental obligations and the limits of transnational citizenship.' *Political Studies* 57: 280–97.

Maxwell, J. C. 1999. *The 21 Indispensable Qualities of a Leader*. Nashville, TN: Thomas Nelson Publishers.

Mayer, M. 1990. *The Greatest Ever Bank Robbery: The collapse of the savings and loan industry*. New York: Collier Books.

McPherson, M. 1983. 'Imperfect democracy and the moral responsibilities of policy advisers.' In D. Callahan and B. Jennings (eds). *Ethics, the Social Sciences, and Policy Analysis*. New York and London: Plenum Press, pp. 69–81.

MED. 2007. *Financial Advisers: A new regulatory framework*. Regulatory Impact Statement. Wellington: Ministry of Economic Development. www.med.govt.nz/upload/47854/financial-advisors-ris.pdf.

Meinshausen, M., N. Meinshausen, W. Hare, et al. 2009. 'Greenhouse-gas emission targets for limiting global warming to 2°C.' *Nature* 458(7242): 1158–62.

Melzer, A. 2007. 'On the pedagogical motive for esoteric writing.' *Journal of Politics* 69(4): 1015–31.

Merscorp v. Romaine NY Int 167 (2006, New York Court of Appeals).

Meyer, L. H. 1998. 'Community Reinvestment Act in an era of bank consolidation and deregulation.' Remarks before the 1998 Community Reinvestment Act Conference of the Consumer Bankers Association, Arlington, Virginia, 12 May. www.federalreserve.gov/Boarddocs/Speeches/1998/19980512.htm.

Meyerson, D., K. E. Weick, and R. M. Kramer. 1996. 'Swift trust and temporary groups.' In R. M. Kramer and T. R. Tyler (eds). *Trust in Organizations: Frontiers of theory and research*, Thousand Oaks, CA: Sage Publications, ch. 9.

Mill, J. S. 1859. *Utilitarianism and On Liberty*. 2nd edn. Edited and with an introduction by M. Warnock. 2003. Malden, MA: Blackwell Publishers.

Minsky, H. P. 2008. *Stabilizing an Unstable Economy*. New York: McGraw-Hill.

Mintrom, M. 1997. 'Policy entrepreneurs and the diffusion of innovation.' *American Journal of Political Science* 41: 738–70.

Mintrom, M. 2003. *People Skills for Policy Analysts*. Washington, DC: Georgetown University Press.

Mintrom, M., and P. Norman, 2009. 'Policy entrepreneurship and policy change.' *Policy Studies Journal* 37(4): 649–67.

Mitchener, K. J. 2007. 'Are prudential supervision and regulation pillars of financial stability? Evidence from the Great Depression.' *Journal of Law & Economics* 50(1): 273–302.

Monaghan, A. 2009. 'FSA treats mortgage lenders like "drug dealers", says CML chief.' *Daily Telegraph*, 13 November. www.telegraph.co.uk/finance/newsbysector/banksandfinance/6562111/FSA-treats-mortgage-lenders-like-drug-dealers-says-CML-chief.html.

Moroney, R. 1981. 'Policy analysis within a value theoretical framework.' In R. Haskins and J. Gallagher (eds). *Models for Analysis of Social Policy: An introduction*. Norwood, NJ: Ablex Publishing Corporation, pp. 78–102.

Morris, S., and H. S. Shin. 2008. 'Financial regulation in a system context.' Paper prepared for the Brookings Panel meeting, 11–12 September 2008 (version dated 7 September 2008). www.brookings.edu/economics/bpea/~/media/Files/Programs/ES/BPEA/2008_fall_bpea_papers/2008_fall_bpea_morris_shin.pdf.

Mortgage Insurance Companies of America. 2006. Letter addressed to the Board of Governors of the Federal Reserve System, the Federal Deposit Insurance Corporation, and two others, 29 March. www.fdic.gov/regulations/laws/federal/2005/05c45guide.pdf.

MSD. 2008. *The Social Report: Te Pūrongo Oranga Tangata 2008*. Wellington: Ministry of Social Development.

MSD. n. d., a. *Code of Conduct*. Wellington: Ministry of Social Development.

MSD. n. d., b. *Our Vision, Values and Purpose*. Wellington: Ministry of Social Development. www.msd.govt.nz/about-msd-and-our-work/about-msd/our-vision-values-and-purpose.html (accessed May 2010).

Murphy D. 2009. 'Rendering to Caesar, and a nod to God.' *Sydney Morning Herald*, 31 October – 1 November.

Nagel, T. 1970. *The Possibility of Altruism*. Oxford: Clarendon.

Nagel, T. 1977. 'Poverty and food: Why charity is not enough.' In P. Brown and H. Shue (eds). *Food Policy: The responsibility of the United States in the life and death choices*. New York: Free Press, pp. 54–62.

Narvaez, M., and D. Lapsley. 2009. *Personality, Identity and Character: Explorations in moral psychology*. Cambridge: Cambridge University Press.

Neumayer, E. 2000. 'In defence of historical accountability for greenhouse gas emissions.' *Ecological Economics* 33: 185–92.

Neumayer, E. 2007. 'A missed opportunity: The Stern Review on climate change fails to tackle the issue of non-substitutable loss of natural capital.' *Global Environmental Change* 17(3–4): 297–301.

Nielson, K. 1983. 'Emancipatory social science and social critique.' In D. Callahan and B. Jennings (eds). *Ethics, the Social Sciences, and Policy Analysis*. New York and London: Plenum Press, pp. 113–57.

Nordhaus, W. D. 2009. 'Economic issues in a designing a global agreement on global warming.' Paper presented at Climate Change: Global risks, challenges, and decisions, Copenhagen, Denmark, 10–12 March 2009. http://climatecongress.ku.dk/speakers/professorwilliamnordhaus-plenaryspeaker-11march2009.pdf.

Nozick, R. 1975. *Anarchy, State and Utopia*. Cambridge: Harvard University Press.

NZPA (New Zealand Press Association). 2009. 'Leaky homes bill likely to top $11.5 billion.' *NZ Herald*, 18 August. www.nzherald.co.nz/nz/news/article.cfm?c_id=1&objectid=10591520.

Obama for America. n. d. *Barack Obama and Joe Biden: New energy for America*. www.barackobama.com/pdf/factsheet_energy_speech_080308.pdf.

OECD. 2000. *Building Public Trust: Ethics measures in OECD countries*. PUMA Policy Brief No. 7. Organisation for Economic Co-operation and Development.

Olson, M. 1971. *The Logic of Collective Action: Public goods and the theory of groups*. Rev. edn. New York: Schocken Books.

Orr, D. W. 2004. *Earth in Mind: On education, environment, and the human Prospect*. 10th anniversary edn. Washington, DC: Island Press.

Ostrom, E. 1990. *Governing the Commons: The evolution of institutions for collective action*. Cambridge: Cambridge University Press.

Ostrom, E. 2000. 'Collective action and the evolution of social norms.' *Journal of Economic Perspectives* 14(3): 137–58.

Ostrom, E., J. Burger, C. B. Field, et al. 1999. 'Revisiting the commons: Local lessons, global challenges.' *Science* 284(5412): 278–82.

Ostrom, E., J. Walker, and R. Gardner. 1992. 'Covenants with and without a sword: Self-governance is possible.' *American Political Science Review* 86(2): 404–17.

Page, E. 1999. 'Intergenerational justice and climate change.' *Political Studies* 47: 53–66.

Page, E. 2007. 'Justice between generations: Investigating a sufficientarianism approach.' *Journal of Global Ethics* 3(1): 3–20.

Page, E. 2008. 'Distributing the burdens of climate change.' *Environmental Politics* 17(4): 556–75.

Parfit, D. 1984. *Reasons and Persons*. Oxford: Oxford University Press.

Parfit, D. 2000. 'Equality of priority.' In M. Clayton and A. Williams (eds). *The Ideal of Equality*. London: Macmillan, pp. 81–125.

Parliamentary Library 2002. 'Leaky buildings.' *Background Note* 2002/10, 6 November. www.parliament.nz/NR/rdonlyres/464AB9F9-B197-4B53-BE9F-4F411CB67877/360/0210LeakyBuildings1.pdf.

Parry, M., N. Arnell, P. Berry, et al. 2009. *Assessing the Costs of Adaptation to Climate Change*. London: International Institute for Environment and Development.

Parsons, W. 1995. *Public Policy: An introduction to the theory and practice of policy analysis*. Aldershot, UK and Brookfield, US: Edward Elgar.

Pasternack, L. (ed.) 2002. *Immanuel Kant: Groundwork of the metaphysics of morals, in focus*. London: Routledge.

Petrie, M. 2002. *Institutions, Social Norms and Well-Being*. Working paper 02/12. Wellington: The Treasury. www.treasury.govt.nz/publications/research-policy/wp/2002/02-12.

Pielke Jr, R. A. 2009. 'An idealized assessment of the economics of air capture of carbon dioxide in mitigation policy.' *Environmental Science & Policy* 12(3): 216–25.

Pittman, M., and B. Ivry. 2009. 'London suicide connects Lehman lesson missed by Hong Kong woman.' *Bloomberg*, 9 September. www.bloomberg.com/apps/news?pid=newsarchive&sid=aNFuVRL73wJc.

Plante, T. G. 2004. *Doing the Right Thing: Living ethically in an unethical world*. Oakland, CA: New Harbinger Publications.

Pogge, T. 2005. 'Severe poverty as a violation of negative duties.' *Ethics and International Affairs* 19(1): 55–83.

Pogge, T. 2008. *World Poverty and Human Rights: Cosmopolitan responsibilities and reforms*. 2nd edn. Cambridge: Polity Press.

Pogge, T. (ed.) 2007. *Freedom from Poverty as a Human Right*. Oxford: Oxford University Press.

Pollitt, C. 2003. *The Essential Public Manager*. Philadelphia, PA: Open University.

Porritt, J. 2007. *Capitalism as if the World Matters*. London: Earthscan.

Povey, D. M. 2002. *How Much is Enough? Life below the poverty line in Dunedin*. Dunedin: Presbyterian Support Otago.

Presidential Working Group on Financial Markets. 1999. *Over-the-Counter Derivatives and the Commodity Exchange Act*. Washington, DC: US House of Representatives. www.ustreas.gov/press/releases/reports/otcact.pdf.

Preston, N. (ed.). 1994. *Ethics for the Public Sector: Education and training*. Leichhardt, NSW: Federation Press.

Quinn, R. E. 2000. *Change the World: How ordinary people can accomplish extraordinary results*. San Francisco: Jossey-Bass.

Quinn, R. W., and R. E. Quinn. 2009. *Lift: Becoming a positive force in any situation*. San Francisco: Berrett-Koehler Publishers.

Rabinowicz, W. 2009. 'Broome and the intuition of neutrality.' *Philosophical Issues* 19: 389–411.

Radin, B. 2000. *Beyond Machiavelli: Policy analysis comes of age*. Washington, DC: Georgetown University Press.

Rajan, R. G. 1998. 'The past and future of commercial banking viewed through an incomplete contract lens.' *Journal of Money, Credit & Banking* 30(3): 524–50.

Rapid Evidence Assessment Toolkit. n. d. UK Government Social Research Service. www.civilservice.gov.uk/my-civil-service/networks/professional/gsr/resources/gsr-rapid-evidence-assessment-toolkit.aspx (accessed May 2010).

Rasch, P. J., S. Tilmes, R. P. Turco, et al. 2008. 'An overview of geoengineering of climate using stratospheric sulphate aerosols.' *Philosophical Transactions. Series A, Mathematical, Physical, and Engineering Sciences* 366(1882): 4007–37.

Rawls, J. 1971. *A Theory of Justice*. Cambridge MA: Harvard University Press.

Rawls, J. 1972. *A Theory of Justice*. London: Oxford University Press.

Rawls, J. 1999. *The Law of Peoples; with, The Idea of Public Reasons Revisited*. Cambridge, MA: Harvard University Press.

RBNZ. 2008. *Financial Stability Report*. Wellington: Reserve Bank of New Zealand. www.rbnz.govt.nz/finstab/fsreport/3311557.pdf.

Rea, D. 2010. *Would New Zealand's Economic Performance Improve if We Were More Ethical?* Working paper 10/05. Wellington: Institute of Policy Studies, School of Government, Victoria University of Wellington. http://ips.ac.nz/publications/publications/list/7.

Read, P. 2008. 'Biosphere carbon stock management: Addressing the threat of abrupt climate change in the next few decades – An editorial essay.' *Climatic Change* 87: 305–20.

Rehmann-Sutter, C. 1998. 'Involving others: Towards an ethical concept of risk.' *Risk: Health, Safety and Environment* 9(2): 119.

Rein, M. 1983. 'Value critical policy analysis.' In D. Callahan and B. Jennings (eds). *Ethics, the Social Sciences, and Policy Analysis.* New York and London: Plenum Press, pp. 83–111.

Reinhart, C. M., and K. S. Rogoff. 2009. *This Time is Different: Eight centuries of financial folly.* Princeton, NJ: Princeton University Press.

Reisinger, A. 2009. *Climate Change 101: An educational resource.* Wellington: Institute of Policy Studies and New Zealand Climate Change Research Institute, School of Government, Victoria University of Wellington.

Reynolds, P. D. 1979. *Ethical Dilemmas and Social Science Research.* San Francisco: Jossey-Bass.

Rhode, D. (ed.). 2006. *Moral Leadership: The theory and practice of power, judgment, and policy.* Hoboken: Jossey-Bass.

Ricoeur, P. 1992. *Oneself as Another.* Chicago: University of Chicago Press.

Ringius, L., A. Torvanger, and A. Underdal. 2000. *Burden Differentiation: Fairness principles and proposals.* Working paper 1999:13. Oslo: Center for International Climate and Environmental Research and Netherlands Energy Research Foundation.

Rittel, H., and M. Webber. 1973. 'Dilemmas in the general theory of planning.' *Policy Sciences* 4(2): 155–69.

Robson, J (ed.). 1966. *John Stuart Mill: A selection of his works.* New York: Odyssey Press.

Rochefort, D. A., and R. W. Cobb (eds). 1994. *The Politics of Problem Definition: Shaping the policy agenda.* Lawrence, KS: University Press of Kansas.

Rose, A. 1992. 'Equity considerations of tradable carbon emission entitlements.' In S. Barrett (ed.). *Combating Global Warming: Study on a global system of tradable carbon emission entitlements.* New York: United Nations Conference on Trade and Development.

Ross, W. D. 1930. *The Right and the Good.* Oxford: Clarendon Press.

Roth, A. E., V. Prasnikar, M. Okunofujiwara, et al. 1991. 'Bargaining and market behaviour in Jerusalem, Ljubljana, Pittsburgh, and Tokyo: An experimental study.' *American Economic Review* 81(5): 1068–95.

Rudd, K. 2006. 'Faith in politics.' *The Monthly Magazine,* October, no. 17. www.themonthly.com.au/print/300.

Rudd, K. 2008. 'The children of Gordon Gekko.' Extract from speech by the prime minister in Sydney, 3 October. *The Australian,* 6 October. www.theaustralian.com.au/news/the-children-of-gordon-gekko/story-e6frg7b6-1111117670209.

Runciman, D. 2009. 'How messy it all is.' [Review of *The Spirit Level.*] *London Review of Books* 31(20): 3–6.

Russill, C., and Z. Nyssa. 2009. 'The tipping point trend in climate change communication.' *Global Environmental Change* 19(3): 336–44.

Salmon, F. 2009. 'Recipe for disaster: The formula that killed Wall Street.' *Wired Magazine,* 17 March. www.wired.com/techbiz/it/magazine/17-03/wp_quant.

Sampford, C. 1994. 'Institutionalising public sector ethics.' In N. Preston (ed.). *Ethics for the Public Sector: Education and training.* Leichhardt, NSW: Federation Press, pp. 14–38.

Sample, S. B. 2002. *The Contrarian's Guide to Leadership.* San Francisco: Jossey-Bass.

Sandel, M. 2009. 'Markets and morals.' First 2009 Reith Lecture. www.bbc.co.uk/programmes/b00kt7sh.

Sanders, J. R., et al. 1994. *The Program Evaluation Standards.* 2nd edn. Thousand Oaks, CA: Sage Publications.

Sandler, R. L. 2007. *Character and Environment: A virtue-oriented approach to environmental ethics.* New York: Columbia University Press.

Scanlon, T. 1975. 'Preference and urgency.' *Journal of Philosophy* 72(19): 655–69.

Schelling, T. C. 1996. 'The economic diplomacy of geoengineering.' *Climatic Change* 33(3): 303–7.

Schlesinger, M. E. 2009. 'Planetary boundaries: Thresholds risk prolonged degradation.' *Nature Reports: Climate change* (September): 112–3.

Schneider, S. H. 2008. 'Geoengineering: Could we or should we make it work.' *Philosophical Transactions of the Royal Society* 18(08).

Schön, D. A., and M. Rein. 1994. *Frame Reflection: Toward the resolution of intractable policy controversies.* New York: Basic Books.

Schultz, B. 2004. *Henry Sidgwick: Eye of the universe. An intellectual biography.* Cambridge, UK: Cambridge University Press.

Schwartz, B. 2004. *The Paradox of Choice: Why more is less.* New York: HarperCollins.

Scott, C. 2008. 'Enhancing quality and capability in the public sector advisory system.' Lecture to the Institute of Policy Studies Futuremaker Series, Victoria University of Wellington, 23 September 2008. http://ips.ac.nz/events/downloads/2008/ScottFuturemakers%2023-9-08.pdf%20 (accessed May 2010).

Searchinger, T., R. Heimlich, R. A. Houghton, et al. 2008. 'Use of US croplands for biofuels increases greenhouse gases through emissions from land-use change.' *Science* 319(5867): 1238–40.

Securities Commission. 2002. *Investment Advisers: A case study. Gideon Investments Pty Limited – Morison Guildford & Associates Limited.* www.sec-com.govt.nz/publications/documents/morison_guildford/index.shtml.

Segall, S. 2005. 'Unconditional welfare benefits and the principle of reciprocity.' *Politics, Philosophy and Economics* 4(3): 331–54.

Selden, J. 1679. *De Synedriis & Praefecturis Juridicis Veterum Ebraeorum.* Three volumes. Amstelædami: Ex officina Henrici & Theodori Boom, & viduæ Joannis à Someren, 1679.

Sen, A. 1985. 'The moral standing of the market.' *Social Philosophy and Policy* 2: 1–19.

Sen, A. 1985. 'Well-being, agency and freedom: The Dewey Lectures 1984.' *Journal of Philosophy* 82(4): 169–221.

Sen, A. 1999. *Development as Freedom.* New York: Anchor Books.

Sen, A. 2009. *The Idea of Justice.* Cambridge, MA: Belknap Press.

Sen, A. 2009. *The Idea of Justice.* London: Allen Lane.

Sepielli, A. 2010. 'Normative uncertainty and intertheoretic comparisons.' *PhilPapers: Online research in philosophy*. http://philpapers.org/rec/SEPNUA.

Shue, H. 1992. 'The unavoidability of justice.' In A. Hurrell and B. Kingsbury (eds). *The International Politics of the Environment*. Oxford: Oxford University Press, pp. 373–97.

Shue, H. 1996. *Basic Rights: Subsistence, affluence and US foreign policy*. 2nd edn. Princeton: Princeton University Press.

Shue, H. 1999. 'Global environment and international inequality.' *International Affairs* 75(3): 531–45.

Sidgwick, H. 1898. *Practical Ethics: A collection of addresses and essays*. London: Swan Sonnenschein. www.archive.org/details/cu31924031432275.

Sidgwick, H. 1907. *The Methods of Ethics*. 3rd edn. London: MacMillan.

Sidgwick, H. 1907. *The Methods of Ethics*. 7th edn. London: Macmillan.

Singer, P. 2008. 'One atmosphere.' In T. Brooks (ed.). *The Global Justice Reader*. Oxford: Blackwell, pp. 667–88. (First published in P. Singer. 2002. *One World: The Ethics of Globalization*. New Haven: Yale University Press, pp. 14–50, 205–8.)

Singer, P. 2009. *The Life You Can Save*. Melbourne: Text.

Sjöberg, L. 2000. 'Factors in risk perception.' *Risk Analysis* 20: 1–12.

Smith, A. 1762. 'Lectures on jurisprudence'. In R. L. Meek, D. D. Raphael, and P. G. Stein (eds). 1982. *The Glasgow Edition of the Works and Correspondence of Adam Smith*. Vol. 5. Indianapolis: Liberty Fund.

Smith, A. 1776. *An Inquiry into the Nature and Causes of the Wealth of Nations*. 5th edn. Edited by E. Cannan. 1904. London: Methuen. Available from the Library of Economics and Liberty, www.econlib.org/library/Smith/smWN.html (accessed 17 October 2009).

Smith, A. 1790. *The Theory of Moral Sentiments*. 6th edn. London: A. Millar.

Smith, A. 1776. *The Wealth of Nations*. Edited with an introduction and notes by E. Cannan. 1994. New York: Random House.

Smith, J. B., S. H. Schneider, M. Oppenheimer, et al. 2009. 'Assessing dangerous climate change through an update of the Intergovernmental Panel on Climate Change (IPCC) "reasons for concern".' *Proceedings of the National Academy of Sciences* 106(11): 4133–7.

Solomon, R. C. 2005. 'What's character got to do with it?' *Philosophy and Phenomenological Research* 71(3): 648–55.

Sorkin, A. R. 2009. *Too Big to Fail: The inside story of how Wall Street and Washington fought to save the financial system – and themselves.* New York: Viking.

Sornette, D. 2009. *Dragon-Kings, Black Swans and the Prediction of Crises.* Research paper 09–36. Geneva: Swiss Finance Institute.

SSC. 1995. *Principles, Conventions and Practice Guidance Series.* Wellington: State Services Commission. www.ssc.govt.nz/display/document.asp?docid=5798 (accessed May 2010).

SSC. 2001. *New Zealand Public Service Code of Conduct.* Reprinted 2005. Wellington: State Services Commission.

SSC. 2007. *Standards of Integrity and Conduct: A code of conduct issued by the State Services Commissioner under the State Sector Act 1988, section 57.* Wellington: State Services Commission. www.ssc.govt.nz/display/document. asp?DocID=7063 (accessed May 2010).

SSC. 2007. *Understanding the Code of Conduct: Guidance for state servants.* Wellington: State Services Commission.

SSC. 2008. *Political Neutrality Fact Sheet No. 1: What is 'political neutrality' and what does it mean in practice?* Wellington: State Services Commission.

SSC. 2008. *Political Neutrality Fact Sheet No. 2: Political views and participation in political activities.* Wellington: State Services Commission.

SSC. 2008. *Political Neutrality Fact Sheet No. 3: The relationship between the public service and ministers.* Wellington: State Services Commission.

Staff Writers. 2010. 'All things being equal.' *The Listener* 223(3651). www. listener.co.nz/issue/3651/features/15346/all_things_being_equal.html.

Starling, G. 2008. *Managing the Public Sector.* 8th edn. Boston, MA: Thomson Higher Education.

Stern, N. 2006. *The Economics of Climate Change: The Stern Review.* Cambridge, UK: Cambridge University Press.

Stern, N. 2010. *A Blueprint for a Safer Planet.* Vintage Books.

Stewart, J. B. 1992. *Den of Thieves.* New York: Simon and Shuster.

Stock, J., and M. Watson. 2002. *Has the Business Cycle Changed and Why?* Working paper W9127. National Bureau of Economic Research.

Stout, L. A. 1999. 'Why the law hates speculators: Regulation and private ordering in the market for OTC derivatives.' *Duke Law Journal* 48: 701–86.

Sunstein, C. R. 2007. 'On the divergent American reactions to terrorism and climate change.' *Columbia Law Review* 107(2): 503–58.

Taleb, N. N. 2007. *The Black Swan.* New York: Random House.

Taylor, J. 2006. *Creating Capitalism: Joint-stock enterprise in British politics and culture, 1800–1870.* London: Boydell Press.

Tett, G. 2009. *Fool's Gold: How the bold dream of a small tribe at J. P. Morgan was corrupted by Wall Street greed and unleased a catastrophe.* New York: Free Press.

The Merchant of Venice. 2004. Directed by M. Radford. Culver City, CA: Sony Pictures Classics.

Tilly, C. 2006. *Regimes and Repertoires.* Chicago: University of Chicago Press.

Tol, R. S. J., and G. W. Yohe. 2009. 'The Stern Review: A deconstruction.' *Energy Policy* 37(3): 1032–40.

Toulmin, S. 1976. *Knowing and Acting.* New York: Macmillan.

Toulmin, S. 2001. *Return to Reason.* Cambridge, MA: Harvard University Press.

Townsend. A. 2009. 'Hector Sants says bankers should be "very frightened" by the FSA.' *Daily Telegraph*, 12 March. www.telegraph.co.uk/finance/newsbysector/banksandfinance/4978496/Hector-Sants-says-bankers-should-be-very-frightened-of-the-FSA.html.

Transparency International. 2009. *Corruption Perceptions Index 2008.* www.transparency.org/policy_research/surveys_indices/cpi (accessed 24 October 2009).

Treasury. 2008. *Briefing to the Incoming Minister of Finance: Medium-term economic challenges.* Wellington: The Treasury. www.treasury.govt.nz/publications/briefings/2008/big08.pdf.

Treasury. 2009. *Financial Statements of the Government of New Zealand for the Year Ended 30 June 2009.* Wellington: The Treasury. www.treasury.govt.nz/government/financialstatements/yearend/jun09/05.htm.

Tversky, A., and Kahneman, D. 1992. 'Advances in prospect theory: Cumulative representation of uncertainty.' *Journal of Risk and Uncertainty* 5: 297–323.

2025 Taskforce. 2009. *Answering the $64,000 Question: Closing the income gap with Australia by 2025 – First report of the 2025 Taskforce*. Wellington: New Zealand Government. http://purl.oclc.org/nzt/r-1252.

Uhlmann, C. 2009. 'St Kevin's halo may choke him.' *Weekend Australian*, 24–25 October.

Uhr, J. 2005. *Terms of Trust: Arguments over ethics in Australian government*. Sydney, NSW: University of New South Wales Press.

Uhr, J. 2008. 'Distributed authority in a democracy: The lattice of leadership revisited.' In P. 't Hart and J. Uhr (eds). *Public Leadership: Perspectives and practices*. Canberra: Australian National University E-Press, pp. 37–44. http://epress.anu.edu.au/anzsog/public_leadership/pdf_instructions.html.

UN (United Nations) Department of Public Information. 1997. *UN Conference on Environment and Development (1992)*. www.un.org/geninfo/bp/enviro.html (last revised 23 May 1997; accessed February 2010).

UNDP (United Nations Development Programme). 2009. *Human Development Report 2009: Overcoming barriers – Human mobility and development*. Houndmills, Basingstoke, Hampshire: Palgrave Macmillan. http://hdr.undp.org/en/reports/global/hdr2009.

UNFCCC. 1992. *Report of the United Nations Conference on Environment and Development*. United Nations Framework Convention on Climate Change. A/CONF.151/26 (Vol. 1). www.poptel.org.uk/nssd/otherdocuments/Agenda21.doc (accessed February 2010).

UNFCCC. 2009. *The United Nations Framework Convention on Climate Change*. Bonn, Germany: Secretariat of the United Nations Framework Convention on Climate Change.

UNFCCC. n. d. *List of Annex I Parties to the Convention*. United Nations Framework Convention on Climate Change. http://unfccc.int/parties_and_observers/parties/annex_i/items/2774.php (accessed February 2010).

US Bank National Association v. Ibanez 29 October 2009, Commonwealth of Massachusetts Trial Court, Misc. Case No. 08-384283 (KCL). www.boston.com/business/articles/2009/10/15/ibanezruling.

Valencia Sáiz, A. 2005. 'Globalisation, cosmopolitanism and ecological citizenship.' *Environmental Politics* 14: 163–78.

Van der Veen, R. 1991. *Between Exploitation and Communism: Explorations in the Marxian theory of justice and freedom*. Amsterdam: Groningen.

Van der Veen, R., and P. Van Parijs. 1986. 'Universal grants versus socialism: A reply to six critics.' *Theory and Society* 15(5): 723–57.

Van Parijs, P. 1995. *Real Freedom for All: What (if anything) can justify capitalism?* Oxford: Oxford University Press.

van Vliet, J., M. G. J. den Elzen, and D. P. van Vuuren. 2009. 'Meeting radiative forcing targets under delayed participation.' *Energy Economics* 31(Supplement 2): 152–62.

Vaughan, N., T. Lenton, and J. Shepherd. 2009. 'Climate change mitigation: Trade-offs between delay and strength of action required.' *Climatic Change* 96(1): 29–43.

Verdier, J. M. 1984. 'Advising congressional decision-makers: Guidelines for economists.' *Journal of Policy Analysis and Management* 3(3): 421–38.

Victor, D. G. 2008. 'On the regulation of geoengineering.' *Oxford Review of Economic Policy* 24(2): 322–36.

Wall Street. 1987. Directed by O. Stone. Beverly Hills: Twentieth Century Fox.

Wallis, J. 2010. *Rediscovering Values: On Wall Street, Main Street, and Your Street*. New York: Howard Books.

Ward, T. 2009. 'Punishment and correctional practice: Ethical and rehabilitation implications.' *Policy Quarterly* 5(2): 3–8.

Wardekker, J. A., A. C. Petersen, and J. P. van der Sluijs. 2009. 'Ethics and public perception of climate change: Exploring the Christian voices in the US public debate.' *Global Environmental Change* 19(4): 512–21.

Warren, M. 1992. 'Democratic theory and self-transformation.' *American Political Science Review* 86(1): 8–23.

Warwick Commission on International Financial Reform. 2009. *In Praise of Unlevel Playing Fields*. Coventry: University of Warwick. www2.warwick.ac.uk/research/warwickcommission/report.

Weimer, D. L., and A. R. Vining. 2005. *Policy Analysis: Concepts and practice*. 4th edn. Upper Saddle River, NJ: Pearson Prentice Hall.

Weiss, C. 1983. 'Ideology, interests, and information: The basis of policy positions.' In D. Callahan and B. Jennings (eds). *Ethics, the Social Sciences, and Policy Analysis*. New York and London: Plenum Press, pp. 213–45.

Weitzman, M. L. 2007. 'A review of *The Stern Review on the Economics of Climate Change.*' *Journal of Economic Literature* 55: 703–24.

Weitzman, M. L. 2009. 'On modeling and interpreting the economics of catastrophic climate change.' *Review of Economics and Statistics* 91: 1–19.

Wells Fargo Bank v. Larace 29 October 2009, Commonwealth of Massachusetts Trial Court, Misc. Case No. 08-386755 (KCL). www.boston.com/business/articles/2009/10/15/ibanezruling.

Westberg, D. 1994. *Right Practical Reason: Aristotle, action and prudence in Aquinas.* Oxford: Oxford University Press.

Westpac Banking Corp. v. Commissioner of Inland Revenue 7 October 2009, Harrison J, HC Auckland CIV 2005-404-2843.

White, L. J. 1991. *The S&L Debacle: Public policy lessons for bank and thrift regulation.* New York: Oxford University Press.

White, S. 2004. *The Civic Minimum: Rights and obligations of economic citizenship.* Oxford: Oxford University Press.

WHO. 2004. 'Causes of death.' *Data and Statistics.* World Health Organization. www.who.int/research/en (accessed 1 October 2009).

Wildavsky, A. 1987. *Speaking Truth to Power: The art and craft of policy analysis.* New Brunswick, NJ: Transaction Books.

Wilkinson, R., and Pickett, K. 2009. *The Spirit Level: Why more equal societies almost always do better.* London: Allen Lane.

Williams, B. 1981. *Moral Luck.* Cambridge, UK: Cambridge University Press.

Williams, B. 1993. *Ethics and the Limits of Philosophy.* London: Fontana Press.

Williamson, M. 2004. *The Gift of Change: Spiritual guidance for living your best life.* New York: HarperCollins.

Williamson, O. 1985. *The Economic Institutions of Capitalism: Firms, markets, relational contracting.* New York: Free Press.

Winston, K. 2002. *Moral Competence in the Practice of Democratic Governance.* KSG Faculty Research working paper series RWP02–048. http://web.hks.harvard.edu/publications/workingpapers/citation.aspx?PubId=1145 (accessed May 2010).

Winston, K. 2008. *What Makes Ethics Practical*. KSG Faculty Research working paper series RWP08–013. http://web.hks.harvard.edu/publications/workingpapers/citation.aspx?PubId=5613 (accessed May 2010).

Winston, K. 2009. *Moral Competence in Public Life*. Occasional paper 4. Melbourne: Australia and New Zealand School of Government and State Services Authority. www.ssa.vic.gov.au/CA2571410025903D/WebObj/OccPaper_04_Winston/$File/OccPaper_04_Winston.pdf (accessed May 2010).

Wolf Jr, C. 1979. 'A theory of non-market failures.' *Public Interest* 55: 114–33.

Woodward, A. 1994. 'Making ethics part of real work.' In N. Preston (ed.). *Ethics for the Public Sector: Education and training*. Leichhardt, NSW: Federation Press, pp. 219–36.

World Bank. 2001. *World Development Report 2002: Building institutions for markets*. New York: Oxford University Press. econ.worldbank.org/external/default/main?pagePK=64165259&theSitePK=469372&piPK=64165421&menuPK=64166093&entityID=000094946_01092204010635.

World Values Survey (n. d.) Online data analysis. www.wvsevsdb.com/wvs/WVSAnalize.jsp.

Yohe, G. 2009. 'Toward an integrated framework derived from a risk-management approach to climate change.' *Climatic Change* 95(3): 325–39.

Zak, P., and S. Knack. 2001. 'Trust and growth.' *Economic Journal* 111(470): 295–321.

Printed in Great Britain
by Amazon